LONG MARCH TO FREEDOM

Tom Hargrove's Own Story of His Kidnapping by Colombian Narco-Guerrillas

LONG MARCH TO FREEDOM

*Tom Hargrove's Own Story of
His Kidnapping by
Colombian Narco-Guerrillas*

Thomas R. Hargrove

BALLANTINE BOOKS • NEW YORK

Library of Congress Catalog Card Number: 95-95163

ISBN 0-345-40508-0

Manufactured in the United States of America

First Edition: November 1995

10   9   8   7   6   5   4   3   2   1

Dedication

To my wife, Susan, and sons, Miles and Geddie, who never gave up the faith and the fight. Without them I wouldn't have survived the Valley of the Shadow of Death.

To my brother, Raford Hargrove, who brought new meaning to the term "my brother's keeper."

To Robert Clerx, who became the voice of my family.

To Uli, Claudia, Peter, and Dina Greiner, who adopted and cared for my family from the morning I was kidnapped until the night I returned home. Their friendship knew no boundaries.

To the other members of what Dina named "Team Tom," who worked so diligently for my release: the "Three Davids," Linda Ercole-Musso, Andres Naranjo, Vivianna Perez, Ray Schamback, and Bill Smith.

To Oscar Tejeda of the FBI, who was Susan's rock.

Contents

Acknowledgments

Without the help and support of the following, my family would never have been able to overcome the difficulties of the last year:

Regina Once Betancour de Liska, Michael Balgley, Allycen Brady, Donald Conover, Bernabe Cortez, CGNET, Dennis and Faridah Friesen, Helga Fries, Myles Fisher, Pam Fisher, and the staff of Comil, the "Friends of Tom," Don Fields, the FBI, Ambassador Myles Frechette and his staff at the U.S. Embassy in Bogotá, H. Garcia, David Hammit, Lana Hargrove, Mark Hargrove, Tom Hargrove, Tiff Harris, Guy Henry, Harro and Uschi Klein, Doug Laing, Carlos Lane, Lee and Linda Lanning, Armando Lara, Fabio Larrahonda, Becky and Kinney McKinney, Joe Miranda, José Apolinar Molina, Jose Tomás Moore, Humberto Morales, Manuel Muñoz, Annie and Isabela Naranjo, Bruce Olsson, Brother Oscar, Ross Perot, LaRue Pollard, Ed Price, Ruth Raymond, Shirley Roman, Barbara Rose, Nathan Russell and CIAT's communication department, Francisco Santos, Sid Sers, Marjorie Sheldon, Miles Sheldon, Marlene Smith, Ed Sulzberger, Mauricio Salazar, Ashley Wood and the members of the Agricultural Communicators in Education, Hubert and Ilse Zanstra, and Bill, Amy, Dan, Michael, Tom, Scott, Christian, Raul, and John.

The Hargrove family is also grateful for the prayers of thousands of friends and strangers around the world that were offered in many languages and faiths.

And finally,

When Owen Lock of Ballantine Books (who published my last book, *A Dragon Lives Forever*) learned that I had kept a diary during my captivity and smuggled it out, he flew to Texas, collected the bits of paper (some with writing only an ant could read), took them to New York, and set thirty typists to transcribing.

This is the second time that Owen has shown faith in my work. This book would not have been published without Owen and the others who worked with him:

George Davidson, Fred Dodnick, Caron Harris, Alex Klapwald, Steve Palmer

Betsy Elias, Mark Rifkin, Kathleen Fridella, Laura Wise, Ann Pulido, Kristen Eberhard, Lisa Lester, Marty Karlow (copy editor supreme)

Ruth Ross, David Stevenson

And the army of typists and proofreaders, among them Scott Briggs, Sandra Childress, Louise Collazo, Tony DeGeorge, Gioia DiBiase, Shani Friedman, Amy Gibson, Emily Gray, Brian Holmes, Bob Katel, Suzanne Miller, Danielle Moore, Pam Pfeifer, Benita Richards, Karole Riipa, Ilse Schrynemakers, Jennifer Scott, Jenny Wesselmann, Leah Weatherspoon, Capers White, and Eva Young.

Introduction

I knew that Colombia was notorious for kidnapping, averaging some 6,000 kidnaps per year. But my profession is international agriculture development—applying science to agriculture to improve the lives of the world's poorest farmers. That mission is similar to that claimed by the guerrillas who are responsible for most kidnapping. My colleagues and I thought we were immune to kidnapping and other acts of terrorism.

But first let me explain how my family and I came to Colombia. I was raised on a red-dirt, dryland cotton farm near Rotan, in West Texas. I was one of three children of Tom and Bargy Hargrove. My sister, Becky, is four years older than me and Raford, my brother, is four years younger.

I received a double degree in agricultural science and journalism, along with a commission as a second lieutenant in the U.S. Army, from Texas A&M University in 1966. I then went on to take an M.S. degree from Iowa State University. During that time I married Susan Sheldon, who is from a pioneer family in Rotan but was raised in the Aleutian Islands, Canada, the Philippines, Kuwait, Iran, and Switzerland.

I reported to Infantry Officers School at Ft. Benning, Georgia, in June, 1968. A year later, I was assigned as a first lieutenant to MAC-V, the Military Assistance Command—Vietnam Advisory Team 73. We were advisers to the South Vietnamese military and government in Chuong Thien, one of Vietnam's most war-torn provinces, almost at the southern tip of the Mekong Delta.

Because I was a farm boy with advanced degrees in agriculture, I was assigned to advise the local agricultural officials, in addition to the regular duties of a junior grade officer.

IR8, the high-yielding variety of rice that revolutionized rice production in developing countries, had been released in 1967, and its seeds were just reaching Vietnam. I helped spread IR8 seeds across Chuong Thien Province, traveling mostly by sampan on the brown-water canals and rivers with Vietnamese agricultural cadre and soldiers. The improved rice varieties doubled and tripled yields overnight in areas where production had remained stagnant for centuries. Those rice seeds were the only good thing I saw happen there.

After the army, I worked for a couple of years as a science editor at Iowa

State University. I then returned to Vietnam on a consultancy for an animal health project of the University of Minnesota and the U.S. Agency for International Development.

My son Miles was born in late 1972, soon after I returned from my second, civilian tour in Vietnam. A few months later, I joined the International Rice Research Institute in the Philippines. IRRI is where IR8 was developed. Thus, my profession became the Green Revolution—the development and spread of the improved crop varieties and technologies that have revolutionized agriculture in the Third World. Tom G., who is now generally known as Geddie, was born in Manila in 1973. In 1976–77, I returned to complete the remaining coursework and dissertation for my doctorate degree at Iowa State University.

In 1988, I returned to Vietnam and went back to the former Chuong Thien Province. There, I met ex–Viet Cong who said they could have killed me two decades before but had spared me because I brought the new rice seeds to local farmers. By then, rice had become my life. Now I realized that rice had, indeed, saved my life years earlier. I wrote about my experiences in Vietnam, about working in the Green Revolution, and about returning to where it all began in my second book, *A Dragon Lives Forever: War and Rice in Vietnam's Mekong Delta 1969–1991, and Beyond* (Random House/Ivy, 1994).

By late 1991, I'd lived in Asia and worked with rice for most of my adult life. I felt it was time for a change. What about Africa, Latin America?

That's when I started flirting with the International Center for Tropical Agriculture, based near Cali, Colombia. The Center is commonly known as CIAT, for its Spanish name el Centro Internacional de Agricultura Tropical.

CIAT was the third International Agricultural Research Center, started in 1967 by the Ford and Rockefeller Foundations, in cooperation with the government of Colombia. Today, there are 16 such centers around the world, sponsored by the Consultative Group on International Agricultural Research (CGIAR), a consortium of about 40 nations and international organizations that support agricultural research for development.

CIAT scientists work to develop improved varieties and technologies for four crops that feed hundreds of millions of the world's poorest people. It has a global mandate for beans, cassava, and tropical pastures, and it works to improve rice production in Latin America and the Caribbean.

In January 1992, I began work as head of CIAT's communication program. I found CIAT a lot like IRRI. The scientists have the same idealism and work ethic. They're sincere and dedicated men and women who want to help humanity feed itself in the coming decades as populations increase dramatically and land available for farming shrinks. The centers want to find ways to grow the extra food to feed those populations without damaging the environment.

The CIAT research center and main experiment farm are near Palmira, about a 50-minute drive from our home in southern Cali. I was 10 minutes away from home and driving fast at 7:30 in the morning of 23 September 1994, embarrassed because I'd arrive late for work at CIAT. Instead of studying Spanish through cassette tapes, as I normally did on the way to work, I was engrossed in an audio book—*Tucker's Last Stand*, a Southeast Asia thriller by William F. Buckley Jr.

At an intersection, I had to decide which of two main routes to take to CIAT. One is a nerve-wracking drive through the heavy traffic of suburban Cali. The other route takes a bit longer, but is through the beautiful Colombian countryside.

I thought I remembered one of the rules for a better life that Robert Fulghum used: "Always take the scenic route." I turned right off the Pan-American Highway and took the scenic route to work. That was the last decision I'd make for almost a year. . . .

Editor's Note

Long March to Freedom is composed of the lightly edited diary entries that Tom Hargrove maintained, almost without break, for the eleven months of his captivity. Full entries were written in his Rotan, Texas, checkbook and in two children's notebooks he was given by the guerrillas. Backup entries, calendars, notes, etc., were kept on the back of blank checks from his account at the Banco Real de Colombia and on scraps of paper.

The section titled "The Retén" was written and repeatedly revised during Hargrove's captivity and largely recapitulates material from the 23 September entry of the Checkbook Diary.

When captured by the guerrillas of FARC, Tom Hargrove was carrying several hundred dollars' worth of Colombian pesos in his pocket and an American one-hundred-dollar bill in his wallet. Finding that much money so easily, the guerrillas never thought to look closely at Hargrove's belt, hence never realized it was a money belt. And it was there that Tom kept his backup notes, calendars, etc. The main diaries were carried in Tom's clothing so that he had control of them at all times and so that they could not be discovered casually when the guerrillas inspected his belongings.

ROADBLOCK
"The Retén"

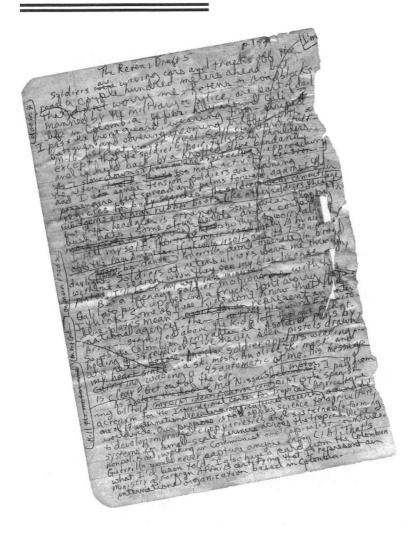

Soldiers are waving cars and trucks off the road a couple hundred meters ahead, but that doesn't worry me. *Reténs*, roadblocks, manned by the military or police, are part of the daily life in Colombia, especially around Cali. I pass the front guard, wearing tiger-striped fatigues and covering incoming traffic with an M-16 held at waist level. Still standard stuff, except that the soldier's hair falls to his shoulders and is held back by a knotted olive bandanna.

I feel uneasy as I slow down, approaching the *retén*. Too much activity, and I sense tension. Soldiers are leaning passengers, feet spread and palms forward, against the vehicles for body searches. Like other soldiers, these wear camouflage uniforms and high rubber boots, but their headgear is strange. Some wear floppy bush hats, some olive berets, and a couple wear bandannas. Nothing to worry about, I tell myself. I'm only ten minutes off the Pan-American Highway itself, and it's 7:30 A.M. Guerrillas don't operate on main roads in broad daylight. Soldiers at *reténs* always wave me through without a search when they see my blue license plates. I'll be on my way in a minute.

But a teenage soldier motions with his Israeli-made Galil assault rifle to pull up behind a truck. Don't worry, I think. Some of these kids don't know that the blue plates mean I represent an international agency. Then I see the word *ejército* [army] stenciled above the kid's left fatigue pocket. So it's the Colombian army after all. A soldier runs by, holding a .38 revolver. I've never seen pistols drawn at a *retén* before. Another soldier appears wearing—oh my God—a ski mask. An olive ski mask, and waving a .45 automatic at me. His message is clear. Get out of the car.

As I kill the Nissan's motor, I pull my CIAT identification card from my billfold. CIAT is the Spanish acronym for the International Center for Tropical Agriculture, one of 17 international agricultural research centers worldwide. Our purpose is to apply science to agriculture to develop improved crop varieties and sustainable farming systems for small-scale farmers across the tropics. We're nonpolitical, working in both communist and capitalist countries. Guerrillas would never capture anyone from CIAT. That's what I'd been told. I also have a card from the Colombian Ministry of Foreign Affairs certifying that I represent an international organization based in Colombia.

I hand Ski Mask the ID cards with my right hand, clutching my billfold with my left. He takes both. "I work for *el Centro Internacional de Agricultura Tropical*, or CIAT," I explain in Spanish as Ski Mask skims my identification. That doesn't seem to impress him. Ski Mask speaks—rapidly—to a *guerrillero* with an AK-47. I catch only one word: *gringo*. The two guerrillas push me forward and we trot past soldiers who are frisking passengers and searching the other two trucks and three cars. Another car approaches the *retén*, and is pulled over for the same treatment.

We turn down a side road of dirt between sugarcane fields. There, a new Chevrolet pickup sits beside a beat-up Chevy van and a Toyota van whose side displays the decal *Ingresos de Cauca*, or "Earnings of the Cauca Valley." The pickup and Toyota van were obviously taken at the *retén*. All vehicles face away from the highway. Ski Mask and his friend turn me over to another armed guerrilla who guards a couple of *campesinos* who've passed by at the wrong time, and hurry back to the *retén*. The guard motions me into the back of the pickup. A *guerrillero* runs up. "Propaganda!" he shouts, and my guard pulls a sheaf of leaflets from his fatigue jacket. The portrait of the revolutionary Che Guevara, wearing a black beret, is printed on the front.

"Who is this group?" I ask.

"*Las FARC*," the guard says matter-of-factly.

Oh God, I think. FARC. The *Fuerzas Armadas Revolucionarias de Colombia*, or the Armed Revolutionary Forces of Colombia. One of the world's last communist guerrilla armies. These guys routinely kidnap wealthy Colombians and, when they get a chance, foreigners with multinational corporations. That's one way they finance their operations. But FARC wouldn't kidnap a CIAT scientist, not purposely. CIAT makes no profit, sells nothing, exploits no natural resources. Our purpose is to improve the lives of the world's poorest farmers, and of urban dwellers who depend on their production. Ski Mask just doesn't understand. When I meet someone with authority, I'll be let go.

A shout! Guerrillas begin to move backward step-by-step, automatic weapons fanning their paths from the *retén*. They converge on our cluster of vehicles and two jump in the back of the pickup with me. One has a baby face and can't be more than 13. But he carries an AK-47, and two bandoliers of .30-caliber ammo for an M-60 machine gun crisscross his chest. The other teenager carries a Galil and wears a bandanna. He motions me to sit flat on the pickup bed. We speed away from the *retén*.

As we bounce down the dirt road at breakneck speed, the muzzles of both *guerrilleros'* weapons keep swinging in my face. By accident, sure, but those weapons are heavy-duty and loaded, and one little slip can blow me away. I motion to the kid with the Galil to *please* move its muzzle out of my face. Please? He does, but the weapon swings back and I'm looking into its muzzle again a couple of minutes later. The vehicles brake at an intersection, and the drivers talk rapidly. Our driver throws the pickup into first and guns it. The lurch takes Baby Face by surprise and he falls backward, almost out of the pickup, but clutching the tailgate with both legs and one hand. The other hand clings to his

AK-47. I grab Baby Face's forearm and pull him back into the pickup bed. He's more embarrassed than grateful.

Another half hour of hard driving through cane fields takes us into the Cordillera Central, the beginning of the Andes. We meet an Indian descending the road on horseback. The pickup stops. "Is the army or police ahead?" our driver asks. *"No, señor."* We speed on. Higher in the mountains, the three vehicles stop by a small roadside store. The guerrillas buy *gaseosas*, soft drinks, and offer me one. No thanks. A *guerrillero* pulls a .22 revolver, confiscated at the *retén*, from his belt and fires two shots at rocks on the mountain slope. Another *guerrillero* takes the pistol and fires wildly into the air, laughing, until the cartridges are spent.

The men gather in a circle and, like soldiers anywhere after an action, start telling war stories, things that happened at the *retén*. Ski Mask, who by now has removed the mask, is the center of attention. Maskless, he's pudgy and could be a clerk in a grocery store.

"I'll pay! Don't kill me! I'll pay anything," Ski Mask shrieks, palms pressed together as if in prayer. He's mimicking a panic-stricken detainee back at the *retén*. Ski Mask hams it up, the guerrillas laugh madly, and I feel sick. Whatever happens, Hargrove, try to keep your dignity, I think. You can't break and provide entertainment for these bastards.

I'm put in the backseat of the Chevy van, and we drive on. *"Me llaman Rambo,"* the driver says. "They call me Rambo." He has a rough beard and mustache, and wears tiger-striped fatigues with a slouchy jungle hat. One brim is cocked up, Australian style. Ski Mask sits in the passenger seat.

"You've made a mistake," I explain to the two guerrillas. "I work for the CIAT."

I tell them how CIAT develops improved varieties of beans, cassava, tropical forages, and rice not only for farmers in Colombia, but worldwide. Rambo and Ski Mask don't seem impressed.

Finally, I change the subject. "What happened to my car?" I ask Rambo.

"We left it on the road." I guess FARC steals only four-wheel-drive vehicles, but someone else may have use for an empty 1993 Nissan Bluebird sedan, keys in the ignition. I doubt that I'll see that car again.

"What happened to my billfold?" I ask. "Will you give me my money?" I had 200,000 Colombian pesos, about US $230—plus a green US $100 bill for emergencies—in the billfold when Ski Mask took it. Ski Mask ignores the question.

Meanwhile, Rambo is on the radio coordinating movements with someone called Gato Negro—Black Cat. Forty-five minutes later we enter a mountain village and park along the lower side of the hillside plaza. I look for a sign that tells me the village's name, but see nothing. A small, whitewashed Catholic church looks down from the upper side of the plaza; at the far side is a broken-down Ferris wheel. FARC obviously considers this a secure village. *Guerrilleros* in fatigues bask in the sun on concrete park benches and stroll the streets. Rambo and Ski Mask tell a group of teenage soldiers to guard me, and leave.

"I work for 'CIAT,' I tell the soldiers. No response. "Do you know what CIAT is?"

"CIA," a teenager says. He pronounces it "ssea-a." "That's the intelligence agency of the United States."

"No!" I cry. "Not CIA—CIAT. *El Centro Internacional de Agricultura Tropical!*" I stress the first letters of the first three words and start talking about beans, cassava, poor farmers. A guerrilla brings me a plastic cup of apricot yogurt. As I eat, one guard puts a tape into the Chevy van's tape deck and we listen to the revolutionary music of the FARC guerrillas.

A *guerrillero* walks up carrying a black briefcase—my briefcase—obviously stolen from my car. He hands me what he thinks I may need from the briefcase—a stack of CIAT business cards, bound by a rubber band, and two checkbooks. One is for my U.S.-dollar account on the First National Bank of Rotan, Texas. The other is for my Colombian peso account, on the Banco Real of Cali. I doubt that I'll be writing many checks, but I take them.

"How much money do you make?" my guard asks, eyeing the checkbooks. "I make three million pesos a year." I know that's about $3,700 U.S. dollars. "How much do *you* make?" the guard repeats.

"No entiendo," I say. I don't understand your question.

Rambo and Ski Mask return, and we drive down a side street and park in front of a stucco house with a red tile roof. A civilian emerges and hands me a plate as Rambo and Ski Mask leave again, leaving me with a teenage guard. Rice and potatoes, and a broiled chicken wing. I'm not hungry, but figure I'd better eat.

"Do you like the food of the *indígena*?" the civilian asks.

"Mucho," I lie. "You are an *indígena* [Indian]?"

"Sí, señor. Everyone in this village is Indian."

"Then Spanish is your second language?"

"Oh, yes, señor. We all speak Páez."

A *guerrillero* comes to the van and shows me a revolver taken at the *retén.* It looks like the one the boys were shooting earlier. "Is this your pistol?"

It may be the one the boys were shooting earlier, [illegible] *"Pero si quiere regalármela, acepto con mucho gusto,"* I say. No, but if you wish to give me it, I'll accept it with great pleasure. "With bullets, please!" The guerrilla laughs, and goes off to tell his amigos what the *gringo* prisoner said. Rambo returns and gets behind the wheel. As we drive out of town, I notice bold letters painted on the sides of buildings. "What does 'JBC' mean?" I ask. "The Jaime Beckemann Callon Front of M-19," Gato Negro says. M-19. That's another communist guerrilla front. A pretty Indian girl works in the garden of a house that we pass. Rambo stops the van and smiles at her, squinting his eyes, tips his hat, waves, and guns the motor. The girl waves good-bye. A kilometer down the road another Indian girl is riding a pony. Again Rambo puts on his killer smile and squint. They exchange looks and a few words, then Rambo rides off again. This guy considers himself God's gift to the Indian girls of this village, I think. There's a leather handbag that a *guerrillero* had thrown in the backseat with me.

I see a cluster of keys and I know that they are mine—because I doubt that many Colombians would carry a key ring with a brass plaque stamped "Redneck." So I doubt that my Nissan will be stolen. We drive, higher and [illegible] 45 minutes then pull up in a valley. There the two other vehicles from the *retén* wait, along with another group of about 25 uniformed guerrillas. I'm ordered out of the van. Rambo meets with a group of men, then one *guerrillero*, with an AK-47, walks from the group toward a clump of trees along the stream below. *"Venga!"* he says, Come. Two more men walk up behind me. One motions me forward with his Galil. It hits me—one man in front, two behind, taking me away from the group to a clump of trees. I hadn't thought, until then, that these men might kill me. They think I'm worth more alive than dead, otherwise they wouldn't have taken me. Still there was that misunderstanding about CIA and CIAT, and this is the way the bad guys rub out the good guys in the movies. I walk, scared but not terrified. We reach the tree clump, but keep going. I pick my way on slippery rocks along the stream. *"Arriba,"* the *guerrillero* in front says, motioning toward the mountain slope that faces us. Up. Then I realize that a tree line, several hundred steep meters up the slope, is our objective. Cover from aircraft that might be searching for me. We reach the tree line and the other three *guerrilleros* relax. One asks me, "How do you like living in Colombia?"

I can't believe this. "I liked it a lot—yesterday," I say. But the question really pisses me off, so I add, "How can you ask such a question—holding an AK-47, and having kidnapped me?" The *guerrillero* smiles and looks at his feet.

We lie in the mulch of leaves the forest has left. I'm more frightened by the boredom that I know must come than by the prospect of immediate death. And I'm really concerned about how my wife, Susan, will take this. I look at my watch. It's 2:30 P.M., so I was kidnapped about seven hours ago. By now the others at the *retén* must have reported that FARC took a *gringo* captive, and CIAT must have recovered my car. So surely Susan knows by now. I wonder how CIAT told her. By phone? Did someone come to our home?

At about three P.M. I survey my possessions. Not much. The clothes I'm wearing, a watch with a broken band, 2 checkbooks, 35 business cards, and—I count my money—650 Colombian pesos—about 75 cents. But I'm thankful for one possession. When captured, I had a Random House pocket dictionary, English-Spanish, in my front pocket. How lucky! I wish I could start writing some of this down, I think. Take notes at least. I'd learned from my days in Vietnam how quickly you forget, even powerful things you "know" are fixed in your mind forever.

The English-Spanish dictionary has several blank pages at the back, I see. And I could write more notes in the page margins throughout the dictionary. No, I can't do that, I think. What if the guerrillas see that I'm writing and confiscate my notes? I can't compromise my dictionary; that leaves . . . my business cards and the checkbooks. I look at the checkbooks. The dollar checkbook has more blank pages. Then I realize that the front of both my dollar and peso checkbooks have records of checks written, deposits, withdrawals. I'm not wealthy; I earn a good salary, about what a professor at a U.S. university with similar professional experience and education would earn. Still, that must look like a lot to these guys. I silently tear the front deposit-and-withdrawal sections from both check-books and thrust them deep into the mulch of decaying leaves.

CHECKBOOK DIARY
"The National Bank of Rotan"

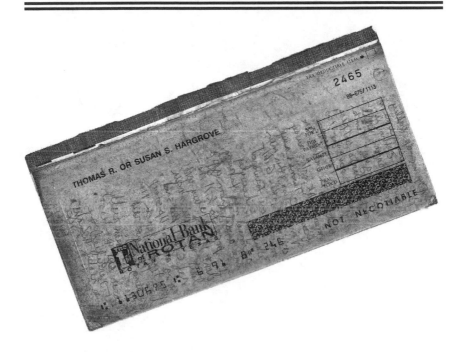

Friday, 23 Sep., *Retén* 1994

[*gap*] but looked different. Soldiers more animated, alert. Then ski masks—olive drab—park—ID, wallet—motion down side road Back Chev. pickup. Two teenage soldiers. Soldier ran up to one man and said, "propaganda." Reached into shirt and handed sheaf of leaflets with image of Che Guevara.

Drove like hell. At two teenagers in back with me. AK-47 and Galil. Too careless. Stop, shoot pistol. Village. Indians speak Páez. Lunch: chicken and rice with piece potato. No appetite. "You must eat, long journey." Is 1200h. Guerrilla shows me a .22 pistol, asks if mine. *"No, pero si quiere regalármela, acepto con mucho gusto."* Everyone laughs. One guerrilla tells others. They own this village. In the open. Church on square. Also a Ferris wheel that looks abandoned.

Drive up valley. The driver's name is Rambo. Other is Gato Negro. Call me *"grinque."* Rambo stops, flirts with peasant girls. He obviously the stud of FARC. Finally stop. Get out, in valley. One man with AK walks away from group. Turns and says, *"Venga."* Two other men, one with AK, other Galil, motion me forward. Why are three heavily armed men taking me away from group? It's possibly to kill me—don't think they would, but that misunderstanding regarding CIAT. But said get going, *"Arriba."* Up steep mountain. Finally reach tree line. There we rest. Getting cold.

1455h: Have not been really scared yet. At least, not terrified, and I never really thought I'd die. At least, not now. But I am frightened by the boredom that surely must come. And I'm really worried about how Susan will take this. She must have learned several hours ago. I asked Rambo what happened to my car. Left by the road. Later, I see that it's true because I see my keys in a leather handbag that one of the guerrillas has thrown in back of Chevy 6-person van. Doubt many Colombians would have key ring with brass plaque stamped "Redneck." As [we] climbed mountain a guerrilla asks me how I like Colombia. A lot, I respond. Especially being kidnapped while driving to work. Survey my possessions, clothes I'm wearing. When guerrilla took briefcase, gave me my dollar and peso checkbooks. Bury checks. Also 35 business cards with rubber band. A watch with broken band. Two packs of Post-Its. Key to closet. One

11

ballpoint. And I should be thankful for one thing. A Random House English-Spanish dictionary that was in my pocket. As for money, I have. . . . I reach in both pockets . . . Colombia $610—about 75 cents. Decided to write in checkbook. Not dictionary. If guerrillas confiscate, couldn't stand to lose dictionary.

Thank God I have paper of some sort and a pen. I can at least write . . . for now. 1535h: Still waiting. Getting chilly. Believe mountains here 3,000 meters. I make a lot of jokes with guerrillas. Not real jokes, just sarcastic wisecracks. I'm asked again how I like Colombia. *"Me gustó muchísimo—ayer."* That gets a laugh. Juaquil is swarthy, wears a tiger-striped T-shirt without sleeves. Farmer grows *papa*, maize, *frijol*, and *arveja*. Is vague whether one or two ha [hectares] but says owns land. I've noticed what appears to be the mouth of a cave. No, it's a large rock. Can we go see? "I may as well be a tourist—and this tour is free!" Bury peso checks. I have a feeling that being kidnapped is going to be awfully boring. I should list what I must do. Keep track of days. Keep my health, but a lot of that may be out of my hands. Don't get depressed, keep sense of humor. Juaquil even said, *"Hay esperanza."* There seems to be no chance of escape. I don't even know where I am—but it seems to be FARC country. I wonder if I'll be able to write to Susan. For medicine I have two Zyrtec tablets. I'm on three medicines, twice a day. What will happen when this wears off? I'll explain about allergies when I meet someone with authority. I wonder if everyone assumes that I am safe or, at least, alive. CIAT policy on kidnapping doesn't particularly assure me: it's that CIAT will not pay one peso of ransom for anyone. Of course, this [kidnapping of a CIAT senior staff member] has never happened before. The third guerrilla shows color photos to others. I ask to see. Him in full uniform with Galil. Macho stuff. I say, "When I leave, I hope you give me that as a souvenir." No one laughs. They must think I'm serious. Careful, Hargrove. I ask Juaquil how he likes the life of a soldier. *"Es muy burgués."* I look up burgues=bourgeois. Must have another meaning. He then says, *"Trato malo."* At the stop this morning where guerrillas were firing the confiscated pistol—Ski Mask and others started telling war stories—things that happened at the *retén.* Ski Mask mimicked a panic-stricken man, his palms together in prayer, begging and saying, "I'll pay, I'll pay." I decided then that, whatever happens, I must keep my dignity although all so far have been polite, treated me with dignity except for calling me *gringo* or *grinque.* I wonder what lies ahead. It may be a long time before I see Susan, the animals, *la Unidad.* I've often thought about how horrible being a prisoner would be for me. Especially with not even anything to read. Whatever happens, I must keep the right to write. I must have that. The satisfaction of recording what is happening in this mutilated checkbook diary. And the dictionary. Thank God I have that. I really worry about Susan. If I'm still held captive two weeks, a month, from now, what will she do? Could she stay in Cali, alone? I think not. And it would make no sense. We must be 600 to 700 meters above the valley floor, but I can hear the river rushing clearly. We climbed until we reached trees at the mountain crest. Now we're walking under a canopy of brushy trees and vines. To avoid any chance of being spotted by air, I guess, although I haven't seen a single aircraft all day. I doubt there's any search out for me. We'd be impossible to find in these vast and rugged mountains. 1655h: Waiting, with nothing to do. It's getting chilly. And my hands are breaking out. Do I use the Zyrtec or save it for a major eruption? This entire episode has gone pretty much like in a movie. And my God, this is unbelievable. I've been kidnapped by communist guerrillas and am being held on a mountain crest by three teenage guerrillas with AKs and Galils.

I wonder what James Springer would think. Have his Rojan bank checkbooks been used as a diary before? 1710h: Again and again, during my first four to five hours of captivity, I asked for my *billetera*, my billfold, and my money. While in the village, my guard asked if I'd buy him a soft drink. "I would," I said, "but your group took my money. Are you guerrillas or thieves?" Then I thought: Cool it, Hargrove.

The guards entertained themselves in the village by reading the titles, registration forms of the vehicles they stole. One vehicle that came all the way to this valley had a sign on the side: *"Ingresos de Cauca"*—Investments of the Cauca Valley. Must have been taken at the *retén*. But I'm apparently the only person who was kidnapped. 1720h: I wonder what type of messages I may be asked, or forced, to send back. I wish I could at least let Susan know I'm okay. Safe? Not quite. But okay. 1750h: We're back in the valley. Will meet someone who'll take us to a house for the night, Raúl says. Coming down the mountain in my Justin Roper boots was rough.

"Lo siento, señores," I said. "When I dressed this morning, I didn't expect to go mountain climbing. Had I known, I'd have worn other boots." Raúl said maybe they could find rubber [boots]. I was interrupted by command to continue march. Am now sitting on a bed made, apparently, of cornhusks covered by a "tent" of military canvas. We're beside an abandoned barn or house . . . it's hard to tell, we arrived after dark. The travel was hard, all up- and downhill. Seven guerrillas and me. One was female, the only female guerrilla I've seen. She carries a battered M-1 .30-caliber carbine, while every other guerrilla has an M-16, an AK-47, or an Israeli-made Galil 7.62. After arrival, we lay on the grass and talked for 30 minutes. I asked one guerrilla how long he'd been with FARC. "Three years."

"How old are you?"

"Fifteen."

"Then you joined at age twelve?"

"Sí."

"As a soldier?"

"Sí."

I asked these teenagers why they joined.

"Because only a few rich people own all the land. The *campesinos* are treated as slaves." 1925h: Interrupted by a guerrilla who looks about 13. He brought me some water and a piece of candy. (I had asked earlier if we were going to have dinner.) I'll trace the piece below to show its size: [diagram] They told me their ideological leader is Che Guevara, and seemed impressed when

I responded, "From Argentina; killed in Bolivia in 1968." At every opportunity, I describe the work of CIAT: how we are an international center with
80 or 90 scientists from around the world, how our purpose is to develop improved varieties of beans, cassava, pastures, and rice to help small farmers
worldwide, etc.

I asked what will happen to me. The answer was *"nada,"* but in a matter-
of-fact tone, like they're surprised I would ask. "Tomorrow we'll show you
around."

"When can I return home?"

"In a few days. The valley is beautiful," he adds. He also said I'll see fields
of poppies. Hmm.

At an earlier rest stop a guerrilla asked what I'd like for dinner. "Do you
have a menu?" I asked. No, he just wondered. "A big steak with champagne and
strawberries and cream for dessert." He looked puzzled. When the guerrilla
showed me this "bed," they asked if I liked it. "I'd prefer a room at the Inter-
continental Hotel in Cali," I responded. Then I added, "But I don't have any alternative, so this is fine." I'd better be more careful with my joking. Some of
the few cross-cultural problems I've had in 20-plus years abroad have been
through jokes; I was joking, but the Filipino, whoever, was offended. Offending
someone in these circumstances could be . . . dangerous? But somehow I can't
help being sarcastic, bringing out a black sense of humor, in these circumstances.
I guess it's better than worrying about what could happen . . . will happen. I also
told the group that my biggest worry is my wife. That I'm very concerned because she doesn't know if I'm alive or dead. All agree that that's bad. I'm trying
to build a case for somehow sending Susan some sort of message that I'm
okay—at least for now.

This is very empty country. I could see only one light in the entire valley.
2035h: Can't sleep. Can't imagine why. Maybe it's too early. Or maybe it has
something to do with realizing that . . . this sounds corny, or trite, or? . . . but I
was kidnapped on my way to work this morning. And now I'm a prisoner of one
of the last Marxist guerrilla armies on earth. This is FARC—*las Fuerzas Armadas Revolucionarias de Colombia.* One guerrilla corrected me: It's [illegible]
FARC:EP, *"Ejército Pueblo"* or Village Army. One guerrilla asked what I knew
about FARC.

I didn't want to answer with complete honesty, so I just said, "Only what
I read in the papers." I'm now sitting on a mound of earth, writing while holding
a penlight flashlight that a guerrilla gave me, after I requested a light. Two
guards stand, cradling AK-47s, about 6m from my "bed." Later. I can see millions of stars here, we're so far from any sort of artificial light. A soldier with
a voice as soft as the light of those stars comes up to talk. "Tomorrow we will
take you to see the fields of poppy," he says. "They are so beautiful."

"That will be very interesting. Very few foreigners have seen those fields,
I think."

"Yes, very few," he replies. His name is Ramiro, I learn, and he is from

Buga, near Palmira. He later brings me a bar of strong blue soap, for washing clothes. I've already been given an aluminum army mess kit, the kind with a lid. After a while I pull out my checkbook, my penlight, and my ballpoint and start writing. "What are you writing?" he asks. I hesitate, then think what the hell.

Saturday, 24 Sep., Day 2

I have been a *prisionero* almost exactly 24 hours now. [*Eduardo me prestó la luz.*] I hardly slept last night, my "mattress" was so hard, I couldn't stay long in one position. The guerrillas are sitting around a fire in the mud hut. A pot of water boils in a battered tin pot. I accept a cup of sweetened coffee and look back. My last real meal was Thursday night, 22 Sept. I didn't have breakfast on Friday. So in the last 36 hours I have eaten one cup of tea, one cup yogurt, one chicken wing with some rice, one Coke, and this morning, one cup of sweetened coffee.

The guerrillas are around me right now, asking what I am writing. They seem fascinated that I am writing about what is going on. I now know that I can't keep it a secret, so I tell them I'm keeping a diary.

"Of what?"

"Of everything that is happening. *Está malo?*"

"No." They ask more, so I read to them, in Spanish, all I wrote after "Day 2" on p. 14 [of the diary, i.e., the 14 lines directly above this one].

I'm asked, again and again, "Isn't this valley beautiful?" And it is. "Isn't the water pure?" And it is. The best, sweetest water I can remember having, flowing cold from the spring. But don't get the idea I'm falling in love with this place. The toilet is some bushes.

I've learned that Juaco is in command. I'm going to try to place a call to Susan if he'll permit. They have cellular phones. Later: Juaco brings me a plastic sack with a toothbrush, a tube of Colgate toothpaste, a roll of toilet paper, and a bar of soap. *"Con esto puedo sobrevivir,"* I say. He also brings a cold roll. It's tasteless and chewy, but I'll eat at least half of it. I have to keep up my strength. I must do everything possible to maintain my health, to not get sick. Thank God I'm not prone to getting colds. Sleeping in the cold dampness, with rain splattering on the canvas cover above you, is a good way to get sick.

0830h: A soldier offers *sabayón*, a milky drink made from *aguardiente*. It smells good. I say I'll try it *con mucho gusto* tonight, but don't want to drink in the morning.

I meet again with Juaco. "When will I be able to go home?"

"When we get permission from our superiors."

"Are they near, or far away?"

"Muy lejos." Very far.

"Does that mean I can't leave today?"

"No, that's not possible."

Juaco took a list of the allergy medicines I need and promises to get them—if they are available in that Indian village down the valley. I doubt that they will be.

I also ask if I can call Susan, just to let her know I'm alive and okay. He'll have to check with his superior. Will let me know this afternoon.

I have in no way been mistreated, threatened, harassed, especially not since coming to this company. In fact, I'm treated with a great deal of respect. This life is hard, but the guerrillas are making me as comfortable as they are. In fact, these soldiers seem so gentle. But it's not because FARC is so benevolent—it's because these are Colombian peasants, very humble people. And of course I also realize that in situations like this, the captors often build you up so that they can later tear you down and break you. I wonder if that will happen to me.

At first, I had qualms about even saying *gracias* to someone who does something nice. These are kidnappers, for God's sake, and I'm here very much against my will. But these boys didn't kidnap me. They were ordered to take and guard me. I must care for my possessions; I have so few. The most valuable thing I now own, by far, is my glasses. Next is this checkbook diary. I have another, my Colombian peso checkbook to start on when this is full. By then, maybe I'll have a notebook—or maybe I'll be free. But who knows? These soldiers assure me that I'll be released as soon as HQ approves it. I'm not so sure that will happen. This company doesn't make FARC policy.

Last night Ramiro gave me his personal pen—as a *"recuerdo."* I turned on the penlight to examine it. Would you believe it's a camouflage pen, with the same tiger-stripe pattern of the uniforms that many of these boys wear?

My third-most-valuable possession is, of course, my pocket Spanish dictionary.

La señorita is Leidi (Lady), 28 years old. From Cauca. I ask about (Javier sketches) the insignia on her left sleeve. It's of *La Gaitana*, the FARC insignia. It's a very British looking form holding a sword of equal height. That's all. I like the FARC insignia much better. *Later.* No, it's a *dragón* holding the sword. That's better. [Javier] then brings me a red armband with that insignia. I ask what the armbands are for. "For when we run *reténs*, for example." I wince. I was captured at a FARC *retén*.

Ramiro is young, curly hair, wears machete in yellow holster. Is 15, been in FARC four years. Joined at 11. Leidi has been FARC one year. Has Walkman in ears most of time. M-16.

Javier and Ramiro mention *amapola* [poppy] again. "Have you ever seen it growing?" Ramiro asks. No. They lead me up to the field of onions that the guerrillas have planted behind the house. The *amapola* is intercropped with onion. The leaves are pale, open, and jagged. Some of the plants are topped with red flowers even though they are only 30 cm. tall. They are of poor quality, Javier explains. He says the plants were introduced from Asia.

A meal is served at 1000h. The main dish is minced fish from can. Also noodles cooked in a sauce and some Vienna sausage, sliced, in rice. We eat from bowls, with spoons. No forks. I ask Leidi how many years of school she had. Two years. Javier had five years, Ramiro, two years. Javier wears a grenade, no more than three inches in diameter, on his web gear. Made in Ecuador, he says, with as much blast as the larger type. They say they buy most of their weapons—they get some U.S. weapons from Belgian arms dealers. Others, they capture in battle. How often do they fight? 12, 15, 20 times a year. The symbol of *la* FARC. Sketched by Javier [see photo insert]

Everyone called me *gringo* at first. But during a rest stop at dusk yesterday, during the march to this place, I said, *"Mi madre, la señora Hargrove del Texas, me dio el nombre Tomás. No gringo, sino Tomás, algunos de mi amigos me llamaron Tom."* Since then I've been called only Tomás or Tom.

It's 1045h and I'm wondering how to spend the rest of the day. If only I had a book to read. I don't want to go back to sleep—because I want to sleep easier tonight.

How long will this last? What if FARC holds me for ransom (that is, after all, its main reason for kidnapping) and CIAT won't pay? I'd then be pretty useless to FARC. Would FARC turn me loose? Or would that be a bad example. So what would they do with me? I don't know. I'll worry about that later. It won't happen today, anyway. 1110h: I lay down for a while. No, I ask Ramiro what we'll do the rest of the day. "We'll stay here," he says.

"Can't we go see the countryside?"

"It all looks like this place. Mountains and cows and grass."

I ask about the *amapola* fields.

"Muy lejos." Very far. Maybe someone squelched the idea of showing me those fields. It seems that Ramiro is specifically assigned as my guard. I ask if there is anything to read. He searches the hut, asks his comrades. He finally presents me the single piece of reading material here. A pamphlet, *"Consolidar el Camino a la Paz Democratica Estatatutos"* published by *el Partido Comunista Colombiano.* Somehow I've missed reading the statutes of the Colombian communist party. May be fascinating reading before this is over.

Why did you join FARC? Because the poor are slaves—the rich are oppressors, etc. Javier's response. But I was asking, expecting to get some personal answers: they killed my lover, or something like that.

Javier tells me that I made the news last night. Just that *una columna de la FARC* had a *retén* 10 minutes out of Cali—it was more—and they kidnapped a *gringo* who works for the CIAT. Javier was part of the *retén.*

It's no surprise, but I'm glad to learn that everyone knows exactly what happened, and that I'm with FARC. That's better (I suppose) than being kidnapped by common criminals. With that, I'm fairly sure that Susan assumes I'm alive.

The "team hut" seems old, like it has been abandoned for years. It has three rooms, no doors separating them. One is the kitchen where I'm now sitting by a wood fire. Leidi is cutting onions. Two pots of something are simmering over the fire. One corner is fueled by a pile of firewood. The walls are of hewn logs, caulked with dried mud, a lot of which crumbled away. The floor is earthen and is not even smooth. The roof was certainly once of tile, but now of galvanized iron forged to look like tile.* I've been teaching the boys how to count to 10 in English. That, and reading the statutes of Colombian communist party.

These guys are pretty careless with weapons. One just drew a bead on Ramiro with his Galil and pulls the trigger. *Click.*

No round in the chamber.

That really bothers me. I can't stand to see people point weapons at one another. "I didn't know the gun was loaded" is the worthless refrain to any country song ever written. As I write this, Ramiro is drawing a bead on the other fellow with his M-16. This reminds me of speeding away from the *retén* yesterday in the back of that Chevy pickup with two guards.

Later. Just looked at my watch. Damn! It's 1310h. I thought it would be much later. I had a good idea for something to do: move a woodpile and wooden bench so I can move my bed closer to the wall. That'll block more of the wind. The job might take 30 minutes or, if I do it right, an hour. Ramiro says no, I'll be moved inside to sleep tonight. Oh well. That gives me something to do later in the afternoon. Quit feeling sorry for yourself, Hargrove, it won't change things, can only hurt you. The guerrilla gave me another blanket, a big one this time that would cover me entirely. I was warm for the first time, drifted off, and slept deeply for two hours. I didn't intend to do that; I want to stay awake as long as possible so I can sleep tonight. But I must have really needed the sleep.

Juaco just came back. I guess he'd been to the village. Must have walked; this unit doesn't have a vehicle. Brought supplies, some coffee, candies (divided equally among all), a pint of brandy, and a children's notebook for me. I said it was just like Christmas.

1535h. We were all outside when I heard an aircraft in the distance.

"It's searching for you," Leidi says.

I don't know if she's joking or not, but we're all ordered inside. Juaco puts a *ruana*, a peasant shawl, over his uniform and returns outside. The sound gets nearer, then fades away. The only plane I've heard in 1.5 days. I don't believe it's looking for me.

I have very little hope of being rescued. I don't even think about it. We're too remote, the mountains are too rugged. And they are dotted with little farmhouses like this one. From the back of the hut I can look across this part of the valley and see a dozen farmhouses. And this valley goes on and on, and on the other side of the mountain ridges, more valleys, more mountains.

These soldiers don't have much to do but seem quite content doing what I hate so: doing nothing. I wonder if this is typical of their day-by-day life, or if all seven have been ordered to stay here with me, to make sure I don't try anything funny.

The sleep may have done me good. I feel more content to sit here and look across this rugged and beautiful valley. Wish I could go sit by the river that I

---

*Later. There is a fourth room attached; that's apparently where Leidi lives.

hear so clearly, a couple hundred meters below us. You may as well adjust, Hargrove, because I've got a feeling I'll be here for a long time. Most of the forest has been cleared from the mountain's floor, a rotating slash-and-burn agricultural system. They grow potatoes, beans, onions, cabbage, maize, and, of course, *amapola.* A special type of palm grows on the mountainsides. It grows very straight, with bone-white bark and topped by a bunch of leaves that grow vertically, then spread. Reminds me of the hair of cartoon characters in the 7UP ads. They look more like date palms. I ask, but it doesn't seem to have a special name—just *la palma*—and the boys tell me it bears no fruit. But their white bark contrasts beautifully against the green of the valley.

I don't think I'll even bathe up here—too cold. And I will never wash my clothes. It would take days to dry them up here. And I have nothing to wear except what I arrived in. I can't borrow from the soldiers; I'm a third larger than any.

One regret, though, it's not my fault. But I can't help it, it keeps running through my mind. I was carrying a roll of [several hundred dollars in] 5,000 peso notes in my pocket. This night, I transferred all to my billfold. So all my money went at once when that bastard took my wallet at the *retén.* If I had money, these guys would buy me things. If only I had some money . . . But I don't, so forget it. Just like I wish I'd been carrying, say, an unabridged edition of *Ulysses* or *War and Peace* when I got out of my car at the *retén.* I didn't, and I should be thankful, so thankful, that the Spanish dictionary was in my pocket. The checkbooks were in my briefcase, the one Susan and the boys gave me for Christmas. The guy who stole the briefcase gave me my checkbooks.

Actually, I'm about as pampered as a prisoner can be . . . in this environment. The boys are continuously asking if they can get me coffee, food, water. They'll share anything they have—they just don't have much to share.

Juaco says my medicines will arrive tomorrow (Sunday) morning. He also says I can call Susan tomorrow. I believe the first, but the second . . . ?

The hut is 17 paces (15m?) long, maybe 5m wide. The walls and ceilings are a creamy brownish black, seasoned by years of smoke and grime, molted white splotches where the clay has crumbled away.

I'm awfully glad that I speak as much Spanish as I do.

If this had happened a couple of years ago, it would have been horrible, not being able to communicate. I just wish my Spanish were better, though.

The novelty of my writing all the time is wearing off for the guerrillas. Watching me was great entertainment yesterday and this morning. They are going to be disappointed when I finish this checkbook, though. Because I plan to start on my peso checkbook, instead of the notebook they gave me, entitled *Contigo Soy Feliz*, With You I'm Happy. The title continues to the back cover, *Porque Eres Muy Especial*, or "Because You're Very Special." In the familiar *tu* form, of course. But I can put the checkbook in my . . .

Sunday, 25 Sep., Day 3

. . . pocket; I'd have to bend the notebook and pages would fall out. I wonder if I would feel this need to write it all down had I not had that incredible experience with a diary I never wrote—but did*—in 1987. Probably. I have virtually nothing to do. Keeping the diary doubles the value of what things I do, or observe, or feel, that are even vaguely interesting (i.e., experiencing it, then writing about it).

I don't even miss my IBM PS-1 computer with 30 MB hard disk. That's so far away, it's not even worth thinking about. Like the idea that a swarm of choppers may appear from up the valley between the mountains, and soldiers will overwhelm this hut and this FARC company with massive firepower, I'll dash to a chopper, scramble aboard, and be flown back to Cali. It can't happen, so don't think about it.

1750h: It's getting dark, and Day 2 as a prisoner is closing. I'm proud that I've kept my spirits fairly high; I haven't come close to breaking down. And I won't.

I wonder if Miles and Tom G. know yet, and if so, what they think. Would Susan have told them, or would she wait until she knows more? My father and Raford, Becky and Kenny, Mrs. Sheldon? Don Fields, who honestly tried to convince me to leave Colombia.

When I interviewed for my CIAT job, I was told that no CIAT scientist had been directly affected by the *narcotráfico*, the Cartel, the guerrillas—the violence and absurdity that composes the darker side of Colombia. I've told others the same thing. Well, looks like that's no longer true, and look who breaks that peaceful tradition. But I was only driving to work, for God's sake.

The guerrillas ask me again and again if I have sons, and I tell them about Miles and Tom G. If I had a daughter, I'd have to force that bad news on them.

1805h: Ramiro comes out to talk. I ask if he received pay as a soldier. "No, only my clothes, food, things necessary to survive. And hospital care if I'm sick or wounded. We are *revolutionaries!*"

Then he points to the notebook they gave me, with a giant yellow duck on the cover. "Your notebook—it's beautiful, isn't it?"

"Yes, it's beautiful," I reply.

2035h. I'm sleeping inside tonight. On a pad of 1/5-inch-thick foam rubber over hard wooden slats. One's ideas of luxury can change fast.

Dinner was a soup of noodles, potato, lentils, and rice. Not bad. I don't even miss beef and pork. Sure.

I still find it hard to believe that I've been kidnapped and am being held either captive or hostage (the former, I hope). I've been thinking about groups that could pressure FARC for my release. Looks like there's only one, outside

*While in Vietnam I kept a diary which, for almost two decades, I'd completely forgotten about—even forgot I'd written it—until my son Miles brought it to my attention. Parts of it are included in my book *A Dragon Lives Forever*.

Colombia, and that's FARC's political mentor: Cuba. And I can't see anything developing that way. [cc]*

Started Day 3 as a prisoner with lukewarm, highly sweetened coffee, served in a mess kit. The "bed" I slept on was, I think, abandoned with this farmhouse years ago. Its bamboo slats were rotten and brittle. Half broke during the night. I had to shift constantly to keep parts of my body on solid bed. Back home we have a king-size bed, the most comfortable I've ever known. I think I'll sleep on the floor tonight.

Now that I've finished this checkbook, I wonder if I made a mistake. FARC must have foreign accounts, to buy weapons, ammo. Maybe I could have worked out a deal to deposit dollars to a FARC account abroad, and use at least some of the dollars in pesos, to buy things I need here. Too late, and best not to think about it.

1000h: Well, I found something to do. Juaco said I could not talk to Susan directly, but could write a message, which a guerrilla would read to her via phone. I asked if I could also send the same message, in Spanish, to our neighbors, the Greiners; because I'm not sure how well the English will be read, and Susan's Spanish isn't so hot. Juaco agreed. I wrote: "I am okay. I am living with FARC in the mountains. My health is good, and my spirits are high. I live almost exactly like the soldiers who guard me. They are getting allergy medicine for me. They will release me when permission comes from FARC HQ. Soon, I hope. I asked FARC to send this message. I was not forced. As proof, I will add something personal, that FARC could not know. My brother's name is Raford, his wife is Lana. My sister is Becky. Her husband is Kinney. I love you, and will be with you soon. Tom."

I translated the message word for word, for Juaco. He said it was okay.

---

*I wrote the initials "cc" here to record—in a way the guerrillas wouldn't recognize if they read my diary—the other group that might pressure FARC: the Cali Cartel, now reported to control 80% of Colombia's drug trade.—TRH

NOTEBOOK NUMBER 1
"Contigo Soy Feliz"

Sunday, 25 Sep., Day 3 (continued from Checkbook Diary)

After Juaco approved the letter, I translated it into Spanish, to be read, also by phone, to Dr. Uli Greiner or Señora Claudia Greiner or Peter Greiner. Juaco checked and approved that message, and commended me for the Spanish. "I write Spanish better than I speak it," I say. "Because when I write, I can take the time to think about the verbs, the tenses, etc."

Juaco let me copy the English message to Susan before taking it away. I added: "P.S. I think about you, and the boys, constantly."

Writing the messages, and reading them to my guards, my captors, was emotionally exhausting. The nearest I've come to losing control of my emotions. I saw the messages being passed around, so I guess most of the *guerrilleros* read them.

An old lady and a little girl moved into the attached room last night. Indians, I assume; I think everyone in this valley is Indian. I don't know how they, the woman and child, fit into the picture. They brought a dog, who looks like an ugly coyote. I'll try to make friends with him for something to do. But I'll save that for later.

1130h: The morning is going better than expected. I'm lying in the sun talking with Luis Antonio, an Indian who also lives in the attached room. His uncle owns the farmhouse and this land. He says the entire valley, practically, is Indian, of the Páez tribe. The dog's name, he tells me, is Honey.

They have a little girl named Susana. Ramiro joins us as Antonio says that there are deer, bear, and three types of tigers in the forest above us. "Lend me your rifle," I tell Ramiro, "and I'll go up the mountain and shoot us a deer for dinner." Ramiro grins, and shakes his hand. "I promise to return early."

I had talked for 30 minutes with Luis Antonio before Ramiro came. Luis Antonio had asked who I was. "A prisoner, kidnapped by FARC," I said.

Luis Antonio was surprised. "I heard about you on the radio. But," he said, "the radio report said only that a CIAT employee was kidnapped. It did not say the kidnap victim was a foreigner." Then he said something that made me laugh. Really laugh, because it was both funny and ironic. "I thought you were the

25

commander of these soldiers," he said. "Why?" I asked incredulously. "Because you are dressed well, and the others are so poor. And they keep serving you things—like coffee and water." Reflecting on it, I can see how he could think that. I wrote earlier that I'm treated with courtesy and respect. That continues. It's almost embarrassing, considering my role in this . . . I don't have the word for it. Absurdity?

Yet even as I write this, Ramiro reappears and hands me a canteen cup of Coca-Cola. Yes, Coke. I have no idea where they got it. I share mine with Susana, who is, I guess, about two or three years old.

I ask Juaco about the military structure of FARC. It has ranks—private, sergeant, etc.—like the regular army. Juaco is a *teniente*, a lieutenant. He is 17 years old.

Luis Antonio told me earlier about the way the people in this valley support the guerrillas.

I ask Luis Antonio if he's heard of CIAT. Yes—but only in the news about me, he says. So my kidnapping is accomplishing something positive for CIAT's public awareness program (which I run—or should say *ran*?).

I wonder how the life these *guerrilleros* live—that *we're* living—compares with the lives of my other friends, Victor and Charley, that I knew two decades ago. Pretty much the same, I suspect. Living sparsely but fairly secure, in a valley they control. Convinced of the justness of their cause, although their explanations of it are prepackaged in communist texts. But these texts were penned by Che Guevara, not Ho Chi Minh.

The team hut is dark inside, and cluttered with gear, ammo, along with the Walkmans, transistor radios, and cassette tapes that one would expect in a group of teenage boys. Yeah, I bet Victor and Charley, in the Asia of my youth, lived just about like my present hosts live today.

Luis Antonio is more curious about me than any of the guerrillas. And about how I view the world in general. "Bill Clinton is your president, no?"

"Yes," I assure him.

He asks a lot of questions, including, "Clinton is poor, no?"

"Not really," I say.

"Pero, era pobre, no?"

I hesitate. I'm looking directly at the one tiny room, about 4x4 meters, where Luis Antonio, his wife, and daughter are crammed. It can't even be closed here in the cold mountain air. It has a single door of wooden planks, 1½ meters high. The roof is 2½ meters high. The difference is open space. The floor is earthen, and the walls are of dried clay.

No, I'd better not try to explain. *"Es verdad,"* I say. "President Clinton was raised poor." Bill Clinton, I wish you could see the life of these Colombian *campesinos*, who have heard that the President of the United States was raised poor, like them.

We talked about the white-barked palms that stand so majestically on the mountainsides. He says they produce *cera*—which I finally figured out is sap, or oil, which they take to a *fábrica* to make into *velas* (candles).

I go out to inspect the opium poppies intercropped with onions in the field in front of our hut. There must be 50 or 60 plants. Only a few have flowered, with bright red flowers. The green pods hang down on stems below the flowers. In photos of opium poppies grown in Asia, the pods stand erect. I wonder how they harvest the sap. I'll ask Luis Antonio later.

It's now 1320h. I feel somewhat better—a sense of relief, perhaps—having sent that message to Susan. At least, she'll know I'm alive. I wonder if she's ever thought I might be dead by now. I wonder what the chances are that I might, indeed, *be* dead before this is over, that this little adventure might be the last of my life. I write that with little emotion. I'm honestly not very afraid. Not for myself, anyway. But I really don't know how this story will end. The assurance that I'll be released soon—coming from my teenage guards high on this remote mountainside—really doesn't mean much. And it doesn't fit the pattern of Colombian kidnappings. Oh well, *qué será, será.*

1400h: At lunch, I entertain the entire guerrilla unit by reading "Useful Phrases" (*Locuciones Utiles*) from the back of my English-Spanish dictionary. They think I'm a very funny *prisionero* indeed. The favorite phrases are:

"Is service included in the bill?"

"Do you accept traveler's checks?"

"Where can I get a taxi?"

Breakfast this morning was rice and noodles and hot chocolate. Lunch was rice topped with a mixture of pastas and chopped sardines, with a canteen cup of Coke, which, I see, they've brought from the village rebottled in empty liquor bottles. A sack of fresh provisions has arrived and I checked it out. Rice, spaghetti, lentils. I think we still have chopped fish. So it looks like we'll dine like *kings.*

During lunch Tony ran up the mountainside, barking menacingly. *Guerrilleros* grabbed rifles and headed outside. It was just a cow, but it must show that the guerrillas are uneasy. Maybe.

"I'm very lucky to have such a wonderful opportunity to practice Spanish," I told the group after lunch. *"Claro que sí."* All agree that I'm fortunate. They think I'm serious, for God's sake.

I just thought. Peter Kerridge paid a lot of money for a "total immersion" Spanish course, and I'm getting the experience free. An Australian, Peter was also stopped at a guerrilla *retén* en route to Quito to take that course. They let him go. Mark Winslow, another American, and his wife were also held by the guerrillas, in the mountains near Palmira, for three hours, then let go. But that was two years ago.

Of course, the U.S. Embassy issued warnings three or four months ago that at least 10 U.S. citizens were being held hostage in Colombia—the most ever. Eleven now, I suppose. I wonder if the U.S. Embassy has been notified? And what it might do. Change the statistics on the advisory, I guess.

I wonder if the fact that the U.S. Embassy warns all U.S. citizens not to even visit Cali or the entire Cauca Valley will have any bearing on its attitude

toward my case. No one from the U.S. Embassy is even allowed to visit the
Cauca Valley, so I don't expect an embassy representative to call on Susan.

Later—Leidi interrupts my writing to *charlar*, or chat. The female guerrillera wears fatigues and boots like the men, stands about five feet tall, has a shy
but sincere grin, and carries a pearl-handled (yes, really a pearl-handled) .45 automatic tucked into the front of her trousers.

She is 17, from a poor Indian family that grows cassava and beans near
Santander, and seems to have a thing going with Juaco. I think FARC assigned
Leidi to this company to do "women's work." She offered to wash my clothes,
but I'll wait for a sunny day. It's drizzling now, and is damp and clammy.
Drying my clothes would take days in this weather. I'm the first foreigner Leidi
has ever met, and I'm sure the first any of these kids has met.

1610h: These guys are really careless with their weapons. I sort of wish
they wouldn't be. My uncle Rex Fields could teach them a thing or two about
gun safety, like he taught me so long ago.

I seldom have access to my dictionary now. All the guerrillas are borrowing
it, copying words they want to learn. I can ask for the dictionary back, but I
don't like doing that. I may want some *compañeros* who speak English if I stay
here as long as I fear.

1700h: Dinner was served at 1645h. Rice topped with lentils. These people
eat as much rice as Filipinos. Honestly. I wonder if they'd continue eating rice
as their staple if, suddenly, they became wealthy. An Asian would, of course.

I assume that CIAT learned on Friday of my abduction, so my absence tomorrow morning won't surprise my communications unit. Wish I could send a
message to Nathan and Walter, María del Carmen and Alex and Pacho, Becky,
Gail, Gladys . . . all of them. But I won't ask. I doubt that they'll allow me to
send many messages, and I want to contact Susan again.

1810h: It's almost dark. Five of the guerrillas are standing together, joking
and smoking at the far end of this house. The other two are asleep in the adjacent room. And I've been in the kitchen, alone. The temptation . . .

But I'm proud of my conduct, at the close of my third day of captivity. I
haven't been depressed; my spirits are high. I'll see this through.

2330h: Somewhere in the mountains. When I wrote the above I thought the
day was almost through. I was wrong! At 1835h, after dark, Leidi told me it was
time to march. I put my few possessions in a plastic bag and we picked our way
in darkness down to the road by the river, where a truck drove up 10 minutes
later. And who was driving the truck? Rambo, the *guerrillero* who seemed to be
in charge of the *retén* where I was captured. Rambo, God's gift to the Indian
girls of the unnamed valley where we'd stayed the past two days. Rambo, who
called me *gringo*, and who I hoped to never see again. Rambo, wearing tiger fatigues, high boots, and a floppy jungle hat, one brim pinned up Australian style.

A motorbike passed as we loaded; I had to sit on the truck bed, surrounded
by soldiers so I couldn't be seen.

We drove about 15 minutes, then stopped at a point where two horses and
a mule were waiting. The *guerrilleros* packed supplies on one of the horses. I'm

given a woolen *ruana*, the typical shawl worn by peasants in the mountains of Colombia. Sleeveless, it has an opening for your head, then hangs, front and back, from your shoulders. Dark blue, but I won't know that until tomorrow. I'm also given a woolen scarf. "Can you ride a horse?" someone asked. "Of course." But then Rambo took the horse, and I mounted the mule. Damn! Later, I'd be grateful.

(I'll continue the story of last night's trip as I get the chance.)

Monday, 26 Sep., Day 4

It wasn't hard to get me up at 0630h. I'd been freezing all night. I pulled on my boots and stumbled outside, curious to see what this hut, this terrain, looked like. The front yard of our hut was a pen where a single heifer stood. A panorama of green mountains and valley lay before me. To my right, a *guerrillero* stood watch on a crest, cradling an AK-47. His bright, pinkish-red *ruana* was almost fluorescent, and contrasted sharply with the olive of his fatigues and the green of the mountainside. What a photo! If only I had a camera. The colors won't help security much, though.

Fog soon rolls in and the valley disappears. We're in a misty, ghostlike atmosphere as *guerrilleros* drive our two horses, mule, and burro into the pen and start packing provisions. I inspect our hut. It's made of logs crisscrossed horizontally by a double row of branches, with mud and straw packed between the branches. Five rustic rooms, all with hewn-plank floors and a roof of wooden branches topped by asbestos (I think) formed like tile. Behind, the forest has been cleared for slash-and-burn farming for about 200 meters. Then the forest begins.

(Back to last night.) We travelled 4½ hours, hardly stopping, over what I surmise was incredibly beautiful, and know was incredibly rugged, terrain. Rambo and I were mounted, leading a packhorse, and the soldiers were on foot. I'll say this for the FARC guerrilla: those little guys can *march*. We crossed streams crashing down over slippery trail, little more than a meter wide in places, with an almost sheer drop-off leading to a cold, rushing river that you could hear and feel, but not see, a hundred meters below. The phrase "as surefooted as a mule" keeps running through and reassuring my mind. *Keep your damned horse, Rambo.* I'm happy with my unromantic, but surefooted (I hope), mule. A *guerrillero* leads the mule, but the leash is six or seven meters long, so the mule picks his own way. I long ago quit guiding him and trust he knows better than me.

My saddle is western style, with a high pommel. The stirrups are typical South American, forged of metal with open backs and a solid front—like putting your foot into a half shoe. Far more practical than the stirrups in Texas.

We're joined by more soldiers and a tough little burro loaded with supplies, somewhere in the night. After two hours of travel, we reach the crest of the mountain. Almost. Then the trail disappears and we face only a face of almost sheer rock. Wrong trail, wrong mountain. We turn around, backtrack across all those rivers and ravines, and start up another mountain.

An hour later Rambo's horse gives out and he, too, is walking. I'm grinning as we plod along, me and my mule.

At 2300h, we finally reach a mud house near the crest of a mountain. A farmer guides us inside. The *guerrilleros* spread packs and prepare a bed, of sorts, for me.

Rambo comes in and we talk for 30 minutes before going to bed. He's 22 years old and has fought with FARC for 10 years. I'm surprised to learn that he's a Peruvian who came to Colombia to join the revolution. He's a communist who admires Che Guevara greatly.

"What do you think of *Sendero Luminoso*," I ask, referring to the Shining Path, Peru's Maoist revolutionary group.

"Terrorists," Rambo says. "I hate them."

I can't believe this. I'm riding a mule, wearing a *ruana*, and guarded by a platoon of Marxist guerrillas, headed from one camp to another . . . who knows?

"Have you ever met an American before me?"

"Only one—in a village called La Buitrera, near Palmira, about a year ago."

I know that village. Alexandra Walter, one of my CIAT employees, has a farm there. Susan and I visited La Buitrera several times.

"Did the *gringo* know you were a *guerrillero*?"

"Oh, no. He had no idea."

"Did he speak Spanish?"

"Yes, but poorly. He lived in La Buitrera and worked at CIAT."

Then it hits me. "His wife is from South America?"

"Yes, and they have two children."

That can only be one person, Dr. William Bell. Bill Bell. I can't wait to tell him.

I find it hard to believe, but Rambo is the most interesting person I've met since the kidnapping.

The night was cold and damp. I hardly slept.

[start Day 4 again] Breakfast was a stew of thick beef bones and lots of meat—my first meat in five days—and bowls of sweetened milk.

1210h: We left camp at 0900h and have ridden steadily—south, I think— until now. We have stopped to rest the horses at an abandoned house over- looking a beautiful valley with a wild river flowing below.

I ask Rambo if my mule has a name. *"Sí, Batalla."* *Batalla.* Battle. What an appropriate name.

I'm sitting on the porch and a

[gap]

will be eight hours. We're going to the *sede*, the headquarters of FARC. There, I'll learn my fate. Everyone assures me I'll be set free, and I'd like to think that. But if so, why this trip? Couldn't I have been freed by radio? This caravan includes 15 *guerrilleros*, 3 horses, and a mule named Battle. Just to take little ol' me to FARC HQ?

We rode along slippery trails through ephemeral primeval forests cloaked in mist. Past waterfalls and across rushing streams. Along steep mountainsides. Through the ghosts of rain forests, marked by tombstones of dead stumps. How did they get the logs out, from regions so remote? Down the rushing stream below, I guess. But the stream looks too small and rocky, the water too wild, to float logs.

Tuesday, 27 Sep., Day 5

As we rode yesterday, the terrain changed from forested and deforested mountains to a beautiful terrain that had, obviously, never had trees. *"Sabana,"* Rambo said, but it's not like the Colombian savannas I've known. The mountains are still steep and rugged. Clumps of grass grow in swampy mountainside [*illegible*] and are topped by the palmlike plant Maguen called *frailejón*. I picture in my mind a squad of Blackhawk helicopters—the Colombian army— emerging from the horizon. But not to rescue me. No, to take advantage of this wonderful opportunity to put superior firepower to work against a column of guerrillas in the open. But that prospect doesn't seem to concern the guerrillas. I could be killed by "friendly fire." I mention the potential danger to a *guerrillero*.

"Helicopters can't operate here," he says. "Not with these clouds, this fog." He's right, I guess. The clouds clear only briefly, then cover the valley again.

It began to drizzle, and the soft rain continued as we rode across mountain ridges and valleys for what seemed to be the next four hours. We crossed several mountains and valleys. I couldn't locate the sun. Too much overcast, too much drizzle. I was absolutely amazed at the sheer rock mountainsides that we climbed, up and down. Sheer, wet stone, 45 degrees or more. I should have been terrified, but I knew that, somehow, the mule could make it.

We reached our destination at 1710h—eight hours' ride, like Rambo said. Then I had to stand in woods and we waited until it was totally dark. Then we ascended into another valley, wading down a stream of icy rushing water, slipping, groping through the mud. Ramiro offered a hand and we edged our way together. We had to cross two flimsy bridges over rushing rivers below. The first was two bamboo poles with a higher, parallel pole to grasp. Not so bad. But I couldn't believe the second bridge. It was like a 10-meter ladder, one meter wide, thrown over the icy river, rushing white among huge boulders. Rotten wooden slats crisscrossed two beams every few feet. Nothing to hold on to. A slip would throw us into almost certain death. I hold Juaco's hand and we cross, step-by-step. "Don't look down!" Juaco shouts. Ridiculous. The steps aren't evenly spaced. I look down, all the way, as my feet connect to the rotten steps, but trying to block out the white foam rushing below.

We waded through more mud, crossed more streams until, at 2030h, a dark empty hut appeared. No need to describe the hut; pretty much like the others.

Someone had provided the guerrillas with a pan of cold rice topped with chunks of salty beef. I wasn't hungry, but hadn't eaten for more than 12 hours. I have to keep up my strength.

0900h: I can't walk around here, like at the other camps. I'm kept shut in this dark room where I spent the night.

Breakfast is brought to me. A broken orange plastic bowl of cold rice topped with a single fried egg. I'm so lucky I wear boots. If I wore shoes, how could I have survived the walking, climbing, the 1.5 hours of wading through cold mud last night. My Justin Ropers have slick leather soles, which isn't good. But they haven't leaked. My socks, boots are soaked—but from water seeping through the leather.

Maybe I reached my lowest point last night, waiting in the forest for it to be dark enough to continue. I fully realized then what I've known all along. They're not going to let me go when we reach the camp. Not after all this.

Somehow my bed last night was the best of the three I've had so far. I was also warm, for the first time. I woke in the night thinking about how hopeless my situation is. No, Tom, I thought, you're warm. You've slept four hours. God knows you need the sleep. Don't ruin it by lying here feeling sorry for yourself. You probably won't have this chance tomorrow night.

I went back to sleep, and slept well. I even dreamed. I don't remember what I dreamed, except that the dreams were happy, about somewhere else.

I ask for a razor. Have been trying to decide whether to continue on a beard—I have a good start—or shave. Maybe it's better to shave, for the same reason the British in India and Africa dressed for dinner. To maintain who they really are.

I hear a distant shout, and a guerrilla answers. Someone is approaching. I'm hustled away from the fire in the kitchen, into a dark back room where I can't be seen. A tiny, glassless window lets a stream of light in. There's an AK-47, with a full clip inserted, right beside me, and I'm alone in this room. I wish they wouldn't do that.

Back to shaving. I ask for a razor, but none is to be found. None of these kids really shave, they have only hints of beards. Rambo, of course, doesn't shave anyway. Probably violates some revolutionary principle.

My black pen has finally died. A *guerrillero* gives me this blue one. The black pen has a white tag "TOM" taped on by María Iglesia, my secretary at CIAT. That tag is a link to who I really am. But I can't carry anything extra. I try to transfer the tag to my new pen, but I can't. I must leave the pen behind. Somehow, that hurts.

Juaco shows me a homemade fishing rod this morning and said we'll fish for trout. I had joked about stopping to fish as we crossed so many beautiful mountain streams. I guess he thinks I'm really gung ho to fish. And I want to fish, when we get the chance.

But now we're packing to march to yet another camp. Will I change camps every day or so, as long as I'm held? Probably. It's done that way in the movies, and this whole experience is like a movie.

In *Vietnam at the Movies** Lee Lanning wrote that the Vietnam War at the movies is nothing like the real Vietnam. Well, [being] kidnapped by the South American guerrillas follow[s] a movie script pretty closely.

I'm drying my boots as we sit around the fire, waiting to go. That's when I notice a metal gadget, also drying. No, that can't be what I think. I pick it up. It's so hot, I can barely hold it. Yes, it's a clip of 30-caliber ammo that Leidi had left on the fire to dry. "I'm going to leave, if you're not more careful," I tell the guerrilla.

Rambo gave me a new pair of trousers last night. I can't believe it, but they fit. They are 100 percent polyester, so they aren't as comfortable as cotton, but I'm not complaining. I wore them as pajamas. One reason I was so warm. I'm now wearing the muddy trousers I was captured in. Unless we settle down somewhere, I'm going to continue using the new trousers only as something dry to sleep in. Juaco tells me I'll soon get some socks (my one pair already has two holes) and rubber boots. Underwear, too, maybe. Maybe even a second shirt. I'd really like more socks and boots. I'd like to leave this fire, but if I do, my only socks and boots will quit drying.

The climate here is, maybe, about like Agostura, a fishing camp high in the mountains of New Mexico, where we went on vacation when I was a kid. Except it rains all the time and is colder.

My possessions are increasing. I now have a towel, two candles, and a little box of matches. Also, a porcelain coffee cup that I snatched two camps ago. It goes in a bag along with my soap, towel, etc. on the packhorse. If I had to carry the cup, I'd throw it away. Later I've put on my socks and boots, even though they're not yet dry, because I have to write something. Something hard, and I don't want to be in the midst of the guerrillas when I write it. But maybe writing it will make it easier to accept.

I'm not going to be released. I've known that really, for several days. But they kept telling me I'd be set free in a day or two.

I confronted Rambo directly this morning: Am I being held for *rescate*, ransom? Yes, and a letter is being sent to the CIAT. There. That wasn't so bad, writing it. Why did I fear it would be?

What I had pictured won't happen. I thought, maybe, I'd be taken to some FARC official who'd apologize for the mistake, tell me how proud he is that his country, Colombia, is host to CIAT, and shake hands. Tomorrow, a hard day's ride through the mountains to some village, where I'll be given bus fare to Cali. I'd take a taxi home, knowing that Susan, or one of our neighbors, could pay the cab.

No, that's not going to happen. And writing it is facing it. I feel a little better. But as I write, the brief sunshine has gone, and a cold breeze has picked up in this muddy valley. And I'm *not* writing symbolically.

1210h: Still waiting. I'd have thought we'd be on the trail hours ago. Rambo has gone with the horses. Maybe to get more supplies.

*Fawcett Columbine, 1994.

Here he comes now, with Erika, on horseback, leading two donkeys with packs. Where's Batalla, my mule? A live chicken is lashed to Erika's saddle. Tonight's dinner? This camp is obviously a way station for FARC units who pass through. It's stacked with cooking pans, dishes, cooking oils, etc. I amble through, looking for something to steal to make life a bit more comfortable. There's nothing. What did I expect to find, a well-stocked library? What *could* make this life more comfortable, anyway? I really can't think of much.

1325h: A *guerrillero* appears, leading Batalla, and we leave at 1215h. Batalla is exhausted. My "surefooted mule" slipped a couple of times on level mud before we started straight up the mountains.

Javier led the mule by a rope. He kept slipping. Then Juaco tied his backpack to the side of my saddle. That much weight to the right threw the mule off balance. We approached a level area where Rambo and Erika are waiting. I say, where Rambo can hear it clearly, "The mule can't maintain his balance with all that weight to one side." Rambo observes, says something, and Juaco slips the pack back onto his own back.

Higher up, Batalla can hardly climb. I get off and climb by foot, Javier behind me leading the mule. Higher still, I stop and sit on a stone, waiting. Finally—here they come, and I curse. Javier is riding Batalla! "That's my goddamned mule!" I say in English, and Javier understands. He dismounts, and I take his place. Sorry, Batalla, I was trying to make it easier. But I'll be damned if I'm going to climb through mud by foot, so that a smart-ass 16-year-old can ride you in my place.

We reach a high, sloping valley of mud at about 1320h. It's covered with swamp, clumps of grass, and the palmlike shrub the guerrillas call *frailejón*. We'll stay here, Rambo says. I'm disappointed. I'd rather be riding with nothing to do. The hut here is another way camp, but it's only one room, and there are holes 1.5 meters long and almost one meter high in the mud walls. While the others are unloading the packhorses, I go inside and look around. On a broken bamboo bed along one wall I find a pile of moldy medical supplies. Cotton swabs, antibiotics, etc. I sift through, hoping no one walks in. I finally find something worth stealing. Maybe. It's one of those two-piece waterproof plastic boxes, the kind that the army issues. It's the size to hold a pack of cigarettes. It's not really waterproof anymore, it's broken and held together by dirty, moldy adhesive tape. Still, the plastic box should keep my matches dry. I slip it into my pocket.

Later: Watching the group unpack our supplies makes me uneasy. Seven cans of sardines, 10 of chopped fish, seven packets of chocolate, five of coffee, three plastic dishes of Axion soap to wash dishes. How long will we stay here? Of four camps so far, this is the worst. Easily. About two kilometers high, the guerrillas say.

Later, I learn. Plans are to stay here 10 days. A wooden and bamboo bed frame stands outside along one side of the hut, like at our first camp. The soldiers hang a canvas half tent, from the hut's roof over the bed. Someone lays one of those one-inch pads of foam rubber over the bed frame, then some blankets. Erika proudly leads me to it. I have my own tent. I can pull the canvas side down, and sit on the bed in private in my *casa acuática*, my tent. I'm grateful, I guess. I really don't know how to handle things like this. Should I be thankful for making me a tent, when I wouldn't need a tent if they hadn't kidnapped me?

1430h: I'm back in my tent. Something terrible has happened. I had one pair of socks, one fucking pair of muddy soaked socks. I was sitting around the fire barefoot, talking with the guerrillas while drying my boots and socks, when I look, and one sock is burning! I grab the sock and put the fire out with my hands, but it's too late. The sock is burned almost into two pieces. That was too much. Everything was swirling and I thought I'd cry, and in front of the goddamned guerrillas. I pull on my wet boots and rush out to my tent. I pull myself together. It's not so bad. My boots fit well, and if my feet are wet all the time anyway, maybe I don't need socks. It's just that I have so little. The less you have, the more each thing means to you. Maybe I'll learn some humility from this entire experience. And this alleviates another problem. I'll wash the burned sock, tear it in two, and I'll have two rags that I can carry like a handkerchief. I don't have a handkerchief, and I miss it. I'd used mine to wipe spilled tea off the dashboard when I left home last Friday, and it was lying there, in my car, when I was taken away at the *retén*.

1645h: I'm back in the tent. I don't want to stay here all the time, but it's a cold, steady drizzle outside. Ramiro pops in to visit and asks why I'm not using the beautiful tiger-striped pen he gave me. Out of ink. He takes the cartridge, rolls it between his palms, bangs it against a log, and puts it back in the pen. My "*recuerdo*" pen functions once more. For a while Ramiro asks what I've just written. I translate and say, "We can continue this all day." That's really funny. We laugh a lot.

Ramiro tells me that it's his personal tent I'm using. Now, for *that* I'm truly grateful. Rambo and Erika appear with a present: a beautiful pair of green woolen tube socks, size 10–13. "USA 94" and a U.S. flag are woven into the fabric twice, obviously a reference to the 1994 World Cup games, held in the U.S.A. I guess they thought I was pretty upset over the burned socks. I'm not going to wear them with my boots, but will save them to sleep in, dry. I've found that I can still wear the burned sock. The front part works just fine, and the heel's not so important anyway. I wonder how much of the next 10 days will be spent like this, sitting in the tent as it rains outside. Rambo says we will go trout fishing tomorrow, if the rain stops. Hope so. I haven't been trout fishing since that wonderful trip with the Robies in Iran the summer of 1970.

I wonder what Susan is doing now. I hope her mother comes down. But what if I'm held for months? She can't stay alone in Cali. It makes no sense. I wonder if my message to her was really sent. I feel awful for the pain, the trouble all this is causing, but there was never one single thing I could have done to change fate. I drove into that *retén*. And now all I can do is survive. I will.

1750h: Leidi comes in with two more blankets, and arranges them. "I'm not a man who gets sick easily," I tell her. "But I must be especially careful

now. For me to get sick here would be bad—not only for me, but also for you."
She agrees. I'm very lucky. I've been cold and wet almost continuously for five
days, yet I've never even had a sniffle. Not only is this valley a swamp, the
mountainsides are, too. I know that sounds contradictory, but it's true. Hundreds
of little springs seep from the sides of the mountains. A thick layer of grass, a
cloverlike plant, and, I think, moss, absorbs and holds water like a sponge.

The valleys here are savanna, then a broad belt of forest covers the mountainsides about halfway up. The upper half or third of the mountains is, again,
savanna.

1910h: Well, I'm in my tent for the night, a guard outside. I'm not used to
going to bed so early, but . . . The chicken that rode up here strapped to Erika's
saddle becomes the second, and last, meal of the day. Cooked with potatoes and
noodles into a stew. And guess what? No rice!

The allergy seems to have gone away, up here in the clear mountain air. A
good thing, because Juaco never brought the medicines he promised.

Wednesday, 28 Sep., Day 6

0730h: I am sitting in my bunk. Have been awake about an hour, but
haven't "gotten up" yet. My God, I've spent more than 12 hours—half a day—
shut in this tent since 7:10 last night. Plus hours yesterday afternoon as it rained
steadily. The guerrillas start getting up around 0630h, but some will still be
sleeping. I don't have much incentive for rising early to face the day. I have only
three things on today's agenda: 1) Rearrange the bedding, to make this bed more
comfortable; 2) Go trout fishing, if it's not raining. But it's raining steadily, as
it did all yesterday afternoon, and all last night; 3) Find something to keep in
the tent as a temporary urinal. Now, that's really practical when you consider
that I'm locked in this tent—flaps staked down from outside—for 12 hours at a
time. The floor of the tent is mud and a few slippery wet stones. There's about
1.5 meters of the floor from the edge of my bunk to where the tent flap *almost*
reaches the mud. The outer edge of the tent area is pools of water.

0755h: Okay, Hargrove, you have to get up. That means taking off my
warm green socks and putting on those cold wet boots, barefoot. I put my
"burned" socks on a stone below to dry last night. This morning, I can wring
water from them.

0830h: I am sitting by the fire in the hut with the guerrillas, drinking a
lukewarm *tinto* of sweetened coffee. The smoke inside is so thick, I'm going to
return to my tent. Inside, the hut is about 10x7 meters, with a single door and
a window, 1x.5 meters, without glass. About 20 percent of the area is taken up
by the "fireplace"—a raised portion in one corner on which the log fire is built.
That's where eight guerrillas sleep. The only advantage of the hut is its dry floor.
I prefer my tent. Two are women. The third woman, Erika, left yesterday afternoon. She came by to say good-bye, and wish me well.

We talked about slavery, and I don't think she liked the conversation. I'll
miss Erika. She was someone to talk with. I must describe her because she, too,

seems from a movie set. Erika is almost 18, stands about 5'8", and is a stunning woman. She has long, reddish-brown hair, bunched in the back and flowing over her shoulders. In her form-fitted, tiger-striped fatigues, high boots, and cradling an AK-47, she reminds me of Patty Hearst in that famous photo from around 1968. The guerrillas call her "La Italiana," so I thought she was really Italian at first. She's Colombian, of course.

Patty Hearst. The wealthy heiress was kidnapped by an off-the-wall revolutionary group and held for ransom in the late sixties. But while in captivity, she apparently became mesmerized, and joined forces with her captors. That won't happen to me, but I wish I'd read more about the psychology of being a prisoner, a hostage, a kidnap victim. Plenty has been written, after the Vietnam POWs, the U.S. Embassy hostages in Iran, Terry White and all those hostages in Lebanon. Susan has read more of that than me, and would know what a prisoner should watch for. One thing, I think, is becoming emotionally attached to your captors. One thing I really regret about Susan's situation is that our electronic mail system at home was out when I was abducted. Susan loves e-mail, and it would be so good for her to have contact with Ken McKinney, Bill Smith, Ricks Pluenneke, and others in this time. "E-mail is something you never miss until you've had it," Susan says. "But once you've had it, you can't live without it." God, I wish for some way to contact Susan, discuss this situation and how we should approach it, both from her end and mine. I know that what is happening will change our lives—but I'm not sure how.

1000h: Breakfast was crackers and coffee—nothing more. The rain has stopped, although the sun isn't out. I can't stay here in this pale green light under the tent all morning. I'll put on those wet boots and go outside. But to do what?

1015h: I was wrong about breakfast. Either a late breakfast or early lunch is now served. A bowl of rice topped by boiled potatoes, and a piece of the neck of that chicken we stewed last night. I'm not hungry, but I eat. I've never been hungry since this began, but I eat to stay strong and, maybe, warmer. Ramiro and Javier are digging a well and trench to divert water from the spring closer to the camp. Afterward we'll go fishing. Leidi has to mend my khaki trousers, underwear, and burned socks and will wash them while I'm gone. She swears the trousers will be dry, to sleep in tonight. I sure hope so. I won't wear socks; I must have the dry socks for tonight.

One aspect of this experience is *not* like I'd have imagined it. I have not met a higher official. I wonder if there really is one? Am I a hostage of the higher, nationwide FARC, as I assumed earlier, or of this unit, the Cauca Front, that took me? The latter, I'm beginning to suspect. Wow. Has a ransom letter gone to CIAT yet? If so, for how much? And how was the *rescate* determined? I suspect the letter has been sent. And I doubt it matters whether I work for CIAT, or British Petroleum. I may have said something to improve my situation that, ironically, worsened my situation. On Night 2, up on the mountain in our second camp, Rambo came in to talk. I told him about CIAT, the centers, our mandate, etc. Rambo said something about CIAT being a *gringo* organization.

"Oh, no," I said. "We're funded by 20 countries and international agencies," and named the major donors. I was not only trying to establish that CIAT is *not* a U.S. organization, I was also stressing our internationality. For obvious reasons.

When Rambo later told me I was, indeed, a hostage, I said that I doubted CIAT could pay the ransom. Rambo actually—DAMN! A gun just went off in the hut about three inches of mud from me. One of these damn kids playing with his weapon, no doubt. If I were in charge of FARC, I'd teach some principles of firearm safety, and enforce them. Everyone is laughing, like a weapon's going off by accident is really funny. (Resume:) Rambo actually seemed surprised. "But isn't your salary paid by 20 countries?" he said.

I tried to explain, but it's hopeless. If this group indeed sets the ransom, that information may have doubled it. A good example of how well-intended public awareness information can backfire. And whatever CIAT is and does, doesn't seem to make a damned bit of difference with this group.

1320h: The rain stopped for a couple of hours, and the guerrillas started building a stone path to the new well. I may as well do whatever I can to improve my own living conditions, I thought. I went to work as much for the physical exercise and to escape boredom as for what improvements I can make. I'm not one of those men who can do anything with his hands. But I dug a little ditch to drain the pools of standing water from inside my tent. I gathered wood and rotten bamboo and make a sidewalk, sort of, so I can step outside the tent without sinking to the ankles in mud. And I found a piece of log, sawed smooth on each end, that I've moved into my tent as a little table. Then it started raining again. Someone had painted on the log "Carlos. FARC: EP" (EP = *Ejército Pueblo*, or Village Army).

I can set my coffee cup on it, and maybe other things, if it dries out (but *how can* it dry out?). I like having my own coffee cup, but I'm no longer proud of stealing it, because I now realize that I didn't steal it from FARC, I stole it from the poor Indian family whose house FARC had taken over. And I realize—so much clearer now—how much little things mean to people who have almost nothing. I'd give the cup back, if I could. But I can't, so I may as well enjoy having it.

The improvements the guerrillas are making are further evidence that we'll be here a long time. This is the most miserable—yet the most beautiful—camp yet. Ranges of steep mountain on all sides, covered with dense forest and culminating in jagged peaks of stone. Down the valley, a waterfall's cascades fall almost straight down sheer mountainside. The waters stand white against forest that's so green, it's almost blue. I can always hear the river rushing below us.

Lunch was a stew of potatoes, and noodles, with a can of chopped fish thrown in for flavor. The guerrilla call the fish *atún*, or tuna—but I looked at a can. The manufacturer didn't have the guts to call it anything more aristocratic than *pescado* [fish]. Dessert was hot *agua panela*, made from sugarcane.

1515h: I stood outside for a long time, watching the water from the spring flow. But my feet were freezing, and it started raining again, so I came back to my tent. The guerrillas are all in the hut, sleeping, cleaning weapons, or just sitting on their bunks. I doubt that they ever get bored. There is nothing to read. I wonder if any of them have ever read a book, or a newspaper, for that matter.

One thing I have to avoid is smoking. *Guerrilleros* are always offering me a cigarette. It would be awfully easy to start smoking with this kind of heavy depressing boredom. I told them how I quit smoking 13 months ago, using acupuncture. Needles in my body, pins in my ears. I don't think they believed a word.

I'd like to go to sleep, but that would be a mistake. My nights start at seven P.M., and I seldom sleep before the early morning hours. Know what I think I'd like, more than anything else to help me survive this? Sleeping pills. The nights here are so long, with nothing to do but think. You want to shut off the thinking, but you can't. And tomorrow will be the same. And this may go on for weeks, months.

1607h: Ramiro comes by and helps arrange the tent again. Gives me a lot more room. He notices holes in the tent, from stones that last night's guard set to hold down the flaps with a boulder. I apologize for the torn tent. "No, it's not your fault, it's the guard's fault. *Puta*," he says. Whore. No, but I still feel bad. This tent is probably Ramiro's most prized possession. I'm sure of it. Ramiro's a good kid, really, and seems smart. Too bad he'll probably die some rainy day, in these mountains. On a *retén* that goes bad. And for what?

1645h: The rain stops and a *guerrillero* takes the single pole and heads for the little stream behind the hut. I asked if I can go. He said to ask Juaco. I'll be damned if I will. Juaco knows that I want to go trout fishing more than anything else I could do here. Ramiro says that Rambo will return tomorrow with more supplies, including fishhooks. We'll go trout fishing tomorrow.

1710h: It's getting dark, and my sixth day as a prisoner is ending. And my sixth 12-hour night shift, in this tent, will soon begin. There's nothing to do but bear it. I think about Miles and Tom G. I wish I could let them know I'm all right.

I hope Rambo brings news—as well as fishhooks—tomorrow morning. I've asked for a newspaper, a magazine, anything, but gotten nothing. I can't help hoping, of course, that Rambo will bring news that I'm free. But I know not to hope that too much.

1830h: I am shut in already. Ramiro and Leidi come to say good night. Leidi washed my khaki trousers. Those two and Juaco will be my guards tonight. Each watches a two-hour shift. Ramiro is such a little lost kid. I'd like to adopt him. Instead, he's standing outside my tent with an M-16, to make sure I don't escape. Would he really shoot me if I tried? Probably, he'd have to, for his own survival.

Thursday, 29 Sep., Day 7

0850h: Last night was forever. It was freezing, and wet. The bamboo poles on my bunk collapsed, and there was no way to make even a semilevel surface to lie on. The nights are the worst. If only I could just sleep through them, like nights are meant to be handled. Six P.M. is about the time I usually get home from work. Then we do so many things before going to bed. Susan and I have drinks, talk about the day, watch the news on CNN. Preparing dinner is a major activity and one that's fun. Then I may write on my computer, or we may watch a video, or read, or all of those things. Then a bath and to bed. Sleep usually comes easily. Here, I'm getting in my tent cell at six P.M. I can't read. I can't even sit on the side of my bed because my feet would rest in the mud . . . with nothing to do but try to be comfortable and warm—and try to sleep and to fight off *those thoughts*, the destructive, dangerous thoughts that come with the cold and the dark.

Last night I heard a distant scream that could only have been a puma, a mountain lion. An owl hooted steadily. And there were other night animal sounds that I couldn't recognize.

I drifted in and out of sleep through the morning hours, then finally woke up at 0700h to something incredible. A guard had pulled up the flap from my tent, and sunshine flowed in. Pure, golden, delicious sunshine. The warmest, softest sun I've ever known, and it's pouring from the east directly onto my clammy bunk. The sky is indigo blue, with just a couple of whiffy, snow-white clouds sailing overhead. I go into the hut and bring a canteen cup of sweet coffee back to the bunk. There, I lay everything out to dry. My towel, socks, blankets. Also, my Checkbook Diary, which was becoming damp and moldy, and I'm afraid that pages will soon start falling out.

This high valley, bathed in sunshine, is more ruggedly beautiful than I'd imagined. The rocky crags above us stand defiantly, like they're guarding the valley. I'd described the forest, in the mist and rain, as so green, it's almost blue. Now it's a dark, olive green, the color of an army fatigue jacket before it fades. I take off my shirt—the first time in six days. I roll up my trousers and bask. I feel like my body is a living battery. The sun I store now will help me through the cold, wet days that will surely resume. I remember a hymn, from the Methodist church in my boyhood days in West Texas. "Suddenly there's a sunshine." It was about being lost in darkness, and despair, and then "suddenly there's the sunshine . . . and hope and love begin." Something like that. Or was there really such a hymn? Is it only in my mind? It doesn't matter, that's how I feel.

It's about 1030h. I ask if it's possible to take a bath. Eduardo and Leidi shoulder their weapons, we all gather soap and shampoo and head for the river about 200 meters below. The stream flows fast and clear. The stream is about 1 to 1½ meters wide and half a meter deep. We reach an eddy, about two meters wide, behind an embankment. I stay there sitting on a level spot inches from the swirling water. It's truly a beautiful sight. I strip and absorb a few more minutes of sun, then plunge into the stream. It's an exhilarating shock, icy and electric. The water is a little more than a meter deep and even in the pool, flowing fast. Back onshore, soap all over, work shampoo into my hair, scoop water on by hand to rinse, and add more shampoo. This time it works into a thick, creamy lather. In the sun 10 more minutes then plunge in again, forcing myself to submerge, letting the cold current wash the soap and shampoo away. Ashore, I lie against the bank, naked, and listen to the roar of the stream. The sun dries and warms me slowly. Six days' accumulation of filth is washed away, and I feel squeaky clean. And I'm warm, what a delicious feeling. I think of baths I've had in the past, warm and soapy, that were comfortable. But not one bath stands out as really special, different. That won't be so in the future. I'll remember this bath the rest of my life. And I hope that's a long time, I can't help but reflect a bit caustically. I think it will be. The sunshine changed the colors of everything and brings strength.

Eduardo finally calls. I wrap my towel and climb the embankment. Eduardo is stripped to his shorts, and Leidi is scrubbing his uniform with a bar of hard blue soap and rinses it in the stream. She offers to wash my trousers and shirt. Better take advantage of this, Hargrove. A chance to be truly clean. Okay. I remove the belt—ironically, a money belt without money—and buckle it around my waist to hold my towel. Ramiro appears from nowhere, along the opposite bank of the river. He presents me with a homemade fishing pole and a single worm. I cast the bait into places where the water is calm, but no trout bites. It doesn't matter.

Later, we walk back to the camp. I'm naked except for a towel and my Justin Roper boots.

Lunch is rice sprinkled with canned chopped fish, and a bowl of *agua panela*. Eduardo produces a pocket mirror, and I look at myself for the first time since my capture. My face is covered with rough white whiskers that have nowhere nearly merged into a beard. I look like a bum. I wonder why I can't shave. Is it a rule left over from days before the throwaway razor, to avoid the chance that a prisoner might commit suicide? Or do they want me to lose my former identity, for the same reason the army cuts a new recruit's hair? Or is it just that these teenagers don't have razors to share? The latter, probably.

Leidi talks with me for half an hour after lunch. Talks a lot about FARC, how poor she was. And how fortunate I am, because I'm one of the very few *gringos* who's lived with the guerrillas, shared their hardships. I'm also lucky, she says, because I'd never really have known how the poor really live, were it not for this opportunity. Leidi also talks about fighting for *derechos humanos*. What happened to *my own* human rights? I don't get a very good answer.

In the afternoon, Ramiro invites me back to the *quebrada*, the stream. There, Eduardo, or Conejo [rabbit] and Gustavo are hard at work, digging along the bank, hauling logs. I'm bewildered. "What are you doing?" "Building a *charca*, a pond, where the water is still to attract the trout," Ramiro answers proudly. I sit in the sun and watch the boys work. Ramiro and Conejo start an impromptu mud fight. It's funny, children soldiers are among the tragedies of war. *Lia sua*, we called them a long time ago. Milk soldiers.

Back at the camp, I see that Rambo has returned. Rambo sits on a stone in front of the hut surrounded by coils of wire. I ask what it's for. "Radio antenna," he says. Hot damn. We'll have instant communication when I'm set free.

If I'm set free. Valley clouds block out the sun and fog covers this height again late in the afternoon heat. A few raindrops fall, and I go back into my *casa acuática* for the first time today. Ramiro has repaired my bunk again, so tonight may be more comfortable.

A prisoner, I'm learning, spends a lot of time doing things to make his life just a little more comfortable. I spend an hour adjusting my slab of foam rubber that serves as a mattress, and tucking my four blankets in just right, so maybe my feet won't stick out from under the covers again tonight. FARC doesn't issue form-fitted sheets.

The rain stops and I leave the tent. Rambo is horseback riding back down the valley and behind him rides someone with long, reddish hair. It's Erika. I didn't know she was here. I'd have enjoyed talking with her.

Cirle brings dinner, a stew of potatoes and noodles at 1730h. Later I stand outside until darkness covers our valley, then return to my tent, to begin another 12-hour night, at six P.M.

6:20 P.M.: But somehow it's not so bad this time. The sunshine, and the bath, and clean clothes and watching the boys build a trout pond on the stream . . . Those things made so much difference. And I feel like I have a new reserve of energy and spirit from the sunshine. Whatever comes next, I can take it. I wish I could let Susan know that I'm doing fine, mentally and physically.

2000h: I've folded back the tent material and carved a little niche in the mud wall that my bunk stands against. Thus, I now have a candleholder. That makes writing easier. It would also make reading at night easier—if I had anything to read. Even the urine problem is solved. I found a pile of old rubber boots outside the hut, selected the best, and brought it into my *casa acuática*. Lyndon Johnson once commented on the intelligence of a political rival (was it Hubert Humphrey?) and I paraphrase: "That guy couldn't pour piss out of a boot." Well, Lyndon, I'm smarter than that. And pretty soon the comforts of my little *casa acuática* will rival those of a room at the Hilton.

Friday, 30 Sep., Day 8

0830h: Today is 100 percent different from yesterday. It dawned overcast and cold, after raining all night. And I was cold all night. Have given up on tucking in my blankets. That leaves too much air around the body—and that means too much cold. I have to just wrap the blanket around me, as tightly as possible.

I should have a plan for each day, but for today, I can think of nothing. Maybe we can try the new trout pond, but it's so cold and wet. Rotten bamboo slats of my bunk broke again, so we can repair that.

But I have an idea. I was taken hostage seven days ago this morning. Later that day I recorded "Keyword Notes"—but they would make sense only to me. I'll take the notes from my "checkbook diary," and reconstruct what happened that morning. I'll start that on a new page.

Later. Leidi wears a green cap with UCLA stenciled in front. I ask if she knows what the letters mean. No. I tell her, and she seems pleased. But she's never heard of "California" or "Los Angeles." The boys are playing a cassette of revolutionary music. I ask them to play their favorite song, and help me transcribe it.

If I weren't keeping a diary, I doubt I'd know today is Friday, or that this is Day 8 of captivity. It's already running together. Losing track of time would be so easy. Whatever happens, I must record each day.

Breakfast was arepas. Didn't look good, so I skipped. It's the first meal I've missed. But I won't use much energy today, anyway.

I wonder if I'm losing weight. I should be. I eat enough, but never stuff myself—mainly because the food is so unappetizing. Food [here] is fuel to keep the body, the mind, and the spirit working—not a luxury to enjoy. Our meals are so starchy. We've had no meat since that *gallina*, How many days ago? And absolutely no green vegetables since the first two nights when our camp was the Indian's house, in front of his field of onion and opium.

1200h: I'm called for lunch. Have been sitting on a log on the mountainside overlooking the valley, writing and studying Spanish. I get up and find the seat of my trousers are wet. Another reason for staying in my tent, where the bunk is fairly dry. Drying these trousers will be a lot of trouble. But if I don't, I'll be miserable tonight.

Lunch is a mixture of beans and potatoes, served over rice. Strange that this is the first beans we've had. *Frijoles* are a staple of this region. That's why beans are one of the four crops on which CIAT focuses research. Nor have we had cassava, another CIAT crop. Of course, the altitude is too high to grow cassava. Potatoes grow this high, and potatoes and rice have been our staples.

But in reality, I haven't seen a field of any kind for days. I don't remember seeing any agriculture other than cattle once we were an hour past Camp 2. Nor did I see any *amapola* fields! Even though two *guerrilleros* told me how beautiful those fields would be as we rode from Camp 2, I'm almost certain that we routed one detour so I wouldn't see those fields of opium poppy.

I haven't heard the sound of an aircraft since Day 2. Nor have I seen a motor vehicle—or even a road—since we left Camp 1. (I've lost my pencil. I had a short pencil in my pocket at the *retén*. Now I want to use it to edit text so later I can follow my editorial changes easier. How could I be so careless? The guerrillas have no pencils. I hope they have another ballpoint; this one has to run out of ink someday.)

1400h: Javier and I walk down to the stream and watch the water run. In 4½ hours I'll be locked in that bank cell for 12 more hours. Am getting depressed thinking about it. Also, a bit claustrophobic. No, don't think about that.

1415h: The rain stopped again, so we're back at the camp and I'm in my tent. Have taken my bunk apart and am trying to figure out how to replace the rotten bamboo that broke last might. Those were replacements for rotten bamboo that broke the night before. If the rain stops, maybe Ramiro and I can go cut some tree branches. But I have to do something; my back really hurts from sleeping half in and half out of that big hole in my bunk.

My feet and legs and shoulders are also sunburned from yesterday's orgy of sun. How ironic! One nice day emerges in the midst of this cold wetness, and I get sunburned!

1600h: I wonder what this experience would be like if someone else were here to share it? When I thought we were going to FARC HQ (were we? did we pass it?) I thought maybe some of those other Americans held hostage in Colombia will be there and we can talk. But that was not to be. I haven't talked to anyone in English—except Tom Hargrove—for eight days now. The oldest person I've met—Rambo—is 22 years old. The highest level of education is, I believe, fourth grade. And I wonder if part of that was in FARC schools, learning Marxism and the teaching of Che Guevara. I can see, I think, 40 km along this valley. And other than our hut, I see no evidence that humans have ever been here. The most modern thing in the hut is the transistor radio and Walkman—next, I guess, is the M-16 or the Galil.

1715h: Dinner is served. A mixture of lentils and pasta, served over rice. I eat. This is one of the strangest, hardest things to get used to. I've always looked forward to lunch and dinner as two of the day's main pleasures, not as an obligation to myself and my family. I wonder . . . to how many people, other than the very sick, is eating an obligation rather than a pleasure? Eating to stay alive, but with no appetite, that must be a trial of those who are very poor—but not starving. I wonder, if the guerrillas think this is good food. They probably consider it okay. Not really good, but okay.

1820h: In my tent cell. Thank God for this diary. What could I do if they wouldn't let me write? If they hadn't given me this notebook? What would I do if, when I'm released, they take my diary away? That thought is so terrible, I push it out of my mind when I can.

My CIAT communications unit should be in good hands with Nathan Russell, but it's awfully shorthanded. I was going to help him get the annual report out on a push basis. Did Rebecca realize that the Seeds of Hope documentary I was working on was for the annual report, and turn it over to Nathan? The Wild Savanna is almost done; Alex can see it through. But I never sent Larry Klaas my last draft of Carolina Gold [a variety of rice once commonly farmed in the American south—before cotton became King]. It's on the hard disk of my home computer. CIATDiar\OranDra4, I think. But there is no way I can get that information "to" . . . anyone.

I'm going to try to get another message sent to Susan when this unit next has contact outside. We are totally isolated here in this valley, without even radio communication. I don't know how contact would be made. Mail would probably have to go to Cali first. They wouldn't mail from the nearest village. Wherever that is; that would leave a postmark. Telephone? From where? And again, the danger of tracing. I don't know what happened to the radio Rambo was setting up. He obviously has another camp down in the valley far below. Maybe it's there.

I wonder how far "civilization" is, if one could move freely, not as guerrillas. Surely closer than the 1.5 day march that brought us here. But I'm not sure. These mountains are vast, rugged, and empty.

Saturday, 1 Oct., Day 9

Slept better last night, after Juaco somehow found some flat planks to replace the rotten bamboo slats in my bunk. I ask Juaco if this unit was in the previous FARC *retén* on the Puerto Tejada road, where four or five *mulas*, the huge trucks used to haul sugarcane, were burned. That was three or four months ago.

We weren't involved, Juaco says. "That was the Jaime Beckemann Callon Front of Incidencia de M-19.

"M-19? But the newspapers reported it as a FARC action."

"It was M-19." M-19; so at least two guerrilla groups are working the Puerto Tejada road. . . . I remember seeing "JBC" painted on the walls of the Indian village where I was first taken after the *retén*.

2000h: Among the clothes drying around the fire I noticed several socks stitched like my sleeping socks, "USA 94." They must have bought a case of the socks at discount; it can't express a political preference.

I ask Juaco if it's possible to send another message to Susan. A pack train will arrive with more supplies on Monday. Juaco says, "We'll see if it can take a message when it leaves." Monday? But today is Saturday. We have no communication out of this valley for the next two days?

"*Es verdad.* We're very isolated. The nearest village is four days' march through the mountains."

"Four days? But it took us only about two days' march to get to this camp." Only two days, I think. Perspectives change.

"Yes, but we can't take that route again." Why not? The weather? Juaco nods, but I'm not sure the weather is the reason. The four-day march may, of course be a fabrication to discourage any thoughts of escape. A town may lie over the next ridge, with police, hotels, restaurants, phones and buses. Maybe, but somehow I doubt it. "The pack train will also bring your medicines." I don't need the medicines now. The allergy has gone away in this mountain air! But if I needed them desperately I'd probably be dead now.

"The boys made a beautiful trout pond along the stream two days ago." I say, "I'd like to go trout fishing today."

"That would be fine. But we had only one hook, and it was lost in the river yesterday." Lost in the river! It must have been Javier. Only he could lose our only fishhook. "But don't worry," Juaco says. "The pack train will bring more fishhooks on Monday." Sure.

My burned socks don't seem so important anymore. I never wear socks during the day and probably wouldn't if I had socks to wear. It makes no sense. My boots are always soaked through and my feet always wet; socks would just hold more water around them. But maybe that's not right. When scuba diving, you're warmer [when] wearing clothes because body heat warms the water, trapped in the cloth next to the skin. Hargrove . . . what the hell difference does it make? You don't have socks, so drop it. I wear my trousers tucked into the tops of my Justin Ropers, to keep mud off the cuffs. For underwear I have one pair of Jockey shorts. I wear them two days, then wash and let them dry one day. Wish I had a second shirt. Eduardo (Conejo) lent me his jacket. The sleeves come halfway up my forearm, but it's a damn sight better than nothing. I like wearing my *ruana*. My khaki trousers are expensive and Susan warned me not to wear them more than two days between washings. Sorry, Susan. I keep forgetting to change.

1200h: Talking with Gustavo. He's an Indian from near Silvia, is 16 years old, joined FARC at 13. Third-grade education. Native language is Páez. "*Qué lástima*, that we can't fish in the new pond," he says.

"I thought you Indians could spear fish or catch them by hand," I say.

"That was the Indians of long ago. Not us of today."

I also talk with Cirle. She is 17, has a second-grade education. Is from Ginebra. Says she has met other foreigners before me, while selling candies in Cali, and apparently has seen other hostages. Joined FARC four years ago and hasn't seen her parents since. "Do you send them messages?" I ask.

"No, how could I?" She admits that she joined FARC partly for the adventure, doesn't give me the standard political line.

She makes Colombia $3 million per year: $3,750/yr or $312/month (Colombia $250,600/mo.). A *guerrillero* on Day 1 also told me he made Colombia $3 million. I ask about money taken at *reténs*. "That's very little," Cirle says. "It must be shared among so many." I decide not to ask about ransom money; other guerrillas have told me that every *departamento*, or state, in Colombia, including Bogotá, has a FARC front. By now I'm sure I'm the exclusive property of FARC/Cauca.

1230h: Lunch is pasta cooked with a little fish for flavor, served over rice.

1500h: A soccer ball appeared this afternoon apparently from the camp below. The boys made a homemade *fútbol* [soccer] field on a flat piece of cow pasture between swamps. Two bamboo stakes at each end as goals. After watching awhile, I join in—as goalie for Ramiro and Javier, who play against Eduardo and Gustavo. Later Ramiro and I play another hour. My first time to play South American *fútbol*, but I know the rules, *más o menos*, from watching the World Cup. Good exercise. I'll play again tomorrow. My feet must be getting tough. I've walked four kilometers, waded mud and streams, climbed mountains, and now played *fútbol* without socks. No problems. Finally got some reading materials: a 91-page pamphlet, titled (in Spanish) "What, and why: Is the Struggle of the Colombian Communist Party?" (1987), and the July and October 1988 issues of *Resistencia*, the FARC magazine. Okay. I've always enjoyed reading communist propaganda.

1715h: I've just noticed that the sole of my right boot has cracked horizontally through the leather. It now looks like in 15 minutes' more walking, I'll have a hole in that boot that will put my bare foot in direct contact with the water, mud, and rocks. Juaco said they've ordered me rubber boots like the *guerrilleros* wear. But will they be large enough? Will they come on the *tren de ca-*

ballos that arrives Monday? This is really serious. Scary. In a situation like this, one must care for his feet. What will my life be like if these rubber boots don't arrive on Monday? Or if they don't fit? It would probably be another week before other boots could get here. The other side of getting new boots is, of course, the uneasy thought [that] if FARC is buying me new boots, it must be prepared to keep me a long time.

1915h: Moved into my tent 45 minutes ago. Dinner was the worst yet. A mush of rice, milk from powder, of course, and sugar. I couldn't eat it. I asked if we had any more of the stuff we had for lunch. We did. It tasted a lot like whatever we had for lunch, but warmed over. I've noticed Leidi studying between cooking and washing dishes and clothes. Good kid, I thought. Probably preparing to go to high school someday. This afternoon I asked what she was studying. "The statutes of FARC!" she said proudly. Christ.

Sunday, 2 Oct., Day 10

0700h: It rained all night and I could never get warm. My covers aren't long enough [for me] to tuck my feet in and be covered to my head. Was going to wear my new polyester trousers today and rest the khakis till tonight. But I found the new trousers are wet. That says something when you consider that I was using them as a pillow. A cold breeze blows through the valley, but the sun fights its way through scattered patches of blue that break the thick gray clouds to the east. Maybe today will be okay. I inspect my right boot in the clear light. There's still a layer of leather between the cracked sole and my feet. I'm back in my tent. I shouldn't complain about being locked in the tent 12 hours; otherwise I'd be in that one-room hut where the seven guerrillas sleep. In five bunks. Two are women; of course, girls is a better term. Female anyway. I wonder what happens when a female *guerrillera* gets pregnant? It must happen. This is hardly the life for a mother to be and less so for a mother and baby. Maybe they're sent back to some more or less stationary base camp.

0845h: Leidi and Juaco found BBC World News on the shortwave (which is always tuned to Colombian stations on MW [AM]). The situation in Haiti scares me. Somalia once again. Some news came from Vietnam and Juaco asked me questions about the U.S. role in the Vietnam War. I answered, but purposely with little sophistication. After all, I was a student during those days and avoided serving in the army. Part of the FARC rhetoric one gets is how FARC is fighting to end slavery. The rich hold the power, own the land, and hold the masses as virtual slaves. Etc. Maybe that's true, but the audacity of these bastards to talk to me of their noble goal of eliminating slavery . . . What is kidnapping but a form of slavery? Humans are systematically captured for one reason: to sell. It's worse than traditional slavery in some ways. A slave is captured, sold, and bought for production, for the work he or she can do. The only products sought through the enslavement of kidnapping are fear, grief. The hypocrisy, to tell me of their noble goal of ending slavery. (Maybe I should insert this earlier, because I've thought of it for days; just hesitant to write it down.)

I want to leave this tent, but how? I put on those wet boots earlier, and my feet are still numb, even sitting in the tent. Feet wrapped in woolen blankets. This is the coldest day yet.

Breakfast is rice mixed with pieces of pasta, and *harina*, fried bread.

1205h: The boys have invented a new game. They discovered boxes of medicines in the medical supplies abandoned in the hut. They're now sprinkling clumps of grass with medicine vials and setting the grass on fire. They then lie below the grass clump, heads covered, until the vials explode. Like soldiers throwing grenades into bunkers.

1230h: The boys are burning clumps of grass all around the hut, playing their game. With all the burned-out clumps, it would be easy to spot this hut from the air as inhabited. But this group seems to feel impervious to air assault. I guess it is. (I went back to my tent, lay down . . . and fell asleep for an hour. Dream sleep. I can't do that, not in the day; my nights are too long.)

1340h: Lunchtime: Lentils mixed with pasta and some rice. Cirle brings me a cup of hot chocolate made with powdered milk. It's pretty good. And warm. When I get back home I'm going to have lots and lots of veggies. I wonder what's happening ref. this at CIAT. I asked Juaco several days ago if a letter had been sent. He really didn't know. Obviously I am more than curious about how CIAT will react. This has to be a big deal. No one has been kidnapped before in the CGIAR* system. I wondered about the World Bank and what WB policy is on kidnapping. I wonder about a lot of things. It's best not to write at this time about many of them. But I know I'll survive and, somehow, go free. I just don't know when. The secret must be, as others have written, to take it one day at a time. I'm lucky in some ways. My health remains good. I haven't been sick at all. Partly, I think, because I am determined I won't get sick. And my spirits are pretty good. A lot of men taken from a comfortable life at age 50 and thrown into this situation would lose hope, get sick, and die. I asked Juaco what happens if one gets sick up here. FARC has a hospital and excellent doctors, he assured me. Sure, I believe that. And what might be a relatively minor illness back in civilization, like pneumonia or dysentery, could easily be fatal up here.

Anyway I have—I must have—confidence that CIAT is doing, and will do, everything possible to get me out of here.

1630h: Day 10 is drawing to a close. We'll eat in an hour, then back into this tent again with a candle for another 12 hours. And tonight will be cold. What is Susan doing right now? I hope her mother is there. I wish I knew something. I have absolutely no idea what has happened there. If only I could get some feedback, talk with someone, exchange ideas. I have to leave this tent, walk in the cold, move some more before the long night begins. I take the half-flat *fútbol* down to the field and with no opponent score some spectacular goals. Ramiro joins me and we play half an hour—enough to exhaust me. "Tomorrow

*Consultative Group on International Agricultural Research, a consortium of 40 nations and international organizations that support agricultural research for development.

the *tren de mulas* arrives with fresh supplies," Ramiro tells me while resting. Including *frijoles*. Sounds good.

1730h: Ramiro has kitchen duty today, it seems, which means he cooks and washes dishes. He brings me dinner on a plate. Rice, lentils, and I can't believe it. Sardines! Three big solid sardines, the kind that come in a tall can, packed in tomato sauce. I've had only one piece of solid meat in 10 days—that chicken leg five or six nights ago. I take the plate inside my tent and pull the flap. If Ramiro is slipping extra portions of a delicacy to his amigo, the *gringo rehen*, I don't want some passing *guerrillero* to notice it. I'm back in my tent for the next 12 hours by 1815. The extra protein from the sardine makes me feel strong, good. And tomorrow the packhorses, or mules, come bringing not only *frijoles*, but also my new rubber boots!

Monday, 3 Oct., Day 11

0720h: As I lay on my bunk, I hear over the radio in the hut of a new antinarcotics operation in the Valle de Cauca involving five hundred men, with U.S., Germany, France. He won't name it. How might that affect me?

0730h: Just heard it over another radio station.

0815h: Heard about Operation Margarita Two again. Five departments. This can't help me personally in the short term. Also on the news: 12 persons killed in riots over the weekend in Agua Blanca, an impoverished, mostly black barrio of Cali. That's where Patricia, our maid, lives.

0845h: Today will be a real bitch. The clouds are so thick and low, you could cut them with a knife. But don't; that would release tons of ice water. Instead of the steady drizzle we have now. It looks like the clouds have won and the sun has been driven off, never to return.

0910h: I've thought about Dr. LaRue Pollard lately in a mood of black humor and irony. We've known one another 26 years. Since Sept. 1968 when I entered graduate college at Iowa State University and she was a professor of science journalism. She later joined me as editor at IRRI. Well, LaRue has a dubious distinction. Two of her former student advisees—Terry Anderson and now me—have been kidnapped and held hostage by revolutionary groups abroad. Anderson was head of, I believe, Associated Press in Lebanon when kidnapped. Hope I'm eventually released, as Anderson was. But I also hope that unlike Anderson I'm not held two to three years first. So here's to you, LaRue, friend and mentor. Probably the only professor in the USA who was adviser to two hostages. I should send a note about that to the *ACE Newsletter* and the ISU journalism and alumni papers when I'm released.

0930h: Breakfast is served. Plain white rice and fried bread. I decline.

1040h: Back in the tent, feet like ice. Today is the coldest yet. How cold is it? I don't know. Water doesn't freeze, but my breath is frosty. The wetness must add one hell of a chill factor.

I worry about my father back in another time and place called West Texas. He's 83, and Mother died 11 months ago. I wonder if Daddy knows about this. I see no reason to tell him. But he could die, be buried, and I'd not know it.

It's so smoky in the hut you can hardly breathe. My tent is even smoky from smoke that enters through chinks in the common mud wall. The four huts we've been in have all been the same: an open, built-up bed in a corner of one room (here, there is only one room!) on which a wood fire is made, for cooking and warmth. There is no chimney; the smoke fills the room and escapes through the one permanently open window and the door. Thousands of Indians have lived in these huts throughout these mountains for centuries. Why haven't they discovered the principles of the fireplace, which draws smoke upward and throws the heat outward?

The mosquitoes up here are enormous but somehow benign. They seldom bite. Too cold, I guess. I can see four right now, clinging to the inside canvas of my tent. I imagine they'll become active when it gets warm. I should kill them all, while they're numb and still; if they continue to leave me alone, I'll leave them alone.

1140h: I have to leave this tent. I guess I've been spending 18 hours a day in the tent. When you consider the base of 12 hours to start from . . . 1200h: I'm back in the tent. Makes no sense to go outside. I can only stand in the rain, my feet in the mud, or go into the hut, which is no warmer than my tent and where the smoke chokes me and burns my eyes. I'd love to get some exercise and will when I can, but—again, if I could wish for anything to help me through this period, it would be a huge jar of knockout sleeping pills, and I've almost never in my life taken a sleeping pill. The lack of movement in the tent bothers me a lot. I can't stand; far too low. I sit on the edge of my bunk because the floor is straw-covered mud, always wet. And I can't put a semidry blanket down there to wrap my feet in. So I must sit up in the bunk or slide onto my back and lie down. My hips are so sore from this. That's why I want to stand up.

1250h: Lunch is boiled beans served over rice. A big improvement over lentils. But I thought we had no beans. The mule train sure hasn't arrived with new supplies. I wonder how long it takes, without vegetables or citrus, to develop scurvy? My teeth feel loose . . . just kidding. I see now that the radio antenna that Rambo was setting up a few days ago was for regular commercial radio—not two-way communication. So we remain unable to contact or be contacted by the outside world.

1810h: Am in the tent for the night. Today was a nothing day. So was yesterday. The mule train or horse train (they call it both) didn't arrive, probably because of the weather.

Late in the afternoon the rain stopped and I jogged/walked for 30 minutes in the mud. Ramiro saw me, brought the ball, and we played *fútbol* for an hour. Dinner was a yellow mush of rice, potatoes, and pasta. It tasted a little bit better than it looked. I should collect the best of this group's recipes and when I am released publish them as *The Guerrilla Gourmet Cookbook*. Especially for those who want to cut back on eating. I've always been a big meat-eater, especially beef. But I know I can live without meat as long as I have lentils, beans for protein. But a diet totally without vegetables or fruits? This can't be good.

Tuesday, 4 Oct., Day 12

800h: I'm not going to write that last night was the coldest ever because I've written it before . . . and they all are. You wrap the blankets around you like a mummy to keep the body heat close.

The day is cloudy, cold.

1005h: I am reading "Standards of International Human Rights Applicable to Armed Conflicts" published in the FARC magazine *Resistencia* Oct. 1988. It is abstracted from the standards presented by the International Red Cross. The standards refer to the rights of "captured combatants," "civilians" controlled by the opposing side," "civilian population," and "civilians." No mention of the rights of kidnap victims who have no role whatsoever in this conflict. Even some parts which surely should apply to me are being ignored, including (prisoners) have the right to exchange news with their families. No person will be considered responsible for an act he has not committed. The parties in conflict must always distinguish between the civilian population and combatants, protecting the civilians. Neither the civilian population nor individual civilians can be the objective of attack. I'll show these to Juaco and to Rambo (who I last saw six days ago). They'll probably say, "Gosh, we don't know this. We'll release you right away." Actually it's interesting that although the FARC abstracted these "standard human rights" from the International Red Cross, there is no mention of kidnapping of civilians in a conflict.

Am getting sores on my shoulders and back. Probably caused by getting sunburned six days ago, plus the dampness, and not exposing my skin to air for six days. Plus the dirty clothes. I'm sitting on a rock overlooking the camp, writing. I hear a flutelike sound. It's Cirle, wearing a tan-and-dark-brown *ruana*, walking across the valley, her hands clasped into a natural flute. The scene is timeless and the sound hollow and lonely, like her life must be. It's a scene of the South American *campesino*: cold, hopeless, without direction. Cirle approaches my rock and we talk awhile. The sun is trying to shine, and I've been airing the sores on my back and shoulders. "Don't worry, the *tren de mulas* arrives today," she says. "It will bring lotion for your *llagas*, and dry rubber boots, another shirt, and socks, underwear, everything you need."

"The *tren* was due yesterday, but didn't arrive," I say.

"But it's so far. Four days by foot to the nearest village. Celina has made the trip before and describes the cold, the wind, the dangers. The route is so uncertain. You can travel only by day. The rocks fall easily." She obviously dreads that journey, which must follow when I get my freedom. Cirle's descriptions make this camp seem warm and comfy.

Lunch is a soup of potato and pasta. Our potatoes, I'm told, are home— FARC—grown. They're from a potato field farmed by guerrillas in the valley below.

1230h: When we arrived at this camp seven days ago, Rambo said we'd stay for 10 days. Yet I see that Eduardo is building himself a new bed. "You must think we're staying here much longer," I comment.

"Sí, señor."

"Qué bien. Buenísimo." No one gets my sarcasm.

1525h: Am on the mountainside overlooking the camp, at the flat place where I sometimes jog. It's strange, about 5x5 meters, and almost perfectly flat, like it was carved for a little house that was never built or that rotted away long ago. Looking down at the valley I see five head of cattle and I know that FARC owns them. Eight of us—seven FARC guerrillas and me—have been here a week. Our only food other than potatoes has come from a sack or can and has mostly been starch. There's a nice steer down there, and a heifer, weighing 600 to 700 pounds each. Why can't a guerrilla kill one of those animals so that we could have some beef? The meat would last a week without spoiling, in this weather, and some could be smoked. Could the sores I'm getting be caused by this diet of starch?

1715h: Ramiro and I played *fútbol* for an hour. Now am in my tent.

1915h: Dinner is a greasy piece of fried cheese and a greasy piece of fried bread which Cirle calls *harina* (but that means flour). And chocolate. The rain was starting again at 1820h and it was . . . almost totally dark. I was about to turn in when—a *guerrillero* rode up on horseback, leading a mule loaded with three sacks. The long-awaited mule train, or at least our part of it, had arrived! The packs are untied and thrown into the hut to be opened tomorrow. Leidi and Celina throw fresh wood on the fire to cook cheese and bread, the horseman pulls the *caneca* of brandy from a pouch and pours thimble-size shots for all. I've considered Colombian brandy pretty bad, but this rivals the finest cognac.

Apparently a good liquor supply arrived. I go to bed, but a party has started in the hut. It's getting louder and louder. At 2000h, Conejo comes to my tent and gives me a *caneca* (375 ml, i.e., between half a pint and a pint) of brandy. My share of the liquor shipment, I suppose, and he doesn't want the boys to drink it on this binge. I stick it under my bunk. As the party noise increases, I hear another ominous sound: rifle bolts being slid, ammo clips inserted. Then things and the clicks quieten and *bambambabam*! Someone cuts loose, from the door of the hut, with an AK-47 on full automatic. An M-16 joined in, rock-and-roll. The noise is deafening and I almost roll off my bunk into the mud. I hear drunken shouts, and someone shooting a .45 into the air, and I realize what's going on. Still I'm uneasy. The way these guys handle weapons—even when sober—scares me. As I'm contemplating this, a *guerrillero* runs past my tent, spraying a clump of bushes on full automatic, hot, spent cartridges bouncing off the canvas. After an hour, another bottle of brandy, and a couple hundred more rounds, the shooting stops. I think of Christmas Eve 1969, and the thousands of rounds we shot into the air. But that was different; we had unlimited ammo. Maybe these guys do, too.

Wednesday, 5 Oct., Day 13

Conejo and Javier came to my tent at 0645h this morning, lift the flap and they're in. They've unpacked the packs from the mule train and have come to bring my new things. I sit up as they thrust goodies at me. These kids are so excited they remind me of Miles and Tom G. at Christmases past in the Philippines. The first item they show me is a new pair of high rubber boots, Venus Llanero brand, same as the guerrillas wear. I praise the boots and put them aside to try on later in private. I'm so scared that the boots won't fit and then what will I do? My leather boots are shot for this kind of life. The hole in my right boot has broken through the sole, and mud and water now enter the boot freely. The iciness almost burns, and my feet are always numb.

A plastic bag contains a new notebook so I can be a bit more liberal with the space I use to write. And a new pen. The one I'm now using. I have two more pairs of socks, still the '94 USA type, plus three shorts and two handkerchiefs. A new shirt and I note its size, "XL." Another toothbrush and tube of toothpaste. Two throwaway razors, although now with almost two weeks' growth, I'm going to let my beard grow some more. Another sack yields a flashlight—a real, honest-to-God, made-in-China Tiger Head brand flashlight, the kind that holds two "C" batteries and really lights up the dark. No matter how often I dry my matches by the fire, they still stay damp, so it's hard to light a candle in the middle of the night. Medicines are in another sack. Enough of two of the three allergy medicines to last five days. I haven't had that problem here in the mountains, so I'll save that. I had asked for and got a bottle of Benadryl. As a medicine, I said, but really because I know that's the main ingredient in Sominex.

Conejo disappeared as I was opening gifts, but he now reappears with the last one, a ski mask, just like those worn in the *retén*, except mine is brown, not olive. This is no joke, of course; I know that a great deal of body heat is lost through the head and I have been trying to keep my head covered at night but with little luck. My blankets are too smoky. This will help.

The others leave and I try the boots. They fit! Thanks, God. They're a bit wide, but long enough, and that's what counts. I wear the boots and my USA '94 socks outside. I walk through mud over slippery rocks. I climb the mountain slope to my jogging platform and return to the camp. My feet are dry. The boot soles are of hard acrylic that could grip ice. Juaco left with the mule train this morning. I wrote a note to Susan, my second since captivity—in English and Spanish. A copy (the first draft) is at the back of my new notebook. Juaco says the messages will be sent to Cali and phoned to Susan and the Greiners. But it takes four days to reach the nearest village. God only knows when she'll receive it.

Like before, I write my note in English then must read it in Spanish for Juaco's approval. All the guerrillas gather around to hear what I've written. I choke, I almost break down. I've almost broken down twice. Both times were when I had to read my notes to Susan to these son of a bitches.

Juaco will be gone for five or six days, but didn't say where. "Who is in charge while you're gone?" I asked.

Juaco looked surprised. "I am."

I meant "during your absence." It's obvious that no one is named acting commander, so I drop the subject. That's how this army is run.

1200h: Lunch is rice with enough sardine mixed in to add flavor, and a piece of white cheese. I don't think the mule train brought any new food. Later: Gustavo is sitting in my tent and confirms no new food. God, our gourmet food is about exhausted; we'll soon have to eat common food. He says another *tren de mulas* will come on Monday (today is Wednesday) with food. "Will the *tren* bring vegetables?" I ask.

"Oh yes, Gustavo says. "Cassava, plantain, potato. Vegetable."

I ask if the guerrillas ever gather and eat wild plants from the forest. "Never," he says. I was joking earlier when I wrote about the danger of getting scurvy. I'm no longer so sure it's a joke. These people have no concept of nutrition. Food is food. I wish I had one of those books that describe wild foods to gather from the forest. I'd do it. The only plants I recognize as edible are mushrooms, and I'm not about to experiment with them.

What will my first meal be, when I return home? My friends would, I'm sure, say, "The biggest, thickest T-bone steak that Comil has to offer." That sounds good, but I'd prefer a medium-size T-bone with lots of vegetables. Or maybe stir-fry beef with lots of onions, broccoli, cauliflower, mushrooms, green peppers, cabbage. I'm surprised that I miss vegetables so much, and so soon. But I do.

1710h: As I write this, Celina appears at my tent with dinner. It's a yellow goo of lukewarm pasta mixed with, maybe, one can of sardines for the seven of us. Yucky—but I eat it. This would be better if I could look forward to the food tomorrow. But I know it'll be worse than today's food, as our supplies dwindle. I'm sure FARC song and lore are full of how the guerrillas live off the land. Bullshit.

It's 5:50 P.M., and Javier is shutting my tent for the night. (Gustavo, Conejo, Ramiro, and I played *fútbol* for an hour this afternoon, before the rain started to fall again. I reminded my three guards and fellow players that my age—50—is greater than their three ages combined—47.)

I hope this morning's supply issue to me didn't sound too much like Christmas. But each of those items will make my life easier or maybe help me survive. Especially the boots. I can move now. And it's almost an alien feeling for my feet to be . . . not exactly warm, but think of Christmas 1989 in the Philippines, when the boys got their first motorbikes—Tom G. said, "You can't imagine how much difference having your own wheels makes."

But again, I don't want to fall into that trap of being grateful to my captors. If the bastards hadn't kidnapped me, I wouldn't need the damn boots.

Leidi told me this morning that another FARC unit will arrive at any time to relieve this one. That makes sense—tomorrow marks two weeks that from 7 to 15 guerrillas of this unit have guarded me. But I hope it's not true. I know these kids now—every one of them—and they know me. And if this unit leaves, will Eduardo take his jacket. Of course. Worse still: Will Ramiro take his tent.

Thursday, 6 Oct., Day 14

0930h: The day is cloud-covered, rainy, and cold. Breakfast was fried bread and fried cheese. I just remembered that Ms. Vrinda Kumble was to arrive over the weekend for a six-week assignment as visiting editor at CIAT. Accompanied by Babs, her husband. Vrinda asked me, via fax, if Colombia was safe for a foreigner—she'd heard, and read, so many negative things. I assured her that Colombia was perfectly safe—especially for someone on the CIAT senior staff. What did she think on learning that I, her old friend of many years who arranged her assignment and assured her of its safety, have been kidnapped?

1245h: Lunch is rice topped with a mixture of lentils and pasta, with a piece of sardine. Gustavo is cooking. (It seems that Lcidi's job is cooking and washing the dishes when the troops are active. But it becomes a rotating duty during "stand-downs" of limited activity, like this.) Spent most of the morning writing about the *retén*—things that happened two weeks ago, before I started my checkbook diary. But that is almost finished. What will I do the rest of the afternoon? Tomorrow? The next day? What a depressing thought.

1510h: Went back to the tent after lunch. I lay down and curled into a ball to stay warm, listening to the raindrops hit the canvas in the soft green light. Woke up two hours later. Why can't I fall asleep so easily at night? And tonight I'll pay for that sleep this afternoon. Tonight begins only about three hours from now.

1630h: Rain stopped. Played *fútbol* for an hour.

1710h. Dinner; rice, lentils, and pasta. I can't eat it. But I do. I honestly believe the food would have been better as Victor's guest [i.e., living with the Viet Cong]. At least, he knew the value, for both taste and nutrition, of green things. And he'd have found a few little fish to mix with the rice.

1810h: In my tent for the night, my 14th day of captivity was a nothing day.

This is supposed to be a communist revolutionary army, but I see little communism. No study sessions for the troops, no confessions. Just the standard memorized response about ending slavery and bringing human rights to the people, when you ask about motivation. I wonder if FARC has political officers to motivate the troops and make sure they think correctly. I doubt it; certainly not at this level.

Friday, 7 Oct., Day 15

It's now been a full two weeks since I was kidnapped. And this is the 10th day in this our fourth camp. Rambo said we'd stay here 10 days. I wonder, if we're going to move? I wouldn't mind leaving here. We have two climates: cold, cloudy, and raining, and cold, cloudy, and raining.

It's like I was snatched up and put on another planet. I have no idea what effect my kidnapping has had on others, what efforts are being made for my release, what FARC is demanding, how Susan is taking all this, whether it is known outside CIAT, etc. And I don't see how CIAT could even be sure I'm still alive.

910h: I'm in the tent, writing about events during and after the *retén* two weeks ago today. "Don Tomás!" It's Eduardo, who asks me to return his jacket for the morning. He wears web gear and ammo clips, so I ask where he's going.

"Below, to get more powdered milk," he says.

"Is it possible to get vegetables?"

"No, no hay." ("No there's none.")

1220h: I wrote most of the morning, recording what happened two weeks ago, before I started the checkbook diary. What will I do with this diary when I'm finally released? That I'm thinking about a third book is obvious. But is there a book here? The story starts with color and excitement and, for me anyway, adrenaline. But after a few days it all levels off into . . . this. Day after day of the same nothingness . . . but a nothingness that I must *not* let slip into hopelessness. I'll worry about what to eventually do with the diary later. But for now, just having the diary is one of the most important factors of my existence. I asked to switch the radio to shortwave and search for news at 1200h. Found Voice of America. Iraq moving troops toward Kuwait. China tests nuclear weapon, etc. Nothing about Latin America except something insignificant regarding Haiti.

1240h: Lunch is rice with boiled beans.

1500h: Yeah, I lay in my bunk and fell asleep, again, for an hour.

Day 15 of captivity will soon end, and I know no more about my situation than on Day 4. If I only knew that something was happening, that some sort of action is under way to get me out of here, whether it works or not. At least Susan is back at Cali. I know she'd raise hell if I were being forgotten—which I'm sure I'm not.

1805h: Am shut in my tent for the night. Raining steadily. Cold and getting colder. Dinner was rice and beans.

Saturday, 8 Oct., Day 16

0800h: Cloudy but not raining. A *guerrillero* arrived from below by horse last night. I see that he brought three 12-volt batteries.

They're to run the radio. That, plus the fact that the guerrillas have rearranged the hut, adding homemade panels to make their bunks semiprivate, makes me feel they're to stay here a long time.

0830h: Some blue sky to the south. Maybe, just maybe, we'll have sunshine today and I can bathe and wash my hair again. It's been 10 days.

I keep thinking of the possibility that I might be released through some sort of prisoner exchange. International Centers Week begins the week of 20 Oct., and Colombia will be there for the first time as a new CGIAR donor. That will draw applause and attention. But won't it be embarrassing if, at the same time, the first center scientist ever to be kidnapped is held hostage . . . in Colombia? I don't know, of course, whether the Colombian government holds any FARC prisoners of value. And I'm not a Colombian government asset to trade. But it's something to hope for even if unlikely. Rambo hasn't been around for the past 10 days. Could he be back around Cali, handling my ransom arrangements?

1015h: Javier just told me not to climb the mountain slope behind the hut anymore; to stay right here next to camp. I told Javier to go fuck himself and walked away. What's the little son of a bitch going to do, shoot me? I guess I'd better be careful; it's getting to me. This is Day 16 of being held by a group of 16-year-olds with third-grade educations. I'm back in my tent, angry and thinking what I'd like to do to this group. That's not going to improve the situation; I can't help it. I'm a prisoner who's committed no crime. Captured, like a slave, to sell. By an organization whose portrayed motives are to bring about human rights, end the slavery of the countryside. What hypocritical bullshit. Be careful, Tom. Keep your mouth shut. Letting loose of your built-up anger, contempt, and frustration for a couple of minutes could really hurt you. These kids couldn't change anything if they wanted to. Your job, Hargrove, is to survive. Anger and self-pity won't help you. Being smart will. Maybe I can bathe if the sun comes out.

1100h: I'm being more low-key about writing in my diary. These contemptible bastards know how they can hurt me most. And don't say the things to them, Hargrove, that run through your mind. Protect yourself, use your intelligence. It's the only weapon, that you have, they don't.

1150h: Raining again. Prospects for sun and bath are shot. I went to our cow pasture *fútbol* field and ran to try to dissolve my anger. Twelve laps, walking one after each fourth lap. Ramiro came out and we kicked goals for 30 minutes. I'm still pissed off. Eduardo took his jacket back yesterday morning and rode down to the valley below. Since then I've worn only a shirt and this thin *ruana*. It's okay now. I guess I can sit in my tent and wrap up in blankets. But this won't do if we have to march or ride again.

1315h: Lunch. A gruel of oatmeal (I think) and pasta, with a can of sardines mixed in, for the seven of us. I have to go back to bed; it's too rainy and too cold to do anything except wrap in blankets. Listened to BBC World News at 1500h. More Iraqi troops moving toward Kuwait. I assume Miles and Hilda and the kids are in Kuwait now. Poor Susan. Something else for her to worry about.

1750h: Dinner. Pasta over rice.

1810h: In tent for night. Raining.

1900h: I can't believe the mosquitoes here. First, they're as big as small sparrows. And as nonaggressive. I don't see how they survive. They cling to the canvas ceiling of this tent all day, never moving. But when I light my candle at night, they play kamikaze, diving at the flame, singeing their wings and falling to be encased in the melting wax below.

Sunday, 9 Oct., Day 17

0800h: This, my second [sic] Sunday in captivity, starts cold, cloudy, and dark. I woke to a cold, icy shock. Someone had tucked the side flap of my tent under the end of the piece of foam rubber that serves as my mattress. That channeled rain during the night beneath the foam rubber until it formed a puddle under my back. How will I dry all of this by tonight? I have no idea.

1045h: I made a calendar this morning. Realized the need when I wrote, above, that this is my second Sunday of captivity. It's the third. Tried to fill in calendar dates with significant events. Not much.

1100h: Take it easy, Hargrove. Calm down, you're going to hurt yourself for nothing. It's been established, informally over the last week, that I can listen to the news over VOA or BBC shortwave, once a day. It's usually at 1100h or 1200h. Eduardo has moved the radio/cassette deck into his new cubicle. At 1050h, no one was even listening to the radio. I asked if I could catch the news. "No," Eduardo said.

"Why not?"

"Because I'm busy."

You smart-ass little shit, I thought, then said, *"Lo siento mucho"* with lots of sarcasm, and spat. What's behind it, probably is that I took back Eduardo's jacket this morning, which Juaco had assigned to me. Anyway, insolence from an illiterate 16-year-old doesn't sit well with me. Even one with a Galil. But I have to control my temper. These pitiful contemptible children aren't worth it. I'd better go run.

1205h: I ran 12 laps. Short laps, around our cow pasture *fútbol* field. But it is hard to run in high boots through standing water and mud. I have to stop this anger. It can eat away at my soul, undermine my will to survive, overpower hope. Now it's raining again heavily. I pull down the sides of the tent and I'm locked again in my little green world.

1400h: Lunch is rice and a mixture of pasta and lentils. I have a piece of rubbery white cheese that I hid away when we had cheese for dinner a few days ago. I crumble some cheese to give the goo flavor, then think I don't want to use up that piece of cheese, I want to save it for an emergency . . . or maybe an opportunity. It's like the green $100 bill I always carried in my billfold, for emergencies. (Didn't do me much good, though, did it?) One month ago today, Susan and I and the Greiners went to that little Colombian village where the Swiss guy lives and had a Sunday feast of ham, sausage, pickles, and brown bread. Will we be able to do that again? Maybe not. That village was a lot more remote than the road where I was kidnapped. I sure hope Susan has e-mail again, by now.

1815h: Dinner was lunch, warmed over. Am in tent for night.

Monday, 10 Oct., Day 18

0730h: Day 18 cloudy and overcast. But it didn't rain last night—for the first time since captivity? And the clouds seem high. Maybe, just maybe, it'll clear off and the sun will come out. This is also the third Monday that the *jefe* hasn't shown up for work at CIAT. I wonder what it'll be like when I finally return. I get choked up, want to cry, thinking about it. But what if no one has missed me? Well, I've missed them. . . .

I checked some of the guerrillas' camouflage fatigues drying on a fence a couple of days ago. Just as I suspected: "Made in the USA."

Monday. Surely, surely, I'll know something of my fate by the end of this week.

1220h: Lunch is rice and lentils. How could I have thought today might be clear? It rained all morning. I sat in the tent and rewrote "The *Retén*." Caught the VOA news at 1100h. Am relieved to hear that Iraq is pulling its troops back from the Kuwait border.

1430h: Tom, you have to control it. You've got to control the rage and despair. You have no rights. Only those with the guns have rights. And they have almost total control over your life. They can make you miserable. They can kill you, and they may before this is over. The only thing you control that they can't take away is your spirit.

1600h: I ran I-don't-know-how-many laps because I can't run laps. The field is too deep in the water. Day 18 will end soon, and I know nothing more about my situation, my fate, than I knew on Day 2.

1810h: Dinner was rice and beans. Am in tent for night. It was a bad day. I hope Susan's day was better. And I hope she has e-mail.

[*Susan Hargrove and Claudia Greiner received telephone calls from the kidnappers asking for a way, other than the phone, to communicate.—Susan Hargrove*]

Tuesday, 11 Oct., Day 19

Juaco returned last night and we talked this morning. The process, again like a movie, has reached the stage that I have anticipated and dreaded. But I thought this stage might be bypassed because this requirement should have come before Day 19. Juaco has met with the *comandante* of the Cauca Front of FARC. Here are my instructions: I am to write a letter to Susan in Spanish asking that she pass my request for help to CIAT administration. That's all. Juaco stressed that the letter must be written very clearly and that I must not try to set a trap, pass secret information, etc. The letter is to go out tomorrow. This puts me in a position I don't like but that, of course, I expected. If the final letter includes no more than the above, then I have no great problem. Everyone knows that kidnap victims are forced to write such letters. I asked about my ransom. Juaco said he doesn't know what amount has been set. "I suspect that whatever is set will be too high," I told Juaco. "It's better to go ahead and kill me now."

Juaco looked shocked. "We're not going to kill you," he said.

No. Not as long as they think they'll get ransom. Without that, though, I can't see that I'm of great value to FARC. They don't have seven full-time guards on me because they like my personality.

This letter will be hard to write. Or maybe not. First, I'll try to write it as simply as described above. Juaco brought back a two-way radio. He said he'll read the letter to the commander for approval before it goes out. The letter will be sent by mail to Susan at home and c/o CIAT. I don't know whether to believe this or not, but Juaco told me this letter will open formal communication with CIAT. So I'll obviously be a hostage quite a while longer at best. Later: Juaco approved the letter. I'll copy to other notebook.

1230h: I don't know what's going on. Maybe it's "Mutt and Jeff"—kindness and cruelty [used on purpose to manipulate a prisoner]—to . . . what? At 1145h I was washing underwear in the spring when Leidi, Celina started crying "¡Venga, Don Tomás, almuerzo!" They were excited as little kids. Leidi brought the lunch to my tent and Celina sat inside to talk. The lunch was fresh cabbage plus boiled carrots and big potatoes (over rice, of course). Anyway, the first vegetables in 19 days! Juaco obviously brought [them] in by horse last night. Real veggies served like a Christmas gift. I finished and Celina stayed in the tent talking. Meanwhile the sun came out bright and clear and the sky is blue. For the first time since 29 September, 12 days ago. "Let's sit outside," I say, "in the sun."

"No, you cannot leave the tent for two hours," she answered.

"Why?"

"I don't know. Those are my orders."

I'm so angry. Why? Are they trying to break me? For what?

1500h: I don't know what's going on. After an hour I asked to see Juaco. I told him I wanted to go to the stream and bathe while there is sun. He agreed and sent Eduardo as my guard. The water was so icy, but it feels so good to be clean, even if I had to put on the same filthy clothes afterward. I was careful not to sunburn this time.

1530h: Am rushing into the tent. Apparently some *campesino* is wandering down the valley and they don't want him to see what's going on.

1535h: I think the *campesino* is in the hut, only two inches of mud and a few feet from me, having coffee with the guerrillas.

Eduardo is trying to get me to give his jacket back! Offered to trade his big heavy wool *ruana* for it. No way! Unless ordered to give it back, I'm keeping the jacket. It's way too short, but more important it's also too tight. When [it's] fastened, I can keep this diary inside with no chance of losing it. Also I keep my checkbook diary zipped up in the side pocket. You see, this—nightmare?—will end someday. The only thing I can possibly salvage of value from the experience is the diaries. They can be the basis of a book. My most depressing, no, truly heartbreaking, thought is that when the guerrillas release me, they'll take the diaries. So I'm keeping this diary out of sight and I only write in it in private. Am hoping it will be forgotten. I use only the second notebook to draft my letter to Susan, etc. If I took Eduardo's I'd have no place to hide the diaries. Also, if I were to be rescued in some Tom Clancy–type operation—which I know can't happen—I'll have the diaries with me on my body. When I'm finally released, I must wear my khaki trousers and be in Jockey shorts. That will make the diaries easier to conceal.

1900h: Eduardo caught some little trout with a net. For dinner, I had two. The bigger one was the length of my hand, the other half that size. Plus a couple of bites of cabbage and carrot and rice.

The letter goes off tomorrow. By mule that is. If the trip "outside" really takes four days, it could easily be a week before Susan and CIAT receive them. Will this *really* be FARC's first contact with CIAT? The introduction, after which a ransom letter will be sent? Haven't I read that kidnappers sometimes wait several weeks before making the first contact—to "soften" the target? To build anxiety (i.e., is the victim alive . . . or dead?)?

So the letter had to be written. Anyway I had no choice. I wrote pretty much what FARC told me to write: asking CIAT for "help" in my release and telling why. Juaco insisted on adding—in fact, dictated—the last paragraph. (Please don't send the police or army . . . !)

Wednesday, 12 Oct., Day 20

0950h: The "cowboy" who came yesterday afternoon, which kept me shut inside my tent for three hours, may have brought supplies. I see two big sacks of potatoes. Wish they were more carrots, onions, cabbages, etc. The boys caught 20 more little trout by net last night.

I realized something when Juaco was reviewing my letter to Susan/CIAT last night. He can't read. Rather, he can barely read. I finally started reading the letter to him word by word and pointing to each word as I read. No wonder when I've asked Juaco to check things I've written in Spanish, he's always said my Spanish was perfect. I don't think that any of these guerrillas can really read.

The latrine is three logs over a ditch of spring water that empties into the stream. The camp is a mire of mud. There are patches of blue in the sky today. The sun is amazingly warm when the sun shines, then a cloud covers the sun and it's cold again, immediately.

The cowboy brought a dog yesterday who seems to have decided to visit us for a while. His name is Oso—Bear—and he's really ugly. He has no interest in making friends with a kidnapped *gringo*. I'd like to spend half an hour playing with Cuchara and Snowball, our dogs in Cali! God! I can't believe that. Captivity must be getting to me.

1045h: I try to pet, make friends with Oso. He just sticks his tail between his legs and runs to the huts to be with his FARC friends. Somehow that almost makes me cry. Really, I mean Oso's a dog no one could love. Mangy, skinny, flea-bitten, stupid. Probably never petted in his life. And for good reason.

1130h: Ran 13 laps.

1415h: Lunch was rice and a mixture of lentils and potato with a few spoons of cabbage and carrot. Raining, raining. I wonder what Susan and I will do when I am released. Immediately, I mean. Maybe home leave in Texas. I should think it could be good to get out of Colombia for a while. If I get out with this diary, I'd like to somehow meet with some agents or maybe Owen Lock [my editor at Ballantine Books]. Also, what about the long term? After an experience like this—on both Susan's part and mine—I don't think one can just pick up and resume life as if nothing happened, like coming home from Vietnam. I wasn't the same person who had left; Susan wasn't the same woman either. Nor was America the same. When I return, even the CIAT will have changed. It must. CIAT can no longer bury its head in the sand and claim to be apart from the insanity that eats away at Colombia's soul. What about CIAT's image as a "stable" center, a place to invest research funds? What about international recruitment: "Any problems with security? I've read so much about violence in Colombia."

"No, relax. Cali is a lot safer than Washington, D.C., or Los Angeles. . . . Sure, a communist guerrilla group kidnapped one CIAT senior staff, but it wasn't a big deal." No, this kidnapping will affect CIAT. It could have been Guy Henry or Carlos Lascano or Tony Bellotti or anyone, but it was me. And that has to mark me in some way, professionally as well as personally.

I could very well be an embarrassment to the CIAT, maybe to the CGIAR. What if I make this diary into a mass-market book? CIAT probably wouldn't like that; it would draw attention to the things mentioned above. Would CIAT tell me not to publish? If so, what will I do? Could be nasty. I've certainly been thinking about that anyway; would that be a mistake? International agricultural development has been more than a career, it's been my life. And it's generally been a good life. Travel! . . . Lots of it, and to many of the world's exotic places. Adventure, sure. (Including this one, I guess.) Professional satisfaction—lots. Prestige. A good living; not rich, but comfortable. A legacy for our kids; Miles and Tom G. know that they were raised in a rare and special way. Can I give all that up? Can *we* give it up? I don't know. . . . My future has been almost entirely out of my hands since that FARC *retén* on 23 Sept. I guess what I wonder most is: After my release, how much will that *retén* and the events that followed continue to influence, shape my destiny?

1650h: Dinner is served. Rice topped with a type of potato salad and some cabbage and carrots. I eat all of the latter, every sliver. Lord, what I'd give for a big piece of beef. I don't fantasize, though, about a big steak. No, what comes to mind is a huge bone; one that I have to hold with both hands, covered with juicy meat. I gnaw the meat directly from the bone. As day 20 ends, I know that my release won't come soon. But I'll be okay through the long night that begins in a few minutes. Then tomorrow, I'll live through tomorrow. Then tomorrow night. I don't know why prisoners have written of taking it one day at a time. It's not that way. It's one day. Then one night. And the night is as long as three of the days. But I'm learning how to handle it all.

1815h: In tent. I've noticed something odd. These kids don't play any games. There's no cards or dice or any kind of game to kill time. That's especially strange for soldiers. I wonder if FARC prohibited such frivolity, or if their lives have been so limited they haven't been exposed to games. The latter probably. I'd teach them tic-tac-toe (Cat and Rat), but I don't want to use any precious notebook paper.

Conejo came riding up the mountain on a mule late this morning with, of all things, a generator! A small gasoline-powered Honda generator. Juaco and Ramiro have worked all day and finally got it running about sundown. It's running in the hut right now, generating power for a single electric lightbulb. Thank God I'm not in the hut with the noise and gasoline fumes added to the wood smoke. And what good is a lightbulb, really, if you can't read? We'll see.

But the scary thing is . . . a generator? These boys expect to be on this mountain for a long time. And obviously, with me.

1850h: Ramiro came by to talk. Asked if I was writing. He obviously wanted me to read what I've written to him, like I did before. I said, sorry, but I don't write anymore. Nothing to write about. I'm trying to downplay that I've ever written anything so my diaries may be forgotten. But I felt bad—almost ashamed—about not reading to Ramiro, the kid liked that so much.

Thursday, 13 Oct., Day 21

0830h: I have a terrible time sleeping on this bunk. It's a frame of logs with a bed of planks and bamboo covered by grass and straw, then 1 inch of foam rubber and a blanket. My back, shoulders, and especially neck ache all night. Makes it even harder to sleep.

The boys separated the calf from one of the cows last night and milked the cow this morning. So we now have fresh milk. I'm sure the cow has been tested for brucellosis. Sure. The cow looks like a Holstein-Hereford cross.

A well, then customized bunks, a generator, now a dairy. This is how man ceased being a hunter and settled down to a sedentary, permanent life as a farmer. Next, we'll be planting our own potatoes. Settled here permanently? I don't like it.

1030h: The front door to my tent was mire. This morning I gathered pieces of wood, rotten bamboo, and rocks; put them onto a layer, then covered with wood chips. Did the same for part of the inside of my tent, although it's drier.

1100h: Took my bunk apart and rearranged the straw, etc. But I already feel new lumps to replace the ones I fixed. I spent the entire morning trying to make my tent space and bunk drier, more comfortable.

1200h: This looks like a day of never-ending rain. I doubt I'll even be able to run. I look at what I accomplished this morning. I felt proud until I really looked at it. Nothing but a floor of mud, now covered mostly by pieces of soggy, rotten wood and bamboo partly filled with wet wood chips. It's pitiful. And I worked all morning in the rain for that? But it helped the time pass. What else would I have done with the time?

1300h: Lunch was the best in a long time. Rice and pasta with some sardines and two little fried trout. One trout was one fourth, and the other one half, the length of my hand. I ate 2 of them entirely: head, bones tail. Delicious. Reminds me of the baby catfish Susan and I used to eat in Augusta, GA, when I was assigned to Fort Gordon. We also had hot chocolate made from fresh milk.

1530h: Still in tent. Raining and cold. Have learned to break my candles into three pieces and put them in a triangle in the middle of my little table made from a cut log. That put out three times the heat and I can sit on my bunk and warm my hands over the side. Also, I can circle the flames with damp socks and dry them. I think about Susan a lot. What is she doing now? How often does she talk to the boys? How are they taking this? I hope Susan is still studying Spanish and has e-mail.

1820h: In the tent. Dinner was rice cooked in milk and sugar. I hate that dish. Talked Celina into making me, instead, a plate of bread, white cheese, and sardines. It's 1825h and I won't sleep for hours. Maybe I should describe the inside of my tent. It's 10 feet long six to seven feet wide. I can sit up in my bunk but can't stand anywhere. To my right is the mud wall of the hut with one candle in a niche. To my left is my little log table, 1½ feet high, on which three candle stubs burn. The canvas roof slopes then drops straight down to my left about 3½ feet from the bunk. The left wall is 3½ feet high. I've already described the "floor" I made today. An old rubber boot at the end of the bunk is a urinal. A cheap plastic belt came with my second trousers; I've made it into a clothesline along the wall that will hold some socks. What else? Nothing, That's it. When I "turn in," I put my glasses, flashlight, and notebooks in one of my boots to my left, to stay dry. It's cold and wet in here. The bunk faces south. I probably average 18 hours a day in here; 20 today.

Friday, 14 Oct., Day 22

I have heard nothing from [the time] I was kidnapped three weeks ago this morning. There are no prospects of which I'm aware that I'll be released in the near future. That is a grim outlook indeed. Eleven October was my father's 83rd birthday. I should have called. Really I'm quite worried that something will happen to him during this time and I won't learn until I'm finally released.

What will I do today? I haven't the faintest idea. Same as yesterday, I guess. Nothing. How do these son of a bitches—my FARC hosts—feel about all this? Does any feel any [pangs of] conscience about kidnapping and holding a man prisoner? I don't think so. Intelligence is not a dominant characteristic of this group. I doubt that any would even think about having nothing to read as an inconvenience. The age breakdown is 17 years old, two; 15, two; 16, three.

I found a plastic knit sack near the camp this morning. In big white letters against a faded background of red, it says, "Canada Wheat 50 kg." I wonder how it got here. It's dry, anyway, and I'll make it part of my mattress.

1105h: Haven't heard the news for four days. Batteries down on radio. I don't know what happened to the generator.

1200h: Lunch is rice and cabbage-carrot.

1545h: Ran 14 laps. Juaco, Javier, Eduardo took the net and went to seine the stream for trout after lunch. They could have taken me, but didn't. What the hell ... I hope they get some fish.

About the generator. The boys made a shed up the hill and installed it this morning with a line to take electricity to the hut. They haven't tried it out yet.

Not only is there nothing to read here—there's nothing to write about, anymore. I've written everything there is about this life. Except maybe I haven't captured the emptiness, the nothingness, the sick frustration at your helplessness. Yeah, maybe the helplessness is the worst. I cannot control a single aspect of my future and I see no change in sight. And the loneliness. If I had someone to talk with. And that problem is not language. Having someone to talk with in Spanish—who could *talk*—would be wonderful.

1600h: Stop, Hargrove. Feeling sorry for yourself won't help. It's only two hours until night, and you can't afford to be down when that long nothingness begins.

1610h: In tent. Dinner was two of those tiny but delicious trout, with rice and lentils.

Saturday, 15 Oct., Day 23

0945h: Rained all night. Cold this morning. I've been digging ditches to draw water from around the tent, and filling in ponds where water stands. The only problem is, when I dig mud to fill in a pond, my excavation makes another pond. It's Saturday morning and I'm starting my fourth weekend as a hostage.

1145h: Found the battered lid of an aluminum pot, brought it into my tent, collected fresh wood chips, and built a small fire. A lot better than burning candles. And keeping the fire going—it's fun—something to do. The first SW radio set is broken. Juaco brought a new one. Tried 45 minutes to pick up VOA or BBC. No success. I haven't heard international news for five days.

1520h: Lunch was rice and boiled potatoes. Ran eight laps, then [it] started raining. Am in tent with woodchip fire. Building fire, watching it burn, keeping it going is therapeutic. Especially when it's cold and you need a fire.

1610h: Dinner was potato soup.

Sunday, 16 Oct., Day 24

My 24th day kidnapped opens cloudy but not rainy. If I only had a date, if I knew when this will be over and I'll be freed. No. Maybe I don't want that. I'd love to have such a date if it's within, say, two weeks. But what if my freedom is two months from now? Or six months or one year? What if I were to learn that I'll never be free again, but will die in these mountains—of sickness or execution ... ? No, it's better not to know what happens next and live one day at a time. I know I'll survive today, and if so I'll make it through tonight. I'll worry about tomorrow tomorrow.

0910h: Eduardo is a pyromaniac—is that the word? He loves to start fires. Harmless enough, I guess, considering the fires. Almost every evening he heads in a different direction, setting fire to the tall clumps of grass that characterize this terrain. You can see a trail of smoke and know he's there. The grass itself is interesting. The top parts of the clumps will always burn—even right after a rain. Must be nearly pure cellulose. Is this the same grass that ranchers in the savannas systematically burn off so more tender grass will emerge?

0940h: As I was writing the above, Eduardo and Celina were preparing to go by foot to the camp below. They've left and I can see already a trail of smoke.

1030h: This morning is one of those rare, sunny days. Went to the stream, with Ramiro as guard, and bathed, washed. There were burned clumps of grass—Eduardo was here. Strange; clumps of grass that burn so easily growing in perpetual swamp.

1305h: The sunshine has ended. It's raining again. Lunch was rice and lentils and cabbage-carrot. My clothes, hanging on the fence, were almost dry. I have no place inside the tent to dry clothes or even to store clean clothes. After my bath I came back to the tent. The sunshine on the canvas made the tent deliciously warm, especially after the shocking coldness of the stream. I fell asleep and slept soundly for an hour.

1720h: Dinner was rice and lentils with a piece of sardine, and hot chocolate. During my one-hour nap this morning I dreamed that I parked my car on the Puerto Tejada road—and woke up with a gun barrel in my face. But I wasn't kidnapped again—it was only my staff playing a trick on me.

Monday, 17 Oct., Day 25

1030h: Last night was terribly cold, but I awoke to the warmest, clearest day yet. The sunshine on my tent creates a warmth so balmy, so creamy I'd like to bottle and sell it. The tent is not of canvas; it's a light, thin waterproof material. Excellent material. This is the first day I don't need the jacket. But I wear it anyway; otherwise I can't carry the diaries.

1140h: The day continues remarkably warm. I'm sitting on a rock behind the hut, toasting in, soaking up, this wonderful sun. Juaco and Leidi sat with me in my tent for 30 minutes this morning. Nothing bad, they just wanted to visit, and Juaco helped repair my flashlight.

But I wanted to tell them to get the hell out of my tent. They were invading the only thing I could even vaguely call my privacy. Irrational? Yeah. But I've been awfully damned rational since this began. I said nothing, of course. We talked about La Buitrera again. FARC holds meetings there because the population is supposedly pro-FARC. They describe the village as "very rich," and I guess it is. I told how Susan and I had looked for a place to possibly rent and live in there. Juaco asked if we might move to La Buitrera after my release. "Are you joking?" I said. "Of course not."

Juaco looked surprised. "Why not?"

"And run the risk that FARC might kidnap me again?"

"No, señor." Juaco looked almost hurt. No one from FARC would bother

me. Why should I think that? I don't think these kids even realize what a crime kidnapping is. They're so naive.

I do not use the familiar form of Spanish with the guerrillas, even though it would sometimes seem natural. I don't care to become overly familiar with people who have kidnapped and are holding me hostage.

1240h: The weather changes so fast up here—while I was writing, clouds suddenly covered the sun. It became cold—and now it's hailing. Yeah, hail for the first time.

Lunch is rice with boiled beans and a piece of sardine, and hot sweetened milk.

My decision to low-key the diary has deprived me of one small pleasure. The guerrillas used to love for me to read to them things I'd written. I'd only read things about the weather, the food, the color of the mountains, of course. Nothing vaguely critical of FARC or my treatment. I'd sometimes make stuff up as I read. Was good for them.

The rash on my feet has started again and there is no way to get medicine to treat it. I don't even remember the name. But I'm so lucky that even on Day 25 the foot rash has been my worst sickness. I'm sure these kids don't realize that they're lucky, too. What would they do if their *prisionero* became really sick up here? I'll bet it's two days' hard march to the nearest medical treatment. A person could die so *easily* up here. I don't know why we're not all sick. This camp is mud, littered with sardine cans (these folks are not great environmentalists). Potato peels and food scraps are thrown down the hill. Dishes are washed in cold water, and can never really be clean. Maybe the cold weather is healthy. The food scraps, for example, don't seem to rot. But my health is remarkably good. My psychological health, too, I think. Every few days I go off behind the hut alone and allow myself to think about the situation. I cry a few seconds, and feel better afterward. There's nothing wrong with that as long as the guerrillas don't see it. But I don't allow that to happen at night. Not locked, for what seems forever, in the cold and cramped wet darkness of a tent I can't escape. I'd suffocate if I got down during those long nights.

1305h: Susan probably hasn't even received my letter—the letter that is to open FARC-CIAT contact—yet if the trip out of here really takes four days . . . And I wrote the letter so long ago.

1605h: It hailed a second time this afternoon, then the sun came out again. Ran 15 laps.

1620h: Dinner is served. Pisses me off. Lunch was four hours ago and even with time it's hard to work up an appetite for this swill. It seems that whoever is in charge of cooking for a day does his three meals whenever he feels like it. And today, it's Gustavo. Anyway, it's rice and beans, same as lunch, minus the sardine piece—and hot chocolate. I remember and pull out the piece of cheese stashed away. It tastes—and chews—like rubber.

1630h: Dinner is over. I wish they'd pass out one of those forms: "To help us serve you better, we would appreciate your comments and suggestions."

1650h: Was rushed back into the tent and shut in. Apparently someone is coming up the valley and I'm not to be seen.

1845h: The secret of survival here, it seems, is to strike a balance between not giving up hope and not hoping for too much. I don't expect or even hope to learn tomorrow that I'm being released. Or the next day. But I know that someday I'll be released.

Tuesday, 18 Oct., Day 26

Am having a hard time sleeping. The bunk is so hard and short it hurts my lower back a lot. Don't think I ever sleep before 1:30 A.M.

0900h: Juaco and Javier have taken the net and gone trout fishing—or I should say, seining. I wish they'd taken me, anything to get out of this tent and hut for a few hours. I haven't asked; being turned down would be too hard to take. Actually I did ask, last week, or was it two weeks ago? Anyway, I hope they get some fish. Anything to break this rice-lentils-beans business. Have been thinking, even dreaming, a lot about food lately. Too much probably. Mostly about great meals. Those half-pound grilled burgers at Chili's in Ft. Worth; one of Pam's big Comil T-bones; fried chicken like my mother or Susan's grandmother used to make; prime rib of beef like at Blackie's in Washington, D.C.; whole catfish like Gerald cooked; the hams and turkeys we always had at Thanksgiving, and Christmas; baby beef and fried *tilapia* in Cali.

It's 0930h. What in the hell am I going to do with the rest of this day? I can't think of anything except fill in a hole in my patio and go to the spring and fill my two water bottles. What a depressing, devastating thought.

1000h: The two new guerrillas, Melena and Viejito. They arrived yesterday (i.e., the false alarm that had me locked in the tent) and are apparently replacing Celina and Eduardo, who left on foot with backpacks, yesterday morning. When Leidi introduced me to Melena, I said, "*Mucho gusto en conoceria.*" What garbage. I don't feel great pleasure in knowing her. She's here to help guard me, because I'm kidnapped. But what else does one say? I may be here for months with this group. I don't know what the answer is, what's right and wrong protocol in such a relationship. But I feel that getting close—in a friendship way—to your captors is not good.

1030h: It's cold, rainy. Gustavo, the 15-year-old Indian, would obviously like to know me better. But there is the factor mentioned above. Plus, we have little to talk about. Plus something else—that applies to all personal relations here. If I start talking, personally, I'll almost surely say how I feel about all this, what I think of FARC and its hypocritical mandate to end slavery and bring about human rights, etc. And while I'm here, that could work against me. Also, friendship isn't going to play any role in my release or, probably, in my treatment.

God, I hope Susan gets that letter today. For almost a month now, I have been totally removed from my society. Like I've stood still while time moved forward a month. What changes will I face when I go back? I've written of my fears for my father, but many other things can happen, and I know nothing about them.

1215h: Borrowed a metal compact mirror from Leidi (all the guerrillas carry them) and Juaco's Swiss army knife, which has excellent scissors—very sharp. Trimmed my mustache and part of my beard.

1500h: Lunch was potato-and-noodle soup. Later Gustavo, Leidi, and Melena were in my tent, all over my bunk. I'd have liked to read to them but can't. Leidi's Indian, and so is Melena. They say Eduardo and Ramiro are part Indian. Juaco is part Indian but doesn't speak Páez. One reason I have such a hard time understanding what they say to one another is that it is a mixture of Spanish and Páez.

1610h: Juaco and Viejito returned—with about 25 trout. I think they're rainbows. Most are the standard hand size or smaller, but one is about 10 inches long.

1650h: International Centers Week opens on Monday in Washington, D.C. Tiff Harris and Ruth Raymond, Ed Sulzberger, Barbara Rose will all be there. I wonder if they know yet about my kidnapping. This is the first kidnapping of a center senior staff. But will it be ignored at ICW? Will CIAT, the CGIAR try to keep it quiet? What are the implications of Colombia being the newest CGIAR member? It must be embarrassing, if my situation is widely known. If I knew what is known, then I might speculate. But I know nothing. That also means most CIAT directors will be in Washington, D.C., next week—not good for me.

1900h: Dinner was two hand-length trout, rice and cabbage, carrots. The trout were divine; ate heads, bones, all. Makes me realize I still have an appetite; I just hate the slop we're served. It's awfully cold. Rained all afternoon. Still I did my 15 laps. Am now in tent nursing a little fire.

Wednesday, 19 Oct., Day 27

My letters to Susan/CIAT left by horse or mule one week ago this morning.

I'm disturbed at the number of flies—big, fat flies—I saw near the spring this morning. The cause is obvious. The guerrillas [are] now dumping much more raw garbage there (it's where they wash dishes). I'm going to show Juaco, but I doubt he'll do anything. But we're going to have sickness here if this continues. Especially if the weather turns warmer, like today. Also, swarms of bees—I guess they're bees. They're the size of a large fruit fly, have a yellow-and-black-striped abdomen, buzz as they fly, and the guerrillas call them *abulia*. The bees seem to thrive on garbage. I've never heard of that. If our dishes were washed in hot water, I'd be less concerned. But they're not. They're washed in cold water, with, I guess, a little soap. In fact, this entire camp is becoming a garbage heap with cans, plastic, soap, dishes, papers strewn indiscriminately. The latrine situation is fairly healthy, though: a stream down the hill. The place with the fewest flies is my tent. I've lined the floor and the "patio" around it with stones, wood, bamboo pieces, and wood chips. There is no standing water except when it rains, and not too much permanent mire.

1105h: I got mad about this situation and took the shovel, and started hauling dry soil and rocks from five meters away, filling in spots where water still stood, and building up my patio. Ramiro asked what I was doing. "I think this camp is filthy!" I said. "Look at the flies and garbage and filth. I'm cleaning my part up."

"But the flies come from the mud," Ramiro said.

"Bullshit. Look behind the hut. There's mud but few flies. But there are millions of flies in front of the hut, where all the filth is." I think it makes Ramiro mad that I'm covering the mire and standing water by my tent. Maybe he thinks God meant it to be that way. The food is prepared, of course, and the dishes washed where the mud and flies are. So my cleanup job probably won't protect me much. But it looks, and feels, better. Turning cold again. Rain this afternoon, for sure.

1445h: Lunch was potato soup with a couple of those little trout thrown in. Juaco and Leidi left this morning. At about 1400h a packhorse and a pack mule appeared, heavily loaded, with them walking behind. Supplies. Gasoline for the generator, lots of potatoes, some soybean, vegetable-protein stuff called *carve*. Gustavo took the mule back down the mountain and returned with a big spool of . . . barbed wire. It's suppose to pen the calves so they can milk the cows easier. The cattle up here seem to be a mixture of Hereford, Holstein, and maybe Shorthorn. Most cattle down lower are Zebu-Brahman type.

1620h: Dinner served already. Rice topped with chopped fish and some cabbage-carrot salad with—wow!—some thin slivers of onion mixed in. We're really getting gourmet.

The acoustics of this valley are unusual. A lot of echo. But a rifle shot, for example, doesn't repeat itself. Instead, it's a continuous rolling roar for 8 to 10 seconds. At times, the sound of the main river, far below in the valley, suddenly comes up here. It sounds surprisingly like a lot of traffic on a freeway.

When a rifle is fired in the valley below, you first hear a sharp report directly below, then almost—[*interrupted by 3 shots, full automatic*]—almost immediately a roar to the south, then a rolling and broader more muffled roar to the north. Again, it takes 7 or 8 seconds.

Thursday, 20 Oct., Day 28

0300h: *Bam!* Another gunshot. Inside the hut again. Then half a dozen half clips, 10 to 12 rounds each, fired into the darkness. Voices rise above the radio, voices that are too loud, I feel. More shooting. I go back to sleep only to be awakened again at 0400h by 10 rounds, fired systematically on semiautomatic, into the darkness. Then more automatic weapons fire. At 0615h I'm awakened again by a burst of three rounds fired from the door. Maybe some more shooting. I don't remember. I go back to sleep. I get up and leave the tent at around

0800h, half expecting to see a dead guerrilla or two from all the gunfire through the night. Ramiro is outside. "What was all the shooting about last night?" I ask.

Ramiro looks embarrassed. "Nothing."

"Everyone was drunk and just shooting for fun?"

"No one was drunk." Ramiro can't lie worth a damn.

"Sure: I believe you," I said. That's when Viejito emerges from the hut, clutching a brandy bottle in one hand, his Galil in the other. He aims at something along the hill to our east and fires a couple of rounds. That brings Juaco and Gustavo from the hut. Someone fires a few more rounds at nothing. I go into the kitchen part of the hut. There's no coffee. In fact, there's no fire. Leidi and Melena must be sleeping late, after being up all night with the gunfire.

As I return to my tent, I see Juaco walking along the mountainside to the west, away from the camp. Where is he going? I wonder.

The shooting dies down to a round or two every few minutes. I try to go to sleep but can't. The volume of gunfire picks up. The boys are shooting 9 or 10 rounds at a time on full automatic again. I lift my tent flap. It looks like they've set that old dry cow skull out on the little hill about 100 meters to the east. A few cows are grazing nearby.

I may as well get up. Viejito is still clutching the brandy bottle, lying back against the rocks in front of the hut. He stands about four feet tall and the Indian's *apodo*, or nickname, means little old man and it fits Viejito. He has the wrinkled wizened look of a centenarian and is the size of a healthy 9-year-old but is [15 and] probably fully grown [at about 4½ feet tall]. I check the fire— still no coffee. Gunfire continues. Viejito is now up, joining the fun, sending short bursts from his Galil in the general direction of the skull. As I return to my tent, a burst of automatic fire, then I hear some shouts. Different somehow from the drunken yelling of before. I look toward the hill. A cow's lying on her back, feet kicking, and thrashing her head wildly. I can't believe it. Surely not. But yes, it looks like one of the silly little bastards has shot a cow. My first reaction is sheer joy. There'll be trouble over this. Someone is going to be in deep shit. My feeling of satisfaction is like revenge, and it's a warm good feeling. And the meat! That cow's not getting up, not from her back like that. They'll have to butcher her, and that means at least we'll have some good, red meat! The shooting has stopped and Melena runs out to inspect the cow, who's still thrashing. She shouts back that the cow has been shot. No kidding. "Where?" someone shouts.

"Here!" She points a finger toward the middle of her body as she walks back. The guerrillas talk but none leave the area around the hut for 10 minutes. I don't remember how, but I sensed that Viejito shot the cow. Finally, Viejito walks across the meadow cradling his Galil. He inspects the cow, which by now lies still. Then he walks back to the hut; about halfway he swings the Galil, firing a burst blindly past the hut.

1015h: Have been waiting, until the tension and emotion die down to write. Also, must be careful. But finally have some excitement. The [illegible] guerrillas finally shot our milk cow. She's lying in the sun, very dead, about 100 meters in front of me and Viejito is lying on his back in front of the hut, looking very sick and sober. Leidi comes out and hugs him from time to time. Melena just brought me a *tinto* of sweet coffee without milk. I wonder if we'll have milk again? I'm ecstatic, of course. Now we'll finally have some meat. Or will we? Surely they won't leave the cow—all that meat—in the sun to rot. I think they've taken Viejito's weapon. Hope so. We've had enough bullets—maybe 200 rounds—flying pretty randomly around here this morning.

I'd better start at the beginning. At 1220h this morning, *Pow-pow-pow*— three rapid shots were fired in the forest above us. Excited voices in the hut. Then I heard bolts being slid, then the radio is turned on loud, to Radio Recuerdas from Bogotá. To cover the conversation, the orders? Four well-timed shots [are] fired from the hut into the forest. Ten minutes later, about 10 rounds are fired on full automatic. Then *whomp!* A hand grenade explodes in the forest. I'm nervous. Naturally. What the hell is going on? Are we being attacked? I don't think so. Not enough shooting. And who would attack us? Nervous guard, firing at shadows? The guerrillas don't post guards at night. More firing, fully automatic, rock-and-roll, from the hut and in the forest I'm wearing my glasses, and my diary, dictionary, and flashlight are in my rubber boot. Ready for my move. Should I roll off the bunk and lie in the cold, soggy wood chips? At least it's no longer mud. My bunk, cold and hard before, now seems as cozy as our bed back home. Juaco brought a lot of liquor back from the camp below today. I remember, five or six *canecas* of Cinca Estrellas (Five Stars) Brandy were stacked on the shelf above his bunk, and he gave me one *caneca*. Maybe the boys are drunk again and shooting up the forest like before. But I didn't hear any party noises before the shooting started. But a shot is fired inside the hut. Then a clip at full auto outside. They're drunk and playing guns, I think. But that doesn't reassure me; there's only a couple of inches dried mud between me and the weapons inside, and the boys could easily forget that my bunk lies opposite that flimsy wall.

Then I went to the spring to fill my water bottles—as Juaco was returning along the mountain trail from the west. All the guerrillas were inside the hut, so our camp looked strangely deserted. I walked to my tent as Juaco entered the hut. I wonder if he's noticed the dead cow. I thought, then the best place for you, Hargrove, is back in your tent. I expect to hear trouble; shouting, maybe shooting—but I hear nothing.

1115h: The hut is deathly quiet. The sun is shining, so I step outside my tent. Partly to stretch, partly to see if anything is going on, partly so if anyone watches me he won't think I'm writing. Like when I last looked at 1045h, Juaco slumps on the stone in front of the tent wrapped in his brown *ruana*, like in a deep sleep that will make it all go away. He must be in deep trouble. Shooting a peasant's cow must be a real no-no in the FARC statutes, especially if men are drunk and firing wildly—under your command.

Meanwhile the cow still lies in the sun. I get hungry just looking at that stiffening pile of potential beef. If only I could take the ax and a machete and start chopping off meat. I'd gut the animal first, then cut out the liver and heart.

We could fry liver for lunch. Then I'd chop through the backbone and cut out the loin to grill over the fire. One haunch would be cut, stored in a burlap sack, and sunk in the cold spring waters of the trout pond. I'd put the rest of the meat on the pack mule, and send it to the camp below.

1140h: Yeah, it's what I'd do, but will it happen? Juaco still slumps in the *ruana* and hasn't moved for an hour. He could be dead, for all I can tell. And the hut has that unnatural silence, like no one wants to disturb the dead. No, now I hear a sound, a heavy breathing, a woman moaning in the hut a few inches away. It's a strangely sexy cry, increasing in intensity and depth. Orgasmic? No, that can't be. But weird things happen around death, and the comically surreal death of that cow probably more [illegible] for this unit than the honorable death of a fellow guerrilla would be. Now I hear voices. Leidi, Leidi. Scared voice trying to sound calm and heavier breathing, like hyperventilation. It's Leidi in a muffled grief-borne hysteria, the drunken slaughter of a peasant's cow, what an absurd disgrace for the unit. What humiliation for Viejito. Maybe more so for Juaco. What stories will go around the FARC units.

1230h: Juaco is in the hut. Melena is at the spring. I walk over. She's cleaning trout, about a dozen little ones. Juaco caught them with the net this morning, she explains. So that is why Juaco left. Fishing with the net I say, looking at the cow. Melena is sniffling too. She and Viejito came here together, three days ago. None of the guerrillas [illegible] out. Where are Ramiro, Gustavo? I hear only one sound, metal sliding against metal. A rifle bolt, working back and forth. Why? The hard liquid sound penetrates the mud wall easily. I like it less than before. The firing finally dies off sometime in the darkness. Well after 1 A.M., I drift into sleep, despite the blessing of Radio Recuerdas.

1300h: I'm sitting on the floor of my tent, on the floor, for the first time, listening to a rifle bolt being slid, rounds chambered and ejected, another clip inserted. The floor is not very safe, but it's the safest place I can go. And I'm eating my potato and onion. What in the hell is going on? I don't know. But I'm going to eat the trout.

1305h: Viejito has come out. He's walking across the meadow toward the dead cow. No weapon that I can see, thank God. But I haven't even written about what just happened at about 1250h; Melena brought a plate to my tent. Two of Juaco's little trout, grilled with some onion. That reminds me. There's half a raw onion in the kitchen. What a treat. I take my plate into the hut. I'm standing by the fire, back to the door, slicing a thin sliver of onion when [I hear] an explosion, a deafening roar. A gunshot in the hut, directly behind me. I'm so shook that I don't even jump. I finish slicing the onion and turn around. Juaco is lying still, sprawled across half his bunk, his Galil cradled in his arms, muzzle next to his head. He's dead, I think. He killed himself. But I don't see blood. Yet he's lying so still. Or did the shot come from outside? No, and the cordite smells strongly. He must have shot through the wall. Accidentally, or on purpose? A botched suicide attempt, I don't know. Across the hut Gustavo is sitting up in his bunk. He's pointing, his forefinger thrusting at me then at the door. The message is clear. Leave! I take my plate and walk through the door and around the corner to my tent, then sit on the bunk. Juaco's bunk is directly behind my head and from it I hear the metallic sliding [of] cartridges being chambered and ejected. That's when I sit on the floor. This is the most absurd day since I was kidnapped. The air is thick with craziness and doom and blood. Someone may die today in the air. Make sure it's not you, Hargrove, although I could be an excellent candidate.

1345h: Another shot fired inside the hut. I go back on the floor again. Has Juaco gone berserk? I can't believe I'm sitting here on the woodchip floor, writing it down as it happens. How many gunshots since things got serious at 0900h? A lot. Someone's going to get hurt. Is Juaco just shooting through the wall at random? Could he, somehow, blame me for all this? Yeah, easily, especially if he's pain-filled and off balance. This is all my party, in a way. My kidnap party. Were it not for Hargrove, none of this would be happening, none of us would be here in this insane camp in the mountains, cut off from society, civilization, any law except what FARC makes. I could be dead before this day is over. Maybe even accidentally, a wild shot through the wall. Thought I was going to point out the fly problem to Juaco today, tell him he should really clean up this camp. Maybe I'd better forget that idea.

After a while I sat back on my bunk, set my plate on my log-stump table, and finish lunch. Leidi, Melena, and Viejito are all back at the cow, skinning her. Juaco is in the hut, alone. *Bam!* Another shot inside the hut. I get back on the floor. Another shot, inside the hut, a few minutes later. If Juaco leaves that hut, I think, it's best that he doesn't see me. I pull the tent flap down and continue to write.

At about 1405h: There's been no shooting inside the hut for some time. What if Juaco's killed himself? I think. There's only he and I at the hut; the others are at the cow. If they find Juaco dead, and I'm here with him . . . that could look bad for me . . . especially in this insane time. If Juaco is alive, he may start shooting again. Can I go to the cow, join the others? They have guns, too, and that dead cow must be damned humiliating. I decide that the crazies with the cow are safer than the crazy in the hut, and I leave.

As I wade through the muck to the hill, I see Gustavo, Leidi, and Melena skinning the cow. Then I see Viejito curled in a fetal position, lying by the cow. "He's dead," I think. The girls see me.

"Don Tomás, Viejito shot the cow!" Leidi says, as if I didn't know.

"Yes, I came to help you. Why aren't you cutting meat from the cow?"

"The hide is very valuable," Leidi says, continuing to skin the animal.

Then I jump; Juaco appears, from over the crest of the hill. My God, I thought he was back at the hut, maybe dead! He looks devastated, and acts like he's in a different world. I haven't used kindness and understanding when dealing with the guerrillas of FARC. I haven't quite been in that position. Plus, I have no love for those who kidnap me. But this seems a special situation. I'm also thinking about Hargrove's fate, as well as Juaco's well-being, when I approach him.

"Juaco, I know this has been a terrible day," I say softly. "What has happened has happened, now I want to help you in any way I can." Juaco nods, dazed.

"They're skinning the cow, but I think we should remove the intestines so the meat won't spoil."

Juaco stares ahead, but nods. He then sits on a clump of grass, rifle muzzle by his head, and wraps [himself] in that brown *ruana* like before.

I return to the cow's carcass. Gustavo holds a hind leg while I chop at the bone and sinew with an ax until the shank parts. I hold the other leg back while Gustavo hacks the unnecessary part.

"Let's remove the intestines," I say. "I'll help. Give me a knife."

"There are no more knives here," Leidi says. "But I left a sharp knife in the kitchen."

I walk up to Juaco, who stares numbly ahead. "I want to help clean the cow," I say carefully. "I'm returning to the hut to get a knife."

Juaco understands, I think. I start picking my way, from clump to clump of grass, across the swampy meadow.

1440h: Am returning to the cow. Had been to the hut to try to find a knife, a machete to cut and help butcher the cow. Walking across the meadow, three more shots—automatic—rang out from the group around the cow.

Who was it? Did Juaco shoot Viejito? Back in my tent, I can still hear the wailing. Ten minutes later Melena slogs back to the hut, crying.

"Juaco," she says, *"se suicidio,"* and she mimics sticking a rifle muzzle under her chin, pulling the trigger, and the top of the head splattering into the air. She disappears into the hut. Leidi returns a few minutes later.

"Pack everything to march, Don Tomás!" she says. "We're leaving."

"By horse?"

"¡No, de pie!" By foot.

I survey my few possessions. What should I take? How far will we march? What will happen next?

Viejito and Gustavo return and dump Juaco's Galil, web gear, cartridge, clip holders, and *caneca* of brandy onto Juaco's bunk. They pull other items from a shelf, dumping them into a pile on the bunk, then start packing their own possessions.

"Is there a spare pack for me? I only have plastic bags to carry my things." My request makes sense, and there's only one pack available. Gustavo empties Juaco's pack onto his bunk.

I go back into the hut. I've seldom been really alone in the hut and I survey for things to steal, little things that might make my life more comfortable. Juaco's Galil is lying on his bunk, but without ammo. A bottle of brandy is in the pile beside the rifle. I pick it up. The bottle has been opened, but it is still almost full. I stick the bottle in my jacket, return to my tent, and bury it in Juaco's backpack. Oh no, they're returning and the three are carrying something. They dropped it.

Then I heard shouts; maybe that's Ramiro and Javier returning from the camp below, I thought, but I knew it wasn't. Then I heard a deep cry of anguish, a woman's cry. Melena, I think. Then someone—I don't remember who—swung a rifle toward me, motioned to return to the hut. I turned and slogged back through the mud.

1515h: Well, I have Juaco's *equipo*, his pack.

1535h: Must write fast. The others are back by the dead cow, covering Juaco's body with some kind of shroud. Then we march to the camp below. I can't believe today. Especially how prophetically I wrote earlier. I knew there'd be death today, almost from the beginning. Will people believe all this when I return? If I return? All this will affect my future, that's for sure. But I don't know how.

1610h: It was a haunch of the beef carried on a nylon sack. I went out and helped carry it in. "We'll fry this tonight," Viejito says. "Here or below?" "Below." I've now packed Juaco's backpack and trapped my three light blankets. The *equipo* is well made—and very worn. Viejito and Melena and Leidi, trying to call someone on the radio, without success. What I can't or won't carry is scattered around my tent, including the 610 Colombian pesos I carried from that *retén*. That was so long ago. I hate to leave my little patio, in a way. I worked so hard on it. I guess the coffee cup I stole from the Indians must stay. It could never make the trip down. It has five chips around the rim, plus a "V" crack down one side, and a straight crack down the other. But the cup has served me well, and I'd like to keep it as a *recuerdo*. In front of me I see the skinned corpse of the cow whose death started all this. No, *terminated* it might be more accurate. And on a knoll just above the cow's corpse, a brown oblong prone shape that is, or was, Juaco. I offered to help carry his corpse back to leave in the hut, so animals won't get it. *"No, es demasiado pesado"* was the answer. But we'll carry beef down the mountain.

One thing is a relief: I'm not so worried about the guerrillas taking my diary now. If I'm smart and keep it out of sight. Juaco was most aware of it; he was the one who'd remember to take it. I found this new pen by the way, on Juaco's bunk. He can't use it, but I can. So I slipped it into my pocket. Do I feel guilty about stealing from the dead? In this case, not in the least. I wish we'd start the march down the mountain. What are we waiting for? We don't want to climb down in darkness.

1640h: We're waiting until the others—Ramiro and Javier—return from below, then we all march down the mountain together. I may be very lucky I returned to the hut for the knife. Had I been in sight when Juaco decided to end it all, he just might have decided to take the *gringo* with him. The *gringo* whose kidnapping started it all. Now Juaco and the cow who killed him, in a way, are lying, side by side, in this beautiful valley. God, I've been writing about death as it was getting ready to happen to someone, not knowing whether it might be me. And death as she came to my captor by his own hand. How many people experience something like that? And record it as it happens? Not many. How did it happen, for me? I don't know.

1720h: Well, I finally had that big chunk of beef I've been dreaming of for so long. Melena fried and served beef at 1700h. I made a side sauce of ketchup and *aji* and cut a big piece of onion, and stuffed myself. Held the meat in my hands and gnawed. It was chewy but had that strong beef flavor of an older animal fed only on grass. Did I enjoy the meal, after all that happened, after what the poor cow meant? I shouldn't even *think* much less write this, but yes, I enjoyed the meal immensely. In spite of the tragedies that led to it. Or, God forgive me, maybe a little bit *because* of those events. I didn't kill Juaco, he killed himself. In more ways than one.

As we finished the meal, Melena walked back to the knoll where the cow and Juaco lie. *Why?* She returns carrying a clip for the Galil. Someone must have ejected it after Juaco shot himself.

1740h: It's time to go. We leave everything and we never expect to return—I don't. Dirty dishes lie where we drop them. I note that [illegible] with about 10 of the little trout Juaco caught this morning sits by the smoldering coals of our fire. I shoulder the backpack, and we march. The trail along the [illegible] inside is slippery. Melena walks [illegible] carrying a pack and her AK-47—plus Juaco's Galil. She's having trouble and slips several times. I should tell her to remove the clips and give Juaco's Galil to me. I can carry it easily, I think. Then my common sense overcomes my chivalry. Don't be a fool, Hargrove. That 16-year-old girl can carry the load better than you. Besides, you don't know how long this march will be. You may not feel so good by the time it's over.

As we leave the terrible camp, a biblical passage runs through my mind. Yea, though I walk through the valley of the shadow of death, I will fear no evil, for Thou art with me. I've walked through that dark valley and now we're walking out of it. What comes next, I don't know—but it has to be better than this. Thank God I'll never see this Valley of Death again. We [illegible] descend into the deeper valley, the one that runs north-south below us. We're also leaving the clouds trapped in the east-west range. A [illegible], late afternoon. Mountain sunset bathes us in golden warmth. We hurry to get down the steep slope while there's still light. The green valley with its winding river and horsetail waterfall cascading almost straight down the western side is a place of surreal beauty. *Things are going to be better,* I think. *I'm sure of it.*

At the foot of the mountain we pass through a potato field slashed from the forest and planted [for FARC's supplies]. Viejito and Gustavo then go ahead. Leidi and Melena and I then set down on a grassy knoll overlooking the rushing river. They're as glad as me to be out of that high valley. Leidi pulls out a headband I've seen her weaving for several days.

"I made this for you, Don Tomás. I'll give it to you when you're released."

"Then I'll get it soon, I hope. What does it say?"

" 'Our home' in the Páez dialect."

"We were so frightened at noon," Melena says. "We thought Juaco was going to shoot you. Then he fired past his own head [and hit] the roof."

"Yeah, I was so scared I didn't even jump. I know he could shoot me, easily."

"Then by the dead cow," Leidi went on, "Juaco was sitting, wrapped in his *ruana*. Then he stood and took a bottle of aguardiente from his jacket."

Aguardiente—I hadn't seen any of the Colombian liquor around the camp.

"No—brandy," she corrected. "Juaco opened the bottle. I took a long swallow. Then he . . ." She pantomimed again putting a rifle muzzle under the chin and pulling the trigger. So *that's* the opened bottle of brandy [I] stole from [Juaco's] gear. The brandy that's now hidden in [my pack] . . . [illegible]

2220h: Am sitting on a bunk writing in candlelight in a cubicle, about 12x5 feet whose walls are covered completely, with newspaper pages. ERNESTO SAMPER NUEVO PRESIDENTE is the banner headline of *El País*. We're at another FARC camp, a way station by the river in the main valley, far below the mountain camp and its bovine and human corpses that we deserted two marches ago. Camp is called, I think, "Che Guevara." His *rostro* [portrait] is painted across the front. So much has happened since [those] first gunshots at 1220h this morning. That was 22 hours ago. The first time in weeks I can't say this has been a "nothing day." No, I've had enough emotion, fear, excitement to last awhile, thank you. I'll write more—fill in the many gaps—tonight. I've had a stiff drink from a bottle of brandy—again, stolen from Juaco—and I'm suddenly exhausted. Mentally, physically, emotionally. I'll hide my diary, and go to sleep.

Friday, 21 Oct., Day 29

0930h: I'm by the river alone, watching and listening to the cold, clear water flow over mossy rocks. The camp is called La Playa, and sits in a [illegible] valley by the river with steep mountains on both sides, most vertical cliffs behind the camp. Yesterday was so emotionally exhausting, I should have slept well. Yet I hardly slept at all. Up at 0700; Ramiro was saddling a mule to ride to another camp with the news and receive orders for what to do next. He said he'd return with Javier. Ramiro did not know, last night, what happened. He left after the cow was shot but before that bizarre lunch.

I guess FARC will also assign another team leader. Right now no one is in charge. Two persons seem to have been in charge of my kidnapping, hiding, and ransom. Rambo and Juaco. Now that Juaco is dead, where does that leave me? I told Ramiro to tell his superiors that this is no longer with it. That CIAT won't pay; the donors won't allow it. That the kidnapping has brought only tragedy and pain, and will cause great damage to FARC's image in Colombia and worldwide. And that FARC should let me go. Ramiro said he would deliver the message. I doubt that he will, although I think he'd like to see me released. So would Leidi and Melena and another Indian guerrilla. That's not going to happen, but trying can't hurt. The most I allow myself to hope for isn't much; it's to stay here at La Playa—so comfortable in comparison and not to have to return to that terrible valley above us; of all the options, that's the most depressing.

1055h: Am back at the river but this time at a *charca*, or pond, bathing with my guards, Leidi, Melena, and another Indian *guerrillera*; pretty respectable. We have separate sides of the pond, sort of, and everyone wears underwear.

The water was always so icy, but it feels so good to be clean. Only five days since my last bath. This camp has a regular, spring-fed area to wash clothes; I washed the clothes I was captured in, this morning.

It's so sunny and warm down here. I've been watching the area of our last camp—El Valle de la Muerte—all morning. It's been covered with dark clouds the entire time. The mountains and air currents seem to trap and hold clouds, and I go, Dear God, please don't send me back up there. But Leidi said a group of guerrillas (*muchachos*, she called them) went up to the camp this morning and will bring back beef. Gosh, I wish we'd gutted that cow before Juaco killed himself. I wonder if they'll bury Juaco up there in that cold swampy valley or bring him down here. Will there be a funeral?

1140h: Leidi tells me that when they cut the beef haunch yesterday, they also gutted the cow. So the meat should be okay. I'm so glad.

Back of this hut, homemade stocks for M-1 and M-2 carbines are hanging. So the guerrillas make their own gun stocks. I've seen only one .30-caliber carbine, though—the one Leidi carries. I must get started on what must be done: to fill in the gaps and finish the story of what happened yesterday. I don't know why I keep putting it off. Not because of emotion, but maybe because reconstructing it seems such a huge task. It was such a fast blend of absurdity and insanity, and how can I explain the heaviness when you can feel death in the air?

1225h: Lunch was french-fried potatos and rice. Good. Why did we never have french fries on the mountain?

1645h: Thirty minutes ago I was playing *fútbol* with Manuel, a guerrilla at this new camp. We talked while playing. He asked a stupid—but standard—question: "What do you think of us FARC *revolucionarios*?" I hate that question; I'm always afraid my answer will hurt me. I guess it's a character flaw, but I cannot make myself say what they want. "I admire you greatly. Thank you for kidnapping me and showing me what wonderful people you are." That's one reason I avoid being friends with the guerrillas. I want to avoid that dangerous question. "I'd like you a lot better if you were not holding hostage a prisoner who's committed no crime," holding back what I really want to tell the son of a bitch.

"But you're CIA," Manuel answers. Once again, it's CIA. "United States Intelligence," he adds. I explain CIAT again, fast, emphasizing *"Centro Internacional de—"*

Thirty minutes later. I'm in my cubicle determined to write all that happened yesterday. A guerrilla girl from this camp, I don't know her name, enters my room and asks what I'm doing. "Studying Spanish," I reply, and [hold up] my dictionary, which I always keep at my side when writing in my diary. Instead she picks up my notebook—the other one, not the diary—from my bunk—and starts reading. She studies the first page, then rushes out the door with my notebook. I'm confused and irritated—she could have asked—and follow. She has gathered two of the other guerrillas around her and is showing them the draft of my letter—in Spanish—of Oct. to Susan. The third sentence is *"¿Puedes pasar el mensaje que sigue a los oficiales de CIAT?"* She's talking fast and pointing to the word "CIAT," and the reason's obvious. She's found proof that I'm CIA. I start again with the explanation "Centro Internacional de . . ." Then I remember the 30 business cards in my pack. I give her a card, point out to the guerrilla and her friends the name of my institution. She studies the card, then hands it back. "Keep it," I wave. Later, I see her writing something on the back of the card—I have no idea what.

At about 1600h today, Javier came riding to this camp, apparently with someone else. I was shut in my room. Later, I asked Javier where Ramiro is; they were to return together. "He left," Javier answered.

"Where?" I don't know. I asked Gustavo the same questions and got the same answer. Is that the last I'll see of Ramiro? Was he transferred because he was too friendly with me? Ramiro is the closest I had to a friend in this group. I'll keep his *recuerdo*—the camouflaged pen. The *"muchachos"* returned from our last camp with lots of beef, our supplies, etc. They buried Juaco on the hill where he died. "Will there be a funeral, a memorial service?" I asked.

"No, but FARC will try to return his body to Tolima later," a guerrilla answered. "Then his family can have a service."

1930h: I can't stand the cold any longer. I have to crawl on my bunk and wrap in the covers. I'll write more later.

Saturday, 22 Oct., Day 30

Awakened at 0630h. "Get ready, Don Tomás. We'll march soon."
"March? Where?"
"Arriba." Up.
We're going back up the mountain to the Valley of Death, where the clouds and rain are perpetual and the terrain is swamp. How crazy is FARC, anyway? The team sent to guard me went berserk up there. Discipline was lost, the commander committed suicide.

I'm changing back to dirty clothes for the march so maybe I'll have something clean and dry to wear when we reach the Death Camp.

1150h: We left La Playa at 0700h and arrived back here at 0900h. Strange and depressing to come back. I was told at La Playa that we'd stay here only one night then return. Here they say two nights. But I can't believe anyone.

1230h: Lunch was rice and a piece of sardine. I cut a sliver from the same onion I was slicing when Juaco fired behind my head and inches from his. Someone from the *muchachos* who came yesterday took the store of hard candy, money (75 cents), etc., that I left. Otherwise, the camp was pretty much as we left it. I took a machete and went to cut grass straw to make my bed more comfortable this time. Finding good dry straw was hard after Eduardo and the others had burned so much. (I wonder if burning grass is a basic instinct of these Indians?) I'm called back to the hut. It's the same woman who took my notebook with its draft letter that included the word "CIAT," and tried to use it to prove that I'm CIA. Her name, I learn later, is Marli. Oh no, I think when I see what she's holding, a Sony video-8 camera. "We must make a video," Marli says.

"Just like in the movies?" I ask.

"Yes."

"You're like in the movies," I said. No one understood that that was an insult.

"This is to send to your wife," Marli says. "She thinks you're dead."

"Dead? How? Did she receive my last message—the letter to forward to CIAT officials?"

"Yes, but she does not believe the letter is in your handwriting. She says she's sure you're dead."

"If my wife thinks I'm dead, then she's probably returned to Texas."

"No, she still in Cali; she's staying here until she knows that you're dead for sure."

I can't believe this; maybe it's my poor Spanish. I repeat what they've said, but using different words. The message remains the same. I don't believe it, but . . . Now let's make the movie. Video. Making a movie to send to my family. This really pisses me off. "Why don't you kill me now?" I ask. "You will later anyway."

"No! We're not going to kill you," the five guerrillas answer almost in unison. Marli then starts telling me what to say.

"I'm not going to follow a script," I say.

That's when Javier the Jackass steps in. "Do you want to stay here—but over there?" He points to the hillside where the dead cow lies and where I presume Juaco is buried.

"That's a threat?" I ask.

"No, no, no," the others say. "Let's start the video."

Calm down, Hargrove, or you'll hurt yourself.

Inside the hut, they've fixed one wall like a studio, with a blanket for background and lit by a naked lightbulb powered by a six-volt battery. Javier, Gustavo, Viejito, and Melena start getting ready. They put on masks and bring out their Galils and AK-47s. Marli is focusing the camera, checking the light. "Can I go outside until everything is ready? This is going to be hard, so I need to think." No problem. I walk outside, alone. Look, Hargrove, you knew this might come and you have no choice. You have to make this video, so do it with as much dignity as possible. Whatever happens, don't lose your pride, don't break in front of these ignorant children. I decide to cry a little. I don't feel like crying, but I know that forcing myself to cry can purge whatever it is that sometimes makes a man cry. It can help make sure that I don't break down in front of these bastards, like I almost did when forced to read aloud in Spanish my earlier letters to Susan. And the worst thing that could happen is to lose control, to break down or choke during this video that FARC will send to Susan and, of course, CIAT administration. Maybe others. I cry a little but with no tears, and my crying turns to ironic laughing. These jackasses with their masks and weapons, trying so hard to look like something they've seen in movies. Let's get this next absurd chapter out of the way.

Back inside, I'm told I must make the video in Spanish. I wish I had time to practice, but all is ready. The guerrillas put on their masks, brandish their weapons, and pose around me. *"Hola, Susan."* I give the date, and say that my health is fine—and will stay fine. Marli has told me to say I want the boys to return to Cali to be with Susan, but I say, instead, that I hope her mother can come and that the boys can come during the semester break. I don't want them to leave university in midsemester. Marli had me say that I didn't know which *fuerza armada* was holding me, even though I clearly said FARC in other messages. Odd. I laugh and joke a lot during the filming. And please don't send the army or police to rescue me, just like Marli said. Only I know that I'm really laughing at these clowns that surround me. We finish. Not so bad, then Marli remembers something and has us all pose again. I recite my special message to the *dueños* (*owners*—Marli's word, not mine) of CIAT, but I say the entire name, not the acronym. I hope they can help me, I say. I hope they can help me. I don't beg them to get me out of here, like Marli instructed.

After my filming, the group heads across the meadow to a little grave about 10 meters past the cow's rotting carcass. I notice that only the haunches were cut away. The loin, liver, heart . . . so much good meat was left to spoil. I doubt that an opportunity like this will come again. What a pity. Javier, Gustavo, and Viejito pose around Juaco's grave as Marli shoots more video. Maybe to send to Juaco's family, I think, as I stand at the crest of the hill out of camera range. At my feet is the remnant of a first attempt at grave digging abandoned at half a meter deep. Too many rocks, I guess. Viejito comes over and Marli shoots video of him and me standing by that half grave. Why, I don't know. Everyone tells me to wave at the camera. I do. We return to the hut and Marli to her horse, to return to the valley with the film. How will Susan react when she sees that video? It's so much like footage we've seen over CNN, of hostages in Lebanon. Well, Susan, I had no choice. And at least you'll know I'm alive. I hope you like my new beard. And I wish so much that I could explain those sad children posing with their weapons and masks.

I hope it does more good than harm.

1630h: What a day. I'm sitting in my tent, like so many days in the past. Except Juaco's pack sits at my feet. So convenient for storing things—and I'm having a drink from Juaco's last bottle of brandy, the one he opened and drank from just before he blew himself away. Now Juaco's dead and [his death is] ultimately [because of] me, his prisoner, who's still alive. And I have his pack, his pen, his brandy. An absurdly symbolic thought has flown through my mind, again and again, over the past two days. I should save the last drink of Juaco's last bottle of brandy. And as I leave this valley of death, I should somehow make my way back to his shallow grave and pour him that last drink. Is that thought wrong? Macabre? I don't think so. I wonder at which end of the grave they placed his head. . . .

Sunday, 23 Oct., Day 31

I hardly slept last night for the numbing cold. I had to leave two heavy blankets on my bunk when we left here. They were replaced with one lighter blanket. Plus the three light quilts I took with me. . . . I wore all my clothes, two shirts, two trousers, two socks, and jacket, plus I wrapped my feet in the *ruana*. Still not enough.

Looks like Javier is the new team leader. That's not good for me. He doesn't like me. I've given him some BS back in the past. He may be the least intelligent person here. Javier threatened me—asked how I'd like to stay up here *forever*—before the filming yesterday. I have a feeling that if or when FARC decides I'm of no value, and it's time to eliminate me, Javier would do the job *con mucho gusto*. I've discovered new holes in my wall. You can see into my tent from the kitchen portion of the hut. Were the holes made on purpose to monitor me? Or did the flaky mud just fall out naturally? I don't know, but I must be more careful about writing in this diary. I'll plug the holes up and see what happens.

1015h: I talked with Javier—may as well. He's from Corinto, near Puerto Tejada. Says he returns home to visit his family from time to time. He also said that we are not leaving this terrible valley tomorrow. We'll leave when FARC says to leave. And that won't be soon, Hargrove, so prepare yourself, mentally and physically, for a long, cold wait up here. The video won't reach Susan/CIAT until at least midweek, and Havener and most directors are in Washington, D.C.

1110h: A late breakfast or early lunch is served; fried beef, rice, potatoes, and cabbage. I think we have enough beef for one more meal. Most was left at Camp Happiness—La Playa, down below.

1415h: Is raining again. Javier and Viejito have been having fun taking 7.62mm cartridges apart, with ax, knife, and the pliers in Juaco's Swiss army knife. I guess they'll make some sort of cute bomb with it all. Viejito stopped work to take his Galil and fire a shot from the hip in the general direction in which he killed the cow. That's nice. He also made a crude cross from two pieces of wood and placed it on Juaco's grave. Touching.

1800h: In my tent, and it's so cold. Javier says there's no more cover to give me. Son of a bitch. They stripped away those two heavy quilts I left on my bunk to bury Juaco in. Well, tonight, I'll try to double my covers and sleep under a little strip, and stay rolled in a ball. It would be so easy to let sickness and cold take over, and die up here. Many other men would. But I can't. What I'd give to let Susan know now that I'm alive, very much alive, and I'm going to live through this. I'm not going to die at the hands of these ignorant, pitiful little bastards.

Monday, 24 Oct., Day 32

Dark. Cold. Raining. In some ways, early morning is the worst time because I think: What will I do today? Nothing. Absolutely nothing.

0900h: Javier thinks he hears something suspicious on the mountain. He shoulders his Galil and tells Gustavo to come along.

"It's probably helicopters," the little Indian grumbles as he chambers a round in his AK-47. "Or extraterrestrials."

Javier climbs the mountain slope and Gustavo falls back 30 meters, swinging his weapon in front. There's nothing there, I'm sure of it. But still, I must hope. Yeah, my checkbook and two notebook diaries are tucked away on my body. If a rescue mission comes, which it won't, I could leave this place instantly, never looking back.

1005h: International Centers Week opened an hour ago. This is the first time in three or four years that I'm not there. Will my abduction and strategies for my rescue be discussed? Informally, at least? Or am I an embarrassment to be hidden? What if I were in charge of strategies for my release? I'd approach Cuba, through the center with the most influence there. IRRI, probably. And use the Cuban Ministry of Agriculture, try to get their political or foreign affairs arm to appeal to FARC to release Hargrove. I'm not so sure how much direct power [Cuba] has over FARC today, of course. But it's worth a try. The trouble is: I don't think any government or group has much influence with FARC. Except—[My unwritten implication is the Cali Cartel—TRH]

1110h: Ramiro interrupted me. He's returned, with a fellow named Moño— "Ponytail"—who, it turns out, is Juaco's replacement. Thank God, Javier will not be in charge of my ultimate destiny, after all! They came into my tent, brought some snacks and Moño asked if I had problems. I told him about the covers. He indicated that he'd do something. The first guerrilla I've met who was born in Cali. He was holding a book: [one of] Karl Marx's on economic theory.

1235h: I walked around until it got too cold, then returned to my tent. Moño came in alone to talk. He's 19 years old, joined FARC two years ago, was around Cali before that. Moño says I'll be released soon, that negotiations are almost final. I don't believe him, but to hope and dream is okay—as long as I don't hope too much.

1310h: Lunch is rice and *carve*—the artificial meat made from soybean protein, sprinkled over the rice like hamburger. It's as good as it sounds. The last pieces were thrown out this morning, blackened and beginning to rot. But we ate fried beef almost every meal since last Thursday afternoon. The meat stayed fresh for four days without refrigeration. That tells you how cold the climate is here.

1440h: At 1400h I heard over the radio the description of a new rice variety that CIAT is to release to farmers. It describes the rice's grain quality, resistance to insects and diseases. I rush into the hut. Moño is listening.

"Did you hear that?" I shout.

"Yes, a new type of rice," he says.

"It was developed at CIA*T*," I say. "Did you get its name?"

"Yes. *Variadad.*"

"No, no. That's a *type* of rice. It's name—it was Turipaná 7. My good friend Dr. Cesar Martinez tried the rice at CIAT. ICA tested and released it to the farmers. Two weeks before my kidnapping, I went to Montería just to see that rice growing on farmers' fields."

Actually, I don't think the variety described was T-7. But whatever, it was probably, indeed, bred at CIAT.

The program continues. A reporter is visiting Palmira to report on developments in agriculture there. He mentions that Palmira is the home of CIAT and— the station is gone. Melena has come in, bored by the program, and turned the dial. I yell, and we try and try, but can't locate the station.

Still, having a new rice and CIAT on the radio was fortunate. Only a couple of hours before, I was describing CIAT's work to Moño. Maybe that broadcast will help assure that he believes me, and maybe that in some small way will contribute to my release.

My release. Moño said that it's imminent. Can that be? No, Hargrove. These people lie. Don't let yourself believe that, it's only setting yourself up to be hurt.

1900h: Dinner was rice topped by a greasy gob of fried sardines. I ran 15 laps around 1600h. While I was running, Gustavo and Viejito returned from the valley on horse and mule. When I went back into my tent two more blankets were folded and sitting on the bunk. I've written what I think of falling into the trap of being grateful to your kidnappers. But I'll sleep fairly warm tonight, after freezing and almost not sleeping at all the past two nights. Javier would gladly have let me freeze. Is this guy Moño part of a Mutt-and-Jeff game? Moño took Juaco's pack and left me his. Not nearly as good. He now carries Juaco's Swiss army knife in its fancy leather case on his belt.

Tuesday, 25 Oct., Day 33

Raining, as it rained all night. We haven't seen the sun since arriving Saturday morning. I didn't sleep much, but I was warm. Am now in my tent nursing a small woodchip fire.

1210h: The sun did come out, finally, and I've washed all my clothes except what I'm wearing! It was the first wash for the new polyester trousers, which I've worn three weeks.

1230h: Moño, Gustavo, and Viejito have gone fishing, I think. The girls are at the river bathing. That leaves just Ramiro, Javier, and me here. The boys are playing guns again. Ramiro just fired four rounds from his M-16. Not even target practice, but holding the rifle by its pistol grip with one hand and firing toward the mountains. Now they're in the hut, playing with the weapons. That cold metal sound of a rifle bolt sliding, again and again, followed by a click as a trigger is pulled on a chamber that's, hopefully, empty. It gives me chills, and I guess it will the rest of my life.

1300h: The boys brought a live hen up last night, and Melena boiled it with potatoes. The girls aren't back yet, so Javier serves my plate. It's the first piece to come from the pan. A beautiful piece of . . . boiled lower back. Really, now,

I deserve better than that. None of these people would be here if it weren't for me. I'd have gotten a good piece had anyone but Javier served the plate. The son of a bitch can't shoot me, but he's not going to make my life any better than he has to. The chicken itself tastes like . . . a big old hen boiled with potatoes. Still, a good break. A damn sight better than rice and lentils.

1650h: Moño and others had gone to the lower valley by horse. Brought back about 50 trout. None are longer than my hand, but they're trout. I helped Javier clean them. Decent of me. Wish I hadn't washed my clothes. It immediately turned cold, raining and cold. My khaki trousers are coming apart. Spent an hour sewing but doubt it did much good.

Tomorrow morning ends 33 days of captivity. How much longer? Michael Benge spent seven years as a prisoner of the VC and Nick Rowe five years. How did they survive?

I had a terrible nightmare last night. I was being kidnapped. Was trapped on a dark bridge, over a river, and kidnappers almost had me. My only hope was to scream; maybe that would bring help. But I couldn't. Finally, I screamed, and I woke up screaming. Was I really? Or only dreaming? I didn't wake any guerrillas, or at least, none came running. That's my second very vivid dream about being kidnapped. But most of my dreams are okay, not about this life at all. I dream a lot about food, great meals.

Wednesday, 26 Oct., Day 34

Started reading Moño's book on Karl Marx's economic and political theories. It's the only thing I haven't read. Good practice for my Spanish, of course. I read all of this in college—but not in Spanish! Moño has no inside information referring to my release.

"So I'll be released soon?" I asked last night.

"Yes, probably in fifteen days," he answered.

"Fifteen days?"

"Well . . . maybe eight days."

This is Day 3 of ICW [in Washington, D.C.]. I remember that wonderful dinner at the Thai restaurant that the center information officers had last year, along with Ellen Wilson and her husband. And Jack Keyser's cocktail party for us . . . visiting the Pentagon with Tony Bellotti, the "green milkshake," etc.

1305h: Ran my 15 laps this morning. Lunch: rice and sardines. For the first time in three weeks, pulled my Justin Ropers from by the fire and am wearing them just to keep the leather in condition.

1535h: Other cattle came into the valley to our east today. A bull, who looks largely Holstein, went to the corpse of the cow, who was killed six days ago, then largely hacked apart. The bull started a deep, mournful baying. I've never seen that before. Other cows came to the call, stayed around the corpse a long time. The bull keeps coming back and calling, like he's grieving, mourning. No guerrilla has grieved—nor shed a tear that I've seen—for their *compañero* who lies about 10 meters from the cow.

1615h: Fifteen or 16 cows are now gathered around the corpse.

1800h: In tent. Moño went down to Happy Valley. Kept hoping he'd return with good news, but I guess he'll come back tomorrow.

Dinner: rice and fried potatoes. A lot better than rice and boiled potatoes. Others, I saw, also had chopped sardines. An oversight, I assume. I'm always fed the same as FARC except when Javier serves. Come to think of it . . . I think Javier made up my plate tonight.

Thursday, 27 Oct., Day 35

Cold this morning. Very cold.

1000h: Moño is back but hasn't come to see me and we're not breaking camp, preparing to march. He brought Ranitania, the third allergy medicine I asked for five weeks ago. So no news of value, no release is imminent. I sleep here again tonight, and tomorrow, then it's the weekend. My sixth. What will I do today, tomorrow . . . ? I wish someone would shoot another cow—and not just for meat. I'm back into the precow routine of . . . nothing. Would be interesting to see the official FARC report on Juaco's death. . . . I wonder who shot that cow?* The only "neutral" person who may know is me.

1310h: Lunch is a sickening baby-food gruel of rice cooked in milk and sugar. I must eat, but I can't eat this slop. I force down a few spoonsful and throw away the rest. Am in my tent, it's so cloudy and cold. A bad day, and there's lots more of it to go. Maybe worsened by hoping, like a fool, that Moño's absence would be related to my release. Well, it wasn't, and I know that nothing will happen tomorrow, or the next day. Maybe next week.

Hail, then rain, fell heavily. I fell asleep and slept about 30 minutes. Later Moño came into the tent.

"Why do you have me?" I ask. "Can you name me one crime, one act against the Colombian people that I've committed?" Moño shook his head. "I sell nothing, I own none of your land, I use none of your natural resources. Holding me is counter to everything you say or write."

"If it were my decision, I'd let you go," Moño says. "The decision to hold you is from my superiors. I only follow orders. But you'll be released soon—I'm sure of it."

"Yeah, sure." Lying son of a bitch.

I ran my 15 laps.

1650h: Dinner: rice and beans.

Friday, 28 Oct., Day 36

It's like being taken, suddenly, and nailed in a box—or a coffin. You're left there in silence and darkness while the rest of the world goes on. Eventually,

---

*By this I meant: After Juaco was dead, and couldn't defend himself, I was sure that the remaining *guerrilleros* were saying that Juaco—instead of Viejito—shot the cow.—TRH

you'll be released from that box to face the world, and your world, and the changes that have come about. At least, you can only assume and pray you'll be released. But you're not sleeping in that box. No, you're in a state of inertia, but your mind continues to function. And you wish, so much, that it wouldn't. Because you think of only one thing: the day you'll be released from that box. You think of family, friends, work, play—but it all comes down to how those things are affected by your being in the box, and what they'll be like when you're out. And there's that dark fear that they'll never open the box, that you'll go silently insane in the box and then . . . slip away forever.

Five full weeks—35 days—of captivity have passed, and I know virtually nothing about what has happened since 23 Sept. in the world outside, or in my personal world. I haven't heard an aircraft—other than the distant roar of passing jetliners, mostly at night—since Day 2. I haven't seen a motor vehicle—or a road—since Day 3. I haven't seen a glass window since 23 Sept. I've heard international news—10-minute broadcasts on BBC or VOA—three times. The last was 10 Oct.—18 days ago. Nor have I heard international news in Spanish—not on the stations these children listen to. Iraqi troops were supposedly turning back on 10 Oct. But for all I know, Iraq may have invaded Kuwait, and the USA may be at war again. I've taken four baths in an icy-cold river. I have neither spoken nor read in English in five weeks. I've tried, with no success, to pet two dogs. I've sent Susan three written/phone messages and one video—but have no idea if any reached her. The oldest person I met was 22. The person with the highest level of education had been to the fourth grade. I've not had an open, serious conversation with anyone except me, for five weeks—and I'm getting uneasy talking to myself. I might talk myself into depression.

The best day was when a cow, then a man, died of gunfire, one of those rare days when you can feel and taste death in the air. I should add that I have not had any type of sickness in all that time. I've recently wondered if that's a mistake. If I got really sick, they'd have to move me out of here. On the other hand, I might well die in the meantime. No, Hargrove, keep your health. You want to walk out of here, not be carried, or left here with Juaco and the cow.

Moño left at 1010h today for Camp Happiness. Our batteries here don't work, so he can't get radio transmissions, except by going downstairs.

Lunch is potatoes and pasta cooked with *carve*, that awful artificial meat made from soybean protein.

1420h: Hasn't rained today, but there is a sharp, cold wind that makes it hard to stay outside. Am in tent with big rocks holding flaps down.

I think about Tom G. in Egypt—another place where one could be kidnapped easily. If I could send him a message, it would be: Be extremely careful. It would be awful for Susan if something like this happened to him, too. I wish I'd sent him Frank Gillespie's address. I was about to, when this happened.

1600h: Ran my laps, came back, and Ramiro asked if I'm ready to eat.

"It's been only three hours since lunch. What are we having?"

"Rice and lentils."

"Maravillosa."

I don't think I can stand to eat that crap again. And I'd better stay as far from everyone as I can, because that deep anger is building again, and I could say or do something that will only hurt me.

It was about this time three years ago that I returned to Texas A&M for the 25th reunion of the class of 1966. IRRI. I think of my Filipino staff there often. Such good friends. Ram and Vicky, Santi, Elma, Glo, Mayette, Ed, Ongleo . . . I'd like to visit them when this is all over.

Saturday, 29 Oct., Day 37

My sixth weekend as a prisoner begins. I should plan weekends carefully: time flies so fast when you're having fun. Will I spend a seventh, (eighth, ninth) weekend here? Lord, I don't even want to know.

1220h: Lunch: rice and fried potatoes. Next time we have onions, I'm going to steal a whole one to keep in my tent.

Moño still hasn't returned. He said that he'd let me go (bullshit) but his superiors refuse, so I spent this morning drafting a memo to his comandante of FARC/Cauca, explaining CIAT, and requesting a meeting or my freedom. If FARC is as protocol conscious as other communist organizations, it might actually reach him.

I brought two magazines up from Camp Happiness last week: *En Foque*, a USSR magazine, and *Margen Izquierda*, published by the Partido Comunista Colombiano. Both are dated April 1988. The two copies of *Resistencia*, FARC's magazine, are also from '88. One starts on page 1 (inside cover), then page 25–26, 15–16, 13–14, 3–4. That's it. I've read all from cover to cover.

1410h: It's so cold, windy, cloudy I can only stay in the tent.

1650h: Dinner is a plate of rice and two potatoes baked in their skins. That's all.

Sunday, 30 Oct., Day 38

The weather seems to be changing—for the worse. We seem to have less rain, but it's colder, with lots of biting wind and always cloudy. When Moño returned yesterday, I read my memo to the FARC commander. He approved the idea and offered to borrow a typewriter from Camp Happiness below. At 0730h today, a portable Brother typewriter was, somehow, here. I don't know if my letter will actually reach the FARC commander, or if this is just a way to keep me busy and thus less trouble. If the latter, it must be working. Spent the morning typing, reviewing, correcting the one-page letter. Will retype this afternoon. Moño said the letter will be sent tomorrow, but again, it will take four days to reach the commander. I also wrote a note in Spanish to Susan. It's so hard to write because you're always afraid that if you include anything even slightly suspicious the letter will never be mailed. I asked Susan to send Frank Gillespie's address to Tom G. I didn't mention Egypt.* Hope that little out-of-the-ordinary request doesn't kill the letter.

1800h: Dinner was a plate of rice with two of those baby trout. A mule train with fresh supplies is supposed to arrive tomorrow. Finished the letter to FARC commander. Suggested he send someone to visit CIAT and see for himself. Gave Alexandra Walker as a contact. Also suggested that Alex could provide two videos that describe CIAT work: *A Fragile Paradise* and *Wild Savanna*—I know the latter isn't ready yet, at least not in Spanish, but if they ask, that request might tip Alex off that I'm behind the request. Alex is the CIAT person whom I'd want to explain CIAT to FARC. A long shot.

---

*Our younger son, Tom G. (also known as Geddie), was a student at Texas A&M University, and Miles was studying at Texas Christian University, or TCU. At the time I was kidnapped, however, Tom G. was spending a semester at the American University in Cairo. Frank Gillespie, a close friend from Vietnam days, was stationed with the USAID mission in Egypt at the time. I didn't want to mention studies in Egypt because I was concerned that it might make me appear, to FARC, more affluent.—TRH

NOTEBOOK NUMBER 2
"Andaluz"

Monday, 31 Oct., Day 39

Mother died a year ago tonight. Actually, it was 1:00 or 1:30 A.M. on 1 November. I had told her it was time to go about 40 minutes before. A tough time. Mother's death, in many ways, marked the end of an era for our family. She became a matriarch in her time, and in her own way. What would Mother think about this if she were still alive? It would be awfully hard on her. Don Fields flew out from California—much appreciated, and it gave an opportunity to get to know one another again. Mother would have liked that. Don almost pleaded with me to get out of Colombia—and continued to do so afterward. Maybe I should have listened. Jim Lanning—Big Hoss—conducted the most appropriate funeral service I've ever attended: country, earthy, beautiful. It's tough thinking about it, especially sitting in my tent here so far from anything of value, so close to man's most ruthless Valley of Death, where it would be so easy to die.

1217h: Javier and Viejito took the net and went down to Happy Valley to fish. The trout are almost fished out of the little stream up here, Javier said.

1250h: The Day of the Shot Cow was 11 days ago. We'd been in this camp 23 days at the time. Life is now about like before Cow Day. I somehow thought that day that the deaths would signal a new beginning, that I'd soon be released. I hardly speculated that we might return to this valley. Why? I don't know. I was sure wrong.

1305h: Lunch is boiled pasta with some potato thrown in. A soggy tasteless mass. I can't even call it soup. But I eat.

1700h: Viejito shot a *pava* (not *pavo*). Looks like a grouse. Cleaned it in front of the hut—feathers everywhere. Moño went to Happy Valley this morning and hasn't returned. I don't think he likes it up here. Jogged my 15 laps (8–7).*

1745h: The *pava* was fried for dinner. Like with the hen last week, I got one piece of the lower back and tail. I can't say how *pava* tastes, because there was hardly a sliver of meat. Also had two finger-sized trout and a plate of rice.

*Means I jogged eight laps, walked one lap, then jogged seven more laps.—TRH

93

Have had bad pains in my lower back and left hip, especially at night. I hope it's from sleeping on hard bamboo and planks—not a disease like arthritis.

Tuesday, 1 Nov., Day 40

Forty days and nights of wandering and fasting in the wilderness. Does that mean this ordeal, like that of Moses, is almost over? Weren't there two biblical references to 40 days? Was the second one with Jesus? The fisherman in Hemingway's *The Old Man and the Sea* went for 40 days with no catch before hooking the giant marlin, I believe.

I woke this morning freezing, the wind whipping tent flaps. Got up and waited until Melena built a fire and made coffee. Now am back in tent.

1120h: Lunch is rice and sardines. We have two more cans, I notice. We're out of almost everything. We had only three candles last night, so I couldn't snitch one. It's almost impossible to build my own fire without the dripping wax from a candle. The mule train with supplies was to arrive yesterday, but didn't. Surely today. We've been out of vegetables for close to two weeks. Maybe tonight we'll have some cabbage, carrot, onion. The children have been playing constantly with that portable typewriter since its arrival.* They'll break it for sure. Thank God my letter is written and on its way.

1450h: After almost six weeks, mostly with the same seven guerrillas, one might expect me to have made special friends. I haven't and for several reasons: 1) It's hard to make friends with people who have kidnapped you and are holding you hostage; 2) Conversation always returns to two subjects: the guerrillas themselves and my situation. I'm angry, and will remain so. I can't hold my temper. I can hardly stand to lie when the guerrillas ask what I think of them while they literally hold my life or death at their fingertips. It would do me no good—and certainly not contribute to my release—to say what I really think. The same refers to my kidnapping. It would piss them off, and I'm hardly in a position to deal with p.o.'d captors. And it could make them think it would be dangerous to release me. I might say, or write, damaging things. 3) I could work and get along—but would probably never be friends with these people under any circumstances. I am very unimpressed with the intelligence of those with whom I've had contact. I've met some really dumb guerrillas—and have met none of more than average intelligence. I've met none who have knowledge of or (worse still) curiosity about the outside world. The subject of communist countries recently came up in a conversation with Moño, for example. I mentioned China, Cuba, Vietnam, North Korea.

"*Y Japon,*" Moño added.

I mean—this is a communist guerrilla group and its leader thinks Japan is communist? These are very shallow people. And I'm talking about natural intelligence and curiosity, not about the education level they've had. (Fourth grade is still the highest education level I've been in contact with.) In summary, I find

*I meant the *guerrilleros.*—TRH

nothing to respect or admire in this group. If today's newspaper were somehow delivered to the hut, I'd be the only one who would read it.

My back hurts a lot, because of this jacket. It's so short and tight, and the bottom elastic band rides around my navel, constantly pulling and forcing my shoulders into a semislump. But I must wear it always, because, first, it's so cold and I have nothing else. More important, I have to carry these diaries inside the jacket. I can't risk leaving them in the tent. If the guerrillas saw all this writing, they'd almost certainly send the diaries off to see what they say and they'd be confiscated. It would also probably hurt my chances for release.

I'm very careful about where I write. Almost entirely in my tent, like right now, with the flaps held down from inside by rocks "to keep the wind from blowing them." I have four communist magazines. When I write, I conceal the diary in a magazine so I can turn a page and it looks like I'm reading. My Spanish dictionary is always on hand in clear view like I'm constantly referring to it. The diaries are the only thing of value I can hope to take from here. I'm not sure of their value, but I don't have much else to put faith in, to give some vague purpose to this existence. Outside the tent, I always carry a magazine in my front pocket in case I need it for cover or disguise.

Writing in the diary is also solace of a sort. I was sick-despondent earlier this afternoon in the cold and loneliness and nothingness and the interminable time. Writing made some of it go away, for a while. Even though I was writing about it, about the pain. Hemingway knew. Yes indeed.

1645h: Ran my 15 laps (10–5). Returned and couldn't find this ballpoint. Scared me so. But I'd put it in a front pocket. Must be more careful in the future.

1810h: Dinner was same as lunch.

[*CIAT received a Proof of Life video of Tom (made 22 Oct.), a demand letter, and a letter Tom had written me.—SSH*]

Wednesday, 2 Nov., Day 41

0700h: Couldn't sleep for the noise next door. Like no one else is here, worse, it's like they perform for the benefit of us all. The tent says [?Cordinadorageriae, xacimonbohlor?]. Wonder what that might mean. Can't find anything in my dictionary, but I thought I heard reference to first part of the word.

I noticed our supply stock in the kitchen. Looks like we're out of everything except rice, pasta, and a sack of lentils. Mule train with supplies arrives today, Moño assures all. It's three days late.

My letter should reach the FARC commander tomorrow.

0915h: The guerrillas constantly borrow my dictionary, now that they have the typewriter to play with. Not for translation, but to see how to spell Spanish words.

"Will you give us the dictionary when you leave?" Moño asks, a few minutes ago.

"*¡Con mucho gusto!*" I say. "Let me go now, and you can keep it."

But Melena wants to keep the dictionary now.

"You won't miss it," she says. "It didn't cost you much."

"The dictionary didn't cost me much, but my life is worth a lot, at least to me," I answer, that dangerous anger-heat rising fast. "And *you* are holding my life!"

Take it easy, Hargrove, there's no point in antagonizing these bastards when—especially when—it'll do you no good. But a good indication of the common sense of your idea not to get into friendly, casual conversation with these people. Your anger is too close to the surface, is too deep, too strong—take care of yourself—control those emotions. If you go too far, you can't go back and undo the damage. You've done okay so far, don't fuck up now.

1125h: I borrowed small scissors and a pocket mirror from Ramiro and trimmed my mustache. I'd like to bathe—it's been 12 days. But it's so cold, windy, no sun.

1250h: Lunch was rice, cooked with some pasta. What did you expect, Hargrove? Grilled swordfish?

1500h: Javier and Viejito returned from Happy Valley carrying a sack on a pole between them. The little yellow potatoes called *amarillos*.

1610h: Ran my 15 laps (11–4). Will I continue the exercise when I return to normal life? I hope so, but it'll be hard. I hate to exercise. It's hard to make myself run even here, where I have nothing to do. Does CIAT have a handball or racquetball court? I could exercise better if it were a game. Maybe. The pack train still hasn't arrived. Glad we have the potatoes, at least. No candles, so no fire tonight. And it's cold.

1650h: What kind of soldiers are these? A good squad of infantry could free me easily, if it could get in here and find this camp. And would if this were the movies. Unfortunately, this is real life. I prefer the movies.

1800h: In tent. Dinner: rice and fried potatoes. Salt for flavor.

Thursday, 3 Nov., Day 42

At 0730h Viejito rode up from Happy Valley on Batalla, the mule I rode up here. He had two bags slung over the saddle—the supplies we've been waiting for. All the guerrillas—and me—gathered around as supplies were unpacked. One sack was cabbage, plantains, carrots, green beans, and I think (hope) onions. The other: living essentials for eight: tubes of toothpaste and bars of soap; little vials of deodorant for some reason (two kinds, for men and women); about 30 AA batteries; plus other supplies in smaller quantities, for individuals. It's been years since I watched kids waiting around the Christmas tree with such anticipation. Me, too. One of the girls got a black nylon bra and panties. My best present was this new ballpoint; the Juaco pen will soon run out of ink, and I didn't know how I'd continue writing. How can I explain using so much ink? Anyway, the shipment included four ballpoints. I told Moño I needed one, and got it without much fuss or attention. I also got two more pairs of socks (yes, USA '94), a container of foot powder, and a small vial of deodorant. I probably need that, but it was pretty low on my priorities. Also, a Gillette (*Presto barba*) throwaway razor. I had thrown away my other two razors when we packed to leave on the Day of the Dead Cow. Why, I'll never know. I somehow thought it was all over and we'd be going home soon.

We didn't get any candles, but I'm going to fill that Benadryl bottle with cooking oil when no one is around, to see if that will serve as a firestarter.

Moño made a point of telling me that no news had arrived.

Later. Now it's 0855h. I have written about my presents. What to do for the rest of the day?

The weather remains cold and overcast. I pray the sun will come out. I need a bath badly. It's been 13 days, and I itch all over, especially at night as I'm trying to sleep.

0930h: I ate breakfast today (I rarely do) because it was fried plantain, which we've never had. The plantain might have vitamins that my diet has been missing.

The guerrillas were all disappointed that mail did not arrive with the supplies. Personal mail? I wonder how they get it? Via a box in a FARC-controlled town? Could there be mail for me? Of course not. Anyway, mail supposedly arrives tomorrow.

Melena came into my tent to talk. I don't really know why. She managed to ask about my house, car, etc. Finally, I said, "I'm not rich."

"Really?" She acted surprised, shocked, then left the tent and went straight into the hut.

"Don Tomás told me he isn't rich," Melena announced to everyone. I heard a comment that seemed based on the word *mentir*, to lie.

What's behind it all? Did she come in to get me to say something about my financial situation? Then left as soon as she had it?

Probably she's not smart enough to handle it in a more sophisticated manner. Reminds me a lot of the bitch—Marli—who tried to pin CIA on me at Camp Happiness.

1040h: Raining, raining, cold. Maybe I should try to go back to sleep.

1135h: Why is it so easy to fall asleep in the day, so terribly hard at night?

1255h: The rain stopped for a few minutes and I walked around, but it's raining again and I'm back in the tent. This seems like one of those days when I spend 22 or 23 of the 24 hours in the tent. But on a "normal" day I usually stay in here 17 or 18 hours.

Gustavo made lunch and I complimented him. A soup of green beans, carrot, potato, onions, and cassava with fried plantain on top. Veggies.

My letter should reach the commander of 6th FARC today. What's the very best I can hope for? That the commander already has doubts, that my letter convinces him that holding a CIAT staff hostage is a mistake, and I'm freed next week. The worst scenario other than being executed in these mountains? That the ransom demand, whatever it is, stands, and the CIAT won't play ball. My family and Susan's then somehow pay a ransom, and I am free. That would be personally humiliating, and would make my return to CIAT very uncomfortable, indeed.

1515h: I've prided myself in staying healthy—never been at all sick since my kidnapping. I've written lots of times. Could that be the wrong strategy? What if I were to become really sick? Could I get sick enough [that] they'd have to release me without [my] dying? How does one go about getting sick? If my allergy came back, I could forget that I have those pills. It's only five days' worth anyway. All those welts and splotches look pretty bad. Could I fake physical sickness to go with it?

The way to really get sick, I guess, is to give up. That doesn't appeal much to me. The reason for getting sick would be to fight this thing, to not give up. It's something to think about, but not to try. Not for now. Stick with being healthy, Hargrove. Other prisoners would probably envy your condition.

This afternoon I collected wide, soft leaves of *trailejon*, that short, palmlike savanna plant, and have lined the hardest parts of my bunk. Seems more comfortable, but night will be the test.

1630h: Jogged the 15 laps (5–5–5, 12.5 minutes). Itched so much I came back to my tent with a cup of water, wet my handkerchief, and took a cold sponge bath, drying behind the handkerchief with my towel. Changed to khaki trousers, not because they're cleaner, but they itch less than the polyester. Put my filthy shirts back on. Now that the weather has turned so much colder, I always wear both shirts, 24 hours a day. That means I really don't have a backup shirt.

I've mostly worn the polyesters for trousers, even though they're less comfortable, because of a silly (sort of) idea: I want to wear the khakis when I'm released. Thus I wash the khakis and "save" them. There is a bit of logic to it, though. The diaries will hide better in the khakis. I'll wear my white cotton underwear that day, too—for the same reason.

1745h: Raining again. Dinner: rice with potato, fried plantain, and a welcome salad of cabbage, carrot, and onion. Still no candles, so no fire. Tonight will be long.

I have lumps on my scalp, and a couple on my forehead. The allergy may be coming back, or immune-system problems. If so, do I take my five days' worth of medicine? Take half doses, to make it last 10 days? Or, as I wrote above, let it erupt fully, then say I have smallpox or leprosy, or something? I don't think the latter is the way to go. I wouldn't get dangerously sick, and I'd just be uncomfortable as hell. That may happen anyway, of course.

1755h: Well, it's almost six P.M., and so dark I can hardly write. Bedtime.

Friday, 4 Nov., Day 43, End Week 6

Bad night. Leaves didn't work. Bed is killing my back. Can't use cover as more mattress; can barely take the cold as is. Maybe I can get Gustavo to help today. Maybe we can cut some tree branches.

Today marks the end of six weeks of captivity. Six full weeks. That's a lot. It's half a summer, 1½ home leaves. In six more weeks it'll be almost Christmas.

By now, Susan has definitely seen the video, knows I'm alive. Or at least, was alive two weeks ago.

The days blend together, almost nothing happens to distinguish one from another. Six weeks since my last discussion with another human, a person I could remotely call a friend. I don't think one of the guerrillas has ever even thought that holding me this way is wrong. None are that deep.

1215h: Stripped a couple of bags of leaves from brush around the camp to add to the straw to pad my bunk. We'll see. Washed one shirt, socks, underwear.

Nothing looks so good, so warm, as fresh, brand-new socks. I wore these new red socks last night and again today. So dry.

The children are playing guns again, sneaking up behind and scaring one another by firing a couple of rounds in the air. My chances of being shot accidentally are probably 10 times higher than chances of being shot for execution. I hate it. I was raised on a West Texas farm where gun safety was sacred.

Breakfast was soggy, rewarmed rice with fried plantain and potatoes. Lunch: a soup of potato, cassava, pasta, green beans, and carrots. I picked out and ate the beans and carrots, left the rest.

1350h: Have been walking on the field where I run, telling myself stories, out loud and in Spanish, and checking my dictionary when not sure of a word. It makes me realize one thing even more. I must avoid getting into a personal conversation with any of the guerrillas. My anger is too deep, and too close to the surface.

Stay cool, Hargrove. This will all end, someday, and you'll go back to a fairly normal life. If you're smart, and stay smart.

The allergic reaction I thought was beginning yesterday seems to have gone away, except for lumps on my scalp.

Yippee! I haven't written anything about that; it's such an irritation, and to write about it will probably look like I'm losing my sense of reality. Or something. And maybe I am. But this started all at once, about three weeks ago. Ramiro, Gustavo, Eduardo started whooping "yippee" all the time. Like, maybe it came from a movie and they thought it was cool. Ever since, they do it all the time. Ramiro is the worst. It's like something a bunch of 15-year-olds would do. And that's what they are, of course, juvenile, childish are these people who literally hold my life in their hands.

1720h: So cold, and raining hard. Am in my tent. Made a nice fire with cooking oil, so I have that to look forward to tonight. A fire and the satisfaction of making it, watching it burn. There's some[thing] magic, almost spiritual about that. It's a basic human instinct, of course, something we've all inherited over millennia. But I've never felt it nearly so strongly as here. Of course, here that fire also fulfills a not insignificant physical function—bringing warmth and light.

The camp gets filthier all the time. But does it really? The weather is also steadily getting colder, and the garbage isn't rotting. Nor do we have flies except occasionally when the sun comes out. How dangerous is the garbage in these conditions?

1830h: Dinner was rice and *carve*, the fake meat. Lousy. My dreams of a fire went up in smoke. Used all my matches but couldn't get it going. The cold coagulated the grease in the medicine bottle and I couldn't pour it like I'd thought. My second shirt never dried, so it looks like this will be a cold night.

Saturday, 5 Nov., Day 44

0800h: Rained steadily all yesterday afternoon, all night, and is still raining. Never ceasing. Like in the Mekong Delta so long ago. Except in the Delta, it sometimes rained two weeks without ceasing. That was warm rain, of course. This is freezing.

Today starts my seventh weekend as a hostage. Yippee! As Ramiro would say.

My bunk was better with the leaves. Still hard as a plank board, after the leaves flattened, but level—the leaves filled in between the bamboo slats. I followed, pretty much, my normal sleep pattern last night; lie awake from 1800 or 1900h until 0100h or so, then fall asleep off and on. I wake every hour or so to shift positions. Arms and legs are constantly numb—"asleep" from cutting off blood circulation. I awake at 0600 to 0630h, then back to sleep until about 0730h, when the camp starts waking. I could sleep as late as I like; the guerrillas have only one job, to guard me, and that's easiest if I'm in my tent asleep. But the hardness of the bed combined with the radio and the noise in the hut (Yippee!) make that impossible. *Tinto*—coffee—is ready sometime between 0830 and 0900h. I take my cracked cup in and have two cups. Then I record the new day in my "almanac," and maybe write something to open the day in the diary like now, except I haven't yet had coffee. Then what? I'm not sure. Then begins the day of waiting, of nothing. Of rereading my USSR magazine, of hoping, of reviewing Spanish words I'd recorded yesterday; of doing nothing, essentially until lockup time again at six P.M.

0855h: Dressed, went to hut. No coffee. Javier is frying bread instead. Back in tent.

By now, the FARC commander must have my letter. Some form of CIAT communication has surely reached him, too, by now. So all I can do now is wait.

I must hope—but I really don't think the explanation of what CIAT is, the appeal for reason—I don't think any of it will work. I don't think FARC gives a damn about what CIAT is . . . they only see me as a *gringo* they've caught.

The seven people guarding me—they don't seem to have much to do anyway: so I wait another week—two weeks—for release. If not, if I'm still here next week, the week after—then what? I can't think of that. Maybe later, not now. And I must stop lying awake for hours, like last night, dreaming about my release, about what it will be like when I first meet Susan, my family, my CIAT staff, our friends in Cali. What do I do then? What will you dream of, Hargrove?

Without hope, you're dead. Javier just called from the hut. *Tinto* is ready. Maybe things will be clearer, brighter after coffee.

0920h: I wish these people would learn to keep coffee hot. My two cups in the morning are a highlight of the day. But usually, like today, the coffee is served lukewarm and getting cold fast, so I gulp it. Coffee time is over in five minutes. Maybe less.

The second part of our supply shipment still has not arrived. It's now five days overdue, and this heavy rain will probably delay it more. We ran out of sardines and canned fish four days ago. The veggies help, but food is scarce.

1100h: The rain stopped and all left the hut. I filled a tuna can with cooking oil and got it to my tent. Gustavo came to the field to talk.

"Do the farmers raise poppies near Silvia?" I asked.

"Yes," he said. "Poppies, potato, onion." He affirmed again that it's four days to the nearest population, by horseback. And that's not even a village, he said, but an area where the Indians have houses along the mountains and valleys.

We went to the stream. It's only a third higher than normal, despite all the rain. This valley is a sponge.

1515h: Javier came to my tent and asked if I would give him one of my CIAT business cards. How strange. What could it hurt? I gave one to him.

1655h: I ran—*slogged* is a better word—my 15 laps. They also asked me to write a letter to Dr. Havener, CIAT acting Director General. Moño gave me the typewriter, but I prefer to write by hand so there can be little doubt that the letter is from me personally.

My diary has gone through three stages of disguise, concealment, and omission, all based on the premise that FARC might discover, translate, and read it. At first, I was hesitant to write about things that, if FARC knew, might make my life less comfortable: the army, etc. The next level: things that if FARC read might cause them to confiscate the diary. I've passed that stage. If they see this much writing, they'll take the diary.

1715h: I have made, *sin duda* [without doubt], the world's best fire. At least, it will be after I'm shut away in about an hour, and light it. I've arranged paper, congealed cooking oil, twigs, and pieces of wood ingeniously. Can't wait. It'll be so warm, and so comforting, so warm.

Walked by Juaco's grave today. The soil has subsided and a pool of cold water has collected on top. If I die, or I'm killed in captivity, I hope I'm not buried in this awful valley. I would be, of course.

1900h: Finally got a nice fire started. Lunch today was rice with fried potatoes and salad. Dinner: rice and a mixture of fake tuna and green beans.

Sunday, 6 Nov., Day 45

0945h: The guerrillas sleep late on Sunday morning; of course, I got up at 0700h—bed too hard to sleep later. Tried to start a fire, but the wood, matches, paper were all too damp. I have a dry piece of typing paper I was given yesterday for the letter to Havener, but I can't use it. I'll want to write another letter sometime, and don't want to use a page from this precious diary. (Precious to me, anyway.) Have been thinking about Larry McMurtry's book *Leaving Cheyenne*.* Am making notes at the back.

Someone brought some more supplies in yesterday: fake tuna, sardines. I saw candles this morning. Will snitch one later. Then I'll have no trouble making a fire.

The "tuna" can labels read *Pescado Tipo Atún* [fish, tuna-type]. Now what kind of fish is a "tuna-type"? I've had my second cup of lukewarm coffee. Now, what will I do the rest of the day? I'll steal a candle and more cooking oil sometime, will write a bit about *Leaving Cheyenne*, study Spanish—without practice, I guess. Maybe the clothes I washed on Friday will dry. That's the real problem with trying to wear clean clothes. Sounds like an admirable objective for a prisoner. But drying the clothes may take three or four days. I like to wear both shirts, but I rotate them, always with the cleanest shirt next to my skin.

1145h: Spent 1½ hours walking in the open meadow, telling myself stories aloud in Spanish, checking my vocabulary with the dictionary. Wish I had a verb dictionary. I'm running out of interesting stories, though. This afternoon, I'll tell myself about Duc, the CORD's security chief in Chuong Thien in 1969—the only other person I've known personally who's been kidnapped. And how I kept him on the payroll, paying his wife (widow) his salary several weeks for two or three months.

1245h: Waiting for Sunday dinner (lunch). Will it be like back on the farm? Fried chicken for Sunday dinner (lunch), potatoes, rolls, iced tea? I bet there was never a Sunday meal we didn't have fried chicken or roast beef. Sometimes we'd even have the Methodist preacher for Sunday dinner. Honest. I also remember going to the Silver Spur in Roby for Sunday dinner after church. Again, all the fried chicken you could eat. Delicious iced tea—and ham, which we had at home only on Thanksgiving, Christmas, and Easter. Charlie and George's barbecue back in Granbury would be good now. Especially if they had ribs. Or one of those double-fried hamburgers at the Gas Station. The special plate at that Mexican restaurant in Snyder. One of Raford's big mesquite-BBQ'd T-bones at his house. And did anyone ever fry roundsteak like my mother? No. And no one could fry chicken like Miss Empress. How about the *lechons*—the whole pigs—at my [IRRI] department's parties, especially Christmas—in the Philippines? Tandoori chicken and mutton in the Imperial Hotel in Delhi. Tamyoon— hot-and-sour shrimp soup—in Thailand. *Chaophya* and noodle soup in Vietnam—Peking duck banquets in Beijing. Those 15-meat-course dinners in Brazil. The fish *sudado* in Iquitos, along the Amazon. The big catfish in the Colombian Llanos. Fried chile crabs in Sri Lanka. *Bulgogi* and *pulk* in Korea. Those huge corned beef sandwiches in NYC. Blackie's House of Beef in Washington, D.C. Again, Mother made the best turkey and dressing ever. Buck Sheldon made the best prime rib of beef. Remember the place in College Station where you bought BBQ by the pound, served on butcher paper with an onion,

*Escaping.—TRH

a cup of sauce, and a butcher knife? Summer sausage, rat cheese, crackers, and beer at Uncle Ed's. *Ripschen mit Kraut* in Frankfurt. Steamed mussels in Amsterdam. Cold fried chicken, potato salad, and deviled eggs at family reunions. Salmon and trout in Oxford. *Cabrito* in Mexico. Shrimp cocktails at Alameda in Cali. Leg of lamb in London. Le Carnivore Restaurant in Nairobi. I've never had red snapper and lobster like on the beach at La Bocana in Colombia. Cold vienna sausages and Spam, cheddar cheese, crackers, Tabasco, and onion on scuba-diving picnics in the Philippines. Tacos at Don Ayala's in Granbury. Chile at John's in Rotan, Texas, or the Roby Truck Stop. More sirloin steak dinners at the Lowake Inn. Half-pound burgers at Chili's in Ft. Worth. Hot dogs for $1 from the little carts on the streets of Washington, D.C.—the world's best. The Sunday buffet at the club at DCBE. The broiled *tilapia* at Balimpasigin in Los Baños, and lots of San Miguel, with my Filipino staff. The fried spinach in southern China. If I leave here alive, I'll never again worry about the cost of a meal. I'll just have the best. I just remembered one of the best meals: fried dove and quail, the way Aunt Pauline used to cook it. Remember buying the buckets of shrimp from the docks in Houston near Becky and Kinney's, taking them back to boil and eat with beer? Tony Roma's for BBQ pork ribs. Back in Cali I'm going to that Swiss place just to order their trout. Fried. And I'm going to get one of those big drinks of *jugo de mora* (boysenberry juice) prepared with milk. Remember dishes of caviar served with chopped onion and bottles of vodka, frozen in blocks of ice—in the Shah's Iran? Fried mountain oysters at the Bobby Cave ranch.

1400h: Lunch is cold rice and topped with bits of fake tuna. And a piece of onion I saved last night. The last time we had onions I saved enough, that way to have onion in my tent for two days after we ran out. Remember how good bacon-and-egg sandwiches used to be? With lots of mayonaise, lettuce, tomato, thick slices of onion, and iced chocolate milk. Also, pork chops and eggs, ham and eggs. Memorable meals. The leg of lamb that Ed Tout and I had as an appetizer in New Delhi. The entire afternoon we spent eating raw oysters and shrimp in D.C., and I was having so much fun he decided not to break the terrible news. A bull's penis at a *kiseng* party in Seoul. Dropping the Thanksgiving turkey in 1968 at Ft. Bragg. Giant corpse-fed crawfish in the Mekong Delta, 1969–1970. Dog, rat, cat, snake, duck embryo—same time, same place. A kilo of duck's tongues at the Genetics Institute, Beijing, 1983.

What is Susan doing now? Still in Cali? Is she making plans for the future? Contingency plans? If we could only talk. It must be painful and difficult for her. How does she know I'll come back? I'm not even sure myself anymore. For how long do you keep hoping every day? When does the next day's pain dull, nullify, block out that instinct? When do you quit hoping and start only surviving? Or is that the day you start to die? I'm not sure anymore how to handle this.

Nor am I sure what I—we—will do when this is over. I'm only sure that nothing will be like it was before. Can I remain in Colombia? Can Susan? If I write a book about this, I'll have to leave Colombia, that's certain. How will I look at CIAT? That depends partly, I guess, on whatever is happening back near Palmira right now.*[1]

Three friends have urged me to return to the USA; all say we can join forces and do well: Larry Klaas, Don Fields, Ricks Pluenneke. I can see working with Larry Klaas most clearly. But he makes ag films and does his own writing, right now. Could the two of us charge double for a project? I doubt it. Could we turn projects around twice as fast? Again, I don't think so.

1600h: Moño returned from Camp Happiness. I had asked him to find me more magazines. He found two, says they are the only magazines in the camp: *Problemas de la Paz y del Socialismo*, published in 34 languages and read in 145 countries (they say on the cover). Issues #2 and #3 of 1980. Both with portraits of Lenin on the cover. A communist journal almost 14 years old. Dull, heavy socialist writing. Two communist magazines in a main FARC camp. That shows how worldly, what thinkers, these folks are. The literature is about as interesting as the food.

1700h: Was leaving to jog, but it started raining again. The clothes I washed on Friday . . . well, maybe they can dry tomorrow, Monday.

1800h: Dinner: rice and beans. Made nice fire.

Monday, 7 Nov., Day 46

Last night I dreamed about using this experience as the basis for a book. But in a different manner than other speculations about a new book. This would be a good way to start a novel—because one's entire world could change while kidnapped. Like being put into a time capsule, you could build a plot, have the hero kidnapped—and he emerges into a totally different world. That type of plot has been used before, of course, but what basic plot hasn't been? And it's plausible. What will I find? What changes will I face? I may well find that my father died while I was away. And Iraq may have invaded Kuwait; Miles, Hilda, Sarah, Laura may all be hostages themselves.*[2] I don't know.

But in what other circumstances does one go into a time capsule? Not many. Being sick and going into a coma; that's all I can think of. If I were in prison or at war with some army, I'd know about the above things.

1420h: Had a scare this morning. Was kneeling on a rock washing my hands in the rushing water of the stream. It would be bad to fall into that water, I thought. But that can't happen. Then I stood up—and slipped, fell halfway into the water, but grabbed a clump of grass and pulled myself out. Wet and cold, but not hurt. But I was shaken, really shook, because a terrible thing almost happened. My glasses were knocked off in the process—but I caught them. What would I do if my glasses were lost in that stream? I get sick just thinking about it. My glasses, after the diary, are the most valuable thing I own.

*[1]Meaning: At the CIAT research center, near Palmira.—TRH
*[2]Miles Sheldon is Susan's brother, my brother-in-law. Hilda is his wife, and Sarah and Laura are their children. The Sheldon family lives in Kuwait.—TRH

Lunch was a soup of potato, pasta, beans, carrots, onion, cassava.

1600h: Raining. A civilian came to the camp at about 1400h today, a young *campesino*. I think he's the owner of the cattle, and the same man who came maybe a month ago. But this time I wasn't locked in the tent; he saw me clearly.

1640h: Dinner: rice, fake meat (*carve*), salad. Nice fire.

Tuesday, 8 Nov., Day 47

I've figured out what's wrong with me! Why did it take so long; it's so obvious. A classic textbook case. I don't like these people; their customs and manners irritate me. They seem stupid. I don't like the food, nor my living conditions. I'd rather be back home. Hargrove—you have culture shock! I must understand that these are humans, just like me. They just have different customs, and different things make them happy. Like kidnapping. I must learn first to accept them, to appreciate and enjoy their way of life. We Americans are so culturally insensitive. We shouldn't be sent to places like the Valley of Death without prior sensitivity training. We should understand other forms of recreation, like getting stoned and playing with guns. We should recognize and appreciate customs like hostage taking; means of livelihood like guarding of poppy fields, and ransom. Hargrove, it's hard to believe that after all these years abroad, of travel and visiting other cultures, you could be a victim of culture shock.

Today is Susan's birthday. Sorry I didn't buy a present, honey, I've been so tied down with my work. No, I feel bad about being here today. I'd never notice, probably, were it my birthday, but things like that are special to Susan. I wish I could do something nice for her, but what? Survive and stay healthy—mentally as well as physically. That's all I can do for anyone, I guess. Including me. If I could wish for a single, practical birthday present for Susan, it would be e-mail. And if she now has e-mail again, it would be that the e-mail continue to work, with no breakdowns or shutdowns on weekends.

1310h: Raining. Back in tent. I tried to write a letter to Susan, but it's hard. First, what do I say? I can write almost nothing of interest because of the censorship. Second, Mono and maybe others here will review the letter. Then it goes to someone else in FARC who reads [it] before putting [it] in an envelope, and mailing [it]. All are suspicious of anything written because they fear a trap. If I write anything suspicious—or something that someone doesn't like—the letter won't be mailed, and neither Susan nor I will even know it. That's also why the letters must be in Spanish. Second, I have to read what I write to Mono because, like Juaco, he can barely read. Reading my personal letters to Susan to these bastards is one of my most emotionally devastating experiences. Sons of bitches.

Lunch: a soup and those little unpeeled potatoes boiled with some chopped beans and carrots. I don't guess we'll ever have any more meat except that fake tuna and sardines occasionally. There are no more trout in the stream. Eat to survive, to stay healthy.

1800h: Dinner: rice, sardines, salad, served at 1640h.

Wednesday, 9 Nov., Day 48

0830h: I'm still in the tent, but the whole group is still asleep except for Gustavo, who I heard slogging by to milk the cow. What soldiers these are. Wish I could sleep late and kill a couple more hours of the day. But my left hip hurts so, I can't lie down anymore. Was in real pain last night. Took two Ponstan 500 mgs [pain pills] and finally went to sleep.

Dreamed I somehow went back to CIAT. The official attitude was that I brought the kidnapping on myself, that I shouldn't have been on a dangerous road, etc. CIAT had washed its hands of me. I awoke, angry and disgusted.

0915h: Well, I've gotten up, dressed (I was dressed already, of course), brushed my teeth, etc. What's terribly depressing is: Now what? I've even written in the diary, and have nothing more to say. Nothing near original. Early morning is the worst, most hopeless time of the day. Maybe. Don't think like this, don't dwell on it, Hargrove. It's this way every day and you survive. All day, and all night.

1215h: Lunch was rice and that awful fake meat. Glad I saved that onion, because we're out. The three pieces that I've saved, combined, wouldn't make a third of a normal onion, but it's better than nothing. I won't run today; running yesterday may have caused the pain last night.

1515h: Couldn't run anyway. Pouring rain. A "new" copy of *Resistencia* appeared: the March 1990 issue. Includes a lot about human rights.

1615h: I returned the *Resistencia* to Moño and commented on the writing about human rights.

"*¡Que irónica!*" I said. "*¿Que pasará a* mis *derechos humanos?* [What will happen to *my* human rights?]" Moño looked at me and nodded. Be careful, Hargrove, you could easily have said a lot more. I have a lot of conversations in my mind with FARC. And I talk with other people about FARC. In Spanish and English. And I'd better keep those conversations internal, not get into a conversation here that could lead to how I despise these bastards.

Almost seven weeks of captivity now, and I'm looking at a harsh reality. If I were to be released anytime soon, I'd have been freed days or weeks ago. Freedom. I don't know what CIAT is doing, but it's not enough. You'd better quit fooling yourself, Hargrove, and put yourself into a mental state to prepare for a long wait. But how long? Six months? A year? Actually, I doubt it. FARC has me for only one reason: ransom. If they could get what they want. FARC has no reason to keep me, but FARC won't let me go, that would be a bad precedent. My life, and my health and comforts, will probably be less valuable as time, with no ransom, goes on. And remember, I'm not a political hostage. What usually happens to kidnap victims if no ransom is paid? I wonder what FARC's record is. I'm really not so afraid, personally, of dying. It happens to everyone and I've lived a pretty full half century. The physical part would probably be over instantly, and that's better than the way my mother died. I realize, of course, that I will become less philosophical as I see that day coming closer. But what about Susan and Miles and Tom G.? I'll survive if I can. By that I mean that I'll continue to live until that decision is taken out of my hands. Okay—if I die, they'll have to kill me.

1900h: Dinner was rice, a sardine, and chopped green beans. Afterward Viejito rode up from Happy Valley, with some supplies. Moño gave me *dulces*— four kid's suckers [illegible] lollipops, a 100-gram can of Nestlé's sweetened, condensed milk. Later: I hate to admit it, but the lollipops taste pretty good.

1925h: The guerrillas are all drunk—or on something. I know Viejito brought brandy. Melena is stoned, crying, cursing the others. There are too many weapons lying around here and [I] don't like it. These fools have too little sense.

"*¡Melena!*" Moño now cries. "*¡Venga!*" Melena is crying again, and curses him. "*Qu[ie]ro usted,*" [Moño says.] That can either mean "I love you" or "I want you." I note that he [uses] the more formal *usted* form rather than the familiar *tu* or *te*. She curses, Moño cries, there's more fighting inside, something crashes to the floor. Moño then cries, "*¡Leidi, venga!*" at the other fe[male] *guerrillera.* Leidi doesn't answer. Moño sobs, curses, yells. The others try to calm him down. "*¡Quiero una mujer!*" he sobs. Then, "Melena! C[ome]! That's an order!"

I recognize Ramiro's voice saying, "Melena, he's the commander. Don't you follow orders?"

Melena curses, [says] something about not being *Moño's* whore.

Moño then [orde]rs Leidi to his bunk. She ignores it. Then more curses and fighting and Moño screams something about the pistol in his *equipo*, or pack. He l[ost], I think, because voices are calmer and more fri[ght]ened again. But I know the others have weapons ready to fire, too. [I scrun]ch down, ready to roll from the edge of my bunk, but can't face the cold wetness again. More muffled sobs, scuffling, then Moño s[ee]ms to be back at the door. "*¡Viejito! ¡Venga!*" he roars, but Viejito's intent to stay in the woods. Moño finally quietens down, and I [see] that he no [l]onger has his pistol. He still yells, "Melena! Leidi! [*¡Veng*]a!" from time to time. But Melena only curses and Leidi stays quiet. I look at my watch: 2220—10:30 P.M.

Thursday, 10 Nov., Day 49

0915h: I feared last night could turn dangerous, and I was right. Melena finally quietened down, but then, around 2015h, *bam-bam-bam-bam-bam* a burst of five rounds fired full automatic from the door. Oh no, it's starting again, I thought. [illegible] then lying back down so I expose less profile. Commotion in the hut, then Moño yells, "*¡Viejito, venga!*" Nothing happens, then a short burst from the woods. "Viejito!" More firing. I put on my glasses, jacket, and boots, and lie off the side of the bunk, ready to fall onto the wet, muddy floor but dreading it and wondering if it would be worse than a 7.62mm round. Another burst. Viejito is evidently stalking and blasting shadows in the woods. Then something happens, changes inside the hut—and for the worse. Understand that I'm lying in darkness [and] I can't see what's going on [illegible] on the floor by my bunk.

I hear drunken, or stoned, cursing, then, *"¡Moño, Moño, calmese!"* then more cursing, that changes to crying, curses intermixed with the [?deep?] *"¡Venga!"*

"Moño, Moño—Henry!" That's the first I know that Moño's real name is Henry. Then that cold sound of a rifle bolt and more voices pleading with Moño. He's apparently pulled his Galil out and chambered a round and is threatening the others. More pleading and the sound of steel against steel as more bolts are pulled. Moño is right behind me—we're separated by an inch of dried mud. Oh God, this is it—they shoot Moño, they'll shoot right through that wall. I get back on the floor. There's a scuffle inside, more cursing, crying. Moño seems to be lying on his bunk. [I] think they have his weapon. I get back in bed.

1015h: I got up at 0915h today—still, before anyone else—and wrote the previous account of last night's activities. Somehow, writing about it in the daylight, the night doesn't seem as insane, as potentially deadly, as it was. It was a dangerous night, all right. A combination of drugs, anger, and automatic weapons. Death could have come last night as easily as it came three weeks ago. Those guys were drinking brandy, but alcohol isn't the chemical that fueled the craziness. It was basuco*, I'm pretty sure.

Moño got up joking this morning, like it was all big party fun.

"¡Viejito, venga!" he yelled.

No one made coffee this morning. I went to the spring to fill my water bottles. Melena is sitting on a rock outside the hut, crying as she cleans her AK-47. I say nothing.

1045h: Coffee is finally ready, so I went outside to get some. Melena still sits on the rock, but no longer cries. She looks very angry—a woman scorned? I don't think I captured her drunken anger and grief last night. Her AK-47 is now reassembled, I note, and a full clip of 30 rounds inserted. Moño is at the spring and I see he now has a deep cut across his nose. Melena keeps turning sideways to glare at him. She wouldn't—would she?

1050h: A bottle flies through the air, hurled from the hut, and smashes on the rocks at the entrance. A liquor bottle from last night? Maybe. Melena follows the bottle, angry, and rushes past as Moño picks up jagged pieces of glass. I like to see trouble within this group, and big trouble would delight me—just as I couldn't help but be pleased on the Day of the Cow. But I'd better not hope for more trouble of that nature, for only one reason: the more chaos, violence, ineptness, and general fuckups I see within FARC, the less likely they might be to turn me loose. They might be afraid that I'll talk—they don't know really that I write—about a side they'd prefer not to reach the public. So, wipe away those violent and morbid fantasies, Hargrove, of Melena, Moño, and that AK-47. You would feel good in the short term, but it wouldn't help your position.

1145h: I just read what I wrote yesterday about my release. Unfortunately,

---

*"Bazooka" in English. A derivative of the cocaine-production process that is sold cheaply and smoked among the poor in South America.—TRH

it still makes sense. I have to think long-term survival, because I won't be released today, or next week, and if I die here—well, I die here. One big regret is ironic: my diary would die with me. But I don't think I have to think about dying—not by execution—until Month 4 or 5. The chances of dying accidentally, but violently, are harder to factor. They're a hell of a lot higher than accidental death in Rotan, Texas. Could have happened easily last night if the boys had taken Moño out. I could have died during last night's bad trip accidentally or by stoned execution.

1217h: Lots of shooting this morning. The chemicals have worn off, I think, but now the boys are acting super-macho. Especially Moño. It's for show, I guess, that last night's pitiful, drunken, crying jag was just part of good ol' boys having fun. I can hear them now, talking about *aguardiente*. Moño is especially loud. Melena now joins. She's such a shallow bitch.

Lunch was rice and fake tuna with something new—I had two Vienna sausages. Delicious. Viejito brought them last night, I guess.

1315h: Such jackasses. Ramiro just stepped from the hut, pointed an AK-47 to the sky, fired a round, and went back inside. No reason, not target practice. I don't think he's even stoned anymore.

Part of the label remained on the bottle Melena threw. It was a liquor bottle; 1.5 liters, I think. Last letters on label "cane."

Raining and cold, am in tent. I wish Nathan could send me a book to edit. Wonder how Vrinda is doing? Think of her often: arriving at CIAT to work again with Tom Hargrove, her old friend . . .

1400h: Went foraging for wood for my little fire tonight. My best source is to tear pieces from the posts of the fence that runs past the hut. The wood is old. Also drier, because the posts stand erect. I've pretty well devastated a couple of posts. That means the *campesino* will have to replace them. Ordinarily, I'd respect the *campesino*'s work and property, but this is different. He'll probably blame FARC for the problem, and that's fine with me.

1625h: Is Thanksgiving the third—or fourth—Thursday of November? The third, I think, and that means—good Lord, a week from today. So I'll most definitely spend Thanksgiving 1994 here in the Valley of Death with these imbeciles. That thought is so damned depressing. . . . Have been thinking more about *Leaving Cheyenne*.* The odds look pretty poor of it to work. . . .

1730h: Dinner was rice and—surprise!—trout. But not much. I had two. Viejito and Gustavo went far up the valley to catch them. It takes a lot of trout, of course, to feed seven guards and me. Incidentally, I'm about twice as big as most of the FARC—but I don't get twice the food. I also ate the last of my hoarded onion with the trout.

*I.e., trying to escape.—TRH

Friday, 11 Nov., Day 50

Today is Veterans Day—November 11—declared the day the guns stopped firing in Europe, marking the end of WWI. I never paid any attention to Veterans Day before, but I watch calendars closer nowadays. I'm a vet, of course, but I never considered Veterans Day as my day; it's something for those veterans of past wars, wars that we won. And there always seems to be something . . . immoral? . . . about celebrating something so tragic as Vietnam.

Two years ago Hugo Melo said to me in the CIAT snack bar, "Lieutenant, do you know what today is?" No. "It's Veterans Day. We should do something." And we should have. Why didn't we? Hugo Melo is the only other Vietnam vet on the CIAT staff. Served with Special Forces—the Green Berets—and was wounded badly in 'Nam. Ironically, but symbolically appropriate, I guess, Hugo isn't a native-born American. He's a Colombian by birth who now has a green card. Hugo Melo is also interesting because his son was kidnapped a couple of years ago—by M-19, I believe. I have to learn more about that when I return to CIAT. My being a Vietnam vet is something I was very careful to keep concealed from FARC. I haven't told them, and I won't. But I'm not paranoid about it anymore. I doubt that if FARC had that information, it would make any difference in my treatment, chances of release, etc.

But don't be too sure, Hargrove. That, combined with the suspicion stimulated by the acronym CIAT, could reopen the issue that I hope is closed. Keep it quiet.

Has being a vet helped me? Surprisingly, when I look at my situation . . . maybe. I may realize, better than others, that man can survive a lot. And as bad as my situation is, I've known men who've survived far worse. It also makes me feel, I guess, that I'm a little bit tougher—both physically and, more importantly, psychologically—than those who didn't go, so I can take more. Probably not true, but living up to that image, if only in my mind, must help in survival, living through each day and night. Having written *Dragon* probably reinforces that . . . what? Obligation? Challenge? Obstinance? An attitude, maybe, of fuck you, you little sons of bitches. I'm superior to you and I'll survive. And I will.

Seven long weeks have now passed. Looking back, I'm proud of my conduct. I've held up well. I've still never been sick, and never let my pride, my dignity, break in front of these bastards. But only I know that. Maybe that's another reason this diary is so important. If I die up here, of course, no one will ever know if I lived—and died—up here like a man, or as a coward.

1030h: I showed Moño that the batteries in my flashlight are out.

"We don't have any more batteries," he said. "But maybe some will arrive with the next supply shipment in eight days."

Eight days. A few minutes later I told Moño that today makes seven weeks of nothing.

"By now your letter has reached the *comandante*," he said. "His answer should reach us in a few days. You'll be free soon."

Lying son of a bitch. Telling me what he thinks I want to hear. I know that

Happy Valley has radio communication even if we don't. If I were to be freed, the order would come by radio. No, Hargrove, you're here for a long time. Look forward to your new batteries that will arrive—maybe—in eight days. Little things mean a lot.

Maybe later today the clouds will go away and the sun will come out. Maybe I can walk in the sun on my little track in the cow pasture, and that will dissipate some anger. Maybe.

Moño's nose is red and swollen. The cut is worse than I thought, and infected. Must be humiliating for a commander to wear that scar—the testimony to how his own men had to beat him while he was drunk, drugged, and crying. A reminder, in front of those same men. I'm so glad.

1050h: Calculating for the long term. If I write one page per day, I have a bit more than 50 days' worth of diary pages left: exactly equal to how long I've been here. And I have a new pen, never used, plus a badly used blue pen in reserve.

1120h: Lunch. Rice and a little piece of sardine, which is gone almost instantly. I'm eating a lot of straight rice, without meat or vegetables. Went to bed hungry last night. Am hungry right now. I need some real food, some protein and vegetables. Maybe there's more sardines, but I hate so to ask. It's like begging.

1200h: I ate a big hunk of the base for *agua panela*.* It tastes like—and is—pure raw sugar with a bit of caramel taste. I got a big hunk of it two days ago and have eaten a lot. I hate to eat straight sugar, but I guess it won't hurt me. I need the energy to stay warm.

1615h: Ramiro is firing his M-16 into the air again, at nothing. Moño watches him and laughs.

If I publish another book, from this experience, I want to retain Spanish rights, or a guarantee that a Spanish edition will be published—and made available in Colombia. Maybe then I'll be able to tell these bastards what I think. Unfortunately, they don't read.

1805h: Ramiro went by horse to Happy Valley today, and brought back seven or eight trout. They were fried for dinner, but none for me. I got two pieces of sardine—and a plate of rice—instead. That's okay, I prefer two sardines to one trout. I've been hungry lately.

Saturday, 12 Nov., Day 51

Another cold, miserable day. Wind is blowing my tent to hell. Couldn't sleep last night until about four A.M., bed is so hard, I constantly wake up with numb parts—arm asleep, etc. Also, maybe I was paying for that one-hour sleep yesterday afternoon.

Stole some squares of bitter chocolate from the kitchen. I took a bite of the

*A sweet drink made from sugarcane and served like coffee or tea.—TRH

unsweetened chocolate, then a bite from the *agua panela*. It tastes like chewing bitter chocolate and a mouthful of sugar together—*algo es algo.* . . .*

I must sleep on my right hip, so I wake up each morning staring at the same scene: the dried black mud of the hut wall, crisscrossed with reinforcing pieces of bamboo. The bamboo is sun-bleached white and looks like human bones, arm and leg. The length and width are about right. And the nodes between pieces look like joints. Sets a mood for the day . . .

I woke this morning, looking at the bones and thinking how I hate these vermin, and wondering how I'll survive this cold and lonely day, the start of my eighth weekend. I will, and the sun may shine later. The beginning of each day is the most depressing time. And that [i.e., *depressing*] is such a cheap inadequate word, it doesn't begin to express how I feel. One can hate upward. Is there a verb that means "to hate, despise, and hold in utter contempt. To consider a form of animal not human life and of no value to humanity." There isn't.

I keep having conversations in my mind. They begin with one of these fools asking, "What do you think of FARC?" The conversations may be good practice for my Spanish, but I'd better not put it to practice. Not until I'm on the other side of the freedom-slavery line. Not till I'm free.

I dreamed this morning of a hard sun that burns away the clouds and fog so Blackhawk choppers can drop in on the Valley of Death. Of violent deaths of all these children. It felt very real, and I felt no sense of remorse, only that instinctual satisfaction I felt when Juaco blew his brains away. A sinful emotion? Maybe, but natural. As human as emotions of the Old Testament. You deserved to die, and now you're dead. Your death somehow seems to transfer, or at least negate, some basic power, and that will help me live. You're dead, Juaco, and I'm alive and I'm glad it's that way. I hope your amigos go in a similar, shameful way. I note with satisfaction that not even your companions, the men you commanded, grieve your passing.

I doubt that any of the FARC have any idea of the contempt in which I hold them. I stay apart, avoid conversation other than communicating the essentials, because conversation can be very dangerous. If I ever really talk, I'll hit where it hurts—at personal self-esteem, concepts of manhood, of being a soldier, of true guerrillas, and of children criminals who play soldier. Stop it, Hargrove, the day is just beginning. Watch the sun. When it shines, wash your socks, shorts, the polyester trousers. They've been washed only once in seven weeks. Read *En Foque* again—that article about the abominable snowman. Practice your Spanish. Don't infect your mind purposely. Someday you might not be able to suppress that infection, the sick yellow pus will explode in stinking bursts that could mean your death.

I had decided to write about religion this morning. It's obvious that thoughts of God, religion, prayer must be part of a life like this one. Especially

*The complete saying is: *Algo es algo, peor is nada* [Something is something; nothing is worse].—TRH

for a West Texas farm boy. But maybe I'll put that writing off until tomorrow, when those instinctual thoughts haven't infected my mind.

I really don't want Larry Klaas, an Arizona filmmaker and friend, to finish the film without me; it's my favorite story from two decades of this work. But he's invested his own time and money in the project, so it isn't fair to leave him hanging until I return. If I return. I was afraid to include the instructions in my letter to Susan because of the codes and instructions on how to access the file on my personal computer. When the FARC censors read the letter, they might think I'm trying to pass encoded messages and kill it. This way, Susan would get the letter that I'm alive (I'm pretty sure). If FARC kills Nathan's letter, well, I tried. . . .*

1745h: Dinner: rice with small potatoes, lentils (cold), and a sardine.

Sunday, 13 Nov., Day 52

1730h: Was in pain through last night, and awoke 0600h in worse pain. An infection in my left ear started three or four days ago. Moño was to request medicines from Camp Happiness but forgot. It's gotten much worse, hurts like hell. Moño says he'll send someone down to Camp Happiness to get medicines this morning. Patricia, I learned, is in charge of medicines and is the informal *enfermera*, or nurse. She's the nice *guerrillera*, who lent me her shortwave radio that night when we marched to Camp Happiness—the Day of the Dead Cow. She also showed me where FARC kept a few magazines—that's how I got the two I have. Anyway, I know an ear infection can turn dangerous; it's so close to the brain. What a place this would be to have a serious medical problem. I'll bet there isn't a FARC-approved doctor, or probably any doctor, within four days' ride of here. And my health has been so good.

0830h: Looking at myself. I'm so dirty. As filthy as this camp. I need to wash clothes and myself, but it's impossible with this cold, wet wind. But the cold still prevents a fly problem. There's standing water outside the door of the hut. It's covered with a film of scum and grease, and garbage thrown directly into it. Even most animals know to keep their living area clean. I'm afraid for myself; my anger and contempt are so close to the surface when I see or hear one of the FARC. I automatically address him or her: "fool," "bitch," "jackass," "asshole," or when appropriate, "queer." I don't say it out loud, but I say it to that fool, asshole, or queer, and actually the word is only one step away. I could also hit one of them. Easily. And there is nothing I can do to change or improve my situation. But I must stay away from them, talk only when essential. Spare myself what I might do to myself. For how long will they continue? I don't

---

*This refers to a letter I wrote to Nathan Russell, my fellow CIAT editor. I knew that Nathan would be in charge of the CIAT Communications Unit during my absence. I had written a letter to Nathan, which FARC promised to deliver, with details on how to finish—and finance—a television documentary that Larry Klaas and I had been making about the odyssey of Carolina Gold—a rice variety that disappeared from the Deep South, and reappeared along the upper Amazon of Peru more than a century later—when I was kidnapped.—TRH

know. It can't end today or tomorrow or this week or the next. Protect yourself, Hargrove. And protect your diary. And God, today is only beginning.

1115h: Humans have always turned to God, to religion, to a supreme being in times of trouble. That's why Jim Lanning went to jails and funeral homes to save souls. Well, I'm in trouble. Deep trouble, no one could deny that. But I haven't turned religious, at least not outwardly so. Why not? I'm not an atheist, or even a good agnostic. I believe in some sort of guidance that can only be termed supernatural; too many otherwise unexplainable events have occurred in my life. I wrote about many in *A Dragon Lives Forever*. For one thing, it would seem hypocritical to turn religious in time of trouble, if one isn't religious in normal times. I've never prayed for deliverance when I thought I might die. Not in Vietnam, either. Also, I find it hard to believe that the ceremony, the act of prayer itself, can make much difference. Surely the way one lives means more than ceremony. I must take care of myself and strive to return to my family, my work. That is faith. It's the way I felt soon after my kidnapping. I thought that with time, the attitude would change. But it hasn't.

1505h: Maybe I'll write more about that later. Right now I have some incredible news. I asked Moño when the medicines for my ear were likely to arrive.

"They don't have those medicines now, Don Tomás. We've requested from outside," Moño also bellowed.

"There are no antibiotics even in the camp below?"

"No."

I find this hard to believe, but why would he lie? This could be serious. I wonder if Moño's lying. I didn't see anyone leave the camp. I haven't seen Gustavo, Viejito, and Javier lately, but they couldn't have gone to the camp and returned then left again without my noticing. And we have no radio communication. I think he's lying. You couldn't have camps like these with no antibiotics. But why would he lie? To save me from having to go to Camp Happiness? None of it makes sense. If the infection gets really bad, they'll have to take me out of here to medical attention. Or would they? I'm not dealing with very intelligent people. The ear feels better right now. That may be because of the pain pill. I sure hope not.

1740h: Gustavo and Viejito returned, on the white horse. Had been fishing in the main river, down in Happy Valley. Caught about 20 nice trout with—would you believe?—hook and line, worms for bait. I helped Ramiro clean them all.

1820h: Had three hand-length trout—the most ever—for dinner, with rice and some little potatoes.

Monday, 14 Nov., Day 53

Something funny, for once—Moño considers himself a potential General Patton and studies military manuals of the Colombian army (which FARC also uses). He reads them aloud, I guess so everyone will know what a military leader he is. And maybe so they'll all know he can read (barely). Anyway, Moño was discussing his military study with Javier, who commented, "*Ud. tienemos tiempo que yo.*" The fact is, no one does anything in this camp besides sleep, cook, eat, and guard me.

Moño also bellowed parade-ground commands—company and battalion level—for our entertainment. At no one, just into the air (like Ramiro shoots his M-16). If Moño is such a soldier, why doesn't he have the troops training, or cleaning up this disgraceful camp? I doubt that he could do it. (I wonder if General Patton's men ever beat him up when the general was stoned? I wonder if any privates with long eyelashes spent hours wrestling and tickling each other and giggling in the General's bunk after lights out?)

0900h: Picked up some nice wood chips for my fire tonight. Building and enjoying a fire is the most comforting, solacing activity. I should remember that in times of trouble after I leave here. A small fire like mine is probably better therapy than a big fire. You can add a lot of wood to a big fire and let it burn. But you must constantly watch a small fire, feeding it new wood, restarting it when it burns out, making sure it doesn't get too big and burn the tent. I usually start my fire right after shut-in time at six P.M., with one large piece of wood and lots of smaller pieces. I sit on my bunk and care for the fire until the large piece burns out at about 7:30 P.M., then crawl under covers for the night. During the 1½ hours of fire, I don't think of anything much except keeping the fire going. I generally use one candle a night and some cooking oil—especially if the large wood is fresh and wet. It's therapy.

1100h: I made and started filling in a new almanac a couple of days ago. Never thought I'd use up the first one. But seven weeks and three days is a long time. I wonder if CIAT is going through the Colombian police and army for my release. Must be. I wonder what they know, what contacts with FARC they may have. To my knowledge, only three non-FARC persons have even seen me since Day 3: the two civilians who rode with us on the Long March and the *campesino* who herds these cattle. As for FARC, maybe 20 persons have seen me.

This camp was probably selected just for operations like this, with its constant mountain-trapped cloud cover. I bet an aircraft could spot our hut less than one percent of the daytime. (But no aircraft have passed nearby.)

1125h: Moño is gone, probably to Camp Happiness, and the FARC are outside cleaning weapons. I wandered into the kitchen and took a candle, two new boxes of matches, and four squares of unsweetened chocolate. Afraid to take more of anything because all supplies are low. We're out of cooking oil. It's hard to supply eight persons in a remote mountain camp by pack mule. Especially if it's [a] four-day trip, one way. This, the mule train, must supply other FARC units, too. Camp Happiness, for example.

I'm not clear about the pack train vs. the mail run. Seems to me the pack train would carry mail, but my letters to Havener, Susan, Nathan are still sitting; have been for nine days. Moño says the incoming mail hasn't arrived, and my mail will go out on the same run. He's lying, I'm sure. Again, why? FARC apparently doesn't want any message from Hargrove to reach CIAT or Susan right now. Again, why not? Does it have something to do with negotiations for my release?

1640h: Moño returned from Camp Happiness with seven cans of sardines, a bottle of hot sauce, and a bottle of eardrops. Then I went with him and Gustavo to bathe in the stream. Oh—lunch was rice and lentils with a piece of sardine.

1800h: Dinner: rice, a sardine, and cabbage that Moño brought from Camp Happiness.

Tuesday, 15 Nov., Day 54

Last night was very cold and my ear hurt constantly. Couldn't help but scratch it in my semisleep.

1300h: Moño visited me in the tent. He asked how my reading was going.

"The last two communist journals you gave me are trash," I said. "No one could read them."

As usual we talked about my imprisonment.

"Fifty-three days have passed—for nothing," I said. "CIAT won't pay your ransom. Kill me now, it's better."

"*Nunca,*" he said. Never. Then: "I think you'll be released in December."

"Bullshit."

Does that mean I should hope for a December release? For Christmas, maybe? No, no, never. That would be terrible, worse than wishing that the news would come this afternoon and I'll start home tomorrow. If I wished for a long-term date like Christmas—40 days from now—what would happen when Christmas comes and I'm still here?

That's asking for real heartache. I wish he'd said tomorrow—which I'd know is a lie—instead of December. I know he was just saying that—but he planted an idea, a hope. How fucking cruel.

1400h: Lunch: rice and beans. Managed to snitch two more candles and a tin can of oil.

1735h: Dinner: rice, sardine, some green beans. My fire is ready to light when I'm shut in, in 20 minutes. Ate the last of my suckers last night—had saved it two days. Lasted 45 minutes.

Seems like I've been here a long, long time. With no end in sight.

My flashlight has been out for days and batteries are to arrive "sometime." Gustavo had an extra battery, which he gave me. My flashlight now works, and I appreciate it. Must remember to repay when new batteries arrive. [old battery = in front by bulb] Gustavo is really my favorite. He helps me from time to time. He also gave me another candle and I didn't even ask.

Wednesday, 16 Nov., Day 55

Last night was awful—the coldest yet. Ice had formed, for the first time, on standing water around the camp this morning. The sun here is strange, I guess because we're so high. When the sun comes out, it's very warm and balmy—you can sunburn easily.

1430h: It was so warm I washed one shirt, dried it, put it on, and then washed the other. It then turned cloudy at about 1400h, and now it's raining—cold, hard rain with lots of cold wind. The weather this morning led to a discussion of [the] altitude of this valley. Moño swears the altitude is around 25 km—about 13 miles. I don't believe it, but we're higher that the 2 km I was told when we arrived. All agreed with Moño. He also said that this area is the highest elevation in Cauca and pointed out that this is the Cordillera Central—much higher than the Cordillera Occidental by Cali. Interesting.

Lunch was rice and beans.

Stole another candle this morning, which means I now have a record 4½ candles.

1715h: Was drying socks over the main "kitchen" fire. I hadn't washed them, but wanted nice and dry [ones] to wear to bed tonight. Went in to check and found that one sock had fallen into a pan of cooking oil. I said nothing and removed the sock quietly. Took it back to my tent and wrung it out over three nice pieces of firewood that I'd been drying because I was afraid they wouldn't burn. No point in wasting oil.

About *Leaving Cheyenne*. The four days everyone talks of to the nearest population is probably true; different people seem so persistent in that number—but that may be following a route that FARC considers safe. In other words, there could be populated areas closer—only not under FARC control. But how to tell? Cali is northwest of here, I'm almost sure.

I wonder about Susan a lot. Is she in Cali? I almost hope not; it must be really bad to be there alone with no purpose.

1800h: Viejito caught 20 trout, including some fairly nice ones, in Happy Valley. At dinner Cirle gave me my share: one trout three-fourths the length of my hand. The seven FARCs were talking, at the time, about how lucky they were to have 20 trout. I said nothing, but stood there with my plate until Leidi, embarrassed, added a second tiny fish. Discrimination in the sharing of food hasn't happened much. Not yet. But as I wrote earlier, the longer I stay here, the less an honored guest and the more a pain in the ass I'll be.

Thursday, 17 Nov., Day 56

Awoke this morning depressed. Awfully depressed, a terrible way to start a day of nothing. Which is, of course, the main cause of the depression. My ear infection is better, but I have a new infection—deep inside my right nostril—that hurts a great deal. I want to localize that infection, bring it to a head, but we have no antibiotics.

Moño came to my tent, told me this time that he thinks I'll be relocated in seven to eight days. "I don't believe you," I said. He reassured me, and I said that tomorrow makes eight weeks of captivity. "I'm very grateful to you for everything," I said, and almost crossed into those words I'd use only when talking to myself, talk meant to hurt, embarrass, about leaders and lovers and queers and soldiers and—"No! I don't want to talk with you about this!" I said. "I won't say what I feel!"

Moño didn't know what I meant, and returned to the hut.

I also woke thinking about the annual Texas Aggie Muster in Cali and the name read yearly at the Roll Call of the Absent. A Colombian who got his degree from Texas A&M returned home to Medellín and was kidnapped soon afterward. That was about five years ago and he's assumed dead—although no one knows for sure. But of course he's dead; these son of a bitches don't keep kidnap victims as pets.

1100h: I showed Moño the infection in my nose. "I need antibiotics to stop the spread of the infection," I said. "It's hard to believe that in a camp of soldiers like below, there are no antibiotics."

"I didn't see any." Moño fumbled, and I realized: He doesn't know which kind of pills are antibiotics and didn't ask. He may not even know what an antibiotic is.

"I'll ask again," Moño said.

"When?"

"Tomorrow, when I go down tomorrow." Good Lord, Moño, he has plenty of Ponstan 500 pain pills, and Acido Metenamico 500 mg, he assured me, so don't worry. I guess he thinks stopping the pain solves the problem.

Moño took out the generator [moved] inside the hut a couple of days ago. It hasn't worked since Juaco's death. I don't think it was even used five times. They gave up on two-way radio communication three weeks ago, so we're as isolated as ever. No shortwave since 10 Oct., 38 days ago. That was the last time I heard English or international news. The Day of the Dead Cow was exactly one month ago today. I didn't imagine then that I'd still be here a month later. Where will I be a month from now? If I had the power to forecast, I don't think I'd use it. It might say I'll still be in the Valley of Death.

1210h: Lunch: rice and a sardine.

1355h: Went and stripped fences for firewood. Took more than enough for tonight, but left the rest. Something to do tomorrow. (Last week I tried a game: to think of things, events, happenings in my life that I hadn't thought about since capture. It was awfully hard to think of a person, and event, anything.)

1425h: Ramiro returned from Camp Happiness with supplies. I watched the unpacking of some: lots of rice, 10 big cans of sardines, a bag of potatoes. Oh boy. Raining again. What is CIAT doing to get me released? I have to keep faith, I've never let it waiver, not really. But two months . . . And I can't help but think: If I were Japanese, I'd have been out of here long ago. My government would get involved, pressure CIAT. Same, I think, for Germany, Holland, Australia, etc. Has USAID done anything? Does AID have an "official" interest? I bet not. I'm on my own as far as my government—at least USAID, the link to CIAT—is concerned. I'm on my own here—but I'm really not on my own. I have absolutely no control or influence over my destiny. The helplessness, maybe that's the worst aspect of it all. I can keep my health up, sort of, if it doesn't require things like antibiotics. And my spirits. Nothing else is in my hands.

1600h: Leidi just asked for my shirt and trouser size. How terribly depressing. FARC is ordering clothes. God knows I need another shirt and trousers—but that means there are no plans to release me anytime soon. I wonder—could they be ordering a shirt and trousers to give to me for Christmas? What an awful day. Rain is falling straight down and it's grown chilling cold and I'm crouched in my tent hating and thinking that it's better to hate these sons of bitches, to think how I'd love to kill [them], than to think about my situation and feel sorry for myself. Will I have revenge someday? I think about it a lot, of course, but it almost certainly will never happen.

1645h: Gustavo and Viejito returned with 60 trout caught by the rod. I've started helping clean trout—voluntarily. Usually Melena cleans them. That's good because she always washes my clothes, and gets them so much cleaner. But I didn't like that because I don't like any special favors from these lice. But helping her clean fish makes it more a trade of services—eye for an eye, etc.

1800h: Rather than let the order of clothes depress me further, I asked both Moño and Leidi if they could please order whatever clothes in cotton, not polyester like before. If I'm to be here a long time, I may well be as comfortable as possible, and nothing compares to great 100 percent cotton.

Today was not Thanksgiving. It's the fourth Thursday in November. So there's still a slight possibility that Susan and I will go to 1994 Thanksgiving dinner at Pam and Myles Fishers'. Maybe. Dinner: two trout, rice, beans.

Friday, 18 Nov., Day 57

0730h: I didn't want to get up, but it's too cold, and the bed too hard to sleep later. And the infection in my nose hurts a lot. Old habits die hard. I thought this morning, Oh well, I'll read until the others are up and coffee is made. Then it hit me: read what? This happens all the time. It's not that I am always aware of it. Even though I don't usually dream about being a prisoner, I'm aware of it from the moment I open my eyes. Maybe the cold, the hardness of the bunk tells me before I open my eyes. But reading, if I'm doing nothing else, is instinctual. I constantly find myself reaching for something to read "like I'd once reach for a cigarette" without thinking.

0835h: Two months ago exactly right now, I was on the back of a stolen pickup bouncing and heading at maximum speed, to somewhere. I knew I'd been kidnapped by FARC. But I thought I'd be let go once they realized I was with CIAT. What would happen if I were freed? What would happen if I were freed, and drove into a similar *retén*? I think I'd throw the car into first, gun the motor, and try to drive through, run over people if necessary, and hope they're FARC, not innocent detainees. And get killed maybe. Once through the *retén*, there's still a heavily armed guard in front.

1435h: I've done two positive things today. I picked two loads of leaves to pad my bunk again, and I sewed two broken belt loops and a split seam on the polyester trousers. The real reason for sewing was so I could borrow a needle to open the sore in my nose. Was afraid no one would lend one if they knew the purpose. Drained a lot of pus. Now it feels a lot better, and I feel the problem is over. But it shows that something that should be routine can be frightening and painful, even dangerous when you have no medical care, lack medicines, and live in filth. (Bad experience this morning. While sewing, Melena, the dumb-ass, came into my tent. The sun was shining warmly, so I had stuck my diaries under the mattress so I could take my jacket off. Melena sat on the bunk, on my diaries, but not knowing it. She picked up one of the four magazines and started reading aloud to show me that she can read, I suppose. She stayed 1½ hours and I couldn't do a thing. I couldn't leave the tent because if she found the diaries, I wanted to be there to say they're only notes and Spanish phrases I'm studying. So I sat here by her until lunch. She never felt the notebooks. "Do you recognize him?" Melena said at one point, showing me a photo of Manuel Marulanda Velez, FARC.

"Yes, he's the commander in chief and he's very white," I said.

Then she pointed to a photo of an old man named Jacobo Jimenez. "What about him?"

"Another FARC leader. Also very white."

"*Sí.*"

"But the FARC soldiers are all *morenos*, brown-skinned."

"*Sí.*" Melena wasn't bright enough to get my sarcasm, but it's true, and it seems to me that this group of little brown Indians should think about that. But they won't.

1610h: I wonder if the CIAT's 1994 Christmas card is well under way. I was to meet with my staff about two months ago today. And the CIAT 1995 calendar.

1700h: Dinner at 1640h was rice, sardine, and some boiled potato. This afternoon I walked to the crest of the hill on the other side of Juaco's grave. I found, in the grass, a torn, rectangular piece of olive cloth from a fatigue uniform, about 15 inches long and six inches wide. Also, a hood of olive cloth. Both were probably thrown away somehow at Juaco's burial. But they are good cloth, and clean (cold rain every day). I'll wash them again tomorrow anyway. I'll use the hood to store kindling wood for my fires, and just the other as simply a rag, a towel. I found a little plastic bag a couple of days ago, too. I store *panela* and bitter chocolate in it. And a plastic cooking-oil bottle, with the top cut out, is both a pitcher when I wash my hair and a firewood container. Raining straight down and so cold. Last night I had a surprise: I found another sucker— that I had forgotten—in my pack. Cherry flavor, sickly sweet. Loved it.

[*A CIAT official made a statement to the press that they might be forced to close if Tom were not released. The Hargroves and Greiners received telephone calls from the kidnappers asking why CIAT had not followed their instructions.—SSH*]

Saturday, 19 Nov., Day 58

0700h: Heard an announcement of my kidnapping this morning at 0630h this morning. Couldn't get all, but Moño had Radio Notícias (news) on, and I heard through the mud wall "CIAT, el Centro, etc." Then something about scientists, worldwide, then my name—definitely—the word *"secuestro"* (kidnapped). Something about hoping for release for the *communicador*, I rushed into the hut. Moño heard it, too, but didn't help much. Said the "news" was this: CIAT is hoping for my release. Now going back to sleep, with the radio on low, I can barely hear anything. (I didn't hear the word "FARC" in the broadcast. What I want to know now is what the news angle was. That I'm kidnapped isn't news, not after two months and one day. And my kidnapping was on the radio news the night of 23 Sept. However, whatever the [illegible], I'm extremely glad this was on the news. I've been thinking about that and decided that lots of news publicity would be best for me because it would apply pressure on three fronts: 1) FARC—I'm the first International Agricultural Research Center (IARC) scientist working for agricultural development to be kidnapped worldwide, and since this type of work began in 1962, that could make FARC look bad. 2) Colombian government—this should be embarrassing, especially if the CGIAR is described and the news includes that Colombia joined CGIAR this year. Could help pressure the government to do something. Prisoner exchange, for example. 3) CIAT and the CGIAR—the first kidnapping in the system will look bad—especially for attracting donor funds to CIAT and for recruitment of international staff. Publicity could push CIAT more to close the issue and shut up the publicity, the news is definitely a step in the right direction; I can't see how it can hurt anything. Has the international media picked this up? I hope Tom Quinn of *Time* and David Marcus of the *Dallas Morning News* are aware. But how did Radio Notícias get the story? Did CIAT put out a press release or statement? Did Radio Notícias hear something and call CIAT? Will I hear more? Moño has now changed to another station. I believe Radio Notícias is carried nationwide but "personalized" and rebroadcast from different cities across Colombia. I hope that broadcast was from Bogotá, not Cali.

0750h: Am back in my tent, mainly because through this mud wall is the best way to hear Moño's radio. You're doing something dangerous, Hargrove, and you'd better stop it while you can ... if you can. But I don't think I can stop in this situation; hope must be as natural as breathing. It's now 1020 and I've been thinking about my release for almost two hours. About what to carry or throw away, should I wash clothes now. About the four-day ride, and when and where I'll be released and what I'll do then, will I fly from ... somewhere ... to Cali, take a taxi to CIAT, or to home? Will Susan know I'm coming? Thanksgiving dinner? Just after eight A.M. Moño told me—and I know I can't believe Moño, but this seems so specific—that the Colombian government is negotiating my release with FARC, and that negotiations are almost complete. That the government is being "pressured" by rich countries (I think) to get my release. Moño said that the negotiations were part of the radio broadcast. Although he confirmed that FARC was not mentioned on the radio news, he also said that the same news was broadcast yesterday. He stressed that my release was imminent. Could he lie so specifically? If this is just something to satisfy me, it's the cruelest blow yet, and something I could never forgive. But it may be, Hargrove. Probably is, you've been told shit like this before. Lies. Don't build yourself up for the worst, cruelest fall yet. You'll be here at Christmas, and FARC is even ordering new clothes for you. But what does Moño have to gain by lying? And, I'm on the news without question. Why? If only my release can be negotiated with no ransom paid—especially important—nothing paid by my family or Susan's.

1204h: The weekend—ninth—has begun, so I can't expect anything for several days. If you're smart, Hargrove, you won't expect anything period. I'd ignore all of this had I not clearly heard my name, and CIAT, on the news— there has to be a news angle. And what else could it be?

1240h: I just remembered, I believe kidnapping is so prevalent in Colombia that there is a law. . . . When a Colombian is abducted, his bank account is automatically frozen to prevent ransom payments.

1300h: Lunch: rice and lentils—rice and lentils even more disgusting than usual. Yeah, Hargrove, maybe you should skip lunch; you'd probably have a big T-bone steak at home tonight. Time for an attitude change, my friend. Cloudy and cold all morning. Raining. Now Christmas music is being played fairly often over the radio. Prophetic?

1450h: I haven't written about the flashlight theft because of other news. I noticed on Thursday night that my flashlight had a dent. But last night, I really noticed. Also, that it doesn't work well and is very worn. Then I realized: Someone has switched flashlights with me. Mine was brand-new—was still in the box when I received it, along with boots, pants, and a shirt on 5 Oct. This morning I told Moño that he has a thief among his troops, *sin duda*, showed him the battered flashlight. He said he will check the flashlights of his troops. "It should be easy to check," I said. "Whoever has a new flashlight has mine." Let's see what happens. Nothing, I'll bet—I'm 80 percent sure that Gustavo is the one. It was Wednesday night that he gave me the batteries. I saw then that my flashlight was much better than his. So did Gustavo. Too bad, because he's my favorite. But like I said, Moño won't do anything.

1525h: Went to sleep at 1330h with the rain falling steadily on my tent— awakened at 1500h. I don't think it matters much whether I sleep a little in the afternoon. I don't sleep worth a damn at night anyway. Moño told me that the radio at Camp Happiness, like the one here, is out. So the only two-way communications with the outside world [illegible] is by horseback—how reassuring, especially if it's really a four-day trip. What if Moño is lying about my imminent release? It'll be at least a week before I could even conclude that with communications like they are. Well, if so, I've killed another week, and I'm that much closer to Christmas. I look forward to my new shirt and trousers. What choices do I have? None.

Sunday, 20 Nov., Day 59

0140h: I was shut in my tent for the night at 1830h last night when someone—I have no idea who—arrived. After some talk Moño yelled, "Don Tomás!"

Then Ramiro opened the tent. "A letter for you," Ramiro said, handing me a blue envelope. A *letter? For me?* How? Who? The only thing I could imagine was they let Susan write. I stood outside, and opened the envelope in near darkness. The note was handwritten, on a sheet torn from a ring notebook. At the bottom of the page was signed *"Atentamente"* [sincerely], *El Comandante*. It was a response to my letter to the commander of the Cauca branch of FARC, which left our camp on 31 Oct. The second thing I noticed was the date on the note—18th Nov., two days before. So it's not four days to FARC headquarters after all. The note, in Spanish was mainly an acknowledgment of receipt of my letter, but included, "I read your note, with great care, the data you gave are important. I was especially interested in what you said about CIAT's activities in Colombia. . . . Your family is fine although very worried about your situation. We agree with your family and you in hoping that you will leave soon, and in good health." The *comandante*'s closing paragraph irritated me a little: "I close hoping that your conduct is good. We will treat you accordingly." Not a bad day all and all, I thought, storing the letter in my pack. First the radio broadcast, now this letter. I at least know now that I'm not forgotten—that others remember who and where I am—and that is awfully important. I should write that I slept peacefully last night—but I didn't. I was still awake at 2:30 A.M., thinking of what my return would be like, how FARC would deliver me to . . . where? CIAT, or home? And about each single meal during my first days of freedom.

1010h: Reading back what I've written since yesterday morning . . . I only hope that I'm not setting myself up for an awfully hard fall. If so, getting back on my feet will be tough. But I can do it. Radio is playing in the background. I wish they'd stop playing Christmas carols. For God's sake, Christmas is still 35 days from now. A part for the radio arrived last night. We can now send and receive messages, Moño says, throughout Colombia—even internationally.

1125h: Went and stripped more leaves from bushes to soften my bed.

1215h: Lunch: rice and boiled potatoes. Isolation from affection. It must affect one. I haven't thought about it, but I've had no exposure to friendship—giving, receiving, or sharing—of any kind for more than two months. A strange dog wandered in this morning. She obviously has beagle blood, black and tan, about 1½ feet high, long, floppy ears. Intelligent and affectionate. I called and she came to me. I scratched her ears, under her chin, and she jumped up and started licking my face. Suddenly, without realizing it, I started crying, and couldn't stop. Not "controlled crying" but crying. Thank God I was behind the hut where none of FARC could see me. Why did I react that way? I don't know. I don't remember, but it was the first, the only act of kindness, of friendship, since my kidnapping. Later I learned that the dog's name is *Orejas*—Ears—and she belongs to the *campesino* down in Happy Valley who owns that scroungy dog *Oso*, plus the cows here in Death Valley.

1555h: Putting it all together, I don't think I'll be here one week from now—so I'd better enjoy as much of this life as possible, while I can.

That's [illegible], of course—and if I *am* here next week? I'll just forget this little interlude of ecstatic hope, and be happy that I know I'm at least remembered.

1645h: Javier made dinner: a soup of sardines, pasta, and potato. I'd never had soup made from canned sardines before. It tastes about like it sounds.

1745h: Some son of a bitch broke my coffee cup—the one I stole from the Indians, brought all the way here. It wasn't much; it was cracked in four places, chipped in more; I kept it outside the tent so I wouldn't step on it, and so the rain would wash it a little. I was warming at one of the grass fires 10 minutes ago, and was returning to the mud hut when I saw something familiar in the grass down the hill, 50 feet from the hut. Half of the cup. I recognized the chips. That cup was about the only thing that I could really call my own. I was looking at the cup this afternoon, wondering if I could possibly take it out of here, back to Cali with me as a true souvenir of this terrible experience. The cup was the only thing I had of use that's truly mine. Pull yourself together, Hargrove. Crying over a coffee cup? You're really flipping out.

It's more than a cup, of course. I've got to get out of here. If the current possibility fails—it's time to look seriously at *Leaving Cheyenne*. I've cried twice today, for very different reasons. I can't take much more. *Calmese* [calm yourself], Hargrove. Build your fire and make it through the night. Then take tomorrow as it comes.

Monday, 21 Nov., Day 60

Yeah, the broken cup late yesterday really shook me. Finding the broken half in the mud down the hill, not knowing the cup had been broken, was a little like stumbling upon the corpse of a friend who you didn't know had died. At least the type of friend you might make here. It was dark and cold, drizzling, and almost time to be shut away for another 13 hours. Well, it's now 0915h the next day and the sun is shining brightly.

I'm sitting on the big rock by the spring. Yet still feel tragedy at losing the cup. I waded through the mud, back to the hut, holding the broken half. Melena and Viejito were outside penning the cow. I showed them the broken cup—and they laughed. I threw the cup against the tent. If I'd had a weapon, I would have killed them both . . . easily, and gladly.

Someday I'll read again what I've just written. But I'll read it as a free man, maybe off the computer screen as I sip coffee from one of my favorite porcelain coffee mugs back in real life. Will this emotion over a broken coffee cup make sense then? Maybe not. Reading what I've just written will probably embarrass me. But right now . . . I could find myself crying again easily, if I continue thinking about that cup. It's the nearest thing to death I've seen up here.

And I valued it more than the lives of any of these vermin with whom I've shared the past two months.

1000h: I was through writing—and thinking about the cup. Then I wandered into the kitchen area of the hut and spotted something familiar. There in a corner was the other half of my cup. So the cup wasn't broken when someone stepped on it or by flying wood chips as they chopped wood. Someone took it inside and broke it. Why?

1020h: My socks look funny drying on the barbed-wire fence outside my tent. They're green and brown, each emblazoned with a U.S. flag, and stitched "USA '94."

After two months here, I still totally lack friendship or respect for these people. Not one is, at best, of more than average intelligence. Most are, simply, not very bright.

I've seen little to indicate moral character or ethics. A group of losers.

1120h: I tried to write about what role religion—or its absence—plays in this life, a few weeks ago. I didn't get very far because nothing seemed appropriate. But Christianity is based—or professes to be based—on love and forgiveness. I can't relate to those traits here. They won't help me survive. I think more about hatred, contempt, revenge. Eye for an eye, etc. More natural emotions, aspirations, here in the Valley of Death. Old Testament stuff. And why not? Both the Old and New Testaments are part of the same religion. The OT fit a harsher time. I could pray, if I could ask God to somehow help me get one of these bastards. After two months together, there isn't one for whom, if he were suddenly killed, I'd shed a tear. My emotions would, I'm afraid, be more of secret elation like those of the Day of the Dead Cow. Maybe later, in freedom, I'll think back, of these pitiful and contemptuous little people, with compassion, forgiveness, maybe even love. Right now . . . I can't. I honestly believe that compassion and forgiveness would be unhealthy. How would, say, Jim Lanning [the minister brother of my friend Lee Lanning] feel about my beliefs? He wouldn't condone or approve. But he'd probably understand. Big Hoss has walked through that Valley. I wonder: could I forgive better, if I respected more? I doubt it, but an intriguing thought . . . If I felt they had compassion, any feelings about holding me . . . but they don't. I'm an animal, an object, they captured only to sell. Maybe that's why I can't relate to the FARC. And it's not that their life had hardened and toughened them. It's more like they're children raised with no adult guidance and little discipline. They're unfortunate, but the world would be better without them.

1312h: Lunch: rice and lentils. I don't think the food has to be as bad as it is. *But* these people have probably never known better. Again, underprivileged, and I'm sorry about that, but . . .

I need to change a habit. One reason I can't sleep at night may be that I lie awake for hours thinking about food. Especially of meals I'll have when I leave here, both in Cali, at home, and in the USA at Christmas. I want to say something good about the FARC food. They make two things well. Coffee and hot chocolate. Trout, too, but we never have enough.

1350h: Ramiro's shooting his M-16 again . . . Why doesn't he concentrate on blow jobs and forget being a soldier?

1500h: It's raining and has been, off and on, for hours. No way to wash my khakis today, nor can I even wash the socks and underwear. I washed yesterday. I wanted to wash the trousers for the march that I know won't come—the four-day trip out of here. I have to quit this hoping, planning.

1625h: Moño and Gustavo went to Camp Happiness this morning and returned an hour ago. On foot, no packhorses, mules, etc. And no one has given me any news. So I know I'll spend not only tonight, but also tomorrow night, at the minimum, here. Why do you build yourself up for this, Hargrove? You know that only makes it so much worse.

Didn't hear that release is imminent, that came from Moño. And you didn't know what the radio broadcast said. Again, only Moño's word. Moño also said that we now have excellent radio communication—but we don't. He tries to raise the other end—HQ, I guess—several times a day, but never gets an answer. Look on the bright side, Hargrove. Staying here tomorrow means if the sun shines, I can wash my khakis.

1755h: In tent. Raining, cold to the bone all day. Tonight will be a bitch. I couldn't believe dinner. It was—again—soup of potato, pasta, and canned sardines. My bowl included about an inch of sardine.

Tuesday, 22 Nov., Day 61

1220h: Lunch. More soup of pasta, potato, and more sardines. With very little sardine; that's mostly for "flavor." Awful. I ate one bowl, to survive.

When did we last have vegetables? More than a week ago. I'm in the tent. Cold and raining all morning; will be the same this afternoon and tonight. Can't dry socks and underwear washed two days ago, much less wash the other dirty clothes that are piling up.

I'll never forget 31 years ago today. JFK was shot. I was leaving Duncan Mess Hall at Texas A&M when I learned.

On Sunday I wrote that I doubted I'd be here a week later. Now I'm not so sure. I'll be here tonight, and since nothing has happened, tomorrow night for sure. If I could only hear that radio broadcast again, and clearly. I've based so many hopes on it, yet have only Moño's word that it was about negotiations for my release. I have to be especially careful. I'm getting back into the mind-set where I can't even say thank you to FARC. (By that, thanks for what? For not killing me—yet? For the slop they call food?) None of this is any good, and there's no end in sight.

Dinner at 1630h was rice and potatoes and sardines. That's better, at least, than sardine soup. What a wasted day. Susan must be expecting my release every day now, too, if Moño told the truth. And Thanksgiving is two days from now. I assume that's quarter break for Miles, and he can come to Cali to be with Susan, at least for a few days. If I'm not released soon, I wonder if he could take a quarter of courses by extension and stay in Cali next quarter.

1745h: In tent. When it's really cold and damp, like now, my left index finger gets numb, the finger poisoned by an Amazon catfish.*

Forms appeared outside. Their dancing beams diffused by the rubberized cloth of my tent. One kicked aside a stone and lifted the tent flap. They want to see if my new clothes fit. Maybe they could be bringing one last present that they forgot, I thought, sitting in the darkness at the edge of my bunk. The party's not over yet. Some liquor arrived with the other supplies on the packhorse, and the boys might have come to share a drink. That happened once before during the 60 days I'd been held hostage, and also marked [the] arrival of the new supplies.

An hour earlier, the final shades of darkness were covering the Valley of Death. I heard the arrival of the packhorse. I had retired to my tent. As usual, at around six P.M. I was trying to coax a flame from the wet wood while waiting for a guerrilla to secure my tent from outside for my 12-hour night. I pulled on my rubber boots and went outside to join the excitement. In the team hut, the guerrillas were digging excitedly into two large burlap sacks. This was a big night. Supplies arrive three or four times a year. Gustavo had a bright red shirt, there was a new pair of high rubber boots for someone. *"Baterias,"* Ramiro said excitedly, and pulled out a sack.

"I'll want two of those," I said, and Ramiro handed me two 1.5-volt batteries. Moño's obviously not going to recover my stolen flashlight, so I may as well see if new batteries will make the dented flashlight work. *"Regalo para Don Tomás,"* Moño shouts. *Presents.* A new roll of toilet paper and two new shirts and trousers. He handed me a stuffed plastic sack. I can hardly believe my luck. Two new shirts and trousers will double my supply—and allow me to wear two sets of each when I wash the others. But I don't show much emotion. First, I wouldn't need the new clothes if these bastards hadn't kidnapped me. Second, their arrival—as the guerrillas are assuring me that my release is imminent—seems ominous. Does the investment in the new clothes mean they now plan to hold me here for longer?

I watch the guerrillas sort through more arrivals, then take my plastic bag of new clothes, returning to my tent. There I load the batteries. The flashlight works. Not as well as the stolen flashlight, but at least I'll have light at my fingertips again. I shine light on the half-burned embers of my aborted fire. Is it worthwhile trying to start the fire again? I was thinking when the unexpected visitors entered my tent.

Javier enters first and he's holding something. "Sit there!" Javier says, pointing at the others. Ramiro and Viejito are giggling nervously. Something's wrong. Then Javier holds up the metal object, letting it drop. It's a chain. A chain? He holds my left foot and starts wrapping the chain around my ankles. What's going on here?

*Poisoned last spring when Larry Klaas and I were searching for Carolina Gold specimens, the lost rice variety imported from the Deep South into the upper Amazon by *Confederados*— ex-Confederate soldiers—after the American Civil War.—TRH

"What are you doing?" I demanded indignantly as Javier jerks at the chain, tightening it. He's never liked me, and obviously loves this opportunity.

"We're chaining you."

"Why?"

"Orders."

By now the rest of the hut has turned out. All seven of the guerrillas assigned to guard me are here to watch the show. "You son of a bitch," I say in English.

"Speak in Spanish," Javier says, working the padlock through chain links and shutting it. The chain is the same type you'd chain a big dog with; it even has a clip at the end to attach a collar. "Don't worry, Tomás, tomorrow we'll free you," says a female voice. It's Leidi. Free me? Maybe this is preparation for my appearance at some sort of release ceremony. If [illegible] can take this. I can take anything, if it gets me out of here.

"Wait, you're saying I'll be free tomorrow? Leave the valley?"

"No, no." Leidi laughed. "We'll take the chains off tomorrow morning and leave them off until night."

You whore.

"Are you mad, Don Tomás," Ramiro says, giggling.

The nights of having to listen to the thin-lipped, curly-haired 15-year-old wrestling in the bunk with the other guerrilla, tickling one another, giggling, spitting, came back. "Why don't you go blow someone?"

"Speak in Spanish, only Spanish."

"Fuck you. I hope I'm around when you die of AIDS." By then my ankle was wrapped tightly in chain. Javier slipped the other through a link in the mud wall and someone pulled tight, locked the chain around my ankle with a huge, heavy chain of steel, and everyone laughed at the chained *gringo*. I was chained to my bunk for the night. The guerrillas left my tenting bastion, the flaps with stones from the outside. "I hope you sleep well, Don Tomás," Javier says.

Fuck you.

I lay in darkness for about 30 minutes and cursed under my breath, bouncing my right ankle so the chain links didn't dig so deeply into the skin. Finally, tears rain steadily down my cheeks, a reminder of how helpless my situation was. And I could think of only one thing: how I'd love to grab an M-16 and waste all of their ammo. The rational side of my mind kicked in. Pull yourself together, Hargrove, I thought, cursing, crying; feeling sorry for yourself won't help. This is almost funny, really. This whole experience has been like a movie; the kidnapping, the ride here, being surrounded by masked guerrillas with AK-47s and Galils, Juaco's death, now being chained like a slave, an animal. How could you end this without being chained to your bunk? It's all been theater-of-the-absurd stuff. I began to laugh to myself. It wasn't really very funny, and the laughter was forced. Still, it beat crying.

Light beamed into the tent. It was a guerrilla shining a flashlight through a chink in the mud wall. It's cold. I sat up in bed and unwrapped one of my new shirts and put it on over the other two. I'd at least sleep as warm as possible.

Wednesday, 23 Nov., Day 62

Moño unlocked the chain at 0630h. "What did I do to deserve this punishment?" I asked, rubbing my ankle. But the question nagged at me. What is behind the chain? Why this new policy, after so long. But why would they impose chaining?

"Nothing. And it's not punishment. Anyway, it's only at night."

But nights start at six P.M. and last 12 or 13 hours. I pulled out my letter from the FARC/Cauca commander. "It says here that FARC will treat me according to the way I behave. Why have you started this maltreatment?"

"It's not maltreatment," Moño said, and left. And most groups feed prisoners as release time draws nearer, give them new clothes. Well, I'm getting the clothes, but why would they impose chaining? I had no answers, and finally dozed off around two A.M.

What the hell, I may as well try on my new clothes, I thought, and put on a pair of blue denim trousers. I wore a size 38 when kidnapped; I'd requested size 36. These were size 34 and fit loosely. As I pulled on a wine-red shirt, the tent opened again. It was Leidi. "I came to see how your new clothes fit," she said brightly. Viejito and Ramiro were behind her. It's as if last night and the chains never happened, I thought. These people are like children. Hell, they *are* children. A chubby man in tiger-striped fatigues joined the group in my tent as the guerrillas inspected, touched, and discussed my clothes. I hadn't met him, but know that he arrived with Viejito and the supplies last night. The stranger said nothing. My memory is longer—and harsher—than theirs, but I have to survive, so I discussed each item. The stranger finally spoke. "Were you ever in the military?"

The question shook me. The subject had never come up, and I sure wasn't going to bring it up.

"Do you mean, am I in the military now?"

"Anytime. Did you ever serve in the military?"

That's when it started to hit me. Be careful, Hargrove. Don't lie, you'll get caught. This guy acts like he's onto something. "I served for two years back in the sixties."

"What service?"

"The army."

"What branch?"

"Infantry."

Zeroing in: "What was your rank?"

"Lieutenant."

"Where did you serve?"

"In the United States and a year in Vietnam. Why do you ask?"

"No reason," the stranger said. "I'm just curious."

Oh boy. I guess this explains the decision—which must have come from the FARC commander—to chain me at night. Somehow he learned that I was in the army or Vietnam—maybe something appeared in the news. Or he could have sent someone to CIAT who may have asked about me. Someone could easily have shown them the article published in Spanish in *Arcos** about my book.

I never mentioned military service because it could do me no good, and could potentially cause problems, as it has. But no one ever questioned me about it either.

Lunch: a vegetable soup from the beans, cabbage, onions brought last night. Dinner: fried chicken. My share: two wing tips. Not wings, but the last two joints. Bastards.

Chained again at night.

Talked a bit with "the stranger" around the fire in the afternoon. His name is Martín and he's from Palmira. Knows about CIAT, but did not know what the letters "CIAT" mean. Has never visited. I did not ask specifically if he knew what CIAT does—but I'll bet he doesn't. I doubt that Martín dug up the army info, but I think he heard about it from others, so asked me.

Thursday, 24 Nov., Day 63

Martín left this morning, and carried letters to mail—finally. I read to Moño, and sent my letters to Havener, Susan, and Nathan, written on 6, 8, and 12 Nov.

When Martín left, I was in the cow pasture, walking. He called, then walked out. Shook hands, wished me well—then reached in a pocket and handed me a present—a pocket mirror. I couldn't believe it. I couldn't speak, I was so overcome. It's the kind of mirror all the guerrillas have—I guess FARC issues them. But a wonderful present. I also have another new possession: a pin. It was holding the fold in my new shirt. I wrapped the pin in plastic and stored it under my bunk. I used both the mirror and the pin this morning. Had to open and drain the infection in my nose again—the last time, I think. So nice not to have to beg and borrow a mirror and needle from the guerrillas like before.

Borrowing, that brings up something very unpleasant that I must do: Leidi asked to borrow my razor—a new Gillette throwaway that I received with supplies on 3 Nov.—at 0800h. At 0900h Melena returned the razor. Since I also had my new mirror, I decided to trim my beard. But the razor was so dull, I could hardly cut a whisker. Strange . . . I had used the razor only once. I looked closely and—it's an old razor, dull and stained and even chipped on the head. The bitches switched razors on me. I'll show Moño. What will he do? Ignore it like he ignored the flashlight theft? A real problem with this type of matter is: It's awfully dangerous for me to make enemies with those who guard me. I'm

*The Spanish-language monthly paper for CIAT employees, which had published a human-interest article about my mass-market paperback book, *A Dragon Lives Forever. Arcos* means "arches" and is symbolic of the arches in front of the CIAT research center.—TRH

a prisoner, a slave, without rights. Each one of these people has ways to get back at me, and I'm at their mercy. So many little things they can do to worsen my life. Leidi and Melena, for example, usually serve my plate. What can I do when they give me less meat than the others, like Leidi did last night? Complain to Moño? I did last night, and nothing happened. So what happens next? Well, I have to complain. This razor incident is just too damned blatant.

1240h: Gustavo made lunch: a soup of cabbage, carrots, onion, potato. Quite good really.

Gustavo set "his" flashlight outside the hut this morning. Bright, shiny new. I stared at it and laughed out loud. Pissed him off—he mimicked my laugh—but the flashlight disappeared fast. He knew.[1]

I took the razor incident to Moño. He said I shouldn't lend anything to anyone in the future. I said that refusing to lend isn't so easy when you're a prisoner, at everyone's mercy. Moño brought me a new razor. I took it, but stressed that that wasn't the point. Stealing from me is. But he's screwing both girls, I think, and won't do anything.

Found about a meter of heavy copper wire. Stored it under my bunk. I don't know what, but a use for it will arise.

Good news! *El verano*—summer—begins in these mountains in less than a week. My God! I was kidnapped in September.

1410h: Today is Thanksgiving, and I'm still here. Or maybe Thanksgiving was last Thursday! I'm not sure. A year ago, Richard Pencivil, my Texas Aggie buddy, showed up and I took him to Thanksgiving dinner at Pam and Myles's[2]. Gosh, to know that all my American friends, worldwide, are celebrating today. Susan will be at [the] Fishers' tonight, unless she's in Texas. If so, there'll be a big turkey, maybe a honey-cured ham, too, at my mother-in-law's. Miles, my son, will be there. Maybe Tom G., too, if semester break has come. There'll also be a Thanksgiving dinner in West Texas, probably at Raford's. Becky and Kinney may be there also.[3] Kinney is going out to hunt quail about now. Or will he stay in to watch the Texas A&M-TU [Texas University] Turkey Day Game? Remember how for eight years Mother and Daddy always had Thanksgivings on Friday—because I, then Raford, had to be in College Station or Austin for the TU game. Coming back to West Texas after the game, with Linda Anne Moore, from Roby, driving . . . I guess there have been happier Thanksgivings than Thanksgiving 1994. Now I only pray that our family will be together at Christmas. That's only 31 days from now.

1715h: Gustavo went out of his way to help me this afternoon, giving me his special *agua panela* made with milk. Took my clothes off the fence when it started raining, etc. I swear it's a direct result of my staring at that flashlight and laughing this morning. But be careful, Hargrove, about thinking they're not

[1]Someone had taken my new flashlight and substituted an old, battered flashlight that worked poorly. I was almost sure that Gustavo was the thief.—TRH

[2]Myles Fisher is a CIAT scientist. He and his wife, Pam, a businesswoman, are close friends of mine.—TRH

[3]Raford Hargrove is my brother. Becky, my sister, is married to Kinney McKinney.—TRH

so bad. Gustavo will screw you again if he has the chance. And don't forget.
These bastards were happy two nights ago. They loved seeing the *gringo* prisoner chained. But in reality I think all are too shallow to see the significance of
the chaining. They see it as an inconvenience, but not the humiliation, the immensely deep feeling of helplessness, at being chained like an animal. Well, the
chains go on again in 45 minutes, Hargrove, so get ready.

Thanksgiving in chains. Thanksgiving dinner, at 1640h, was *carve*—the artificial meat—cooked with green beans and carrots, and rice. And a special treat:
a piece of new onion. As usual, I took more than needed, and began the process
of hoarding again. Tomorrow I'll try to steal a whole onion. But stealing has
been hard lately because it's been so cold, and raining all day, so the guerrillas
have all stayed inside the hut around the fire.

1800h: I've been thinking about the girls and the razor, Gustavo and the
flashlight. You know, it takes a really sorry son of a bitch to steal from a prisoner, especially one who has so little as I have.

Friday, 25 Nov., Day 64

I did something last night that will be hard to explain, but the action was
not spontaneous; it was well thought out, even planned. I made a Thanksgiving
toast of Juaco's last drink of brandy. It wasn't exactly a religious ceremony, but
it was inspired by a combination of very conflicting emotions: superstition, hate,
fear, revenge, a begrudged sense of respect for the dead, regret for lost opportunity, all influenced by a West Texas red-dirt sense of decency, morals, and, I
guess, religion. I'll try to explain. I've written about how I stole Juaco's bottle
of brandy on the Day of the Dead Cow, then learned that Juaco opened and took
a last, almost ceremonial drink of that brandy just before placing the muzzle of
his Galil under his chin and pressing the trigger. Learning that pleased me immensely. I stole the rest of the brandy. Back in Death Valley two days later,
stood by Juaco's shallow grave and made a vow. You kidnapped me, you miserable son of a bitch. Now you're dead, by your own hand, and I'm glad, I'm
delighted. The feel, the taste, the smell of your death is exhilarating. I'm alive,
and I leave you here to rot in the cold rain. But before I leave this awful valley
and its fears, its boredom, its freezing loneliness, its hard memories, I'm going
to stand over your grave once more, drink the last swallow of your last liquor,
and push the empty bottle into the mud of your grave with my boot. That'll be
my farewell.

I kept that last drink of brandy during long, cold nights. I thought for hours
about opening that flask over Juaco's grave while exercising in the meadow. I
walked past the grave several times and visualized just how I'd push the bottle
in. Anticipating that last symbolic act of scorn, contempt, hatred, and I guess
victory of a sort, I believe, helped me survive this long.

1555h: As I write this I'm standing in the drizzling rain over Juaco's grave.
It's so tiny. And the crude wooden cross marking the head, I suppose, is at the
south end, not the west end. Two shanks and four hooves of the dead cow lie

to the side, and the still rotting skeleton only 25 feet away; the only memorials of the grave.

1650h: Have returned to my tent. Moño is trying vainly to rouse Farcitta on the radio. Back to the brandy story: As time has passed I began to feel, somehow, strangely uneasy about that vow of vengeance and the last drink of brandy. And again I thought my release was imminent, only to face harsh reality, bitter disappointment, and worse pain and loneliness than before. And I've thought, Is it really right to [illegible] an event will bring immense relief and joy with one [illegible]. Such bitterness, such hatred. The vow began to make me uneasy. Yesterday was Thanksgiving and a very bad day. I thought all about Susan and the boys, family back in Texas, friends around the world. I knew that Susan and her mother and the boys, if they're in Cali, would be at the dinner at the Fishers'. So I made a hard decision: after they chain me tonight and shut my tent for the next 14 hours, I'll build a fire and be with my family and friends back in Cali. I'll share a predinner drink not of Myles's Scotch but of the only drink available, Juaco's brandy. That will not only link me, for a time, with those friends, it will also eliminate the brandy and negate the vow.

And that's what I did. I'd like to write that my fire was comforting and I was warm all over—but it wasn't that way. Rain was falling and the cold cut like a knife. The air was like water and the firewood not much drier. Icy breezes kept whipping through the tent. I made a fizzle that never grew into a fire. Finally, I poured that last brandy into a cup—it filled only the plastic cap of the bottle—and splashed in some water. I drank Juaco's last brandy in the darkness. I then adjusted the covers around the chain locked to my ankle and lay down for the night.

I hope this doesn't sound like I knew what to do and did it, made my peace, and now all is well. Far from it; I'm still as kidnapped as ever—more so, if you factor in the new chains at night. I'm still glad Juaco is dead, and I have a nagging fear that I may have made a mistake in destroying the future promise of a final type of vengeance. I no longer have that option. I've burned that bridge.

1750h: Lunch today: rice and beans. Dinner: the same. I made the news again today. I made the news again today. Was walking around at noon and returned to the hut to find all the guerrillas talking. Radio Palmira announced that a video of Dr. Thomas R. Hargrove, kidnapped on 23 Sept., had arrived at CIAT—proof that I was still alive on 22 Oct., when it was made. My God, it took 33 days for the video to get there? Listened to two stations at five P.M., Radio Caracol [snail] and R. Mundial [worldwide]—both from Cali—and caught the end of the same news on both. Ended with "CIAT is funded by 25 nations." Sounded a bit like CIAT may have put the news out itself. I just thought of something ironically funny, and true: I'd have found handling the news and of CIAT kidnapping fascinating—and that would have been my responsibility, had I not been the one kidnapped! It's seldom that a center information officer handles a story of hard news—and what news is harder than a kidnapping? But it seems to me that CIAT is handling the news well. FARC can be reached only

134 Thomas R. Hargrove

by radio. I've heard at least parts of three broadcasts on three stations. And it's good that the "extra" information—what they need to know about CIAT—is included.

Did I give up something that I could draw on for strength to keep going when other sources are dissipated, or did I discard some unneeded and harmful baggage of hatred that could only hurt me?*

[*CIAT held a press conference to announce that they would not negotiate or pay ransom.—SSH*]

Saturday, 26 Nov., Day 65

I never eat breakfast, but it was a soup with green beans and carrots this morning. Anytime I can eat vegetables, I do. My 10th weekend as a hostage begins this morning. Listened to a range of radio stations, but nothing about me on the news. Talked more than an hour with Moño yesterday; following are some highlights. Both boys are in Cali and have been interviewed for radio news, he says. So has my *jefe* at CIAT. FARC has kept Susan informed by phone. FARC is holding me here partly for my own safety, he claims. "If the Colombian army rescued you, they would kill you and blame it on FARC for propaganda. So guarding you is a big responsibility." I said nothing about "black propaganda" but as an old Vietnam hand, I thought: Yeah, and FARC may kill me and leave evidence that the government killed me in order to blame FARC. Double-black propaganda. Of course, he could be partly right—and a mistake could leave me partly dead. Being a kidnap victim can be a dangerous game. You're outside the boundaries of law, decency, and morality, whichever side you play with. Nevertheless, if I knew a Colombian army unit was over the mountain, and I could escape to it, I'd go without hesitation. I prefer government ethics to FARC ethics.

The International Red Cross has been notified about me, he says. "Ask the Red Cross to send me something to read," I said. CIAT's acronym is unfortunate, and has hurt me. Moño said, "No one in the FARC Command knew what CIAT was when you were captured," he said. "Most assumed that it's part of the CIA. Me, too, when I came to replace Juaco, and to guard a prisoner from CIAT." I agreed sincerely that the acronym has caused problems for me. "FARC officials now know that CIAT is an agricultural organization, but not before. When you return to CIAT, you should convince CIAT *duaños* to change the name. That is *very important*," he emphasized. "It can save you much trouble in the future." I asked why negotiations were going so well a week ago, according to him, then all stopped. Then came the new order to chain me. Are these events related? Moño says he doesn't know, and stresses that the chain policy came from above, with no explanation. "I'm only following orders," he said.

The worst scenario of the chain policy is that it reflects a change in FARC's stance; that FARC will use knowledge that I once served in the army, in Viet-

*When I abandoned my quest for vengeance by pouring the brandy on Juaco's grave.—TRH

nam, combined with CIAT's name problem, to change my status, and I'm suddenly transformed from an economic to a political object. If that happens, I doubt that I'll be with Susan and the boys on Christmas 1994—nor, quite likely, on any subsequent Christmas. And the radio news does *not* mean my status has improved, although the public attention could be, I suppose, a little protection.

1130h: My new clothes came in a big, heavy plastic bag. I saved it, of course. This morning was sunny, for the first time in days, until 0900h. Then it clouded over but didn't start raining until 1030h. Anyway, my bunk has gotten really bad—I couldn't possibly sleep past 0600h this morning. I needed fresh leaves to soften the bunk as a mattress. The sun dried the leaves of surrounding bushes, so I took the bag, filled it, and repadded my bunk. Before the bag, I had to fill [with leaves] my one-liter [plastic] cooking-oil bottle with its top cut out, several different times, to pad my bunk. Little things can become luxuries in some circumstances.

1235h: The FARC have started putting a soft, thick leather around my ankle for padding with the chain. I had wondered where they got it. I looked closely this morning: it's a heavy-duty dog collar. Probably came with the chain. Moño confirms that neither Death Valley nor Happy Valley has radio communication outside. So any news regarding my status must come by horseback. I decided yesterday that I had to bring this army thing into the open. After all, Martín asked those questions—service, rank, Vietnam, etc.—in front of Moño and several other FARC, so I have nothing to lose.

Here's how I led into it. "I've heard you guys joking about eating rats," I said to Moño and Ramiro. "Have you really eaten rat?"

"No, that was just a joke."

"Well, I've eaten plenty of rat."

"Really? Here in Colombia?"

"No, in Vietnam during the war." That led to questions. I told some stories of eating rats, dog, cat, and duck embryos as an adviser, and that led to rice. I made it clear that that's how I got into this type of work. Did it sink in, do any good? I don't know. It's probably better, since the topic had already been opened. Maybe with serious implications (i.e., the chain policy).

1400h: If FARC executes me, I plan to ask Moño, as a last request, to *not* let Javier shoot me. That will force someone who at least doesn't hate me to bloody his own hands.

1530h: Paper is so precious. A week ago I calculated that I had enough diary space to write for 50 more days, at one page per day. But I've used more than 10 pages in 7 days. At that rate, I now have 30 days of diary. I shouldn't even be writing this, but I must, because worrying about the diary is part of this life. I could request a notebook with the next supplies—but that might raise the question: Don't you *have* a notebook? I can't stop writing because this diary is the only really personal thing I have. It's more than a diary. It's what links a hungry and dirty prisoner and Tom Hargrove. Lunch was rice and beans, with a spoonful of "tuna-type" fish. We're out of onion, but I've hoarded three pieces.

1805h: In tent and chained. Dinner: rice and beans and some cabbage-carrot salad.

Sunday, 27 Nov., Day 66

How could I have been so naive, so foolish as to write last Sunday that I felt I would not be here a week later? Here I am, and the only things different are the chain and Christmas carols on the radio.

0800h: I'll read something, I thought a minute ago. God, what will I do the rest of today?

1700h: Lunch: rice, beans, and two small trout.

Dinner: rice, beans, and cassava. Saved paper today.

Monday, 28 Nov., Day 67

It's Monday and I'm always glad to see the weekend over—because I know nothing is happening to get my freedom over a weekend.

Rained all day yesterday and all night. Cold rain. A man and a woman were here this morning, trying to fix the radio. I think the woman was Marli, so I totally avoided contact. I despise her so much, there's no telling what I might have said. In my mind, I started with: "*¿Discubrió unas agentes . . . recientemente?* [(Have you) discovered any (CIA) agents . . . recently?]"

1350h: Lunch: rice and beans. I wonder if FARC might release me for Christmas. That would be a way to get rid of me while saving face. Better not think of that. FARC probably won't release me without ransom. How long will they continue like this? Maybe five months=two-and-a-half months more. Then what? How would FARC get rid of me? Execution doesn't seem likely, although I could simply disappear. But Moño accidentally indicated a way. My death could be rigged to look like a government job—to discredit FARC. That would fit the pattern. But I at least feel better that I've heard about myself on the radio. That means a lot. It's probably also a form of pressure not to kill me. That means a lot.

Melena came to my tent, asked to borrow my mirror this morning. I got mad, said a lot about her and Leidi stealing my razor. Probably sounded like a Sunday-school teacher: "Don't you have any shame?" She denied all. I didn't lend the mirror, and will probably pay the price when my food is served, etc. I'm now carrying the mirror and my spare ballpoint—the only things they could steal—in the pocket of my inner shirt.

1800h: Locked and chained. Dinner: soup of cassava, fake meat, green beans. Today is a day I'll never remember—because it was exactly like yesterday and the day before and, I fear, tomorrow and the next day.

Tuesday, 29 Nov., Day 68

Wednesday, 21 Dec. That can be my target day. I'm glad when each day is over because it's then one day closer—but closer to what? Twenty-one Dec. seems logical because if FARC releases me gratis as a gesture of goodwill, it will be for Christmas. If I'm released before then, it will be for ransom, I fear. Twenty-one Dec. is only three weeks and two days away—23 days. I've already been here 67 days—so I can last that long. What happens if I make survival until then my goal, then 21 Dec. comes, then Christmas—and I'm still here? That's dangerous, I guess. I can hardly stand to think about it now. But I'd survive. Christmas here will be awfully damn rough—terrible—no matter what. This wouldn't make it too much worse.

It's 26 days—22 *shopping days*—till Christmas.

I measured the ground I walk on—ran, before—daily. It's about 230 feet around my "track" once.

Lunch: rice, fake tuna, cabbage-carrot-cucumber salad. Ramiro has been digging a trench all morning on the ridge just above the hut. "Is that another well, to capture spring water?" I asked.

"No, it's a trench."

"To dump trash?" I asked, hoping.

"No—for defense against the Colombian army." The trench faced Happy Valley. So the guerrillas are ready to defend me, protect me from those bad guys who want to kill me. I hope we get to try that trench out soon.

1805h: Why do I do it, why do I let it happen? I was doing okay, but Moño went to Happy Valley and stayed all day. I know better but imagined the delay was because orders for my release had come, and he was arranging for the horses, mules out of here, etc. I built myself up for the fall. Now he's returned and everything is the same and I'm chained until tomorrow and tomorrow will be the same as today. For the record, dinner was rice, cabbage, and two trout.

Wednesday, 30 Nov., Day 69

I earlier wrote that the nights were the worst—but they're not. Mornings are far worse. I rush to get unchained, empty my boot, get coffee if available. Then what? When my fire goes out at night, a day is finished.* Toward what? I don't know, to whatever will eventually happen, I guess. Right now, it's toward Christmas. CIAT will probably try hard to get me out by Christmas—and it's FARC's opportunity to get me off its hands in a fairly positive manner. If I'm still here at Christmas, I think the chances that FARC will kill me increase by 10 times.

But I can't plan for death, because I can do very little to influence that, or its outcome. I can't go buy more life insurance or go back to Cali to wrap up

---

*I had found an old rubber boot that I used as a urinal while shut inside the tent at night. —TRH

jobs at CIAT, say final farewells to Susan, talk with the boys. And death is final—at least, on this earth, in this realm of time. The only thing I can do that might pay off is to plan to live, and what I'll do after this terrible ordeal ends. I should spend a lot of Christmas vacation in Texas making contacts. That's what Ricks, Don can give me: introductions. Maybe I could even set up some jobs in advance, so I can leave CIAT with assurance of some income. Lunch: rice, cassava, fake tuna.

1500h: Talked with Moño. He says it's doubtful I'll be released before Christmas. My God, after what I wrote just a few hours ago! "Talks with the government aren't going well, and there's more fighting," he said. "Also the government insists on militarization of the mountains." FARC wants "free zones." Putting it all together—and the chains—is it possible that the game for me has changed? That it's no longer just ransom, but I've become a pawn in the politics (i.e., government quit operating in mountains and set up free zones)? If so, I'll probably never be freed.

Maybe I should forget a Christmas release. FARC knows that CIAT wants me out before Christmas, so may put up a much tougher bargain. I talked with Moño a little about the morality of this, but that's useless. It always comes down to, "It's not my fault. I'm only following orders." And I'm sure it's true, that he has little or nothing to say. Talking to these guys does no good and can be dangerous. But if only I could talk with *someone*.

I made a clothesline under the eaves of the hut with the wire I found. Now I can put wet clothes there when it rains. Found about three feet more of wire and am saving. Am terribly depressed. I have to shake this off. Wish I could ask Mike Benge what he did to keep from going crazy. CIAT—please, *please* keep up the publicity. International, call Tom Quinn and David Marcus. It may save my life.

1800h: Dinner: rice, squash, salad of beets and cabbage.

Thursday, 1 Dec., Day 70

Made big mistake. Asked Moño if I could write Red Cross for things to read. With my typewriter? Yes, but there is no more paper. Is there in La Playa? No, then I can use notebook paper. Can you get me a notebook? Yes, but don't you already have one? Yes, but it's almost full. The subject was dropped, but that conversation scares me. No matter what, I can't mention notebooks again. I awoke in the night, half dreaming that I'm released, but . . . "Give me your notebook," Moño says. And I lose my diary, the only thing that gives this absurd situation any meaning. That thought terrifies me. I must use notebook paper for my letters, so must do everything to conserve paper. Including collect scrap paper and cardboard for future writing.

1415h: I've thought and soul-searched since late yesterday: maybe I've figured out how to make at least some peace with myself and that will help me survive or face death as calmly and with as much dignity as possible. I've never been religious, and I can't be in the traditional sense. But I feel there is order, direction in the world beyond human control or understanding. Maybe that is belief in God, or its equivalent. I've led a fairly decent life, with more than my share of adventures, extraordinary experiences. I've written two books and seen my sons reach manhood. I want to live, but that may not be in the plan. If not, so be it. I die. If so, I'm curious to see if I'll continue to live on in some manner. If so, maybe I'll see Mother, Ed Tout, Joe Bush, Gene Oates, Donaway and Ard*—wouldn't that be interesting? But I hope—"pray" may be the word—for the strength to die bravely, and for strength for my family.

I want to leave here alive, of course, *with the diary*. The latter only slightly less than to live itself. I'll almost certainly spend Christmas here. The reasons that FARC should release me—CIAT and Colombian government pressures, the emotions that come with the Christmas package—are reasons that FARC will hold out for whatever it's after. And I wonder what that is. How valuable am I? But spending Christmas here doesn't mean I die afterward. I may—by "accident"—but the publicity can help prevent that. To get out of here with the diary, I have a plan. I make Notebook 2 a "dummy." Tear out the most essential pages and hide them with the Checkbook Diary and Notebook 3, separately on body. Then if they ask for the notebook when I leave, I produce the dummy. With luck, it could work. Luck, and, perhaps, help from a force that's beyond me.

I spent several hours this morning walking and talking to myself about this. It's the best plan available that I know. But this morning I talked to myself in a different way. Out loud, for the first time. And I called myself God—in other words, I talked to another entity maybe. Is that praying? If I live, I'm going to give thanks in a church, and see how that feels. If it's talking to myself, maybe it's a source of comfort. I'll try.

Lunch: rice and fried flour (not fried bread, but *harina frita*).

An excellent idea came to me while walking and talking. Why not plan that reunion of Chuong Thien Province [in Vietnam] veterans that Harvey Weiner suggested? I'll do it. Will be fascinating and will help pass time. But will write on a piece of cardboard that I found and saved, not here [in the notebook]. Then I can use that if I need to produce more "dummy" written material when I leave. Dinner: rice and beans and two trout. Played *fútbol* [goal] for second day in a row.

Friday, 2 Dec., Day 71

1015h: The mornings. They're so terrible, as cruel as FARC. My spirits were fairly high yesterday afternoon, but I woke terribly depressed. Today, 2½ months since I was kidnapped and I'm no closer to free than two months ago.

---

*All of those people are friends who are now dead. Ed Tout was an editor at IRRI in the Philippines. Bush and Oates were Texas A&M buddies who were killed in Vietnam. Donaway and Ard were a lieutenant and a sergeant who died in a Viet Cong ambush—that I had personally almost sprung—in the Mekong Delta in 1969.—TRH

I finally broke and asked Mono if I could fish. No, he said—but we'll probably move to another camp this weekend, and there, I can fish. I guess the river must be in sight there. But the FARC are cutting trees like mad for firewood here. The "trench" has become a fortified bunker, with log-soil and plants for camouflage on top. Also—supplies may arrive and mail leave on Sunday. I must write letters. But one page of notebook paper is four to six days of diary. I have almost 45 pages (one side) of paper left. Must let Susan know I'm okay. Must try to let CIAT know to keep up the publicity—the only thing working for me. But whatever I write may also mean FARC kills the entire letter. Not easy to resolve. Worse—should I suggest that Susan return to Texas for Christmas? I won't be freed, and it would be worse for her to sit in Cali, waiting. How cruel for her. But what if I were freed, say, on Christmas Eve? Well, I'd make the best of it and take the first plane to Texas. Also cheaper for her to go to Texas than for both boys to come to Cali. But do I even have the right to advise her? She must know things that I don't know, and must make her own decision. Maybe I should write that.

1130h: Talked with Mono. I don't know why. He says I may be released in five to six days and will spend Christmas with my family. I know not to believe him, but when he says that, I always build false hope. I can't help it, it's natural.

Found a horseshoe in the meadow. Tiny, fits in my palm. Maybe it's an omen, a sign of luck, as folklore says. Used the wire I found to hang it over the entrance to my tent. And the sun came out.

Looked at my teeth with new mirror and found—oh no!—what looks like a big cavity on a back molar. If it is, and exposes a nerve, what will I do? There are no dentists in the Valley of Death. Found mayonnaise jar with lid to store cooking oil. Found second mayonnaise jar lid. Will save. Means another jar for something.

1220h: Melena came to my tent again. Wish she'd quit that.[1] To make it worse, she has a cold. I've washed my cuts, my hands with soap. After 2½ months without a single day sick, I do *not* want a cold. My fastidiousness must seem funny, considering that we live in filth. But a cold is something you can see and fear.

1325h: Lunch: vegetable soup. I was on the news—Radio Palmira—today. Just [that] CIAT had received my last letters and I'm okay. Wonderful! Keep it up, Nathan, Alex, Gail—whoever![2] When I'm in the States, I must try to visit Khang.[3] Maybe combine with meeting Harvey Weiner to plan the Chuong Thien reunion. Must also write regarding Jung.[4]

[1]My unwritten message is that Melena wanted to have sexual relations.—TRH

[2]Nathan Russell, Alexandra Walter, and Gail Pendleton are all CIAT editorial staff who prepare public awareness and news materials.—TRH

[3]My interpreter during the Vietnam War, whom I helped to immigrate to the USA in 1992.—TRH

[4]Another Vietnamese friend with whom I worked closely during the war. Jung is still in Vietnam.—TRH

1750h: Something strange seems to be happening, but I don't know what. A new guy—a tall stranger—arrived. Moño and Viejito left. Viejito shook hands with others and joked about not returning. It's getting dark and cold, yet no one is building a fire. Gustavo said they told him not to make a fire and that I should go lie down in my tent—that's where I am now. Everyone is talking in a low voice. Is this scary or just my imagination? Viejito took his pack, Moño did not. Maybe Viejito was called for a meeting over the dead cow?

1820h: They're making a fire in the hut and cooking something, but I'm uneasy about going inside. Does whatever this is affect me? Probably; everything here does.

1950h: Javier said to stay in tent again. Ramiro brought me my dinner. Beef. Yes, a piece of fried beef. Mostly gristle, but I ate in little strips so wouldn't choke. And with beans. Something really strange is going on. I'm dressed to march, although I don't think that will happen. Why am I kept out of hut? What is there to see?

Saturday, 3 Dec., Day 72

1455h: I've been chained in the bunk in my tent all day and all night. Was I ever right when I sensed last night that something strange—and scary—was going on. Javier and Gustavo came to chain me at about 2030h last night. But this time they didn't have the leather dog collar for padding and locked the bare chain directly around my ankle. Also gave me far less "slack" chain so I could hardly move around on the bunk. "Why?" I asked.

"It's a new policy," Javier said.

"I'm being punished? For what?"

"Nothing. We're only following orders brought by the . . ."—and he used a word that sounded like *"corregidor"* but wouldn't repeat it. There was no point in arguing, so I accepted it. After they left, I tried to build a fire, but it fizzled out. Then I saw flashlight beams and saw that Tall Stranger* was talking with guerrillas: one by one outside. Don't do anything to draw more attention, Hargrove, I thought, and forgot about the fire.

All the guerrillas were up and about at 0630h today—none of this normal sleep till eight A.M. business. I called for someone to unchain me. Javier came—and explained that I could not be unchained. "Am I to remain chained in this tent forever?"

"Sí," he said, adding quickly, "I'm only following orders."

"Can you unchain me only to go outside and brush my teeth?" I asked. That I'd like to also urinate was, of course, implied.

"You can use the floor," Javier replied, and left. It's a good thing I have the piss boot.

I believe I wrote after the chaining began on 22 Nov., followed by questions about my army days, that the worst scenario would be if FARC decided

---

*Tall Stranger was Rambo but, somehow, I didn't recognize him at that time.—TRH

there is something ominous about that and jumped to wrong conclusions. If that's what's happening, I felt I'll be killed for sure. Well . . . "five, six . . . open them pearly gates. . . . Don't ask me 'cause I don't know why. We're all gonna die" as Country Joe sang. Tall Stranger came to my tent around 0830h and handed me a letter, my second letter from the commander of FARC/Cauca. I started reading, and almost fell off my bunk. The second paragraph read: "We have information that you are a full colonel (R [regular]) in the army, a hero of the Vietnam War, an expert in counterguerrilla warfare, a communications expert, and a member of the U.S. Academy of History." Good Lord! Vietnam sure seems to follow one, doesn't it? I was right on when I titled my book *A Dragon Lives Forever*. First Agent Orange poisoning, 25 years later,* now this. Looks like the book itself has done a number on me. For this, surely, I deserve more than the 20,000 copies that Owen Lock [my editor at Ballantine Books] said had been distributed by the time I was kidnapped. If I were writing fiction, I'd have a tough time fabricating more ludicrous—and more dangerous—charges. On the "bright" side (can I call anything bright in this context?), the *comandante* also wrote: "It seems to me that it would be useful if we talked about these issues, and I get to know you better, to know if this information gives a true image of you." The commander then asked that I respond in writing to those charges. "It is not necessary to lie," he wrote. "What is important is that you open a space (*abra un espacio*)" So . . . *writing for my life*. I guess you could say that's what I've been doing this afternoon. The most important (and maybe the last) letter of my life and I must write it in Spanish, no less. If only Earl Martin, my high-school Spanish teacher, could see this (or better, if he could help with the letter).

I've written the letter and kept it to one typewritten page. Responded to the charges, one by one. Tall Stranger leaves to deliver the letter tomorrow. This saga is becoming more and more insane. Hope I live to tell it. If so, I pray that I'll have this diary. One good thing: the food improved with the arrival of Tall Stranger. I was brought a big bowl of boiled beef and vegetables for breakfast, then fried beef, potatoes, and rice for lunch.

1840h: Have been chained, and barely able to change positions, almost 24 hours, and am shut in for the night. Dinner: grilled smoked beef, rice, potato, but I didn't have much appetite. Last night I wrote, "I'm dressed to march." I didn't really expect to march, but knew, somehow, to put on my warmest and most comfortable clothes. Fortunate, because then I was chained. I asked to be allowed to exercise a few minutes this afternoon, but was refused.

Sunday, 4 Dec., Day 73

1600h: Have been locked in this dark room since we arrived at this new camp at 1400h, and it looks like this is my new lifestyle. Moño had told me we

---

*I had filed with the U.S. Veteran's Administration for a disability due to Agent Orange poisoning during the Vietnam War just before I was kidnapped. Agent Orange was thought to be responsible for the allergy problems to which I referred earlier.—TRH

move out of the Valley of Death today—and made it sound like our new camp would be like a country club. Got up, had breakfast—a soup of smoked beef. Asked to go to the latrine, and was unlocked to do so. Got off the bunk, stood, walked for the first time in 36 hours. Hips, whole body was, and is, sore from being in the same position on that hard bunk so long. Tall Stranger had confiscated my backpack, so packed my things in a white plastic tote sack. Maybe 30 pounds. We marched down to Happy Valley, where we remade the sack into an improvised backpack. After 3½ hours we turned up another valley. The travel was tough. Lost trail en route and had to climb up a mountain, crawling through the brush. After 4½ hours, here we are. A plain, plank tabernacle-type building in the forest, with a river below that I can hear but haven't seen. FARC-EP-UP painted across the front. A big porchlike structure about 45 feet long and 20 feet wide, with a couple of rooms at each end. I have one. It's made of half-inch thick planks; you can see through cracks between them. Dimensions: 6½ feet long, 4½ feet wide, 6½ feet high. A wooden bunk covered with bamboo leaves takes up two thirds of the room. There's a wooden shelf with five boards along one wall. The floor is also plank. I can see that the sun has finally come out, but there's no place for light to come in. I can barely see what I'm writing. I'm wearing all four shirts, jacket, *ruana*, two shorts, three trousers, four socks, and I'm still cold. I have only one blanket of my seven. The others will arrive tomorrow. Tonight will be, I'm sure, one of the coldest of my life. Tall Stranger is here: will leave tomorrow with my letters to the FARC commander. All are obviously scared of him. Maybe I'll be treated more reasonably after he leaves tomorrow. When we left Death Valley, I forgot to bring my horseshoe. But I found another one on the trail. Luck? An omen? I hung it over the door of this room before I was locked away. But if I've been having luck lately, I dread my unlucky days.

1650h: Can barely see. I always thought that God—or whatever power— wouldn't allow a person to be punished for something he didn't do, especially not me. Boy, was I wrong. I see two ways of looking at my situation and future in light of the new developments: 1) the charges are so bad, the *comandante* will read my responses, invite me to visit him, then turn me loose. But is that being realistic? Just as likely—maybe more so—is 2) the charges are so bad—and there's no way I can really disprove them—that I'm dead. FARC won't turn me loose and either kills me, through some method, or moves me to some type of more permanent prison, where I stay forever. I guess that either way, I'm hoping these charges and my response bring everything to a head. I'm still not afraid of dying, not really. I think much more positively—of the day I'm released [rather] than of the day I'm executed. But the thought of months of being locked in a cold, dark room like I'm in now, with nothing to do but think, is more scary than death.

I'm writing with flashlight. That's something I hate to do. It may be months before I get more batteries.

2010h: Melena got my plate 1½ hours ago, said she'd return with dinner— but never showed up. Finally, Ramiro appeared outside. I asked and he said there was no dinner tonight! I don't believe him. They just forgot to feed the prisoner. The kitchen and, I think, eating area are in a different building that I haven't seen. I think most FARC sleep there, too. I had a small can—100 grams—of Nestlé's Lechya—sweetened condensed milk. Ramiro punched a hole, and that's my dinner. Ramiro is outside as my guard all night—even though I'm locked in this room. Things are *not* getting better.

Monday, 5 Dec., Day 74

0900h: A terrible chilling thought shot through me suddenly in the cold as I awoke from bad dreams at dawn. Beatings, even torture, may follow as my situation worsens steadily. FARC obviously takes the new accusations—that I'm a full colonel, counterguerrilla warfare expert, etc.—seriously. That's why I'm locked in this dark room. And I can't really disprove anything from here. Will FARC try to make me tell what they think I know? Rough play would not be beyond them. Imagine being tortured to divulge information that you don't have. Could they make me sing confessions? That would fit the picture. I'm not looking forward to anything pleasant soon. The accusations really leave me alone and helpless. I can no longer say that FARC has no charges against me. Now it does—anonymous, terrible charges. I'm now probably beyond any help that CIAT could give. Also the Colombian government and the U.S. government, since I'm not even what they charge me with. I might be better off if I were really a colonel: then there'd be an element with a strong interest in getting me freed, somehow. Hargrove—you're alone. You're totally alone and to survive, at least with your sanity, will be tough.

What about my sanity? I think I'm okay, but I can't be sure. I've been trying "silent screaming"—I scream in the darkness with all the emotion and energy I can—but not making a sound. Does it help? Probably not. I've tried prayer, but that doesn't seem to work either. The best way to pass time seems to be thinking about that wonderful day I'm released, being with Susan and the boys again. But then the fantasy ends and my situation seems harsher, more bleak than before. Like this morning. I was let out of the room to brush my teeth and empty my urine bottle. Was outside in early morning sunshine for four or five minutes. Then was shut back in the room. That was so bad I wished honestly that I'd never been let out. No breakfast this morning, after no dinner last night. Is FARC trying to purposely starve me? To weaken me? To destroy my will? Is this part of the new policy? Could be. It seems to fit the pattern. My last meal was a piece of fried beef intestine and some rice at 1500h yesterday.

I must write something on the bright side. Was worried that I'd soon run out of ink. Well, last night I found this blue ballpoint pen—looks new—under the shelf. Think I'll save it till the others run out. I can stand in this room, but can't pace. Lengthwise, it's three short paces, but I can't turn around because of the shelf at one end. Sitting on the bunk, I could be outside with one short step—but there's a wall and the door, padlocked from outside. Through cracks between the plank walls, I can see outside. A cow is grazing in the sun by the

Sophomore Tom Hargrove as a new corporal at
Texas A&M, 1964.

Tom and his wife, Susan, in the
palatial "Vi Thanh Hilton,"
SRV, 1990.

Tom Hargrove as a U.S. Army agricultural adviser, and lieutenant,
in Vietnam, 1969.

Tom watches a rodeo in the Colombian Llanos (eastern plains). (Photo courtesy of Alexandra Walter)

Tom examines a grave in the Colombian Llanos. (Photo courtesy of Alexandra Walter)

Tom with harvested rice, August 1994, on the north coast of Colombia. (Photo courtesy of Luis Fernando Pino)

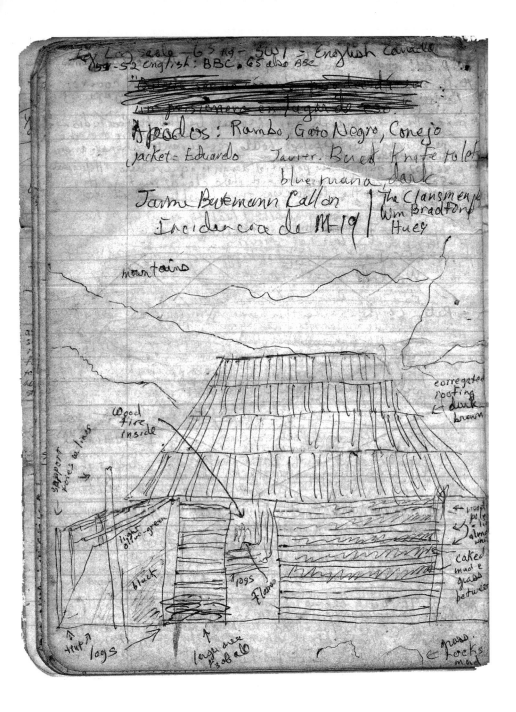

Tom Hargrove's sketch—from his notebook number 1 diary—of his cell/hut in the Valley of the Shadow.

Dic 1°/94.

Dr Thomas R Hargrave

Respetado Dr.

Jo saludo esperando se encuentre bien, a pesar de So situación.

Tenemos información que dice de usted que es Mayor Coronel (R) del ejército, héroe dela guerra del Vietnam, experto en la lucha contra-guerrillas, experto en comunicaciones y miembro de la academia de historia de EE.UU.

Me parece útil que usted nos hable sobre estos temas, para conocerlo mejor; pues como comprenderá si esta información se la manipulan a uno la información dará una imagen subjetiva. Quiero que usted me ayude a tener una imagen objetiva ampliando ésta información.

Tampronto como pueda escribame ampliando esos temas. No es necesario mentir, lo importante es que usted abra un espacio.

Con ésta son dos notas que lehenviado.

Hasta pronto.

Atte. El Comandante.

Letter from El Comandante de las FARC. In paragraph two he accuses Tom Hargrove of being a hero of the Vietnam War, a colonel in the U.S. Army Reserve, an expert in communications and counterguerrilla operations, and "a member of the American Historical Academy."

A blurry screen shot from the proof-of-life videotape the guerrillas made of Tom Hargrove in late October 1994. One of the female guerrillas in the background has trained her automatic rifle on Tom.

The FARC flag, from the author's checkbook diary.

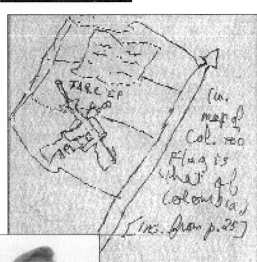

Tom and Susan Hargrove's sons, Geddie and Miles. Miles is holding a proof-of-life photo showing his father holding a copy of *El País* with the head-line visible.

Natalia's sketch of Tom Hargrove in his cell/hut. The details are correct but the dimensions are greatly enlarged. In actuality the hut was about 6 x 4 feet.

Marches of Silence to protest Tom's abduction in Palmira (2 December), near CIAT headquarters, and in Cali (9 December). (Photo courtesy of CIAT)

Members of CIAT's Graphic Arts and Communications staff greet Tom
at his home, 24 August 1995. They took along with them a small band
called a *papayera*. (Photo courtesy of Julio Cesar Martinez)

Almost all of
CIAT's 1,000
employees—
most wearing
Tom T-shirts
and many car-
rying sheaves
of rice—gath-
er for Tom's
return.
(Photos cour-
tesy of
Mauricio
Antorvesa)

Tom Hargrove in Cali, after his release (above), and after his first shave in 11 months, in his hometown, Rotan, Texas.

4 July 1995 backup notes.

9 July backup notes during reassembly.

a cofe roll. It's tasty
and chewy, but I'd
eat at least half of
it. I have to keep up my
strength. I must do everything possible to main-
tain my health, to not
get sick. Thank God I'm
not prone to getting
colds. Sleeping in the
cold dampness, with
rain splattering on
the canvas cover above
you, is a good way to get
sick.
0830. A soldier offers saba-
sabajon, a milky drink
made from aguardiente.
It smells good. I say I'll
try it con mucho gusto
tonight, but don't want
to drink in the morning.
I meet again w. Juaco.
"When will I be able to go
home?" "When we get perm-
ission from our superiors."
"Are they near, or far away?"
"Muy lejos." "Does that mean
I can't leave today?" "No,
that's not possible."
Juaco took a list of the
allergy medicines I need
and promises to get them—

if they are available in
that Indian village down
the valley. I doubt that
they will be.
I also ask if I can call
Susan, just to let her
know I'm alive and OK.
He'll have to check w. his
superiors. Will let me know
this afternoon.
I have in no way been
mistreated, threatened,
harassed, especially not
since coming to this company.
In fact, I'm treated w. a
great deal of respect. This
life is hard but the guerr
are making me as com-
fortable as they are.
In fact, these soldiers
seem so gentle.
It's not because
is so benevolent,
it's because
are Colombian
very humble
And of course
realize that
situations
like this, the
often
So that they can later
tear/break
break down, and
if that will happen
me

Pages 16 and 17 of the checkbook diary.

(But I couldn't believe)

(10-m)

~~The~~ second bridge ~~It~~ was like a ladder, 1m wide, thrown over the ~~river~~. Rotten wooden slats crissed-crossed two beams, every few feet. Nothing to hold to. A slip ~~and~~ would throw us into ~~that~~ icy rushing white among huge bald boulders. (Almost) certain death. I hold Juaco's hand and we crossed, step by step. "Don't look down!" Juaco shouts. Ridiculous. The steps aren't evenly spaced. I looked down, all the way, the white foam rushing below. crossed more streams until

We waded through more mud ~~and~~, at 2030h ~~reached~~ appeared a dark, empty hut. No need to describe ~~the hut~~; it is pretty much like the others. A pan of cold rice ~~topped~~ with chunks of salty beef ~~appeared~~. I wasn't hungry, but hadn't eaten for more than 12 hrs. I have to keep up my strength.

as my feet connected to the rotten steps, but trying to block out

Someone had provided a green a...

Notebook number 1 is written in a large hand and is fairly easy to read.

Notebook number 2 can be tough reading.

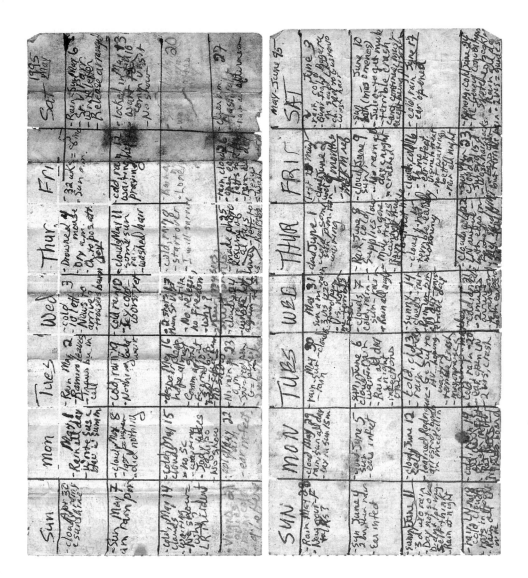

Two calendars.

Dr. Norman Borlaug
por Sra. Susan Hargrove
Ud de Comunicaciones
CIAT
AA 6713
Cali

página 1 de 2
13 de junio de 1995
En alguna parte de Colombia
de: Tom Hargrove/CIAT

Estimado Norm,
Espero que has recibido la última carta, que escribí en marzo o abril. Todavía estoy un preso. Hace 9 meces y unos días hoy me secuestraron. Pero nunca me ha rendido la esperanza que el día de la libertad, llegará. ¿Cuando? No se, pero debo mantener la fe.
Tengo un favor a pedir. ¿Es posible escribir unas líneas del libro que el Random House puede imprimir en la cubierta atrás (back cover) para la imprenta próxima? Eso mi editor me sugerió antes del secuestro. Iba a suplicarte en las vacaciones en los EE UU después de la liberación, pero la oportunidad todavía no ha venido. Mientras tanto, pienso que van a imprimir otra vez pronto
Sería agradecido por el favor

Dr. Norman Borlaug
por Sra. Susan Hargrove
página 2

P.D. Perdóneme. Se me olvidó a incluir las instrucciones a como enviar la escritura del libro. ¿Puedes enviarla a la Sra. Susan Hargrove Ud de Comunicaciones, CIAT, AA 6713, Cali? Ella puede recibir correo electrónico y fax también. Susan puede enviar lo que escribes al editor apropriado en el Random House. Me dicen que todavía Susan está en Colombia esperando para la liberación. ¡Qué prueba dura para ella! Ojalá que disfrutaste el libro. Me pregunto como

Sra. Susan Hargrove
Ud de Comunicaciones
CIAT
AA 6713
Cali
3 de junio de 1995

Querida Susan,
Hoy es 7 días después del envío del paquete a ti con la foto grabación, etc. Estoy esperando para la respuesta.
Ayer fue el aniversario: 9 meces del secuestro.
El verano, como la libertad, todavía no ha llegado.
Me dicen que combate nuevo ha empezado a través de Colombia aun en Bogotá pero de eso, se muy poco. Me pregunto como los consecu...

Sr. Tom Hargrove Sr.
por Sra. Susan Hargrove
Ud de Comunicaciones
CIAT
AA 6713
Cali
3 de junio de 1995

Estimados Pedro, Becky, Ra...,
el verano, como la libertad, viene algún día, pero no se cuando. Mientras tanto, puse asegurarles que vivo todavía. No me he rendido la esperanza que la libertad vendrá algún día.

Unsent letters, written on scraps of paper, to Norman Borlaug, Susan Hargrove, and Tom Hargrove Sr.

porch, not 20 feet away. It's 1100h and sunny, but cold in here. My feet are so cold. If only I had a deck of cards I could play solitaire. Or something to read. But my health is still good, and I think my spirits are as high as anyone's could be in this situation. I'm trying not to look at my watch all the time. Maybe I'll see the comandante in a week, and maybe that will end this. I'll survive.

Tall Stranger showed me a word in the dictionary that he said describes his job: *recompense*. Makes little sense, though. Mosquitoes are bad—you can't stop them, they come through the cracks. Slept in ski mask last night as much for protection against mosquitoes as against the cold. And I was so very, very cold. Unlike in my tent, I can't build a fire. And God help me if [the place caught on fire]. I'd be dead for sure, surrounded on six sides by dry planks, and on a mattress of dry bamboo leaves. After four pairs of socks I wrapped my feet in the end of the blanket, then enclosed my lower legs and feet in the plastic tote sack. But I hurt, ached from cold all night.

1430h: It seems more likely that my worst fears may be materializing. Lunch was finally brought at 1400h—exactly 23 hours after my last meal. It was a plate of rice and beans—but with four (yes, four) beans. Plus 10 pieces of bean "skin." I asked for more beans and Judi said there were no more. Are they now going to starve me, weaken me though hunger? Looks that way, but why? I can think of only one reason: so I'll break and "confess" . . . earlier. What a dangerous and ironic situation. Being prepared to confess—talk—when I have nothing, absolutely nothing, to confess. I decided to finish all the rice, because I may not be fed tonight. But the girl took my plate before I finished the rice. I saw Tall Stranger. I thought my letter might be with the *comandante* by now, but it hasn't even left. Maybe part of this is to show Tall Stranger how hard-ass this FARC unit is on *gringos*. Have been in this room 24 hours now, no end in sight. Maybe can learn how to sleep, others do that in times of stress. That would be wonderful.

1820h: It will be hard to even begin to explain the highs and lows of being a hostage, once I'm free. I think it also has something to do with being on the edge, so close to death. Real death, the permanent kind, as well as living death. Just before Tall Stranger left this afternoon I thought: I should give the *comandante* a neutral way to check my past even if it's impossible to do from here. I need proof of something that I couldn't have done if I were in the army and that I couldn't fake likely, even if I had U.S. intelligence resources behind me. But what? Then it hit me: ACE. In 1988 I received the ACE Professional Award* and the ACE International Award. I wrote rapidly, and I'm sure in atrocious Spanish, a memo to the *comandante* describing ACE and those awards. Wrote that he could have his people in the States ask who is an ACE member at the Ag Info Service of any major agricultural university and ask them to

*ACE is the Agricultural Communicators in Education, a U.S.-based 700-member professional society of agricultural editors. The ACE Professional Award is the highest honor awarded to a single agricultural communicator each year. I was then at the IRRI in the Philippines and was the first agricultural communicator to receive that award while working outside the USA.—TRH

check if Hargrove really received those awards. Also gave addresses of Ashley Wood and Joe Marks. Also wrote that my name is in the senior staff of any IRRI Annual Report from 1973 through 1991 and told where this could be found in Colombia. Got it to Tall Stranger just as he was leaving. Almost missed him, and that scared and depressed me a lot. Maybe this will work. Agricultural communication has been my life's work. Now maybe that profession, through ACE, will save my life. Tall Stranger said my letter, and that memo, would reach the *comandante* tomorrow (he doesn't know that Moño still maintains [that] the *comandante*—and any populace—is four days away). Somehow I feel that memo will help my chances of release—or, at least, survival—immensely. Even if it doesn't impress the comandante, getting the information to him makes me feel more confident, like I'm fighting with real ammunition. And *that* could save my life. The atmosphere changed after Tall Stranger left. I was as low as I've been, and that's pretty damned low. (Write more later). Dinner: rice and beans and one small trout.

1950h: The FARC are loud tonight—too loud. I wonder if a supply shipment arrived today, *with liquor*. I hope there's no shooting. Not tonight, they've built a big fire in the room adjoining this one—also entirely wooden plank. If they [set fire to] that room, with me padlocked in this one . . . well, I won't need to worry about release for Christmas, or even execution, anymore.

1955h: Uh-oh. I just heard that cold sound—one that'll stay with me all my life, of a rifle bolt sliding, loading a cartridge.

2025h: The first shot of the night was just fired, at nothing, in the forest. Please, Moño, keep this group under control.

Tuesday, 6 Dec., Day 75

0810h: Things quieted down after last note last night. No more shooting. Am sitting in my bunk. Most guerrillas are still asleep. What a difference. Yesterday, when Tall Stranger was still here, all were up and busy by 0630h, repairing things, cutting vines, shrubs, getting the camp shipshape. Thank God my own six blankets arrived yesterday. One of my blankets was stolen, but I heard Leidi and Melena complaining like hell to Moño that I have more than my share of cover, so I didn't complain. Those girls—and I do mean girls, not women— are so shallow, and they'll never get brighter. Judi, the new girl, is even dumber. Anyway, last night was terribly cold. What if I'd had only one blanket, like the night before? This camp is built within a bamboo grove, with forest all around. Probably invisible from the air. We're even more remote, less accessible than in the Valley of Death. We moved here for still more increased security after my status changed to bad-ass professional commie killer. A sign across the front reads *"Escuela Entrenamiento"* or Training School. My little room is designated *"Biblioteca,"* Library. All the lumber planks, posts, etc., seem hewn by hand. One thing that makes this room eerie, spooky, is that the sun is shining brightly outside, but it's cold, damp, and dark inside. But light shines clearly through the cracks between the planks. That makes it like a dark jail cell with vented, luminiscent bars for walls. To read I must hold my dictionary sideways so that lines on the page are parallel with the stripes of light. I can stand on a rock, used as a doorstop, and see over the front door to a beautiful mountain coming down the other side. I think it would all be better without the beams of sunlight.

0900h: Judi brought me coffee and let me out for five minutes to brush my teeth, empty my jar, etc., at 0830h, but now I'm locked back in the room. Seems to be no one around but Judi, my guard. The others stay around *la rancha*—kitchen building, which I've never seen—a lot. Moño told me to have letters ready to send out this morning. Lord, I hope they haven't left for Happy Valley already, having forgotten about my mail. Have letters to Susan, Havener, and the Red Cross. In the letters to Susan and Havener, I specifically mention how *pleased* I was to hear *over the radio news*, that my earlier letters had been received. Hope they read between the lines to what I couldn't write: *Keep up the publicity, CIAT. Keep my name on the radio, so it will be embarrassing for FARC if I disappear.* I'm uneasy, of course, that even what little I wrote will cause the censor to kill the letters and Susan and Havener won't hear anything from me. The letter to the Red Cross asks for some books, magazines to read. Moño said that FARC has notified the Red Cross about me. I doubt that, and I don't really expect FARC to deliver the letter, but . . . I also asked the Red Cross to send me a Bible, preferably with Old and New Testaments and an index. I also wrote to Havener, "When I return I want to discuss some problems with CIAT's image, *especially its acronym*, among certain groups in Colombia. It has caused me many problems." Hope it's clear I mean CIA—and hope that may give all a hint of the current problem.

0925h: How I hate this room. I'm so cold. And I hate looking through the cracks at a world of warm, happy trees and grass and cows and sunshine just outside. That's the cruelest thing about solitary confinement in this room. And I can almost feel how toasty warm that sunshine is just by watching it through these cracks. It falls heavy to the ground outside. Susan, Tom G., and Miles—God, how I want to be with you. The days in Death Valley seem almost idyllic now—I could walk outside, in the sunshine, when we had it.

1000h: Don't feel sorry for yourself, Hargrove. You know it can get worse. And you were outside 1½ hours yesterday, and you know you'll get out of this cell—for an hour or so, anyway, sometime today. And quit looking at your damned watch. That only stretches it out. And I feel so much more positive than yesterday. Don't get jubilant, Hargrove. You're still far from free. In fact, your situation is the worst since you were kidnapped. You've been locked in this room for 44 hours, during which, you were allowed to stand outside—chained—for an hour and a half and it looks like that's all you'll get today. Yeah, but at least I know I'm not being purposely starved. That phase is over, for now, at least. Sure, but what happens if the *comandante* decides that you're really an undercover colonel—like has been reported to him. All bets are off then.

The subject of *A Dragon Lives Forever*, my book, came up yesterday. After all, it's now one of my main defenses. "Are you writing a book about *this* experience?" Moño asked. "No, of course not. It's too boring," I said. Careful,

Hargrove. Don't trust him. Don't trust any of these bastards. All he's done is give you subhuman treatment, often inhumane treatment. Remember Mutt and Jeff. Is that what's happening? Tall Stranger plays Bad Guy, Moño "saves" me; I spill my guts to Moño. But I have nothing to spill. He doesn't know that. Be careful. Damned careful. Don't be naive. You're in a perfect set-up position. You've been beaten down a lot, and your treatment has gone steadily worse. You've been totally isolated from your—or any normal—culture for close to three months. But what could they get from me? Nothing. But that's the scary thing. Will they try to make you admit to something you haven't done? Isn't that what happened in the Soviet Union in the thirties? There's a funny thing about punishment, and guilt. Have I read this? Or is it only from my experience here? If you're punished enough, and I guess, in increasingly severe increments, you begin to feel like you deserve it. Why?

1135h: I had to look at my watch. Am I losing my reason? Or am I reasoning better than ever? If this is all a charade—a cruel game to trick me or break me for some reason—then I've been falling perfectly into the trap. Apply more punishment, then relieve it a little, and I'm grateful, to Jeff, no less. I've told both Moño and the *comandante* (and thus Tall Stranger) my really weak point. My paranoia about confinement in this dark room. And the cold dampness of it. And where am I? For 45 hours now, and I was so happy, and grateful as a puppy for that 1½ hours—chained—outside the room yesterday. And for receiving a "regular" meal. This is a very dangerous game. It might be less dangerous if I knew why it's being played. All I know is who makes the rules. I'm not the colonel they want. But is it possible they want to make me . . . that? For propaganda or whatever purposes?

1420h: This is getting crazier—and scarier. Judi brought lunch at 1400h. A bowl of rice with maybe two teaspoons of puréed squash on top. That's all. A repeat of yesterday. Judi let me out to urinate. Moño came by. I asked about the food. "That's what we all had," he said. Bullshit, of course. Said I could go outside, chained, at three P.M., but that it was "too cold" this morning. This room, of course, is where it's too cold. Will I get a reasonable meal tonight? We'll see. What are they trying to do? *This* makes me feel, even more, that I'm not about to be turned loose, that all of this is some insane, preplanned hoax for some reason. And the target of all this right now is my will, my spirit.

1820h: Dinner: a piece of fried bread and a cup of cold chocolate made with water, not milk. Remembered that copies of my honorable discharge and DD214* are on file in Cali. Wrote to *comandante* with enclosed note to Susan, in English and Spanish, to get and give to FARC representative.

[*I received, by courier mail, the 22 Oct. video and instructions on how and when to communicate with FARC via a two-meter-band radio.—SSH*]

---

*Both are official documents that prove I was separated from the U.S. Army 25 years before.—TRH

Wednesday, 7 Dec., Day 76

Lukewarm coffee at 0730. Letters to *comandante* to Moño. Stayed in bunk till ten to experiment with shutting off brain. Last night I was numb—was aware, but shut off thinking process. No, it shut itself off automatically. I knew, but didn't try to turn it back on. Was asleep by 9:30. Best sleep since kidnap. Can I learn to control my mind, turn it off as a weapon, a survival mechanism? What a blessing that would be. Today, my fourth in the Valley of the Shadow (of Death) is better, so far. Yesterday at this time—11:30—I was half-crazy, even though I seem to have been reasoning okay. Did the mind shutdown make the difference? I'll try again—but when things get bad again.

Leidi let me out six to seven minutes at 10:30. Found and smuggled back in two one-foot pieces of electric wire. Trash comes in handy. A piece of plastic holds my soap—but it also hangs over a crack that lets the guards see inside. The day outside is dark and cold—but my eyes had to adjust to the darkness when I returned to this room. Or should I call it a cell? Yeah, that's what it is. At 1450h yesterday, I was let out, chained, to 1800h. But prior, I spent 47½ hours in this cell with one hour outside, and I was grateful as a puppy for that hour. Try not to let them get you in that shape again, Hargrove.

1400h: Already used the piece of wire I found—to measure ends of my bunk. Gustavo helped me turn bunk around where higher end is at wall where light comes through cracks. Gustavo's my favorite, even though he stole my flashlight.

1450h: Leidi brought "lunch"—eight pieces of Aladino hard candy, each the size of a thumbnail. I asked for lunch. Said no lunch—economizing. Did not offer breakfast either. No doubt, now they're starving me. Going to feed me so little, I'm weak. To break me, I guess. But *why*? I feel, more and more, that I'll lose this diary—they'll search me and take it. I'm making a backup calendar on the backs of peso checks. Do they really think I'm a colonel, or is that, too, part of this charade? If they're really checking me, and will release me when I've proved my past, *why starve me*? Releasing a skeletal man won't help FARC's image. Could they want me to die in captivity so they can say I died of natural causes, not executed? Death in captivity looks more likely all the time.

My next letter to Susan is ready. I had written on 5 Dec., after the Mutt-and-Jeff treatment, my spirits having risen because I have reason to believe that we will be together for Christmas. Keep up your faith and hope. It's a shame that I can't explain more. That's not fair to her. I realized when I saw the Mutt-and-Jeff [treatment], the food cut off, I have less reason than ever to expect a Christmas release. I rewrote the letter and told her to talk to boys and do what she thinks is best for Christmas. Oh God. What's happening? And I must quit chewing the hard candies, only suck on them, make them last longer.

1640h: Moño let me out on the chain at 1515h. Leidi brought dinner at 1600. A plate of rice with chopped meat and a mixture of green beans and cassava. Not much but the closest to a real meal in 48 hours.

1945h: If I leave Shadow Valley alive—far from certain—big changes in my life will have to follow; postkidnap will be bad enough, but the FARC charges of being a colonel undercover, etc., will probably follow me forever—at least if I continue in international agriculture as a profession. I'm tainted, no matter what the truth is. This career is probably shot.

Thursday, 8 Dec., Day 77

Am I losing my mind? I've thought so much of ways to prove I spent the last four years with IRRI, not the army, yet only at about 5:30 this morning did I think, in a state of half sleep, of something so obvious: the April '91 issue of *National Geographic* has my photo in Vietnam—the caption tells it all. I got up and, by candlelight, wrote Letter 4 to the FARC *comandante* with a note to Susan to give a copy of that issue to the FARC representative. Also pointed out all the research papers I'd written at IRRI with a note to María del Carmen [my secretary at CIAT] and Nathan Russell [CIAT editor] to provide copies. Used 1½ sheets = three pieces of precious paper. But no one would come to my cell. Moño finally walked by at 0730h. He'd already sent someone to Happy Valley with mail. So too late. A big disappointment. Maybe can go tomorrow. But if FARC *comandante* is really serious, I've already sent enough evidence to make my case. Asked for breakfast, got a plate of fried rice and a cup of warm milk. Crawled back in covers and—how wonderful—slept till Leidi woke me with lunch at 1230h. Rice and lentils, and plenty. I ate a lot in case no dinner tonight. Did I sleep because of "mind shutdown"? Maybe, but also I hardly slept all night because I was thinking about food. Grilled steaks, fried fish and chicken, etc. Also rained all night and was terribly wet and cold. Damn whoever stole one of my blankets.

1910h: Dinner was a plate of rice with some chopped-beet-cassava mixture.

2000h: All the guerrillas have had *candelas*, buckets of coals, in their rooms. I asked Moño and he brought me one tonight. I was probably better off not knowing how dangerous they are. A bucket of glowing coals and pieces of dry bamboo that I blow on every five minutes, spraying sparks in this tiny wooden room with a bed of dry bamboo leaves. But I'm warm for the first time since moving into the cell.

[Miles Hargrove and Peter Greiner received a threatening call from FARC demanding that we follow instructions to communicate by radio.—SSH]

Friday, 9 Dec., Day 78

1215h: Judi brought coffee at 0750. Asked for and got breakfast. Boiled potatoes and pasta. Went back to sleep and woke at eleven. How wonderful to sleep away three hours of daylight solitary confinement. Then only four hours until I'm outside the cell for three hours unless FARC changes the rules again. If only I can control my mind, make it continue—it's survival, a way to stay sane. Then I can stand the night if I can get warm—especially my feet—before going to bed. Somehow, lying in darkness, thinking, is better than sitting in the bunk or standing, thinking, in the semidarkness of this cell during the day. Prisoners describe cells as light and dark bars. Mine is dark with vertical bars of light—cracks between the planks. Lunch at twelve was rice and potatoes and not much of either. I don't think they'll feed me sardines or even fake tuna again. I eat all I'm given, even if I don't want it, because they may start starving me again. Judi is from Popayán, just joined FARC, and is here waiting for the next training course. Will change soon from black [rest of page is illegible].

I had a strange problem—excessive urination from mid—or late—Oct. until early Dec. (about when came to Shadow Valley. Would urinate 20 [times] a night). There was a 375-ml liquor bottle outside and I started measuring: 1.3 liters morning of 4 Nov.; 300 ml 5 Nov.; 0.94 liters 6 Nov.; 800 ml 7 Nov.; 300 ml 8 Nov.; 1 liter 9 Nov. I hit 1.5 liters several times around last week of Nov., then suddenly down to maybe half a liter in 24 hours over last week. Does it have anything to do with weight loss? At about Week 7, [bowel movements] changed from one a day to one every two days. Funny, all I had planned to do when leaving Death Valley: pour brandy on Juaco, etc. But when we left, I forgot about it all, just packed and marched. Was halfway to Death Valley when I remembered, and turned around for a last look. By then, I couldn't even see Juaco's grave. Of course, I had been chained in tent for the previous 36 hours and I couldn't have poured the brandy because no longer could move about. I thought, of course, that leaving Death Valley would be to freedom. But it wasn't, it was to a worse form of imprisonment. Have started moving papers. *Retén* story with letter from FARC *comandante*. Summarized Notebook 2 on peso checks. Must wear my long green socks—the burned ones—at night so always have ready.

Asked for more food at dinner. Was told there's nothing. Then one of FARC walked by and I heard Melena ask, "Do you want to try our soup?" I wasn't even given soup.

Saturday, 10 Dec., Day 79

Christmas is two weeks one day away. How I hope and pray to be with Susan and the boys then. Thank God, in a way, that this cell is so isolated. I can never hear a radio and thus, no longer hear Christmas music. But if I'm here Christmas, well, I have no choice but to survive, do I? And I'd better prepare myself. Somehow, I've built myself up [to believe] that once I clear these ridiculous army charges, I'll be set free. I have nothing to assure, even indicate, that I was held—and not freed—two months before the army charges.

Dinner last night was rice and a thin piece of salted beef about the size of my palm. Mostly gristle and cartilage, but I save and chewed it like gum off and on for several hours. Made a mistake this morning. Judi brought coffee at 0730 and I drank it, but I didn't go back to sleep. Have had coffee last two mornings, then slept. The coffee is made with milk and is the best thing here. 4½ more hours till I can sit outside for three hours, chained. The Mutt and Jeff worked with solitary confinement. I can't help but be elated—grateful, even—to FARC for three hours chained outside this cell.

Lost the old blue ballpoint pen yesterday. How, I can't imagine. Terribly depressing. Now have two: the new one I found in the cell (thank God!) and the old black one. Shouldn't have written so soon about the urine problem. At least 1 liter since seven P.M. yesterday, mostly last night. I think this from body burning fat and maybe tissue.

Received the letter from FARC *comandante* with the army charges only one week ago today. Seems like a month. So many charges, all bad.

1500h: Moño let me out chained at 1200, but he took my shelf from my cell. Some bullshit about will give me a better one. What the hell, I can't do anything about it. Gustavo gave me a *candela*, so I'm sitting on the porch nurturing a fire, showed Moño my urine—almost 1.5 liters (I measured with liquor bottle later). He agreed that much urine didn't seem normal. I told him it's a sign of malnutrition. Got a couple of spoonsful of meat at lunch, with rice and potatoes. Then at 1400, Judi brought coffee with milk and sugar and six crackers. Moño must have ordered it. We'll see. Did a stupid thing. Judi is doing laundry. I gave her my long green socks to wash. Then thought: Why? Sick feeling. I need to wear them when I leave. It turned out okay, though. I saw her with them, hanging them to dry, and asked her for them to dry by my fire. They're almost dry. If I leave tomorrow, I can wear them.

1600h: Found my pen outside. Will be more careful; I seem to misplace things. Maybe hunger and being shut up affect my mind a bit.

1910h: In cell. Moño never brought the replacement shelf. Judi said she would sweep my cell this afternoon. I didn't want it but couldn't stop her. She closed door while sweeping. All my things were on the bunk, waiting for the shelf. Anyway, my ski mask was missing and I'm almost sure she took it. I can't believe these people, stealing essentials from a prisoner. That ski mask is more than decoration—it's part of survival. And I can't replace it. There's not much I can do to protect myself. I can't lock up my things in my cell. I can't keep others from entering, nor can I tell Moño he can't take my shelf.

Sunday, 11 Dec., Day 80

1115h: That old Elvis Presley song keeps running through my mind—not on purpose, though. I just realized it this morning. The refrain is "I'll be home for Christmas." Only, in the last line of the song it's followed by ". . . if only in my dreams." Two weeks till Christmas. It rained all night. The roof leaks. My bunk is wet, also socks [illegible]. It's overcast outside, and cold wind is blowing. There's barely enough light in this cell to write. I can't copy Notebook to Checkbook. I can hold out—mentally, emotionally, physically—until Christmas, but God, please let me spend Christmas with my family. If that's not written, I'll survive, but I fear—yes, fear—Christmas Eve and Christmas Day.

Will I be let out of this cage at noon today, like yesterday? Probably not. Yesterday, Moño came to take my shelves. It's so humiliating, watching the door, waiting to hear the chain rattle, a key in the lock. Like a dog, except scared, and scrambling to hide the diary when footsteps approach. And like a stray, homeless dog, or a whipped dog, grateful for any treatment that's not cruel. Ready to lick the hand that lets me out of this cage, ignoring the 20 feet of chain. I had breakfast—hot chocolate and an *arepa*. Coffee, too, but I poured the coffee through a crack in the floor, hoping to go back to sleep. Didn't work.

Shadow Valley is higher than Death Valley, Moño says, and even colder. I don't think there's been 10 minutes straight of sunshine since arriving here.

A slogan spray-painted across the front of this building is *"Estudiando y combatiendolo y ganamos la victoria."* I don't think that's even correct Spanish. I kept a *candela* bucket burning most of yesterday afternoon and last night. Again, gratitude for [their] being less cruel. Please may I have one today, I'm so cold, and I need to dry my bunk, socks, *ruana*. Gail lent me a cassette book of the "self-help" guy [Robert Fulghum] who wrote *All I Really Need to Know I Learned in Kindergarten*. He gave his "11 elements." One was "always take the scenic route." That made a lot of sense. One reason I took the Puerto Tejada road on 23 Sept, even though I was late.

The only good thing about being locked in: It gives me more time to hide my diary if someone approaches.

Since coming to the Valley of the Shadow, my guards have increased from 7 to 10 or 11. New ones are Victor, Julian, and Judi. Julian is a jackass who sings loudly and badly all the time, showing off. The others are just jackasses.

2000h: Locked in wooden cell with a *candela* bucket of fire. How terribly dangerous. But I don't think, given everything else, that I'm destined to die in an accidental fire. Anyway, there's a fire in every room here; I may as well be comfortable, too. Besides, I know the inhabitant of this room isn't stoned or drunk. And building a fire, caring for it, keeping it going, that's the most interesting, satisfying thing I have to do. Comfort, something soothing about a fire. I don't think so much about my own situation when I'm keeping a fire going. And besides all that—it's awfully cold! Moño also likes fires and likes to come help me with mine. Today I asked Moño if he thought I'd spend Christmas with my family. For the first time he didn't give me bullshit about freedom in a few days. He shook his head and said, *"¿Quien sabe?* [Who knows?]" It didn't bother me a bit because I know things look bad. I'm going to be here Christmas; I may as well start accepting it. I wish I had a Bible; I'd like to read the Nativity part on Christmas Eve. Lunch: rice and beans. Dinner: a soup with trout. Good fire.

Monday, 12 Dec., Day 81

1235h: Breakfast: A hominy in sweet milk. I ate part, rinsed the rest. Made two little bags from plastic sacks, and stored hominy, tied with pieces of electrical wire I found. Can't have done it without the wire. Save things! Helps insulate my bunk. I also found/saved half of a plastic burlap bag. I sit on it when outside. Lunch: rice and lentils. "Out" time is three to six P.M. But Moño let me out at twelve two days ago; two P.M. yesterday; two P.M. Sunday. So I sit here listening, waiting. Worse, in a way, than straight three to six out.

When you live in darkness and filth like animals, that's how your captors start to treat you—even though they make you live that way. I wanted Judi to empty ashes.

"Would you please empty—"

"*No!*" she said, and ran away.

Thought I was going to ask her to empty the piss bucket I'm sure.

1300h: Oh no, I can see through the cracks actual sunshine outside. That's so rare and I need it.

2030h: Dinner: rice and boiled potatoes. Am in cell with fire of wood and *chuzco*, one of three types of bamboo here. Judi threw away, apparently, my shorts and olive handkerchief. When I asked, [illegible] she said, "*No me moleste* [Don't bother me.]" Insolent little bitch. But, *calmese*, Hargrove. Remember, you're a prisoner here. . . . They treat you as a dirty creature that lives in a dark cold hovel with a urine jar under the bunk.

Tuesday, 13 Dec., Day 82

1935h: I'm chained but sitting in cell with door open, waiting for Ramiro, the first guard tonight, to return, unchain me, and lock me in for the night. I feel so much safer writing in this diary when I'm locked inside (and thus, others are locked outside).

Breakfast was two pieces of fried dough. Saved half of one, thank God. Lunch was rice and beans, and dinner, a small plate with rice, three slices of fried potato, and a couple of spoons of beets. I asked for more. "*Apago, Don Tomás.*" Ate the dough and feel a little better, but am still hungry. Also eating the hominy I saved.

This A.M. was very clear, could see, clearly, a snowcapped mountain to the south. Párramo [cold and mountainous] is name, I think. Moño let me out on chain at 0845. Said someone would take me to river to bathe and wash clothes later, but that never happened.

Ironic, but I may be better off, psychologically, for the time in solitary confinement. I'd go crazy, spending the day on a 15-foot chain, had I not spent a far worse time locked up in this dark room. Now I'm almost happy to be chained outside. The flip side of that is, of course, what happens when I go into prolonged isolated confinement in semidarkness again? And it will happen, I'm sure.

Wrote Susan today, asking to contact Red Cross and see if she can send me books, a Bible maybe, some games. Slipped in a request for a notebook. Read to Moño, he took to send out tomorrow.

2045h: There's obviously a playing field nearby. Can hear the FARC playing volleyball late in afternoon, laughing. Also hear laughing now, but can't imagine what is going on. Hard to have indoor games at night without electricity. I have a headache, probably from not enough food plus blowing on the fire.

I probably inhale more smoke blowing on these fires to keep them going than when I smoked.

What I really need right now is a big slice of rare beef. Dream on, Hargrove.

Wednesday, 14 Dec., Day 83

0900h: Judi brought coffee at 6:30, which I put under my bunk to drink cold, later. I tried to go back to sleep, but didn't. Worried so much that I'd agreed that I didn't want breakfast—she asked something, fast, two times, and I finally said no. My stomach was growling. I was hungry. But breakfast now means more than a morning meal. I can get by on half what I'm served, and always save the rest for reserve. Like last night.

Found a plastic vitamin jar yesterday and cleaned it. Then—miracle—I saw something white. It was the lid. I put both away. How will I use them? I don't know.

But breakfast today was that awful hominy in sweet milk. I ate half and put the rest without liquid in the vitamin jar. Will rinse milk off later. Without the milk, in this cold, it should store well. Lord, I hope Moño lets me out of this cell again today.

Am studying my Spanish, especially preparing for the meeting with FARC *comandante*. Learning new words like *confutar* [disprove]. Will there be a meeting? Before Christmas? Was the *comandante* serious about *confutando* the charges? Or is the [charge of my being] "colonel" a fabrication for some reason? Will FARC decide I'll be more ready, mentally and psychologically, for their type of meeting after Christmas? If FARC is serious, I've given enough information to refute the allegations. If FARC is serious.

1000h: Eleven days till Christmas. I have strong and conflicting emotions that make little sense. It's crazy, but a part of me instinctively hates to see each new day—because that's one day closer to Christmas and I'm not free. And one day closer to those two days I dread so. Yet, if time doesn't pass, FARC can't review my case and release me for Christmas. And if I'm not released, it's best to get the entire process out of the way—have Christmas come and go—ASAP. Less pain that way.

1920h: At eleven, I asked to go to the latrine. It was a ruse to get out of this cell. Then, since I was out, I asked if I could stay out. It worked. Lunch was a small bowl of potato soup with only a couple of pieces of potato. I had Victor take me to the stream to bathe and wash clothes. No sun. Cold.

My hair was so dirty, I used two handfuls of shampoo before I could make suds. Saw *la rancha* on the way. Not much. Washed clothes. Set clothes out to dry and studied Spanish rest of afternoon. Am practicing my meeting with the FARC commander—if it happens. Dinner was a plate of cold rice, three small cold boiled potatoes, and a cold cup of *agua panela*. I'm always hungry now and never throw away any food. Are they feeding me less than before? Yes— and no meat, sardines, tuna. I know they have it, but now that I can't see, there isn't any. So less total food = less protein. And I think my body has used all its fat reserves, so I need food as immediate fuel.

If the meals I fantasize are 10 percent as good as I imagine them, I'll have a gourmet's vacation when I get out of here. Recently started thinking a lot about chocolate. And, strangely, strawberries and blackberries [*mora*] and *mora* juice and milkshakes. Chocolate cakes but not ice cream. It's too cold. *Leaving Cheyenne* was never very practical, but now it's virtually impossible; I'm locked in a cell most of the time, and chained the rest.

But I still can't figure why FARC is keeping me so hungry. It's deliberate. I ask for more food all the time. The answer is always "*Acabó* [finished]." Is it merely selfishness? Feed me less = more for them? Or do they want me hungry, weaker for a purpose? This deliberate starvation doesn't strengthen my faith in a Christmas release. But it may be simply selfishness. Remember, these are not very sophisticated people.

2015h: I just had a shock. I don't know how to take this. I had one of the bags of hominy, plus the plastic jar I filled this A.M. I looked in the bamboo leaves that compose my mattress. Couldn't find the bag. Then I opened the jar. EMPTY, and has been washed clean—so someone searched my things while I was gone. And took the food I had put away. Why? And was the search just for food? I was terrified to look further, but did. The notebook pages were still where I left them. I have to think about this. My peso checkbook is still here. Also the draft letter to veterans of Chuang Thien Province. Apparently, only the food was taken. But everything must have been searched. And now I'm hungrier than ever. All evening I'd been thinking about eating that hominy just before turning in.

Thursday, 15 Dec., Day 84

0920h: How utterly frustrating. Melena brought breakfast—a greasy *arepa* and coffee. When she returned for the cup, I asked if she could let me out.

"Not until Moño returns." He's in Happy Valley.

"But last night I asked Moño in front of Leidi and he said, 'Certainly.' Will you go ask Leidi?"

She agreed and left. But 20 feet from my cell, Javier stopped her and started playing grab-ass. They kiss and rub one another for 10 minutes. Finally, Melena left but probably forgot.

1840h: Moño was here and let me out at 10. Later, I asked for water. Melena went to get [it]. Took jar and my water bottle—a 75-ml liquor bottle I brought from Death Valley, returned the bottle without a top. Said it didn't have a top when I gave to her. Bullshit. So now I can't use the bottle like before— can't put behind my head in the bunk.

"*¿Porque lo hizo* [Why did you do that]?" I asked. She laughed. I guess it's continuing revenge for not playing ball when she would visit my tent in Death Valley (I should have said, "It wouldn't be fair to you. I'm a prisoner and

I can't give you the life you deserve.") Plus calling her on stealing my razor and refusing to lend her my mirror.

Cut another notch in my belt. Found and strung more wire across my cell to hang clothes, both to store and to dry.

Christmas is 10 days from tomorrow—but really two weekends and one workweek. I should either be out of here within nine days, or I'm in real bad trouble. I still find it hard to believe that I got into all this just driving to work.

My Justin Roper boots were left in Death Valley, to be brought here later. They're still not here. I haven't reminded Moño because if I don't have the Ropers, I have to wear the tall rubber boots out of here. Talked with Javier this afternoon. He wants me released so he can go home to Corintho for Christmas. Said that guerrillas cannot resign; they must stay in FARC for life.

Friday, 16 Dec., Day 85

Today is three months exactly of captivity. At 0830h Gustavo rattled my door. Came to say good-bye. Is being transferred. Couldn't open the door, so we talked through it. I didn't know he was leaving. That tiny little Indian has been the closest thing to a friend I've had. He's helped me with so many things: fires, bringing wood and *chuzco*, more food, etc. I'd seldom ask him for anything, especially in front of the others, because was afraid it might cause him trouble (i.e., soft on the *gringo*).

"I hope you're released soon," he said through the door. *"Hasta mañana."*

"You mean you're returning tomorrow?"

"No. Hasta luego."

I feel a little more empty, a bit more lonely. Lord, I've been lonely. Three months without a friend, even someone to talk with. Three months without speaking English—except to curse those who chained me the night of 22 Nov.

I guess Gustavo carried my letter to Susan, with Red Cross references, to wherever he's going. I thanked him sincerely for the help he's given, wished him luck. I could have cried. I did. As a prisoner, I can. . . .

1935h: In cell. A lot of things seem to be going wrong. I had the new pen I found and cherish in my front pocket. Sat down and broke off the point. I'm writing by holding the pen together. Lunch was rice and lentils. Dinner a soup of noodles and potatoes. Now that I'm chained and locked in 24 hrs/day, I have no more chances to steal or pilfer. If I could push Christmas back, say, three weeks, to increase the chances that I'd be home with my family, I'd do it. I talked with Moño 1½ hours today, about rice, IRRI, CIAT, Vietnam, how I got into this field. Longest conversation in three months by far. Hope it did some good, but I don't think he has any say. He commands a squad of 14 guerrillas, normally.

No one brought me breakfast or even coffee or chocolate, this A.M. "Economic," they said. Liars.

Saturday, 17 Dec., Day 86

Breakfast at 0730h: Two pieces of fried dough. Saved most of one although must always carry saved food on my body now. I would like to sleep later, but if I do I miss breakfast—and my body needs that nutrition. FARC isn't going to release me for Christmas. It—the evidence disproving the army, charges, negotiations—doesn't matter or neither does whatever CIAT negotiated. FARC will hold me through Christmas out of arrogance—to show who is in charge, that they can't be pushed, etc. I'll continue to hope the government has, but I'll try to downplay, in my mind and psyche, the significance of those two days. Then . . . I'll record what those days are like. I won't let these bastards hurt me like they want to. I won't. Or at least I won't let them know. I don't think FARC will kill me—not in the next few weeks. March will make five months of investment without payoff. Somehow I feel that March is when my life becomes less a capital investment and more a human and financial burden. But I actually feel that I'll live through this. If FARC were to march me out to shoot me this A.M., for example, I feel I'm as ready as I'd be three months from now. And I'd better keep that possibility in mind. This army-colonel business is nonsense, but FARC may not be sophisticated enough to see this. Situation is still extremely dangerous. So hazardous that maybe I should forget even thinking about Christmas. Impossible, of course. 0940h: I hate carrying the fried dough in my pocket; I want to save it for when I need it most—to take away the hunger edge just before I go to sleep. I keep reaching and taking one more bite. Only one-third of second piece is now left. I fantasize, daydream of but two things: my release and food (or vice versa). Often I merge the two. I spend hours—especially between 0930 P.M. and 2 A.M. when I try to sleep—dreaming of food and reunions with family and friends and what we'll eat, our first meals. Even when I'm "full," I'm not; I need some substantial food. I fill up on flour and rice. FARC has sardines, tuna at least. Always has had. But not for me. 1415h: Have been out since 1015h but Moño just now locked me in cell again. I asked if we have a visitor; yes, he said. Don't hope, Hargrove. It won't be a representative of the FARC *comandante*. That won't happen. Spent two hours this A.M. filling cracks on the porch with rocks so my chain doesn't always get hung. Not much work, but it made me dizzy. I think I'm getting weak. Measured urine this A.M.: one liter, same last four days. Now I remember something: my urine became normal in early December. Tall Stranger came to see and we ate beef for two days. Must be function of protein deficiency. Melena gave me cap to water bottle this A.M. Did she feel bad? I've been trying to get the guerrillas to help with my Spanish study. Not much luck. They don't know correct Spanish themselves. 1630h: I can look forward to my release until Christmas Eve. Then I have only that day to dread. Once Christmas is here, it's over—no anticipation, etc. So Christmas Day won't be so bad. Also I'll give myself a page—no, 1½ pages—a day to write after Christmas. I'll worry about getting another notebook. 1700h: Looks like I'll be locked here at least until morning. So cold. Lunch was a soup of noodles and potato. Dinner: rice and beans, both cold. Gustavo came back. There was a mix-up in his orders, he said. I'm so glad. How naive to think the visitor would be the *comandante*'s representative to take me away tomorrow. Don't know who it was, but I'm still locked up. Gustavo built me a fire and got me a candle and water, thank God. A fire brightens the darkest night. Maybe that's why I find the mornings worse than the nights. Maybe the fire really makes a difference. Gustavo acted drunk or something. And I want the water not only for drinking—these fires are dangerous. For the first time, tonight I spilled a bucket of burning bamboo and coals on my bunk, on the blankets. But I don't worry much about a fire; there are too many other ways to die right now. After three months my mind still seems sound, I think. But I'm really not in a position to judge that, am I?

Sunday, 18 Dec., Day 87

0830h: Christmas is one week from today. Woke up hoping the visitor had spent the night and we'd march to FARC headquarters this A.M. But nothing has changed except I've now been shut in solitary 18½ hours. Was it wrong, a mistake to hope? No, I couldn't help it. You must hope. That, or die, I guess. Someone brought a radio near my cell—I heard the melody of "Jingle Bells" a few minutes ago. Breakfast: a soup of pasta and potato. If I'm not released this week—and I doubt I will be—I must write Susan that she should close the house and move back to Texas and start preparing for a new life. She can't stay here forever, waiting. I can't be that selfish. I've thought about my father a lot. Why didn't I send him a personal message? No. I had only a few chances and had to contact Susan. That was the right thing to do. I wish that whoever gave FARC that ridiculous army story could spend 24 hours here, in solitary confinement. Not for revenge, but to see what he's done. Stop it, Hargrove. That *is* revenge you're wishing, and it'll do you no good. I doubt that events after 22 November would have happened had I not written *A Dragon Lives Forever*. But I can't regret that, too. The book is honest and disproves these charges if only FARC would read it, and that regret would lead only to regret that I went to Vietnam and from there, Texas A&M, even born in West Texas. There is no end to it, and regretting can only hurt me. I have enough negative emotions simmering inside me—boiling over occasionally as it is. But Vietnam does seem to follow, doesn't it? Like that song, poem I wrote one night so long ago: Vietnam, you were a slut, a forbidden taste of . . .

A thought: Men and women have been jilted, martyred for writing books controversial or truthful for centuries, But I'm probably the only person who is currently imprisoned for writing in 1994, about the Vietnam War. It's an endless, continuing cycle, one that I thought ended with the publication of *Dragon*. How long will it continue? It pulled me in like into an eddy. Finishing *Dragon*, I wrote, would release me from the cycle. Instead, *Dragon* only drove me deeper into the cycle, opened a new dimension. And I thought I'd had my last adventures and that the complexity of emotions, hopes, guilt, confusion—the *why?* of Vietnam, the greatest tragedy of my life—had ended. No, it's just begun. But my life—at least this one here on earth—may very well may end this chapter. 1000h: But Tom, this is not the greatest tragedy of your life, because it really affects you, your family, and friends. No, Vietnam is still the greatest. But it doesn't matter—it's a continuum, it's not my tragedy, I'm just a little part of it.

1300h: I was let out at 1030h. At 1115h Orejas appeared. Was so surprised. Then . . . the Tall Stranger arrived with Oso. When I saw I thought maybe the FARC commander sent for me. Then: Tall Stranger brought the bad news, now he's here with the good, hiking through the forest to get me, wearing a yellow bandanna and carrying a shotgun. It was just as I'd imagined the beginning of the end. Oh no, I'm going to be locked in for a month was first thought. Fixed *candela*, brought in a year's supply of chutzo, got ready for long solitary confinement. Later Moño appeared with [. . .] I couldn't believe. Two packs of crackers, two cans Vienna sausage, two chocolate candy bars, two coffee, *manjar rojo*, three packs orange drink mix (one liter each), a packet with four rolls, and a can of something (tuna?) without a label, apparently because of my complaint to Moño when I told him of my urine problem. I'd have preferred more protein and less sugar and starch, but I'm sure not complaining. Now: how to ration it out when I don't know how long I'll be here. (Forever seems the safest assumption.) Later. Tall Stranger came to cell. Has *not* come for me and doesn't know if I'll be called before Christmas. Is here, I think, to give classes.

1930h: In cell, locked. Inspecting my hoard. Opened one can Vienna sausage. Had two sausages with lunch then three with dinner. Four of the 50 pieces hard coffee candy. Stuck my finger in the *manjar blanca* three times. Now I'm hoarding food so the guerrillas and especially the women—they're such little people—don't see it. Melena has already been snooping. Will probably come to room when I bathe next. I have two plastic sacks. Put all in one. Also have a piece of paper to wrap and conceal partially. Hard to keep my hands off the food. I've been so hungry for so long. Wish it weren't so much sugar. Or maybe that's best, I really don't know. It seemed decent. Talked with Tall Stranger about whether I could inform Susan of the charges. He said he didn't know if the FARC censor would allow such a letter to go through, but he would carry a letter and submit it for me. Moño brought the typewriter.

I wrote fast about the charges. She needs to know. What I hope is understood is that I was held two months under much better conditions—before these accusations arose. Lunch: rice and lentils and boiled potatoes. Dinner: Rice and boiled potatoes. (Note: Moño wears a red headband and often a red scarf over a gray *ruana*. Javier is skinny, with bad teeth. Melena is chunky with the look of a cow.)

Monday, 19 Dec., Day 88

Christmas is six days away, but Christmas won't happen. Not for me, not at home. It was something I wanted too much. Selfishly, perhaps. The arrival of Tall Stranger yesterday was exactly what I'd waited for, but it was a false hope. Now it's almost too late. I've been regretting—cursing and castigating myself—

for being so crudely selfish and insensitive. I should have sent away my last let-ters to Susan to pass to my father: I love you, and we'll come back to Texas ASAP. Now it's way too late and the next mail is Friday, the day before Christ-mas Eve.

At first I figured that no one had told Daddy about my kidnapping, but he must know by now, and I pray he'll be around and okay when I'm released! But when will that be? Will the FARC commander, like most Colombians, take off from 24 December thru 1 January? Probably. And even when he returns, resolv-ing the army issue doesn't mean freedom. I was a hostage before it arose . . . It's morning. I'm depressed. Must shake it. Make it through today, Hargrove, then tonight, then comes tomorrow. One "tomorrow," someday, must bring free-dom—or death. I had a small Colombian $600 jar of deodorant (of all things) that I received. 22 November, the day of the chain. Gave it to Melena as a Christmas present this A.M. I figured this: Melena is the dumbest of the guerril-las. Also the least secure, most vain, and most dangerous; she likes to snoop. Also, she brings my food half the time and also locks me in at night—that means the potential to bring me hot coffee, not cold, plus extra food, or at least my share. Plus maybe a slice of onion sometime, or, can I wish? a piece of sar-dine? Plus a new candle at night—when I ask for a candle. So I need both to protect myself from her and to court her friendship. And she may be susceptible to a small bribe. I hope so. I have nothing else to give anyone. Only my watch, my birthday present, '94, from Susan and the boys. I can't part with that. Mea-sured urine: 1.15 liters despite the extra food. Think it's protein I need, not cal-ories. Breakfast: noodles, potato soup. 1300h Lunch: rice and beans—Melena brought me plenty, plus a piece of green onion. Dinner: rice and beans with some fresh potato.

Tuesday, 20 Dec., Day 89

Am in my cell listening to guerrillas doing exercises outside—*"Uno, dos, . . ."* Judi brought breakfast: bits of hominy, refused to bring coffee with breakfast. Her arrogance, disdain piss me off worse than . . . Easy, Hargrove—don't let the treatment of an illiterate 16-year-old girl get to you. It's not worth that; you have far worse and more important things to worry about. Like your freedom and even your life? Think how she sees you: a filthy disgusting thing with a white beard living in a scary dark cell where she can't even see, yet she must bring me food. Now the dilemma: Do I ask to be chained and let out or try to go back to sleep? Chains, because I'm terrified that everyone will go off and leave me in this cold dark all day. 0915h: It's cold, dark, and raining like the past three days. Built a fire at 0830h. That may be like moving cocktail up, again and again. Building a fire is by far my favorite activity, and has been a good way to close the day. Lyrics of the Elvis Presley song "Jailhouse Rock" have been running through my mind for days—not intentionally—and just now realized it. "Warden threw a party . . ." Careful, Hargrove. Don't start dwelling on prison songs. Life is depressing enough as it is. Had three vienna sausages yesterday, two at night. Plus some candy. Urine was normal. Did the extra calories—or the protein—cause the change? Not being called by the *comandante* before Christmas may be a very bad omen. But they must not think of Christmas like I do. FARC is officially an atheist organization, I'm sure. [Earlier I don't like to think about one potential scenario: FARC decrees that I'm a Colombian undercover officer in civilian clothes. Maybe FARC already *has* decreed that. Thus, they shoot me, claiming I'm an agent. Punto. The end. It could happen.] 2020h Lunch: rice and lentils. Dinner: a shallow dish of pasta-potato soup. Shut in cell. I opened second can of Vienna sausages. Ate two, there are eight to the can, so that gives me two a night till Christmas Eve, when I open the "mystery can" (the one whose label was lost). Several guerrillas (Julio, Jon), had asked me lots of questions about English. Yesterday, I suggested an English class. Had the first today from 1230h to 1330h, using the wall outside my cell as a blackboard . . . a piece of chalk I found soon finished. Much interest among 5 or 6 of the 10. Several prepared lists of Spanish and English words for me to correct. Their spelling and understanding of correct Spanish itself is sad. Individual consulting continued in afternoon with Leidi until 8 P.M.

Wednesday, 21 Dec., Day 90

0755h: Waiting, praying to be let out. 0955h: Was out at 0815h. Seems like I sleep better at night recently. Maybe because I've exhausted things to think about. There are only two: freedom and food. I've spent hours and days thinking of each, from every possible angle. Other reasons: less urination, some food before sleep. The hypnotic effect of the fire, acceptance that home for Christmas is a fantasy, a beautiful bubble that can only burst in despair. I hate, fear more than ever, being locked in this tiny dark cell during dark night. It's strange that it doesn't bother me nearly so much at night when I can see the light outside. 1125h: Half of FARC is studying English. But they really need to learn to read and write Spanish correctly first. I'm teaching English for me, not for them—to give me something to do.

And indeed it is giving me something to do. Let's see if the enthusiasm continues. Hope they don't burn out.

Meanwhile, maybe my new role will improve my living conditions. Jura brought coffee this A.M. at 0625h, then coffee *again* with breakfast—for the first time, breakfast—fried dough. Lunch = rice and beans. 1435h: What a disappointment. The class this afternoon was to be at one or two, it wasn't clear. But although individuals drifted by, the class itself didn't materialize And it's obvious why: Moño doesn't like it. If he'd said, "Let's begin," like yesterday, we'd have had the class. When I asked about it, later, he said, "The others are all too busy for class today. Most are bathing in the stream. Maybe tomorrow." What's going on? Well, the lessons seem too popular. I guess that makes Moño uneasy. Maybe he sees it as undermining his authority. *Handle this one carefully, Hargrove.* Think it out—You can't afford to alienate Moño—unless you like starving in your cell all day. But you don't have to give up the most positive, uplifting thing you've started. Maybe I'd better talk to Moño, get his input. I've given only one class—yet the possibility of not continuing it frightens me.

Wrote letter to Daddy. Will go with mail on Friday to give to Susan to fax via [my brother] Raford. 1640h: We're out of almost everything, including candles. I have three pieces of candle. Maybe I can have light for one hour tonight, tomorrow, especially if I can keep blazes going in fire. Supplies supposed to arrive Friday but who knows? I had about seven centimeters of *ají*—hot sauce—that Julio gave me but it was stolen from my cell when I went to the latrine. Raining—cold. Would like to start a fire but am waiting for Gustavo. Want to keep him happy. He takes pride in being the supreme fire-starter. Must kiss ass a lot to survive as a prisoner.

There's no more hope of being home for Christmas. Must keep up my courage, spirits, and strength, and accept that I'm spending Christmas in chains. It can be awfully tough, if I'm not both strong and smart. Lunch: rice and beans. Dinner: [illegible] and boiled potato. Wish I had salt, but what would I put it in? 1935h: Have three pieces of candle left. Am using flames of fire for light as much as possible and saving candles. Want to be sure to have light for Christmas. Talked with Moño, asked his suggestions for classes. Think will be okay now. Had enough beans and potatoes tonight so am saving my two rationed vienna sausages, maybe for Christmas feast. I'm hungry, but not like before.

Thursday, 22 Dec., Day 91

I wrote the above too soon. I got hungry last night and urine was a lot. Ate one vienna sausage and had . . . crackers at 10 P.M. Urine last night was about 1.2 liters. Showed Moño and asked if a doctor was available. He agreed not normal, said he'd ask.

I smelled something burning last night. Jumped up. My *ruana* had fallen into the fire, burned away maybe one foot. My luck hasn't been so hot lately. This A.M. shaved around my beard: trimmed my mustache, getting ready for Christmas. May as well. Then Julio took me to the river at 10 A.M. Bathing and washing clothes took up 1½ hours. Moño gave me a book to read. Perestroika! *Nuevo pensamiento: mi país y el mundo*—Mikhail Gorbachev's book. 1425h: Again no one showed up for class. Victor said it's because Moño did not give an order. Leidi would not come out of room when I called to ask her why. This is depressing. I feel like a fool and of course my natural reaction is to say "Screw you," and forget teaching English. But it's also for me, and this has been the most up I've been. I can't just drop it. And I *absolutely cannot* let myself go into depression—not three days before Christmas. But I am, I'm on the verge of plunging really low—but what good will that do me? I have to survive. It's early, but maybe I'll build a fire. And think about how lucky I am to be chained here instead of in solitary confinement. It's Christmas, Hargrove. Count your blessings. I wonder what Susan is doing now. When do I write to her and tell her to go back to the USA, start a new life? If I live to join her, fine. But she can't wait for me in Cali. My hopes of release anytime soon are pretty dismal, now that the Christmas opportunity is past. Again, how long will they keep me before they kill me? If they'll kill me eventually, I think I'm about ready now. This is no life. But no, I'm thinking of suicide and I want to live because I think I'll be free again soon. Breakfast: rice and lentils. Lunch: pasta-potato soup. Dinner: rice and boiled potato, cold. Talked with Moño again. I still think—and he says—a mistake. Must be. Julio, Leidi, Melena, all around my fire one hour before dinner, practicing English, asking questions.

Friday, 23 Dec., Day 92

0830h: Am in cell. Javier let me out to go to the latrine, then, to my surprise, said I must return. I protested. *"Un momentito, un rato;"* he said I'd be locked in only 20 minutes. I don't believe it. He wants to do something so he locks me away so he won't have to worry about me. Just leave me here. We'll see. I practically begged Javier to let me out in 20 minutes. How humiliating to have to beg for everything. But at night the guards check every 30 minutes, shine a light inside into the cell to make sure I'm still here. The cell is padlocked from outside. (Big fire hazard; takes forever to unlock). Moño gone to Happy Valley to get supplies. Took letters to Susan, Daddy. He gave me a candle last night and assured me that I could stay outside the cell today. Hard to figure him. Breakfast: rice and beans. It's three days till Christmas and I changed to solitary confinement—chain all day—three weeks ago. Today makes three months, one week of imprisonment. I could stay outside the cell today.

I have a back pain. Think I pulled a muscle yesterday breaking *chuzco* for my fire, and no wonder. I've had no exercise, except the four-hour march here on the 4th of December, since Dec. 2. Just my cell a minimum of 14 to 15 hours a day plus my world of 15 feet of chain 8 to 10 hours the past week.

I woke up thinking of scenarios. One of the worst: I'm part of FARC's bargaining power in the demand for free zones in mountains. Good Lord, I could be held for years. Ate two vienna sausages last night. Urine not so bad.

First thing when I go out each A.M. is to empty my *candela* so, if locked in again and it turns cold, I can build a fire. I always keep matches (down to two now) and candle stubs on me, plus *chuzco* in the cell.

0900h: Javier let me out. I can't believe it, I'm so used to lies.

1400h: Lunch was different, a piece of salted pork back fat, fried, and rice and fried potato. Delicious; I did not worry about cholesterol. I've been served meat once in the past three weeks; can you call pork fat meat? But I feel a bit uncomfortable, so much grease after almost nothing but rice and potatoes. A terrible thought. My last two vienna sausages are in the can; for tonight. What if they spoil and I have to throw away? After Viejito shot the cow, our beef started spoiling after four days.

1425h: This is the last day of work at CIAT—starting the 10-day Christmas holiday. I just realized the CIAT Christmas party is under way. Right now many of my staff are sitting on the lawn talking, joking, someone is passing around a bottle of *aguardiente*. I wonder if anyone will drink a toast to me.

1650h: Dinner, another piece of fried pork fat with rice and boiled potato.

2030h: Moño told me he had talked to the *comandante* via radio and he said not received any communication from Susan for 20 days. Waiting for responses. What can be wrong? Is she in Texas? Am I concerned about disproving the "army colonel" story? Asked if I could write letters to three neighbors, Frierson, Rao, Greiner (in that order), with instructions on how to find my honorable discharge and DD214 (i.e., proof that I had left the army more than 20 years ago), *National Geographic* article and a copy of *A Dragon Lives Forever*. Moño agreed, sent typewriter and a clean sheet of paper. I tried to make it clear as possible in Spanish. I'm sorry that I forgot to add *Ojalá que pasen un Feliz Navidad.* Later: I don't feel good. Wish I hadn't eaten all that pork fat, no matter how hungry I am. Wrote letter.

Saturday, 24 Dec., Day 93

Christmas Eve: It's been a beautiful, clear morning—I slept on the porch in the sun for, I guess, two hours, what a wonderful Christmas present. Two hours of the day passing in a balmy comfort, without thinking. I don't know what time it is now. Time goes faster if you don't look at your watch. Birthday isn't perfect. Have bad diarrhea, for the first time since being kidnapped; not pleasant, especially when you must ask guards to unlock your cell, or your chain, to go to the latrine—which is anywhere in the bush below this hut.

Just emptied the last of the second of my three packs of orange drink mix into my water bottle. It's mostly sugar and water with the label claims, "VIT. C." I need it all; I'm losing lots of liquid. Not good when you're as weak as I am. Walking up the little hill from the latrine exhausted me. No more pork fat! I'll starve first. On the bright side, I ate only 1 vienna sausage plus a little bit of crackers and candy last night. So my reserve stock of food—which is dwindling fast—will last a little longer. Letters to *comandante* and neighbors went out. Does this mark only the beginning—a delayed start—of the process of investigating and clearing [up] my army background? That the past three weeks have been wasted and this is the worst time to get anything done, especially with CIAT closed the next 10 days? I don't know when or if any of my neighbors are home. I asked also to send *comandante* the IRRI annual report from CIAT library, for example. And even if I clear the army charges, does that put me back to where I was when orders for the chain arrived on 22 November?

Breakfast: crackers (which I added to my stock), a flan-type of food that I didn't eat. Back hurts. Being a prisoner plus 50 years old is a bad combination. Lunch was rice and a potato cake, fried, with awful strips of pork fat mixed in. Couldn't eat it. Ate that last vienna sausage with one of those awful, doughy rolls that taste like flour. A possible thought: if the pork fat triggered this, it's probably not amoebic and will pass.

1520h: Am chained on the porch. The weather has turned dark and cold. Am nauseous now. Need to vomit, there would go the last vienna sausage, almost the last orange drink, and no way to replace. Some guerrillas went to

Happy Valley and Moño asked them to get diarrhea medicine. Hard to believe this group's medicine kit doesn't have that.

I've heard the Nativity read in one form or place or another, just about every Christmas Eve. Wish I had a Bible, I'd like to read it now, with the Spanish Christmas carols in the background (someone has brought a radio around). I vowed long ago that if free, I'd give thanks tonight at the Christmas Eve services in Trinity Church in Cali, in the Episcopal church in Granbury, or the Methodist church in Rotan, Texas. Looks like I'll give thanks from my cell instead. *Why?* On the bright side, this has to be the bottom, the devastatingly disappointing culmination of weeks—no, months of anticipation, prayers. Tomorrow, Christmas will be better, but I've never looked forward to anything like to Christmas 1994 as a free man. Maybe there's a reason for all of this, but it's hard to see.

1630h: I finally vomited a lot then I built a fire. I'm sitting now chained but feeding firewood to my beautiful Christmas fire. Things are better and will get better still. I wonder what *next* Christmas will be like. Will I appreciate it like I'd have appreciated this one? Hold on, Hargrove. You still have Christmas 1994. You're alive and have hope. And no, there's no way you'll spend Christmas 1995 in chains.

You'll be free long before then. No, fight off despair, make the best of what you now have. Think of this as the most special Christmas of them all. You've forgotten many Christmases past—but you'll *always* remember *Christmas in Chains*.

1740h: Christmas Eve dinner is some kind of pasta-potato goop mixed with some sardines, Unlike Christmas Eve '93, no champagne. I can't eat it.

I've tried, but I can't. Moño gave me a pill. We'll see if it works.

1945h: In cell with fire. Each person got a glob of *manjar blanco* [white dish, a local candy] and I notice that guerrillas got a chocolate bar. Two 30-grain chocolate bars were in my clandestine food cache, but I didn't get one of the "official" Christmas Eve bars tonight. I'll bet there was one, but whoever was to give it to me ate it himself. Am eating *manjar* and one chocolate bar and drinking lots of water. I'm really dehydrated and feel really weak.

Sunday, 25 Dec., Day 94

Christmas Day 1994 is cold, foggy, and freezing, and marks three months, one week, and two days of captivity for nothing. Had to go to the latrine four times last night; still have diarrhea, but don't feel so nauseated. Breakfast was hominy cooked in milk and I ate it. Went back to bed at nine A.M. and slept fitfully for 1½ hours. Back to the fire at eleven and now, at 11:30, am sitting by it. Can't help but think of Christmases past. Christmas '89 is [a] real special one; I'll always remember the kids' reactions to their new motorbikes. I wonder where Susan, Miles, Tom G. are now, what they're doing. Keeping me through Christmas is the cruelest aspect so far of the kidnapping.

Will this life be different—easier, maybe, or harder, after Christmas? I've had Christmas to look forward to; to daydreaming and lying awake at night thinking of [it], for so long. But it didn't happen, and I now no longer have even the dream. Is that better? Maybe so—no more false hopes. Just survive, shut mind off when possible. Get through day by day. It'll end, someday. But don't think about when, Hargrove. The disappointments are too painful.

Lunch: a soup of pasta, potato, and some sardines again. I eat.

I wish, so much, for a friend. I wish I had a dog. Even a cat. Something that could give and, maybe even more important, receive affection.

I cry sometimes, of course, for short periods—and always alone. *Never* where they can see. I think crying, in the circumstances, is normal, a healthy way to release some emotion. Wish I'd sent my message to Daddy in time for him to have it at Christmas. But I didn't, so no use worrying about it. Anyway, I thought I'd be home to give him my love personally.

Gustavo is looking for cloth to make something; he asked if I have any old shirts that I'm going to throw away. I couldn't believe it.

Later: move the fire into my cell, but keep the door open. It's so cold, steady rain. Tried singing Christmas carols to myself, but I remember much less than I'd thought.

1600h: Went to bed for an hour, mainly to get warmer—woke up vomiting. I'm losing so much water, and almost none going in to stay.

Diarrhea and vomiting can be dangerous, I know, especially in a situation with no medical attention available. If I went to the doctor, I feel sure he'd give me a sucrose I.V. I want to take better care of myself—but *how*? For better health, I need exercise and good food. I'm getting neither.

1700h: Dinner was rice and lentils. I have no appetite, but force half a plate down. Now, if I can just keep it down. Will be shut in cell in about an hour— maybe I can eat candy. But [it] was no good last night, gave me a terrible heartburn—and nothing I could do to reverse it. Guerrillas have spent all day at the *la rancha*—kitchen area—leaving [me] here alone, except when bringing meals. I suspect they're partying.

Monday, 26 Dec., Day 95

Afternoon. I haven't looked at my watch today. Maybe time will fly. I went to bed at six P.M. last night. A good thing I slept fairly well, out to latrine only once.

Breakfast was fried dough. Maybe the worst is over. I doubt I'll ever eat another slice of pork fat, although I think the problem was beginning before the pork fat. I kept remembering a conversation at CIAT about how fast a person can die of dehydration. I feel I've survived another very dangerous situation— maybe as dangerous as Juaco and his Galil on the Day of the Dead Cow.

Now I feel very weak, but know I'll survive—I don't know how long—but as long as necessary. A deep, almost unthinkable fear is that this is *really* long-term—and I'll be a prisoner at Christmas next year.

But Christmas '94 is over, and I'm glad. It brought only heartache and sickness. It's probably better that I no longer have the "home before Christmas syndrome." Or is it? That was something to pray for, dream about. Did it help me to get so far? Maybe there's a purpose to all this, but I can't see it. But maybe I have a book. I could break *my* story with perspectives from Susan, Vrinda, etc. Now I'm sneaking drinks from the last of my orange drink when no one is around—like a drunk with a secret bottle of whiskey. A guerrilla left a "cushion"—a bag padded with *chuzco* leaves—by my fire a few days ago. I scarfed it. It's now under bottom blanket of my bunk. Makes it a little warmer, a little softer.

I need to sew some things but will wait until I have nothing to do. Right now, just getting over the sickness is something to do.

My jacket is no longer such a safe place to stick my diary because it no longer fits tight around my waist.

1945h: In cell, with another ballpoint pen. But how I got it is another kidnapped movie episode. How many scenarios are left? At 1600h a guerrilla rode on a mule up to the tent. I noticed he was carrying only one thing, a plastic sack with a box.

Strange, I thought. I couldn't help but get my hopes up, though any time someone arrives I hope they're bringing good news.

At 4:45, Moño and the guerrilla rode up, followed by virtually all the guerrillas in the camp. Like for a ceremony. Moño handed me a newspaper. What is this about? Is he about to announce my release, and they're all here to watch? Maybe to congratulate me? I should have known better. These brutes always come in groups to watch when there's special humiliation in store. Remember the night of the chain? I glanced at the paper. EL PAÍS, 20 Dec.—six days old. [I] glanced at a headline and pretended to read "Hargrove is freed." That was my first attempt in months, I guess, at humor. And it wasn't funny. "We're here to take your photograph," Moño said, and I saw that it was a Polaroid camera that the guerrilla had in the plastic sack. I figured it out immediately. No use trying to fight this one. I went first into my cell, but I guess it was too dark, so we moved to the room Gustavo is building next door. As we left my cell, I realized I was wearing my blue short-sleeved shirt—for the first time. Today was the warmest day since the kidnapping. If the folks back in Cali see that, they will think that I'm in the lowlands—not the mountains, I thought, and managed to put on my red long-sleeve shirt over the blue one—oh, so casually, as we changed rooms. No one noticed. "Sit down and hold up the paper," Moño said. I did, so the headlines could be read clearly. They took photos and let me see them. I look awful. Poor Susan. "My poor wife," I said. "Yes, it's for your wife," a guerrilla responded brightly. In one photo I had my hand up like in black power salute. I hope they use that one.

Later Moño and the guerrillas and all the others came back, and I had to listen to the radio, and date and sign what was on the news—to prove I'm living still on 26 Dec. Someone gave me this pen to write—and forgot to take it back. I'm uneasy; someone's missing the pen could lead to a search. But pens keep appearing when I need them. Maybe when the time comes, I'll find another notebook. No one remembered to take back the newspaper. It's under my bunk right now. Says a lot—that not one person showed the slightest interest in reading the paper.

They said the photos would be delivered to my family, and that they're still in Cali. Whatever comes of the army charges, this means I am still in the ransom game. What will come next?

Lunch: rice and beans. Dinner: a watery potato soup, cold. Christmas is bad dream. But I know I'll be out by March 3—my birthday. These guys hardly ever ask about English anymore. They have an attention span about like Cuchara's ("Spoon")—my basset hound. I feel okay, although weak. I've little to eat, but I'm not hungry, not even for my little hoard of candy.

Tuesday, 27 Dec., Day 96

0800h: What I'm doing now, to me, is one of the most degrading acts of this life: sitting in the cell looking through the cracks with my forehead pressed against these cold wooden planks, waiting like a dog for someone to appear who will let me out. And fearing that no one will appear, and I'll be in this cell all day. Can happen easily. They don't like letting me out because it means someone must keep an eye on me.

Later: The guerrillas are having a study session outside, sitting in the sun. Moño reads a passage, then others read something else, somewhat like vacation Bible school. But really, I have [not] seen much political training since the kidnapping.

Subject of drugs came up. Guerrillas seem to have disdain for marijuana, say it causes *locura* [madness]. Obviously use and like basuco, say it's like cocaine, which I'm sure they don't get. Basuco is a by-product of cocaine processing. Read the 20 Dec. paper. War in Chechnya—was that happening three months ago? Carter is in Bosnia—successful again, apparently. Editorial: Why can't Carter come and mediate in the war in Colombia? But would the ex-president risk an encounter with the belligerency and uncertainty of Colombia? the editorial concludes. Gosh, I wish he'd come, but he'd probably get shot or kidnapped.

Also Muñoz Mosquera, "La Quica [the Drug Trafficker]," indicted in the United States for narcotics and the 1989 Avianca bombing that killed 102 persons. So much that concerns both the U.S. and Colombia. U.S. helicopter strayed, crashed in North Korea. Surviving pilot is a prisoner. I feel for him, but at least he has the backing of the U.S. government.

1430h: Never looked at watch all morning, noon. Finally went to bed in afternoon. Slept some. Nice short dreams. It's turned cold. Looked outside. It must be 3:30 or 4 P.M. No, it's 2:30. Why is today so long? Can I make it till tonight? How did I make it yesterday, the day before? I don't know; I don't remember.

Two of the CGIAR sponsors are FAO and UNDP. Is the U.N. doing anything for my release? Seems to me that being sponsored by 20 nations is hurting me—makes us look fantastically wealthy—but I don't get benefit of belonging to a world body. Would they hold an FAO, UNDP staffer? Breakfast: hominy.

Lunch: rice, potato, a spoonful of sardines. Lots of urine—one liter—last night. How? Was reading the Gorbachev book and studying Spanish when Moño came up and asked to borrow my pen. Fortunately, I was using the broken blue pen, not the one I picked up yesterday, which may even be his.

1830. Made it through another day. How strange, how totally different from how captivity is supposed to be. If I can make it through the day, I can make it through the night. How much of it is the fire? There's something hypnotic, almost magically soothing about the fire; I can understand how primitive men worshiped it. In the day I stare at nothing, at night I can stare at the fire. I don't forget my worries or where I am, but it makes things better. It's my favorite thing, my only pleasure. I look forward to the fire like I dread and fear solitary confinement. I wonder if I can have a fireplace in my home someday. Of course, I can, if I survive this. And I will.

Dinner: a shallow bowl of potato soup. I'll eat some crackers and candy in a minute, but really, I haven't been hungry since the sickness. But . . . are they starving me again? If so, why? So many whys and few answers, and so little that makes sense in life anymore. Anyway I'll be out of here by March 3—I'll spend my 51st birthday at home. Not quite like Christmas with the kids, etc., but it will do. And if March 3 arrives and I'm still a prisoner? Can't be rougher than Christmas.

The newspaper has three sections. I read one today, will read a second section tomorrow. But Moño took one section. He said I'll get it back. But the other section is in the cell with me, but I won't touch it. I have my fire.

Wednesday, 28 Dec., Day 97

I am sitting up looking through the crack in the cell wall again. They bring me breakfast at 6:30, but it's eight A.M. and no one has come. I hate watching through the cracks; it's humiliating. Did they forget my breakfast? Will I learn that this is *"economia"* again—which means that they don't feed me at all? But first priority is to get out of this cell. That's so humiliating. I'm not let out automatically, I have to ask. I usually ask to go to the latrine, even though there's no need. Then I hold out my hand for the chain. Strange, but I haven't had bad dreams for months, and I never dream about imprisonment. But I dream on the periphery of it a lot. Last night Bob Kern [a fellow agricultural communicator and personal mentor] came to interview for my job. I introduced him to Gail Pendleton [CIAT editor]. But we were at Iowa State University, not CIAT. Other dreams—meet old friend who just got out of jail. I'm somewhere and realize my hands are filthy from fire.

0840h: Melena let me out for the latrine, then locked me back in. I protested: "Letting me sit in the sun is a policy."

"You have to learn to follow orders," Jhon said. "When we say no, it's no." Bad scene. Moño was by the kitchen, started to call to him then thought: No, that would be a bad mistake. They may leave me in the cell all day now. Just to show that they can. And the sun is so bright outside.

0920h: Still locked in. Also ominous. I'd made a pile of *chuzco* firewood outside my door, broken into pieces the right size, ready to burn. This A.M. the FARC took it all. Why? Are they going to take away my fire? They could have told me to move the pile. Do they know how much the fire means [to me]? Is that why? So far, whenever it's been time for a change, and changes have come, they've made my situation worse. Are we entering a new phase? Do they know that to keep me in this dark, cold cell and take away the fire is the worst thing they can do? Or is this merely random cruelty and thoughtlessness? Scary, but this is an awfully scary life.

I must be getting well. Did not sleep last night for fantasizing about beef, chicken, ham. All meat but fresh pork.

1120h: Still in cell but made fire with *chuzco* I had. Feel 100 percent better, calmer, less afraid of what they may have in store for me.

Observation: These people never use the words "please" or "thank you." I don't say "please" or "thank you" either; seems a weakness in this environment.

1215h: Breakfast: served at eight, fried dough. Lunch: rice and lentil and spoon of sardines.

I can't understand the *purpose* of the cruelty, punishment? I've broken no rules, angered no one. Is the cruelty sadism? I don't think so, but I don't know. I think sadists enjoy inflicting *physical* pain, but maybe not. Maybe this is pure sadism. Cruelty that accomplishes no purpose. The fire is out now, but it did its job. It calmed my soul and warmed my feet. I'm sitting in semidarkness, looking at the sunshine through the cracks, thinking. I pray that this ordeal won't affect me mentally, but how can 3½ months of solitude, being alone with no friends, not talking or even using my mind, how can that not affect one mentally?

1300h: Oh no, this hut is built in a grove of *chuzco* and there is a fire in the *chuzco* outside. I can smell it and hear it popping and exploding—30 to 40 feet away. I guess the fire is under control—but there's no one near. I'm alone and locked in this wooden cell. This hut is dry wood and would go up in minutes, especially surrounded by *chuzco*, which burns like hell.

1305h: Javier came outside. Said the fire is under control. Meanwhile I gathered my letters, from the FARC *comandante*, got ready to flee. But it took Melena five minutes to get chains off my door enough to pass my lunch plate. After all this, I do not want to die in a fire. The sudden change in treatment, as usual, brings up fears that FARC *will* kill me, and maybe soon. If they think they will free me soon, they should treat me better so I'll have a better image of FARC to give the world. Makes no sense.

1920h: Viejito returned and let me out at 1400h. "I left you locked because I was gone," he said. Who knows? That was 20 hours of solitary confinement. I'm sure not up to any more 48-hour lockups.

Dinner: shallow dish of watery pasta, potato soup. Moño opened mystery can: fake tuna. The last of my substantial food. He said I'll get more, but who knows? FARC burning [wood] all around camp. I hate to see good dry firewood go to waste. Jhon took me to the river to bathe, wash clothes.

Jhon, Melena, who spent hours asking my help in English, treat me with total contempt, especially when they can show off for others. I sure wasted my jar of deodorant on Melena. Why didn't I try to trade for a notebook?

Thursday, 29 Dec., Day 98

Didn't sleep last night. Think of food, especially meat. Also freedom. I feel something may happen next week, especially if Moño was telling the truth, that agreement was near when the army charges hit me. Careful, Hargrove. Now I have nothing to go by, to indicate freedom is near. Hope but don't decide, for example, that you'll soon be out. Don't set yourself up for another fall; plan to be here a long time more.

Breakfast: an *arepa*. Out at 8:15 A.M.

Lunch: rice and beans, mixed with cassavas and potato.

Borrowed needle from Gustavo. Leidi gave me some thread. Sewed underwear and jacket well. Then Gustavo gave me bag of straw. Took bunk apart, redid it with *chuzco* leaves as base, lots of straw above.

1500h: It's sunny almost every A.M. now and turns cloudy and cold around 1400h. Like it is now. Nights are colder than ever. Last night was bad.

If, when I'm released and I learn that Daddy died while I was held, I'm not going to let grief spoil my homecoming, my reunion with family. I'm sure Daddy would agree.

1600h: I'm so lonely.

2130h: Dinner for me was cold rice, six tiny potatoes, and a trout's head. Just the head, with no meat, and too big to eat the bones, like I do with little trout. Bastards. Back in cell I ate the other half of my secret can of tuna. Hated to eat the last protein I have. Would have saved some, but it's fish, and today is two days.

Friday, 30 Dec., Day 99

0935h: Have been waiting, watching through the cracks almost three hours for breakfast. Looks like I won't be fed this A.M. I hear someone two rooms away. Otherwise camp seems deserted.

Today is exactly 3½ months. What are Consultative Group, FAO, UNDP doing? What would happen if a World Bank employee were kidnapped? Finally decided to make a fire; used embers from last night.

1615h: Was let out at 10. No breakfast; they obviously forgot. Moño was there when I asked; glad of that. Ramiro took me fishing—first time. Didn't get a bite but got me outdoors. Washed socks, hair.

Lunch: rice and pasta. Dinner: rice, potato, and a piece of fried beef 2x1½ inch. Tore into tiny pieces so I could have flavor of meat with each spoon of rice and potato. When did we last have vegetables? FARC set many fires all around at night to make *castillos* [castles] of flames that shoot straight up along the tree trunks.

Saturday, 31 Dec., Day 100

Breakfast: an *arepa* and another piece of beef. I eat two-thirds of *arepa*, almost none of my beef, even though is delicious. Save for tonight.

Later. Judi borrowed my blue pen. I hated so much lending it. She'll use part of my ink, and has never done anything at all kind for me. (*"No me moleste"*—16-year-old bitch.) But what choice do I have—she brings my food. She doesn't help me now—but can hurt me a lot. Part of the humiliation. Officially I don't even have a pen until she returns that blue pen.

Today is New Year's Eve. The day means little to me; we seldom even go to a New Year's Eve party. But it's the third major holiday as hostage.

Later. I shouldn't find it hard to believe, but Judi returned only an almost empty ink cartridge. She said the broken pen I lent her broke again. Threw the parts away. Lying bitch. She changed pens on me. I was furious but could do nothing. She laughed at me, said she'd give me a new pen, laughed some more. I can hardly hold the cartridge and it's almost out of ink. Later I showed Mono. He said he'll give me a new pen when the next ones arrive, and he probably will, so I'll get a better pen from all this. Maybe.

Why won't Mono discipline them? They bring me my food, I told him. It's easy to take vengeance on a prisoner. He agreed. But how can a person be so low as to steal from a prisoner? The women, in this situation, have far fewer principles and are far more cruel and with less morality than the men. Less intelligence, too.

Lunch: pasta soup with piece of beef.

1715h: Was out and left unchained all day. Mono asked if I like to dance. I think he has a dance planned tonight and probably drinking.

1945h: Yes, there's a New Year's Eve party tonight, with liquor, food. But without Hargrove—I'm in my cell.

Dinner was rice, *abregas* (beans), and a piece of beef.

Ramiro had "*la rancha* [mess duty]" today. I complimented him twice on how good the food was. After dinner he brought me a plate, a piece of grilled beef, *arepa*, a piece of cheese, and a gob of *manjar*—a type of candy. The most food I've had at one time since the kidnapping.

This all makes me wonder, of course, and I can't help but hope. But . . . could FARC be getting ready to turn me loose? Maybe wanting to put a few pounds back on, improve my attitude? No, I really don't think so.

2050h: Ate my beef and *arepa* saved from breakfast, plus some of the new meat and candy. It's hard to believe, but I'll go to bed full tonight. For the first time since the kidnapping. It's hard to stop eating, especially the candy. Will that be a problem when I'm free? Probably.

[Miles and Geddie Hargrove and Peter Greiner received, by courier mail, a Proof of Life Polaroid of Tom holding a 26 Dec. newspaper.—SSH]

Sunday, 1 Jan., Day 101

Happy New Year! New Year's Day 1995 starts, like the others, [with me] watching through the cracks of my cell, hoping, praying that someone will remember to bring me breakfast, then, most important, let me out. Looks sunny outside.

Listened to the New Year's countdown, in Spanish, lying in darkness last night.

"*¡Feliz año!*" several people shouted. Didn't mean much except that I've been here a long time. Too long. Writing this A.M. I'm surprised to notice that New Year's is also Day 101. Later. Cold coffee arrived. I'm really upset, angry, that Judi stole my pen yesterday—so blatantly—yet Moño did nothing. Thank God this black pen—which has half a cartridge—fell into my hands five days earlier. Luck or part of something that's written? Black pen is now [my] deepest secret. To the world, I survive on a smidgen of ink in the blue cartridge that Judi left me. I'll forgive a lot someday. But I'll find it excruciatingly hard to forgive that little bitch. Must ration writing like I ration food. And *protect* what I have when I can. *No more Judis*—will carry black pen hidden in sack, with notebook.

Later. Breakfast: rice and piece of beef. Lunch: rice and beans. Gustavo gave me spoon of *manjar blanco* this A.M. Each FARC got a bag of it for New Year's. It's made in Happy Valley of milk, sugar, cheese, and cocoa.

Moño says the *comandante* is about 80 years old, spent 45 years as guerrilla.

1935h: I made it through another day. To make it through this afternoon, I tried to remember what I did yesterday, so I could do it again. But I couldn't remember. Nor do I remember, really, what I did today. Read, studied Spanish. Maybe I go into a bit of a hypnotic spell, like I suspect at night when I stare into the fire. I still find myself thinking this can't be happening. I didn't do anything. These bastards can't take and lock me up, hold me prisoner. They can't. And it's awfully hard to believe. Now it's survive, day by day. It must end, someday, in freedom or death. If the former, I just hope I keep my mind together through.

What would happen if I went totally berserk? Would they free me?

Dinner: rice and beans and potato. I pointed out to Moño that the skin of my arms is flaky, wrinkled—from dryness, lack of oil, I thought. I now realize: that's how my mother's skin looked when she got worse [before dying]. The wrinkling is from weight loss.

Monday, 2 Jan., Day 102

My favorite fantasy—of the food orgy I'll have when released—has been shattered; I feel sick and weak. It's noon and I'll make it through today. Then I'll survive tomorrow, and maybe tomorrow will be better. Last night I ate half of the steak and *arepa* saved from New Year's Eve. It was 24 hours old but the best steak I'd ever had. Still, I saved back half for another banquet tonight—a piece half the size of my palm. Plus candy made from milk and cheese. Got real sick later, had diarrhea and vomiting all night. The food was too rich for my system. Or had it spoiled? Do I throw away what's left, heaven forbid? Even though food sounds sickening to me right now, was I already getting sick before I ate the steak last night? I was. So what do I do now? Survive, figure it all out later.

At five A.M. Moño gave me a *"sal de frutus,"* which is like an Alka-Seltzer—bicarbonate of soda and *tártarrico* and citric acid. Worked okay, although I'm still nauseated.

Breakfast: an *arepa*. Ate most and went to the latrine, then I was chained and went back to sleep until almost 11. Had to hold arm with chain almost off the bunk, but that was okay. To chain me from outside they had to leave the door to my cell unlocked, which means no need to beg to be let out later. Have enough orange drink mix for 375-ml bottle. Made half because I must need it. Melena returned the tube of my blue pen today—like she and Judi hadn't taken the ink cartridge. Bitches.

Melena goes around a lot without her fatigue shirt—just in a black bra—a lot now. What a shallow dumb cow—but be nice, Hargrove. The bitch controls a lot of your life.

1530h: Moño appeared.

1920h: In cell. Have a stomachache but am also hungry. Melena brought dinner: a piece of gristle covered by a rough yellow substance. Tongue, she said. Just what a sick man needs. Still, I'd have forced it down, but I couldn't even chew it. I'm in pretty bad shape physically and can feel it. And I've thought for the first time, what about my physical health when I leave here? When does this start to do permanent physical damage to a 50-year-old? I've heard of people whose "health was ruined" in captivity. What does that mean? I have a feeling that recovery will be a slow process, that I won't return and start living on shrimp cocktails and one-inch T-bones. Maybe not.

I'm pretty sure the cheese was spoiled last night. Still, I don't think I can eat the rest of that steak; the thought sickens me. What a pity. And to think I went more than three months of bad treatment without being sick. Now it seems to be finally catching up. But I survived the ninth day of Colombia's nationwide shutdown, and today was the first day of business for 1995. I'm hoping that Hargrove's release is high on the agenda. If I give up hope now, I'm dead. Broke water bottle. Sick. Leidi found new one. Physical things mean so much.

Tuesday, 3 Jan., Day 103

Survive today, Hargrove. You already have a good start, until lock-in at six. Then face tomorrow, tomorrow; don't think about release or rescue—just get through today. One day has to be the last. Was very sick all night. To latrine with every change of guard. Nauseous this A.M. Still diarrhea. I am dizzy when I stand. Breakfast was hominy. Ate most. Slept in sun or dozed off till 10.

Lunch: rice, potatoes, a spoon of sardine. Drinking lots of water. More important, am keeping it down. I'll live. I'll live. But I know my situation is dangerous. Why didn't I ever study Transcendental Meditation? I try and try to find ways to shut off my mind, but I can't. If I could prioritize the elimination of everyone of this guerrilla group, there's no doubt the females would go first. They're really unnecessarily cruel, and as I get thinner, sick—more physically disgusting, I guess—their arrogance and contempt increase.

I don't understand why; I've certainly been so nice, it sickens me. No choice. Ran out of toothpaste 9 to 10 days ago and Moño found half a tube. Now that's low. Brush teeth every other day. Ration toilet paper about the same. A disgusting life.

Just realized that tomorrow is Tom G.'s birthday. God, that makes me sick. Four months. I keep thinking four months and out, but that's only 10 days from now, Hargrove. You can't think that. You'll be here much longer than that.

2030h: Dinner: rice and green peas. FARC burning brush, *chuzco* every evening. Five or six fires around the camp. Javier started a fire of a *candela* tree also called *palahojo*. The tree was about 4 feet in diameter at the trunk, maybe 70 feet tall—and hollow. They burned it from the inside. You could see the tree burning, glowing within, through cracks all the way up. A second fire started at a hole about 60 feet high. It finally fell after three hours of burning. Waste of a tree, but an unforgettable sight. Today was very long, but also warm and sunny. Still no appetite. Threw away that piece of steak.

Wednesday, 4 Jan., Day 104

Happy birthday, Tom G.! I thought about you a lot last night, this A.M. I wonder if I'll see you again. I think so, pray so. But am less sure with each day that passes after Christmas. If I could only show you and Miles and Susan how much I love you. Is that chance lost forever? No, I can make it through today, and that's one day closer to freedom. Or death, which is also freedom. But I'm not ready for that step yet. If I knew I'd die in chains, I'd rather die right now. But I don't know that; I'll survive today. Am still sick, especially at night. It's now almost two weeks. "I need medicine," I told Moño. He gave me another packet of *sal de frutus* (Alka-Seltzer). "This is the best medicine."

He doesn't understand about antibiotics, etc. Moño explained to me, very seriously, that I must quit drinking so much water. "Water is very bad for you when you have diarrhea," he said. Its scares me to think about getting really seriously sick. He wouldn't know enough to get me to medical treatment even if it were available. I now have to hold my trousers up with one hand while I walk, despite the extra notch in my belt, plus it's extra thickness.

This A.M. I thought, My life is a lot like that of Spook in the *Wizard of Id*. Dark cell with streaks of light. Footsteps. Chain rattles and I hear a click as the padlock is opened. Then light floods into the cell and a hand thrusts in a bowl and cup. I take it, the door closes, chains rattle again, and I am in darkness with breakfast, which today was an *arepa*. I always know where I am when I awaken—but I have an absurd thought *every* A.M. as I'm half-asleep. They have to let me go now, because I didn't *do anything wrong*. Then I realize they *don't* have to let you go, Hargrove, and they *won't* if they don't want to. And the seriousness of my situation sinks in once more. That may be the most depressing time of each day. I usually cry a little.

1500h: Went to bathe, wash clothes. Returned and saw that Tall Stranger [Rambo] is here. Why? Don't even think it, Hargrove. He brought the first bad news and nothing good the second time. It won't happen. Still, he represents the *comandante* [of FARC].

2005h: I prayed this afternoon, not that the Tall Stranger had brought news of my freedom—but that I'd have the strength to stand it when I learned that he had not. Does that make sense? It does to me. I knew it wasn't freedom, but I had to think of the possibility, to imagine returning home to Susan, the dogs, my friends. I guess both boys are gone by now. Moño finally told me 10 minutes ago that the Tall Stranger had brought nothing for me. And it wasn't so bad. I knew it couldn't be, anyway, and I know that nothing will happen for at least another week; I've had my thrill for a while. I don't feel too bad; I'm feeding wood to a nice fire, and I am clean and I don't have an appetite. When I thought I might go home, I didn't even think about food. But I don't feel so sick.

Lunch: Rice and beans; I hardly ate.

Dinner: A watery pasta soup.

I am still alive and my health seems to be returning. I'll make it through tomorrow. I'll be okay.

Thursday, 5 Jan., Day 105

I know what's happening. It's been my worst fear—one I've not permitted myself to think, it's so awful. CIAT won't pay my ransom, maybe as a matter of principle, maybe because they [FARC] have priced me like a British Petroleum executive. FARC isn't about to let me go without ransom, so I'll sit here until . . . ? Maybe until I have an accident or the government rescue kills me. FARC won't keep 10 full-time people guarding me forever. But this situation must be so bad for CIAT's image. Imagine, trying to recruit new senior staff. It's not realistic to put a scientific staff in Colombia—then [say to them] you're on your own if kidnapped. I've never given up faith in Susan and CIAT, but my faith in CIAT is crumbling. But you can't let that happen, Hargrove. If I lose faith, I die. Maybe from illness, like the past couple of days, and I simply cannot believe I am left on my own. I must survive to publish this story. Or otherwise it's all suffering, for nothing. To write this will be hard. In my first two books, I've tried to show the readers, make them feel what it's like to find sunken ruins, to go to war and return years after, but if I convey the feeling of this life, I have lost my reader.

I'm thinking, in case I die, my body might somehow be returned, someday. Is there a way to let Susan know about the diaries and Checkbook Diary? And other? Too risky to put in letter.

And again—how long can Susan stay in Cali with no job, no reason to be there except me. It might be best for her to return to Texas. But the thought of being totally alone in Colombia . . . but making her suffer, too, makes no sense. If this were her country, she could try to start a somewhat normal life—not quite a widow, but . . . But. I can't ever write her to go back; FARC will never let such a message through because FARC is using her like it's using me. All I can do is wait, and survive. I'll make it through today. Almost four months of kidnapping and I've never yet even talked with anyone who has any control over my destiny. FARC is really big on human rights.

Breakfast: Boiled rice and a little boiled potato.

Lunch: Rice and dried green beans. I asked Judi the Spanish name—she wouldn't even answer me. Such arrogance from an illiterate 16-year-old; she treats me with utter contempt. The women are all so much crueler than [the] men. I guess because their status in the unit is far lower. The three are probably 7 to 10 in status. Thus, I am the only thing lower than them—and I can't fight back. They can take out frustrations, aggressions on me. Made new checkbook almanac page this A.M. Wanted to wait till Sunday, when needed, but Moño and three others went to Happy Valley—took fishing poles—so had more privacy, security today. No longer sick, but no appetite. Maybe my weight and food consumption have reached a low equilibrium.

When I'm free, people will think I had lots of opportunity to improve my Spanish. But, in reality, not so much. I study—with magazines and dictionary—a lot, but have little conversations, far less than in a normal day at CIAT. I'm a prisoner, remember? Can't look at watch, but I believe in two hours I can build a fire. I want the days to be warm—but to turn cold early, so I can build and appreciate fire. More and more I think that, at night, in my cell, the fire hypnotizes me. I'm aware of time passing—but it passes steadily. Someday I'll have a fireplace in my home. If I ever have a home again. I have been thinking about *A Dragon Lives Forever*. It's a good book; I wrote the best I could, but when it was finally published, I never got to enjoy it, to be and feel like an author. I was in South America, I never got back to the bookstores to sign copies, etc. I was to do that on vacation this fall. Will I ever? Will the book itself have destroyed me, in the end? No matter what, I don't regret writing the book. I just hope it's not my last one. Hey, Hargrove, there will be another—about kidnapping in South America. A sequel. Remember: A dragon lives forever.

2100h: I'm getting hungry at night—again—but my food fantasies have changed. I dreamed for what seemed hours last night about a fried-egg sandwich, the yolk not quite hard, with lots of mayonnaise, lettuce, and big slices of tomatoes, onion sprinkled with black pepper and Tabasco but no bacon—I doubt I'll ever be able to eat pork fat again, in any form. Washed down with a chocolate shake. Also pan-fried round steak. Moño came from Happy Valley, as usual with no news. I can't seem to learn not to hope.

Friday, 6 Jan., Day 106

Got *Cambio* 16–30 *agosto* to 6 *sep.* '93. *Cambio* magazine is news and features, like *Time*, the only nonpolitical reading I've had except for the paper on 21 Dec. since my kidnapping. "*El Secuestro* [kidnapping]" is lead article. 1310h: I'm sick. Really sick. Not physically, but . . . I've always believed it's better to know exactly where you stand, no matter what. Now I'm *not* so sure. Gustavo had the magazine mentioned above. I talked him into lending it to me. The lead paragraph described Colombia's anti-kidnapping Law 40 of 1993. It includes five years prison as penalty for anyone who pays ransom to get a kidnapping victim released. Good Lord, that almost negates the possibility that CIAT could pay my ransom and get me out. Especially as a highly visible international organization. And I was wanting more publicity. I have to think about this. But it scares me. Truly.

2000h A.M. in cell with fire and didn't read much more—I'll have plenty of time in the days to come. But six FARC, including all three females, went to Happy Valley. That left far more privacy than usual, especially with women gone. First I borrowed Gustavo's needle and pulled threads from my *ruana* and the woven bag I used to store wood chips. Then I sewed rips in the lining of my jacket again. More protection for the diaries. Then I wrote to the FARC/ Cauca *comandante*, this time explaining about my old Colombian friend from Iowa State University days, Dr. Hernán Pérez Zapata, suggesting that the *co- mandante* contact Hernán, if he knows him. Also included a section on the impact of IRRI and CIAT rices in the world and Colombia, plus Turipaná 7 and Orzica Sabana 6 [both improved rice varieties bred at CIAT]. Mentioned cassava biological insecticide for hornworm control, wild Mexican bean for bean borer resistance [both are nonchemical strategies of pest control], and the CIAT training program. Then I wrote to Havener [Robert Havener, then acting director general of CIAT], asking that he send *Fragile Paradise* and *Savannas* to El Co- mandante plus any other material [videos] that might describe CIAT-Colombia relationship.

I felt a real urgency to get all that done, and the knowledge that CIAT probably *can't* pay the ransom triggered it. I feel, since reading that [article], that my chances of release anytime soon are far, far lower than I'd thought. And I have to do what I can to build an even more positive image for CIAT. The kidnapping article includes photos of 10 kidnap victims: 4 killed, 4 set free (2, 6, 18, and 36 months later), 1 died in captivity, 1 still held. Will I die in FARC hands? Seems more and more likely. I'd better not even think about freedom. That's far in the future, if ever. Survive, Hargrove. Don't think about what it will be like.

Later. Reduction of all foreign support of Colombian guerrilla groups has led to increased kidnapping. From 1987 to July '93, 5,025 kidnappings were reported in Colombia; 723 victims were assassinated; 2,187 were freed; and 2,115 were still held. But author[s] say those were only half the [total] kidnap victims. Colombia was averaging over 4.19 kidnappings a day in '93. Mostly businessmen, cattlemen, landowners. Common criminals were responsible for most, followed by FARC, ELN, EPL, M-19 [all supposedly communist guerrilla groups], then narcos. From a published list only one seemed to be a foreigner, from Texas Petroleum. One Richard Sparr is listed as a biologist, kidnapped in '77, released three years later. Harold Eder, father, I think, of Alan Eder (Texas A&M, class of '66), who was kidnapped in 1965, and killed. In almost all the kidnappings, there was an informant—so all were planned. So I am an exception in many ways. At least I won't wake up tomorrow thinking: Is today the day? Will I be set free today? I feel awfully sick, but I guess it's better to know where I stand. I'll read more tomorrow. I'm in worse trouble than I thought. That's plenty for tonight.

Supplies arrived and as he said, Moño gave me a new notebook and pen, plus batteries and toothpaste. And a bottle of *ají*—hot sauce—of my own.

Breakfast: *arepas*. Lunch: rice and beans. Dinner: two trout and rice. I'm even more alone, more on my own than before. The kidnapping article came as a real shock. In a letter to Havener I thought much about suggesting he contact Dr. Norman Borlaug* to suggest that Borlaug has group make a statement about agricultural development in Colombia, and about kidnapping. Decided can't risk having Havener letter killed when I request materials to send to *comandante*. Will include in letter to Susan right after Havener letter goes. Moño says tomorrow.

Saturday, 7 Jan., Day 107

Moño did not go to Happy Valley this morning. What a disappointment after all that work and worry. Will go tomorrow. Another day's delay. Easy, Hargrove, you probably have months ahead of you. Years maybe. Breakfast: hominy. *Cambio* issue has five or six articles on kidnapping, plus dozens of stories. A regular magazine, the first since I was kidnapped that's not propaganda. How do I ration it? I could read all, easily, this morning. Read one article a day, Hargrove, slowly, with the dictionary to look up all you don't know. My new notebook has 200 pages. How to use it? Not as diary, not till this one is finished. But then tear out pages to hide? Moño certainly knows about this notebook.

My only chance now is for FARC to release me on the basis of CIAT's work and mission. I think otherwise I'm dead, or I'll be here so long that my health—physical and mental—is likely to be gone before FARC gives it up and lets me go. Terribly depressing thoughts. This will be a long day. Orejas came up the mountain with a group yesterday. I almost wish she hadn't; I can hardly stand to see her. Somehow a dog says home, family, love, care—all the emotions and necessities that are missing from my life.

Urine last night 1.42 liters. Lunch: rice and lentils. Later. Judi brought a sardine. I know Moño said to bring it. I wanted to save some, but how? I have

---

*1970 Nobel Peace Prize Laureate, for developing the high-yielding semidwarf wheat varieties of the International Maize and Wheat Improvement Center (CIMMYT) in Mexico. —TRH

no plates, cups, utensils. One little plastic bag and two bigger ones. Putting things up is a problem when you have nothing. Not even a shelf; all my possessions are stuffed into my bunk or are on the floor of the cell with the firewood.

I must learn to shut off my mind, to quit thinking of freedom. But how? Maybe the ability is developing. I didn't think much about food last night. I could shut it out because I know it'll be a long, long time before I see another half-pound burger with a chocolate shake. But I thought about being freed instead. Moño returned from Happy Valley two days ago wearing a green camouflage beret. His new attire. Article: with new law, fewer prolonged kidnappings, more "lightning strikes" of two weeks; attorneys totally against paying ransom. FARC made a resolution two years ago that it's impossible to negotiate with government so changed to radical means, including kidnapping. I think there's still little dialog—Moño said the government is negotiating for me! I rationed well today. I read only two regular articles (same as last night, but thoroughly) plus letters to the editor, short features, and some ads. 1930h: Dinner was dish of potato-pasta soup, nothing else. Am starving. Eating the last of my crackers with mayonnaise and *ají*. But have only a few—then: nothing. Feel sick. Headache. Have a Ponstan but don't want to take it. Headache may put me to sleep easier.

Sunday, 8 Jan., Day 108

Ate cracker sandwiches with mayo and hot sauce. Finished my mammoth bag of candy last night. Shouldn't have. Got really sick—diarrhea and vomiting all night. I can't afford this. Breakfast: *arepa*. Lunch: hominy in milk. Slept some in the sun. Read my third feature in *Cambio*, about Roberto Arévalas, a businessman who was kidnapped and held almost a year by guerrillas. Makes me feel better because so many of his experiences and descriptions are like my own, including things like second-grade education of guerrillas. And one day he found himself in the airport with a ticket home. I'll do the same. [Article] didn't say if ransom was paid, so it probably was. Now I can make one more article. Lost all afternoon, until I built a fire at four P.M.? Moño and three guerrillas went to Happy Valley, took my letters to the *comandante*. However: the *Cambio* issue included a lot of information about kidnap victims released without having to pay ransom. But I worry. These guerrillas have a lot invested in me. CIAT, please put the publicity machine back in gear. I think it's essential. . . .

A terrifying thought is: the *comandante* calls me to HQ! There I'm held in a regular prison compound, kept in a dark cell night and day. P.M. I feel better. Nauseous still, but that's minor physical sickness. My mental health is at least as important. It's a shame that the food I had last night was wasted. 2000h: Dinner: rice and potatoes, some sardine. Jhon locked me in. But he refused to get me water. Said, "It's bad to drink water when you have a bad stomach." I finally got water by pointing out that I'm locked in the cell with a fire and need water in case of an accident. Otherwise, I'd be locked in, dehydrated all night without water. Please, God, deliver me from these imbeciles. But cruel and dangerous imbeciles. Read three articles today, but two were only one page. One was about how screwed up *secuestrados* [kidnap victims] are after their release. But you can't afford to get mad, Tom. It can do you no good, and won't help with the one thing you need—to survive. Seems from what I've read, one leaves this life via two routes: being set free, or death. I've read nothing of anyone escaping. Have started using "please" and "thank you" again. No point in following their example. Arévalas said captors were *campesinos*—but left much of the good things of the country behind. I agree, and it puzzles me. How? Peer pressure, I guess. Once they get to FARC, they act like the others. I'm also being polite to Judi—turn the other cheek. Survival.

Monday, 9 Jan., Day 109

I got through this A.M. without looking at any new articles—just reviewing the six I've already read. What a change from my normal life, to make everything I do go as slowly as possible, make the entertainment last longer— Everything except time itself, which I've always savored . . . time to go as fast as possible, until I reach what? It's all 100% reversed from the way I've always lived. Reviewed [illegible]. Trying to help Gustavo write a song.

These people use such bad Spanish. Amazing that I can correct or edit it. Sick all night. I ate some of the sardine last night with crackers and mayonnaise and *ají*. Hope that's not what caused it. (i.e., the mayo and hot sauce are too rich for my system.) But that means two nights in a row. Ear infected again. If I could only wash my hands, be clean. But I don't have a bowl, not even a cup to put water in. I wash hands by taking mouthsful of water and spitting it on both hands simultaneously. Breakfast: pasta-potato soup. Lunch: rice and beans. Found a battered aluminum pan about six inches in diameter. The boys were shooting at it at Christmas. Thank God they missed. It's been used as a *candela* and is caked with ashes and soot but I'll take it to the river to clean the next time I bathe. Then maybe I can use it as a pan, especially to keep soapy water to wash my hands. Also took two pieces of twine, one of wire from the pan. Minor? Maybe. But the pan may make my life a little more pleasant. Day has turned cold. May rain. Early fire today? Dinner: rice and pasta. Will try to clean my ear but I have *nothing* that's not filthy. But still have some eardrops from before. Hard to believe that I read only one-half of article today. Spent rest of time rereading the first six, studying Spanish, etc. Had the boys recite a song, copied verses. Also clichés, sayings. Being a foreigner will probably help me survive this—bad public image to kill a foreigner. Especially if CIAT is making publicity. Maybe. I don't really know. These are not very sophisticated people.

Tuesday, 10 Jan., Day 110

Am writing letters to Susan and to Daddy. It's so hard to write, partly because nothing happens and partly because of the censorship. Read the other half of article seven, which is only a half article. Was not chained yesterday, maybe because had been so sick, but had to stay in area covered by the chain. This has happened a couple of times. Thought maybe policy was changing, but I was chained again this A.M. In my head, I feel I'm going to be held prisoner about a year. If only I could know that, then maybe could adjust, accept: It's been one-third of a year now—in three days. I seldom have an appetite and I'm not as hungry as before. Maybe my body has adjusted to a survival level, and adjusted food consumption to match. I have fantasized about food the past two nights, but mostly lean, ground steak, maybe a burger. The thought of a T-bone or anything with fat makes me sick. But I've been sick, so nauseous lately—maybe all will change as I get better. Or maybe it's best I don't have an appetite, don't think of food so much. But somehow it was sort of fun when I did. Made time go faster . . . and food consumption to match. Eating is no pleasure; it's an obligation to keep myself alive. Poor Susan, if only I could do something for her. Life must be so tough. Not a wife, not a widow, not a divorcée, not even a working woman, and living in a foreign country. If she goes home, she leaves a husband prisoner in a strange land. She'll have to eventually, of course. But I can't even tell her that in a letter, FARC would never let it through; they want her here, for pressure.

Surely CIAT is in contact with a negotiator by now. That's the one hope I have; that CIAT wants me out of here badly, and *will* work as many channels as possible. I have fantasized about food, about the past. I can't be forgotten, written off. I can't let myself even think about that. And Susan will keep pressure on CIAT. Breakfast: an *arepa*. Lunch: pasta-potato soup. Gustavo asked me today if Martians are *cristianos*. Seriously. Finished letter to Susan, but it was so hard. Don't want to be so negative, but not much bright news to write about. I can't write, anymore, that I'm in good health. I'm not. 1935h: Read article today [illegible] read several others. Turned cold. I was miserable, so built a fire at 1900h. I wish for lots of things but one is that I had some feedback from CIAT or Susan. Not their fault, of course, but I've received no communication from anyone—except the *comandante*, who says I'm a colonel—for four months. Will I ever again? I think so, I think I'll live through this. But I'm not sure. My chances of survival looked a lot better a month or so ago. Spent time today giving Gustavo lessons in Spanish, correcting what he'd written, etc. The guerrillas are almost hopeless for helping me with Spanish. Nouns and words okay. But I didn't even get it across to Moño today why I wanted to know how to say *pedir* in the present, past, and future tenses. Beyond his comprehension. I've read all five articles about kidnapping. Did they reassure me? No. I now realize my position is more dangerous than I originally thought. This thing about not paying ransoms really worries me. Without money, I'm not worth much to FARC. I also don't want to be a martyr.

Wednesday, 11 Jan., Day 111

Today was easier than most. Went for my weekly bath, washed clothes. That took up most of the morning. My one bathing for the week. The afternoon was bearable so I didn't let myself read a single new article; just reread some of the first ones. Breakfast: hominy. Lunch: rice and a spoon of sardine. Dinner: potato-pasta soup, shallow bowl, then sat around by fire and talked. Later Melena brought a surprise: a second plate of rice and a mix of cassava and sardine that was obviously the main dish of the night. Why wasn't I given any in the first place? Selfish bastards. I got that only because Melena felt good. No chain to drag.

Thursday, 12 Jan., Day 112

0900h: The day is cold and overcast. I hope the brief, sunny summer hasn't ended. And I'm chained again. Why? There seems to be no pattern, no policy on the chain. It's not for security, otherwise why was I free all day yesterday? It must be for punishment and/or humiliation—the latter, probably. I did nothing to warrant punishment. But why impose the humiliation or hardship? Those who might pay ransom aren't here to see it. Kidnapping is an art of purposely imposing pain, humiliation, and grief. Letter to Susan and Daddy got off today. I doubt seriously I'll ever see Daddy again. The chances that both of us will be alive in, say, six months or a year are just too slim. Lord, I just thought we would both be dead, easily, in six months. Javier brought me coals to build a fire. He and Julio are both building fires so early in the day. It's going to be a bitch of a day, they say. Later: A visitor is coming from Happy Valley today, Moño says. Oh Lord, don't let me think it, don't let me hope it. But I have no choice. I must think and hope, like the other times. . . . One day a visitor will bring the orders for my release. And four months are complete tomorrow. Breakfast: an *arepa*. Lunch: rice and beans. I lost two articles—Gustavo took back the *Cambio* (it's his) and tore out four pages. How I wish I'd read those articles, but how could I know? I read another article today, about cost of imported luxury autos—because Gustavo said he might want to hang the pics of the BMWs, Bentleys, Mercedes, etc. on his wall as pinups. At 1300h my chain was removed and I was taken to river to bathe—second day in a row. Washed hair again. Dinner: rice and pasta, the kind in a box, with cheese flavor. How long since we had any form of veggie?

Jhon says the summer here is only Dec.–Jan., then it starts to rain steadily—like it is now. Our visitor didn't show up, I guess. Our candle supply is out. I should have a couple of pieces, but I can't use because had to beg Melena to bring me water tonight. "Oh, but you don't need water, it's raining." Real cute.

Friday, 13 Jan., Day 113

Four months ago today that I drove into that *retén*. Sixteen weeks. Even leading a normal life, even having fun, one-third of a year is a long time. One third of a year without speaking, or more importantly, without a friend, without a conversation with someone I trust, one-third without laughing. The weeks of isolation with no communication from outside. I'm so lonely. Maybe that's the worst, the loneliness. And not knowing when it will end. Can I survive four more months? I guess so. What is CIAT doing to get me out? It rained all night, and this A.M. Can the summer be over? If this is my chronicle of what happens to me, then I must write once more about prayer and religion. Like before, I've been putting it off. Why? Maybe because what is happening in my mind just isn't the way it is supposed to be. There are no atheists in a foxhole, they say, and I've never claimed to be an atheist, and I'm in trouble, bad trouble, by any standards.

Prayer hasn't brought me the comfort I seek. Or maybe it has, and I can't see it. I prayed on 1 Dec. and it seemed to work. I talked to God, or to myself, and made a plan to back up my diary with Checkbook Diary, use Notebook 1 as a dummy, etc. And the Chuong Thien reunion. I had discovered something, and things would get better with this new power I'd found. On Dec. 2, I tried, but didn't recapture the feeling. That night began the short chain, the isolation. Thirty-six hours of solitary confinement, the army charges. My life changed afterward—but for the worse. Still, I tried to pray. I continue. I pray every morning, every evening. Sometimes I pray in Spanish. But I don't feel a comfort, a closeness. At first I prayed for deliverance from here, for reunification with my family. Then I thought that may be selfish, so I prayed, "Thy will be done," and for strength. But that's hypocritical, too. I obviously want out of here, more than I ever wanted anything. I pray for strength a lot, strength to get me through another day, and to make it through the day. I pray a lot for Susan—to give her strength, and for Daddy. I feel those are the strongest parts of my prayers, the most sincere. But none of it seems to give me much comfort—at least, not that I recognize. I feel as empty after praying as I did before. But of course, I do make it, day by day. So maybe my prayers are heard, answered, and [I] just can't hear. I've requested a Bible from the Red Cross, from Susan, and from CIAT. Maybe that will help.

The most depressing time of day is when I wake in the A.M. This morning, when I woke, I started to pray. Now wait, Hargrove, I thought, that makes you more depressed; wait until later in the day, when you have hold of yourself. As I write this, I'm sitting on the porch, in the cold. I'm constantly watching because I must hide this, my diary. I just saw that pages 32–56 of my magazine are also missing. Didn't notice before, because, I wanted to read, slowly, from front to back.

I like the line "deliver us from evil." I use it a lot: "Lord, deliver me from this evil, from these evil people." I ask that my FARC captors be forgiven, but I probably don't mean it. Maybe I'm too much a hypocrite to pray. I seldom pray for anything selfish except freedom, and that because it's total hypocrisy not to pray when that's what I want so desperately. But really, I pray for the strength to get me through what is happening until death or freedom ends it.

Breakfast: hominy, Lunch: rice with dried green peas.

Rain all day. All say winter has come—that sudden. Move *chuzco* under porch. Leidi opened ear, drained lots of pus, cleaned it out with sticks and cotton. Hope water was boiled. Put bandage and suture. [illegible] Can't afford infections, especially in ear. I could die of an ear infection here.

My greatest solace is easily fire, not prayer. Fire is getting me through today, will get me through night. It's uncanny. Sometimes I wonder . . . is it possible that God is answering my prayers, is sending solace . . . through fire?

1930h: In cell. I've got a wonderful fire. Moño walked up while I was writing about magazines. Did he know I was working in this notebook? Scares me and reaffirms need for checkbook backup. Melena brought dinner: a plate of cold rice and an *arepa*. Nothing more. I didn't even get a hot *arepa*. I later complained to Moño. *"Economía,"* he said.

Why? I know they have more to eat than that. The punishment part of the kidnapping is so unnecessary. And I'm getting afraid that FARC must be keeping me for special stakes. Otherwise, enough time has passed. I should have been free a long time ago. And this sudden descent of cold, wet winter. If this is really the way it will be for the next month, then I'm in for a bad time. Ear doesn't hurt, I think it'll be okay. Also think I'm lucky. I'll try my best to avoid another ear infection. What more can I write? I can't give up hope. I have to keep faith, keep hoping, I guess that also means keep dreaming of the day of my release, keep thinking it could be tomorrow, keep living. Eat cold rice, it'll keep you alive.

Saturday, 14 Jan., Day 114

Sunny this A.M., but colder than usual. Helped clean front yard of the camp. They allowed me to collect firewood. Ear seems okay. Breakfast: *arepa*. Lunch: rice, lentils, a spoon of sardine. Lost watch—Moño found [it], near trash I had emptied. Watching Melena and Leidi pick fleas from Gustavo's hair makes me wonder, Why haven't I gotten fleas? Everyone else has them. Maybe I do, just don't notice. When I go to bed hungry—like last night—I don't seem nearly as hungry as before. Guess my food requirements have shrunk. But urine increases. Like last night and the night before. I wonder if I have a dubious place in history, the first senior staffer of the IARC [International Agricultural Research Center] system to become a victim of international terrorism? If so, will they hang my picture on a wall of the CGIAR? Or try to bury the news? The latter, probably.

We have a dog in camp now. Ranger belongs to the camp but has been here two weeks. Spent a couple hours gathering firewood. No chain today, only Julio guarding me. Partly to put wood under porch so we'd have dry supply when constantly raining, but also for the purpose of walking downhill, returning with wood, breaking it up, etc., later. Lord, I pray never to use all the firewood I've collected. Dinner at four: rice, lentils, and potatoes, all cold. Eat to survive, Tom . . . until this nightmare ends. Someday, when I'm free, I'll make every meal, no matter how simple, something special.

Sunday, 15 Jan., Day 115

I heard four rifle shots early this A.M.—someone coming up the mountain. Then at 0640, Moño, Julio, Viejito all approached my cell, unlocked it. Why? A delegation coming to tell me something? News received in Happy Valley? No, Hargrove, don't even think it. But I did. The door opened. "Look, Tom!" Moño held out two grouse. I took one.

"¿*Pava?*"

"*Sí.* Viejito shot them this morning."

"¿*Quiere ambas?*" I stuck one under a blanket. Very funny, all left laughing. I cried after they shut, locked door. Can one quit anticipating, shut freedom from mind, without giving up hope? Could I just accept being a prisoner until it's all over? Or is that giving up hope, and the chance of surviving this? Melena didn't bring coffee this A.M., I asked for coffee—later, in front of Moño and five or six others. It's "out," of course. She glared, and I know I'll pay. Careful, Hargrove. A not-too-bright woman out for vengeance can be dangerous, especially if you're a prisoner and she brings food, water, etc. Maybe I screwed up a couple of months ago in my tent in Death Valley. Gustavo later brought me a cup of coffee. At the bottom of the cup was hominy kernels. He obviously retrieved the coffee from the slop when it had been thrown out, but he did it to be nice, not as harassment. I shouldn't have noticed the hominy.

Urine: 1.3 liters. Could probably be partly because of so much rice—two water: one rice. Later, lunch was rice, beans, supposedly *pava*. Melena brought my plate. I got about two inches of the upper back—the part without meat. Peeled off every bit I could of the backbone, but not the ribs, would have been better if no *pava* at all. Each bird is about the size of a small, skinny chicken. It's revenge—but I might not have received more even without the coffee incident. Glad I got firewood yesterday. Melena told me today I can't go to south of hut anymore. Lost blue pen found at latrine—careful, Hargrove—yesterday you lost, and found, your watch. What's happening? Am I losing my reason, my memory? I'm hungry, and lonely.

1900h: Read article about Arevalos kidnapping again, and it inspired me. Dinner: rice and beans (a spoon) and piece of fried dough. I scooped beans and rice onto fried bread and pretended it was a bean *chalupa* served at Don Ayala's in Granbury [Texas, where Susan, Tom G., Miles, and I have a family home]. Almost worked, but Melena brought me only a few beans and whoever heard of a rice *chalupa*? But as Arevalos did, I'll try to live more in the present and think about how good the food is. It's about time for something to happen—it's been too long stagnant. I'm ready, and I say that realizing that most major changes have been for the worse.

Guerrilla pastime: beating the dog. Jhon likes to write in chalk on the walls, *"Jhon es Rambo."* I must get out of here, somehow, CIAT can apply more pressure on Colombian government. But can government do anything? I'll make it through tonight and tomorrow. And I'll join Susan and my father. Read article aloud to Gustavo—Ramiro also, hope [that] ungrateful little bastard [i.e., Ramiro]. . . . Asked for candle. None. Moño says will be 8 more days before next supplies arrive. We've been out of everything for 8 to 10 days already. At least, that's what they tell me. I really have no way of knowing, do I?

Monday, 16 Jan., Day 116

Rained all night and cold, wet today. But my spirits are higher, am trying to be like [a] revolutionary, live in the present. Breakfast: *arepa.* At lunch I savored throughout about how delicious the rice and lentils are. Idea: build a fireplace. Gustavo and Melena agree. Start tomorrow—maybe. Here 16½ pages left and 33 [done].

2000h: Today was better than most. Built a fireplace to the side of the hut. People stood around it all day. Will do more tomorrow. I worked hard, to keep spirits high—to live in the present and not think too much about when I'll be freed. Worked okay. Tried the *"¡Qué sabrosa!"* trick again at dinner—but it's harder to pull off when the second meal of the day is also rice and lentils. Heard guerrilla talking. Lots of fighting and no talks now between guerrillas and government. Great. If the Colombian government is really handling my negotiations, that means no one is worrying about Hargrove. Melena started calling me *gringo* and *gringuez*, which no one [else] does. Part of her way of getting to me. I started calling her *gordita*, which others got a laugh out of. I finally said, "Look, I don't like being called *gringo*, and you don't like being called fatty. Let's just call one another Melena and Tomás, okay?" She agreed. How silly this must sound, to anyone who reads this. But it could be rather serious. I don't want people to start calling me *gringo*, not as a prisoner. Moño said it will be 15 days before the next mail goes out. The guerrillas found an old typewriter ribbon— red and black. They tie pieces to their weapons, gear, etc. *"Sangre y muerte* [Blood and Death]," they say—a battle banner. I mentioned "until you release me or kill me" today in conversation with guerrillas. No one corrected [me]. Ominous?

Tuesday, 17 Jan., Day 117

I asked why the *comandante* hasn't asked to see all the documentation, proof, etc., I've provided. "He's so busy," Moño explained. "Just wait." It's that the kidnappers—not the victim—call the shots. Just as Arévalas wrote, they feel kidnapping is a right. I haven't set new goals for release date. Have set so many in past. One year, Susan's birthday, Thanksgiving, Christmas, four months captivity. All gave nothing but heartache, especially Christmas. I don't pray in the cell in A.M. anymore. It's too depressing, can make me cry. Not a good way to start the day. I wait till I'm out. Now still in cell and cold. Haven't eaten with a knife and fork since I was kidnapped.

2100h: Breakfast: *arepa*. Lunch and dinner: rice and peas. Ramiro and I dug a new *fogón*. It's really nice to sit by. Am burning mostly green *chuzco*. Have been extremely nice to Melena today and we've gotten along fine. Moño said he was going to talk to her, dress her down. Maybe he did. Julio Anderson has been sewing, making a new *equipo*, a backpack, for 8 to 10 days. Said he'd give me his old one, but I didn't believe him. Well, he did, and it's in pretty good shape. Nice of him. I can store things in it, maybe hang it on my wall. But I really need an *equipo* for only one thing: to march out of here, I hope. And soon. Cold and wet today. Had a fire going all day. Now that I have that little tin pot to use as a bowl, I can wash my hands before going to bed. Doesn't sound like a big deal, but if you've had nothing to wash with, then get a bowl, it makes a difference in your life. Clean hands might have prevented that nasty ear infection I had last week.

Wednesday, 18 Jan., Day 118

Dreamed I'd been released last night—unusual, I've never dreamed directly of this life. Maybe getting the *equipo* triggered it. Awake to a breakfast of that awful hominy and milk and reality. I won't be released today, no message will arrive, nor will it come tomorrow. I'm being put away, saved for . . . something. Release may come, but I'll be here a year first. How terribly depressing. Now I'm forcing myself to eat the hominy and waiting, hoping to be released from this terrible cell. If I only had a sign, an indication that this will end. But I must keep the momentum, keep the positive attitude of the past two days. That means, I guess, don't think of the future, but only how to survive, get through right now, today. Stay awake dreaming of food again. What is my favorite? Whatever food comes to mind. Probably a BBQ chicken is my favorite. Chef's salad, chocolate cake, a chocolate milkshake, thick burger, even bacon, sausage, ribs, pork again. Been thinking about the next change that I wrote must be coming. It could well be to decrease guards from 10 to 5 or 6, lowering FARC's investment and store [in] me. . . . Found 1½ inch candle someone lost on porch. Last week found three-foot wire. Noon: came quick [. . .] is really 1130 or so. Can't look at watch. Spent A.M. gathering more wood to keep dry before the winter rains begin.

Lunch was rice, and hominy, I think. Like Arévalas says about how good it is to savor the taste. It works, sort of. Have used one-third of my bottle of *ají* What will I do when it's gone? Maybe I should write and try to meet Arévalas when I'm free. He'll be surprised to learn that he helped a *gringo* survive, who [he] has never met.

P.M.: The sun is out but Moño is gone and no one else can authorize me to go to the river and bathe and wash clothes. I'm afraid there'll be no more sun for days. Worked all afternoon heaving rocks and making a stone-faced fireplace. Includes flat rock at the front where maybe I can boil water in my pan, have hot water to shave and wash with. The work feels good. I must be regaining strength, but can't keep trousers up, even with a new notch and fat belt [where I kept my diaries]. Made suspenders to go over one shoulder from a piece of canvas strap I found and saved a few weeks ago. That's how I'll walk out of here someday. But I don't want anyone to see the suspenders—not now—because I don't want to draw attention to my belt. "Let me cut another notch for you, Don Tomás."

By the way, I use one three-liter jar—but less, the top is cut away—of water per day for drinking, washing, plus another two to three cups of coffee, *agua panela*, or chocolate that may come with meals. That's not much water. I require a full jar each night before I'm locked in.

2020h: Dinner was a plate of rice and an *arepa*. *Nada más* for me, although again, I think for better. Will be a long night. Played *fútbol* for first time since Dec., the day of the short chain. Sat around my new fireplace till 2000h. It's really beautiful; I wish I could take a photo. Big stones, one-foot by one-foot, square corners. I think I'm being stored for something political, not financial. A *gringo* the Colombian government wants badly—because of pressure from CIAT. I don't expect to be free for a long time, and that's too depressing. Especially if you're hungry and don't let yourself think about it.

Sitting on anything hard hurts. So does sleeping on my side. I've a lot less padding between my bones and the hard surfaces.

I think about Susan a lot, also my father. I won't see Susan for a long time. My father—probably never again. Julio has guard. He asked if I needed a candle—I got me one, they're not out of candles, they just don't want to share with a prisoner. Like the food. Yesterday I gathered a supply of firewood. Today, I built a fireplace. What will I do tomorrow?

Thursday, 19 Jan., Day 119

I was blessed this A.M. After breakfast (hominy, terrible) I went back to sleep and awoke at 10 A.M. Day is cloudy and cold—there goes my bath, wash clothes—and the two hours it could kill. *Fútbol* in P.M. Lunch: rice and lentils—why can't we have had lentils. . . . Last night made nice bench from two stones, a plank, in front of *fogón* [fireplace]. Gathered more wood.

2030h: it rained, then cleared off. Dinner: rice and lentils, then more *fútbol*, then sat by fire till sleep. Haven't combed—or cut—hair for four months and one week.

Friday, 20 Jan., Day 120

2045h: Had breakfast—an *arepa*—then went back to sleep again this A.M. Rained all day with that bone-chilling wetness that permeates everything all the way to the soul. I built and fed a fire all day until eight P.M. And gathered *chuzco* to feed it, that's all. And I got through a miserable day. Another one. Lunch: rice and beans. Dinner, at least for me, was a plate of cold rice and a cup of sweet black coffee. Nothing more. I still have some crackers. Took three and made a sandwich. *"Economía,"* Judi said. Did FARC have only rice? Maybe rice, but I doubt it. Supplies to arrive on Sunday, but with this weather, who knows? One-thirty or two, thinking about freedom and food. I can't help it, I can't stop it. I'm hungry right now, I have what's left of my plate of rice and I take bites of cold rice. But it doesn't stop. The hunger. How long since I had meat and vegetables? All this will really end someday? I'm not so sure. Maybe in a year—can I live in these conditions another year? I guess so. If I don't get any serious infections. I'm not ready to die, but it's awfully painful to realize that I'm not going home. Gustavo asked if I had a candle. Yes, part of one, I said, feeling defensive. "Do you need the candle?" he asked. I thought. "Hell yes," I said defiantly, then thought: Better treat Gustavo with kid gloves. He does more to help you than all the others together. "Come back, Gustavo," I said. "You're my amigo. If you need my candle, it's yours." Turned out Gustavo had two candles and wanted to know if I needed one. He gave it to me—a beautiful white candle, never lit. I'm writing at night now. Lesson: Keep your temper. Don't jump to conclusions. Being a prisoner is tough.

Saturday, 21 Jan., Day 121

Woke this A.M. to the steady sound of heavy drizzle—the type of sound that says it'll rain all day—and it has. Breakfast: *arepa* and rice. Lunch: rice, beans. I took the little vitamin bottle, the one where I stored hominy but Melena or Judi threw out so long ago, and filled it half-full of beans in case dinner tonight's, again, a plate of rice. Have done nothing today but keep my fire going. But I'm alive. God, I'm so lonely. So lonely. Go get more *chuzco*, Hargrove. The fire is low—and thinking is unhealthy.

2030h: I got through today, by tending my fire, and now by my *candela*, or firepot, in the cell.

There's a lot of mud and mire in front of my *fogón*. Started building a stone patio today. Will continue tomorrow. Moño brought his radio out and we listened to local news by the *fogón*. The Cuban government has sent someone to talk with guerrillas about peace talks in Cartagena. Right now, I can only hope. Of course, there are a couple of factors that make peace less likely in Colombia than in other countries torn by revolution. Wrote Susan, Dad, Havener, and my CIAT department. Goes out tomorrow, and supplies supposed to arrive tomorrow. Pray for vegetables, meat, any kind.

Sunday, 22 Jan., Day 122

P.M.: Am sitting by my fire. It rained all night and all day. Cold, wet. Had a terrible time starting a fire. Now am drying *chuzco* and wood to use later. My beautiful fireplace collapsed, but that's okay. I'm rebuilding it—something to do.

Last night I fantasized not only about steak, egg sandwiches, chocolate milkshakes, but also about the *arepa* I hoped to get this A.M. I must really be hungry. But breakfast was rice and lentils. Lunch: rice and fried dough. I brought out my little bottle of cold beans and had one of Don Ayala's [one of my favorite restaurants] famous cold bean *chalupas*.

What luxury. Dreamed last night that I was freeing prisoners—POWs—from the Vietnam War, held, somehow, along the creek of the old Hargrove place [in West Texas]. Strange, how my dreams are always on the periphery. I never dream that I'm a prisoner, or about being held in the Andes Mountains. When this is over, people will probably ask how it compared to Vietnam. A logical question, although there's little in common beyond being in another country, lonely, dangerous, at war—well, maybe there's quite a bit in common after all. Anyway, veterans form veterans associations everywhere, after every war. But there are also prisoners—do POWs ever form associations? Maybe, but the only one that comes to mind is survivors of Santo, in [Manila]. But being a prisoner is a far worse experience. Little exciting to remember. Just miserable boredom and loneliness. And heartbreaking uncertainty. Will I ever see Susan again? My sons; Becky and Raford [my sister and brother]; and my in-laws and Susan's mother? Maybe not, I don't know. But can't give up hope.

The weather is about as bad as it can get, but I'm surviving. I will survive. I got a new three-liter water bottle with a top.

1930h: Had the best dinner in months, some baked tuna, some *carve* [fake meat, made from vegetable protein], and rice. Sounds terrible, I guess, but tastes wonderful. Protein at last. And the *carve* was so good. Warmed water in my pan by my fire. Was going to bathe in cell with handkerchief. But washed hands in water so dirty, was afraid to. Afraid will spread infection.

Monday, 23 Jan., Day 123

I crossed a border last night, and I don't know what to think of it. I dreamed of where I am, what has happened. I was a kidnapped prisoner of FARC. They let me go to Texas for my father's funeral. I would skip out, of course, and not come back, except they held my family hostage. Then I awoke. I had found the phenomenon of not dreaming about my kidnapping strange, but a relief. At least I escaped during sleep; I hope I don't start dreaming regularly—and realistically—about my situation. The Cuban-guerrilla talks are in second round, I heard. Would any peace agreement affect me? If POWs are returned, what about *secuestrados*? Or vice versa. What about those army charges? What am I? Whatever FARC wants, I guess.

Moño is gone. Thought I'd be left in cell all day, but Ramiro took me to bathe. There's sun today, but it's cold. Judi is to wash my clothes. Got big lecture from Melena that I use too many clothes, get things too dirty, etc. Bitch. Breakfast: rice, *carve*, and piece of sardine. I saved part of sardine in my water bottle. Lunch: rice and a couple spoons of noodles with tuna. I ate part of sardine but want to save most for tonight, so don't go to bed so hungry. Problem: I can't really wash my vitamin bottle, I don't have any rags. Dangerous, what I'm doing? I sure don't want to get sick again.

I need oil; 120-ml bottle of Johnson's baby oil has lasted four months but almost gone. . . . Each night I wash my face and put oil around eyes. My hands are so dry, cracked, I feel like I'm scratching my face if I rub it.

About two A.M. today I broke down and put some oil on the worst parts of my hands—the pain was too much. Heard on radio of assassination attempt on Colombian president in Barranquilla. How will that affect the Cuba talks?

2030h: Dinner: rice, half an *arepa*, and a piece of salted beef, very salty, half the size of my hand. Where is all the food? I wonder what Becky and Kinney, Raford and Lana think of this? They never thought I was too bright, living in Colombia, or for that matter, the Philippines. I hope Ken's still in e-mail contact with Susan. I worry about Daddy, a lot. . . .

Tuesday, 24 Jan., Day 124

Fourteen pages left = 42 days at 3 days a page: One month ago—actually, one month three days, was Christmas Eve. I was so sick. Where will I be one month from now? Here, I think. In one year? My 51st birthday is 38 days from now. Here? What changes will I face when free? After total isolation for so long. People move, marry and divorce. How many people have such a time capsule.

Breakfast: fried dough and a couple of spoons of fried beef. Tasted rancid. Saved half the dough for tonight. Haven't been chained for several days, but the chain and collar hang outside my cell—a chilling reminder. Gathering firewood. What else to do? Be thankful you have that, Hargrove, and it's part of the fire. I spend a lot of time—maybe an hour a day—planning my fire for the evening. Lest I be accused of not seeing the positive side of FARC—heaven forbid—let me say, when they have milk, they make the best coffee and hot chocolate I've ever had. Wish I had more. Never get a second cup.

Now use the canvas strap as a second belt—under the leather belt.

Lunch: rice and beans and couple of pieces of beef. Saved half of beef for tonight. Played *fútbol*, but soon colors become brighter, things begin to swirl. I get dizzy easily. No Johnson's baby oil in supplies. Moño says next supplies come in eight days. Also next mail out.

2045h: A long, lonely day, but got through it. A growing fear: If Moño was telling the truth, I was about to be freed in late Nov. Then came the army charges. I've received no feedback indicating acceptance of my denials and evidence, and nothing more about being freed. I'm in cold storage and I'm afraid the army charges are still there. Staying here a long time seems more and more likely. So does the possibility of dying here. Dinner: rice and beans, and *carve*.

Wednesday, 25 Jan., Day 125

Cloudy—clear with cold wind. Nights are so cold. I wear my best socks—the red ones—as the "base," for the three at night. I need sleep and figure that I can gather wood and stare at the sky with cold feet. But I can't sleep with cold feet. I wear three socks, three trousers, one shorts, two shirts, jacket, *ruana*, two ski masks, two heavy, three light blankets over me, one under, plus some sacks I found. I don't sleep under covers, I wrap it around me. Still; so cold, I hate to move.

Breakfast: an *arepa* and a piece of the beef. Blankets are filthy and haven't been washed in 4½ months and are locked inside with fire every night. But the cloth never touches my skin, through all the clothes, so I guess it's okay.

The guerrillas are at *la rancha*—the kitchen—around their fire and I hear them laughing, cheering. That happens a lot. I always wonder: Did Moño receive the radio message and he's told them? That I'm being freed, and they'll break camp? But then I know it isn't, because the laughter is too forced, the cheering not spontaneous and happy. These are not happy people, but they try to convince one another how happy and carefree they are.

Gathering dry *chuzco* and storing under eaves of hut for when rains really come.

Lunch: lentils, a spoon of *carve*. And I'm down to 20 percent of my *ají*. What will I do? How will I eat this slop when that's gone. Stricter rationing. I didn't use any *ají* with breakfast or lunch. It's overcast, don't see sun. At about three P.M., I did what I never do, I looked at my watch. It's only 12:45. A long day. Am preparing for a magnificent fire with big logs on three sides.

"It's been four months," I said to Moño this A.M. "Is the problem that FARC still thinks I'm in army?"

"No. You have to be patient; the investigation is still under way."

"Investigation?"

Moño assured me it's a matter of time while FARC investigates my case. But can I believe him? Of course not. But I must because that offers hope.

2035h: "When did the investigation begin?" I asked Moño later.

"Fifteen days ago."

"Will they call me, question me?"

"No." I wonder just what a FARC investigation involves anyway. "When I'm cleared . . . will FARC free me?"

Moño shrugged. "I don't know." Whatever, I'm awfully glad. A chilling thought: What if the investigation concludes that I am indeed an army colonel? Would it be in the head, or in the back? I can't even think about that. But if the investigation clears me, where does that leave me? Free? That's possible, if FARC was really, as Moño said, on the verge of releasing me when the army charges arose. But don't count on it, Hargrove. But I have to grab at anything that offers hope, and this is the only development in weeks, months. If it's true. If Moño fabricated this story, may he burn in hell.

Melena is sleeping with Jhon now, but has an afternoon thing going with Javier. She is certainly a promiscuous thing.

I've had a strange problem lately: overeating. The last two nights I've been given huge amounts of rice. I've been so hungry in the past; I eat it all. Tonight was the same. I threw away some rice. Ramiro saw it and lectured me about wasting food. Lord, I hate taking orders from or being chastised by a 16-year-old illiterate. But not much I can do about it. Now he'll probably tell the others that I'm being fed too much, wasting food. Dinner was rice, lentils, and sardines.

Thursday, 26 Jan., Day 126

I hardly slept last night thinking about the investigation, being freed. Food. What I fear most is what I feel is most likely: that there is no investigation really. Moño just said that, not thinking, and I latched onto it. The evidence is probably there, but nothing is happening. I'm still on ice.

Breakfast: Dough. Lunch: rice, beans; stored some beans away. Played some *fútbol*, am gathering wood, but feel so weak. I feel I need some vegetables most followed by meat, fruits, sugar. I wonder how much exercise you should do when you're weak and you don't get enough to eat. And I need to do something with my mind. I look at this like I'm in a coma for four to five hours—in which I absorb nothing mentally. When I come out, I'll resume. If I come out. But I have faith that Susan is hanging on there, keeping pressure on CIAT, and will be waiting. I must come through this. . . .

2120h: Am in cell with fire. Today was long, today was bad. I guess it's from getting so upset over the "investigation," then realizing it's all bullshit. Probably, I'm not about to be released. I'm on ice. But I have to remember: it could be worse.

This makes no sense, I've done nothing to deserve it, but I could have terminal cancer without deserving it. I could be killed in a car wreck, blinded in an accident. I still have my health, mental and physical, though I'm sure neither is as good as before. There's still hope. And there's still love, though it's a scarce commodity here in the Valley of the Shadow of Death. I have my fire and candles. I'm hungry, but I've been hungry before. I'm alive, and I intend to stay that way. Dinner: rice and noodles, *carve.*

Friday, Jan. 27, Day 127

1645h: Bad day, but I'm sitting by a fresh fire now—so maybe it'll get better. Breakfast: *arepa.* Lunch: rice and lentils. Am not using my precious *ají* on lentils anymore, probably not on beans either. Both are so bad, it doesn't really help the flavor. I'll save the *ají* for better things, not my strictly survival eating. Gustavo and Moño went hunting and shot a *pava.* Wish they hadn't—everyone loves it, it's a partridge. So they cook and I get a piece, which is always the upper back with no meat—and rice. I'm better off with plain old lentils and rice. Actually, I've never really tasted *pava*, except for the bones. Ramiro told me I can't go but a few meters from the hut to gather firewood. The little queer, how I'd like to . . . Calm down, Hargrove. That won't do any good. Rage won't help you survive. Oh—it's starting rain again.

2030h: Dinner was rice and noodles, *carve* and—surprise—half the back portion plus the end pieces of a wing. But I asked for, and got, a second portion of the noodles. Moño says some sort of agreement is being reached in Carta-

gena; the government will pull out of some zones. If so, some *secuestrados*—
like me—will be released. I'm not packing my bags yet (what an expression to
use under these circumstances!). I'll try not even to hope, or notice. Don't want
to jinx things again. But dare I hope that for my 51st birthday, I'll go back with
my staff into Palmira for a special birthday lunch, like [we've done] the last two
years? I'll have baby beef this year!

Saturday, 28 Jan., Day 128

Hardly slept last night thinking about freedom. Will we be released in a ceremony? Will I be taken to an airport and given a ticket to Cali, etc.? Now I realize: You're falling for it again, Hargrove. You never learn, it's like you have
to keep hurting yourself. I checked with Moño again this A.M. The guerrillas
proposed to government that [they] will release *secuestrados* if government pulls
out of free zones. [Colombian president] Samper wants to do it but the military
is dead opposed. I don't believe it will happen—it's too obvious; why do the
guerrillas want free zones?* But the fact that they're talking is good. And
secuestrados are on the agenda. But I don't see a ticket out of here soon. No
chance that any *secuestrados* will be released while this is going on, but that's
better than being forgotten. How depressing.

Breakfast: fried dough. Lunch: rice, beans, *carve*. Saved 58 beans in my
plastic bottle. I save only beans whose skins haven't broken.

In Cartagena three sides are sitting: Cuba, government, guerrilla. Another
development: Peru and Ecuador went to war, apparently, five days ago. That
can't help. Ramiro tells me there are lots of booby traps around here, some left
by the guerrillas, some by the Colombian army. And that he took a nine-month
course, mostly booby traps, given by five Vietnamese, three years ago. Very em-
phatic about it, showed me scar on his knee where he was injured in an accident.
Jhon says he is full-blood Vietnamese. That his father was killed in the war and
that his mother brought him to Colombia as a baby in 1975. Mother joined guerrillas, and was KIA [killed in action] by Colombian army. He could be Vietnamese, is very Oriental. But those who left in '75 weren't communists.

Thinking about life, my situation, etc. I've always craved adventure and
had a lot more than most people. Last June, I was in Rwanda. In April, I was
in upper Amazon of Peru searching and finding a lost rice variety straight from
Gone with the Wind [Carolina Gold]. Have been in a war, traveled in 100 countries, wrote two nonfiction adventure books, but kidnapped by the Colombian
guerrillas in Colombia—too much. Am lucky to still be alive, or unlucky to be
kidnapped. The former is the best way to look at it, I guess. I have no regrets
about coming to Colombia, even taking the Puerto Tejada road to work on 23
Sept. Both were fate. I think I'll survive this, but I don't know. If my last adventure ends in the Cordillera Central of Colombia; so be it. I can't change

*So the Colombian army can't raid the opium fields and the drug-processing laboratories.
—TRH

things right now, so no use regretting. Have shown Ramiro, Gustavo, Melena the trick game of fox, goose, bag of corn. Good cross-cultural gimmick.

Dinner: rice and beans, *arepa*. I asked Melena why we never have vegetables. "The budget is too small. We must feed 10 people plus you on the budget." So it's not just logistics. There are more mouths to feed than [they] can afford. Encouraging.

It's 9:30 P.M. Saturday night in Shadow Valley. Am in cell. Dinner was rice and beans and *arepa*. Saved half an *arepa* and now am having as Saturday late-night snack with some beans. I pull beans from the bottle one by one. Julio asked what is my favorite of the foods we have here. Tough question; for breakfast there are three items: *arepa*, fried dough, hominy. For lunch and dinner, really, it's rice and lentils or beans, day in and day out. Sardines, peas, *carve*, are items that come so rarely I can't call them Shadow Valley foods. Of the Shadow Valley foods, *arepa* and fried dough are my favorites. You know this is a pretty awful life. I don't like any of the food. I eat to stay alive.

Sunday, 29 Jan., Day 129

How long since I laughed. Dreamed I was back in my normal life, at a dinner party with mountains of food. I told about my life as a *secuestrado* and was even amazed myself at how funny it was. The guards used most of my stockpile of *chuzco* last night. Should I be p.o.'d? Maybe not, replaying it gives me something to do. Guard tours are one hour each, start at eight P.M.

It's Sunday A.M. Most seem to have slept late. I slept till 1010, but I try to avoid that. It's so hard to go to sleep at night. When will I get used to it, learn to turn off my mind? Never, it seems, and it's cold at night. This A.M. was as depressing as ever. Will it ever make sense? I don't think so. Ate 14 of the beans and the half *arepa* I saved.

Breakfast: today *arepa*. Lunch: rice and *arvejas*, or green peas. Saved peas with my beans so [I] can eat if we have *economía*—only rice, or nothing at all for dinner. Sunday—a waste—I'm sure talks in Cartagena are off today, but maybe negotiators are planning strategy for tomorrow. Cartegena is my only hope right now.

The sun is under cloud cover, then it appears again. The sun is very warm at this altitude, but it's cold immediately when clouds cover it.

Skimming over this, which I seldom do, I see that I wrote on Nov. 27 that they would probably kill—me after five months. I'm not afraid of that yet.

The Cartagena talks have increased my value even if FARC can't get ransom. But if neither Cartagena nor ransom give results, the day of reckoning must come eventually. I really find it hard to accept that people can be so cruel. There's not a person here who cares anything about me, Thomas R. Hargrove, as a human. Only as something to keep to sell or trade. What will I be like when I leave? Four and a half months without any type of friendship, talk, or laughter, must change one. A lot.

Resupplied my stock of *chuzco* and wood. But this time I left the stack over the knoll, where it's not so obvious, harder to get to. Maybe that'll help.

Should I have the skin transplant operation when I return to Texas? Maybe. Ten days in bed doesn't scare me so much. Not anymore. Especially with books, a TV, a computer, good food. I could probably even order burgers and ice cream whenever I wish. I should probably do it.

Dinner: rice, peas, some *carve*.

Monday, 30 Jan., Day 130

What—oh what—will I do to make today pass and go away? By now I should be so used to this life that I don't have that problem. But I'm not. And if I think about my situation—especially now in the A.M.—I'm as depressed as ever. Worst scenario: All *secuestrados* are freed, except me, because they use that army stunt.

Breakfast: *arepa* and rice. Gustavo has *la rancha*—kitchen duty. Today, he brought me a *tinto*—coffee with milk and sugar—at 10, and it was hot . . . delicious. No one [else] ever does that. When I leave I must think to send him a present. Maybe a watch, or a Swiss army knife. Dreamed last night I went through a prison in the Philippines and thought how much better [a] life the prisoners have than my life as FARC prisoner in Colombia. I must visit the prison in Snyder—especially if I write a book. I have no prisoner experience to compare this with.

Moño and the others went to La Playa—Happy Valley—today. Supplies arrived earlier than expected. Supplies come to La Playa–Happy Valley by mule train. Then must be brought here by foot in backpack. Trip down two to three hours; return: three to four hours. So logistics are another reason our diet is so bad. Mail also goes out. I wrote Nathan and Alex to, if possible, ask Klaas to delay *Carolina Gold* film so I can help if freed via Cartagena. Impossible dream? Probably. Also sent memo to Havener regarding need for [publicity] campaign in Colombia to try to avoid repeating what has happened to me.

Rain gone, I am collecting wood to south and southeast where [I'm] not allowed to go. Why do I resent the guards using my firewood? Replacing it kills time.

Lunch: rice and beans and some noodles. Gustavo sent extra-big plate. What a paradox. I often overeat on rice. Complained to Moño again I am hungry; he increased my rice ration but not the rest. Dug hole in ashes of castillo tree to bury extra rice. Can't turn it back, can't let anyone know that I can't eat it all.

Lit fire about two P.M. because Gustavo wanted it. He asked me to tell stories about Vietnam. I used term *Oriente Lejano* ["Far East"]. "Is that another planet?" he asked, serious.

1545h: The guerrillas are returning from Happy Valley. Melena stopped before reaching hut and stuffed candy from her backpack into pockets—obviously so won't have to share them. I saw other candy in pack. Will I get some? Lord,

I hope so. I'm so hungry for sweets now, I fantasize about chocolate cake and candy now more than about steak.

Dinner: rice and beans sprinkled with fake tuna. But I got a new bottle of *ají*. I'm going to guard it with my life. I didn't believe it when I saw Melena coming with dinner and that bottle. I'm so hungry for candy, sweets, that I could cry. But they'd soon be gone. The *ají* can make dozens of meals more bearable.

2045h: I am so hungry for something sweet, seeing the others with suckers and candy bars really brings it out. For a week now I've thought only of chocolates, and more *jugo de mora* [blackberry juice] like they sell in Cali—for a couple of hours each night.

I made it through the day, but I'm not sure how. Now I have only the night to get through and I mark off one more day. And I'm one day closer to . . . what? The next day, the next week, I guess. I wrote my staff about going to restaurant in Palmira for my birthday lunch, but I don't believe it (baby beef or a big *churrasco*). It'll be rice and lentils here in Shadow Valley.

"You believe in God?" Gustavo asked me today.

"Yes."

"Me, too."

"Are you Catholic?"

"Yes, are you?"

"No, I'm Protestant."

"Me, too."

Gustavo doesn't have a radio—that's what I can send him.

Tuesday, 31 Jan., Day 131

Night terribly cold. Didn't sleep. Morning: clear. Melena restarted my fire this A.M. for no reason—threw on wood and left it to burn out. What a waste. And of course, I must replace the wood. *"¿Hace frío, Don Tomás?"* or *"¿Como amenecío?"* are the most intelligent conversations one gets here. But to be honest, [the guerrillas do] the same with one another, not just with me. Am I here, a prisoner, because of Vietnam? Still being punished for . . . something? Definitely, in one way. After Vietnam, I found life in the States boring, depressingly meaningless. To have excitement and travel and work with meaning, adventure, that led naturally to IRRI in Philippines then CIAT in Colombia and this, my kidnapping. I tried to keep Vietnam a secret here, but she followed me—with a vengeance that still continues and may mean my death here in the cold mountains of South America. Being a Vietnam vet certainly hurts me at the macro level (security, the army charges, etc.), although it probably does not at the personal level. The guerrillas are always asking me to tell Vietnam stories. I seldom do, partly because what I found fascinating about Vietnam is too subtle for them to handle. The movie *Platoon*, which they have all seen, is about as deep as you can go. But if I hadn't had Vietnam, I wouldn't have written *A Dragon Lives Forever*, and if Moño isn't lying, I guess FARC would have freed me by early Dec. The title sounds more appropriate now than ever. The dragon does seem to live forever, and may kill Hargrove. The dragon that lives on is war, the Far East, etc.—not me personally. I'm quite vulnerable to death. We'll see—I've pretty well decided to have the operation/skin graft when, if, I go to Texas after freedom. What does that mean, Hargrove? It's like fantasizing about your big meal after freedom . . . like it'll come any day. Still, one must plan. God, I wish I could talk with Susan.

Breakfast: rice with *arepa*.

Anyway, I thought a lot last night. For the operation, I'll buy a notebook computer with modem, CD-ROM, everything and Windows and use those 10 days [in the hospital] to learn it, work on manuscripts.

It's so bright, sunny, and I haven't bathed for nine days, but Moño says this P.M. Can't argue, but I know we'll lose the sun. Awful, to have no control over your life.

1600h: I bathed, but was just as I feared. Clouds covered the sun, and it was very cold. Oh well, I'm clean, and have built a fire.

Lunch: rice and *arepa*, a couple of spoons of noodles, but I suspect that they have sardines, tuna. Ramiro walked by with water bottle full of Kool-Aid. Wished I could have some.

Moño says that next mail out is 15 days from now. It's usually more frequent than that, he says, but I guess that's the next scheduled trip out— supply-run problems.

2130h: Dinner: rice, lentils, soggy fried potatoes. Melena didn't bring the *sobremesa*—the drink with the meal, almost always chocolate or coffee. I asked, and she said she'd get it. Then went into Javier's room. I waited and waited, but she never came out—till 6:30. I'm really cold. It's more than missing a drink. The *sobremesa* is part of the requirements for *sobrevivir*—to survive—through this. I need that milk and sugar; besides, there's only three things I like here, the coffee, the chocolate, and my fire. Melena has the responsibility to make sure I'm fed. I'll talk to Moño tomorrow. It worked for a while, the last time. She's so pitifully dumb—but there'll be revenge after I talk with Moño. A prisoner doesn't win in these situations. Never.

Wednesday, 1 Feb., Day 132

This is going to be a very long day. Rained last night, is drizzling now. Started a fire already. Maybe I'll only feed wet *chuzco* and wood to the fire, to keep me busy. How strange to find ways to make time go faster with no regard for quality. Today has absolutely no value. It's something to endure, to survive till it's over, *nada más*. I may learn a few new Spanish words, nothing more. The faster I can cut today out of my life, the better. The problem—the terrifying reality—is tomorrow will be the same, and so was yesterday. And there's no end to it, none I can see. If only I knew, that . . . one year, six months . . . if only I had something to read, to learn, to do. Someone to talk with, someone to do something nice for, someone to thank for doing nice things for me, someone to joke with, to laugh with. A book to read, music to listen to. The worst part is, there is absolutely nothing I can do to change things, to influence my destiny, except survive. Quit it, Hargrove. That won't help you survive. Besides, you have your fire. I'm off to collect more wood.

A commotion: The guerrillas are painting Julio's face black with soot, lathering his hair white with soap. Turns out it's his birthday—his 14th. Good Lord, it's midmorning and I don't know how I'll stand the rest of the day. I'm going to tell one of these little bastards what asses they are, that they have no right to hold me, to order me around. What good could that do, Hargrove? Will it help you survive? No. How ironic that I think about Melena—how she has no right to deprive me of my *sobremesa*, how absurd, when I'm here and she has the mandate to serve me—through kidnapping, one of the greatest of crimes, an ultimate violation of rights and what is right. I must hold my temper, I have to make it through this long, wet day of miserable nothing. Then tomorrow. This is one of those times I truly wish I could die, end it all. Why is this nightmare happening? What sense, what purpose could it serve?

Breakfast: *arepa* and soup of noodles and potato. Glad we got potatoes, will add some variety to the rice-bean-lentil diet.

2015h: Yes, the day was long. Lunch was rice and beans—saved about 20 beans. While [I was] eating, Judi asked, "Are you in the army?"

"*Ridículo,*" I said.

"Do you think about when we will kill you?" she asked a few minutes later.

"When is that?"

"When your soldiers come to get you." Cruel remarks from an intellectually deficient 15-year-old. But I take them seriously because they reflect something she's heard.

The guerrillas played *fútbol* this P.M. I borrowed Javier's machete, cut green *chuzco*. Hard work.

Dinner: rice, boiled potatoes, and a handful of beans, supplemented by the 20 I saved from lunch. The beans are cooked with no seasoning, not even salt. So bland.

I wonder if I'll ever eat for pleasure again? That's the same as saying, I guess, I wonder if I'll live through this, the food here isn't going to change. Judi and Melena asked me to give [them] some *ají*, I refused. Later I talked with Javier. Of the guerrillas I know, only he, Viejito, and Juaco were on the *retén* where I was kidnapped. "Were you surprised to get a *norteamericano*?"

"Yes, we were surprised, we didn't plan to kidnap anyone. We planned to get cars."

That confirms what I felt at the time.

Do I write too much negative, too much gloom? Probably, but what else can I write? This is not a very happy place. And my kidnapping is its only reason for existence, for the 10 guerrillas to be here. And I haven't read any good books lately. Maybe I should list some things I'm happy I have here: I'm happy I have the canvas strap I found; without it I couldn't keep my trousers up. My new bottle of *ají*. The pan I found and cleaned; with it I can wash my hands and face. My *fogón, chuzco*. My new notebook and pen. My health, which seems okay right now. Candles, which is how I write every night now.

My pocket mirror. My boots fit well with my three-sock combination. My feet are no longer cold at night even if the rest of my body is. I'm no longer routinely chained through the day. The *equipo*, or backpack, that Julio gave me—when I bathed yesterday, I used it to carry everything of value, like my plastic bottle of reserve beans, to the river with me rather than leave [it] where it can be stolen or destroyed. My dictionary. What incredible luck that it was in my pocket when I got out of my car on 23 Sept. My *candela*, or fire bucket, to take into this tiny cell at night. The plastic bag I found yesterday. Juaco's green cloth bag to hold my diaries. The diaries themselves. Oh, yes. My precious diaries, the only things about this experience that make sense. My special belt and two checkbooks. I'm listing only physical things, not memories, faith, a good family, etc. I have more than I thought. Fire is so important. My 370-ml brandy bottle lets me drink water with meals. And I have six blankets—enough to stay warm except when it's really cold, like most nights here now.

Thursday, 2 Feb., Day 133

Yesterday was bad; so was last night. Hardly slept. Cold, but more because of worry. What Judi said could be bad. How did she know about army charges? I have no reason to believe the charges have been dropped. Still 10 guards, maximum security at night. FARC could execute me anytime. All I know about Cartagena *secuestrado* return, etc., is what Moño told me.

But I feel far better now this A.M. After some probing, Moño said one problem causing delay of your release is that "your family has made this international news." Moño said this. He sounded irritated. I didn't believe it. I asked again and Moño said it's been in the news around the world. "Why would this being international news delay my release?"

"It's made you a political issue, along with troop withdrawal from the free zone."

"Am I being discussed in the talks in Cartagena?"

"Yes," he said, but can one believe him? "I'm not saying I'm pleased," I said to Moño. "But I'm not surprised. After all, CIAT is an international organization with scientists around the world." I'm delighted, of course. I could have kissed Moño when he told me. I may not be released soon, but my chances of survival increased in my mind, then, by 70 times. Moño meant that the international publicity is delaying my release. I see it as an embarrassment to FARC. And to avoid more negative publicity, FARC is less likely to kill me. If I'm wrong, so be it. That's why FARC is unhappy. But I applaud whoever decided to go public with the news. It's what I'd have done. Now I wait and survive. But right now I feel more like surviving. Something is happening, there's hope. Moño also said Samper [president of Colombia] wants a cease-fire, which would be good for me, but the military is opposed. But he also talks about withdrawal of troops from the free zones, which isn't likely. In fact—and this is very bad—he mentioned that I am now a political issue and he mentioned in context of troop withdrawals. And that is what I have feared. "When did I become an international political issue?"

"About three months ago." Uh-oh, better not pack your bags, Hargrove. If FARC hasn't released you over the past quarter of a year, what makes you think they'll release you now? Well, I can do nothing but survive and wait.

Breakfast is fried bread, my favorite meal here. That says a lot more about the food in general than the fried bread. Sunny.

Lunch: rice and lentils. Went to river and bathed. Water so cold. Jumped in deep pool, complained water too hot. All laughed. I should clown more; probably helps my chances of being taken to bathe more often. A thought: I almost certainly have more years of formal education—21—than all 10 of those who are holding me combined. Worked on my letter to Chuong Thien Province veterans this A.M. That killed a couple of hours. Then pen I stole on 26 Dec. from guerrillas who took my photo just ran out of ink. I now have two. Urine last night was 1.6 liters—because of anxiety?

2045h: In cell. Lord, what a difference hope makes. I feel totally different. I know now that I'll live through this. That I'm mixed up in the politics is probably good—better than being forgotten, in which case I'd be killed, easily. I know I won't be released tomorrow, but release will come and maybe in less than the year I've been preparing myself for. I don't know who made the decision to go public, but I commend and will back him even if for some reason I die because of that decision. But I won't. It may well have saved my life. Dinner was rice, noodles, and potatoes. I saved half [of the] fried bread from breakfast. I'll have a famous Don Ayala noodle taco before turning in.

Friday, 3 Feb., Day 134

I didn't sleep at all till about four A.M. Excitement at the new hope brings mainly [illegible] anxiety at realizing that it's nowhere near over. This has gone on for three months already. Plus the cold. It's awfully cold. Tonight I'm going to try to arrange my blankets like a taco shell and roll into them. I hope we have a family reunion this year. Maybe I could help. Dreamed about Tom G. when he was a little kid. Wish he still were. I wish so much I could relive those years as the kids grew up. Too late for that, but I hope I have the chance to know Tom G. and Miles better as young men. If only I could grab and savor the life that is passing me by right now. What will freedom be like? How will I be? Will I appreciate more the things that make life meaningful: food, people, TV, books, laughter, the freedom to move, love, friendship, pets. Breakfast: *arepa* and potato soup. Lunch: rice and beans. Saved 28 beans. Javier was to type a manuscript for Moño. I typed it for him so he could spend more time playing with Melena, who is assigned to take care of me but won't do a damn thing. Javier gave me two candles, so I now have four candles. Maybe yesterday's elation was premature. Seems I'm being held to trade for something the Colombian government can't give: denial of guerrilla-held zones. The international news does assure that

FARC won't kill me. But now the kidnapping of a CIAT scientist is exposed, and FARC can play hardball with me. Not an enviable position. "You're in a heap of trouble, boy." Those words from the song "Sheriff of Boone County" come to mind whenever I analyze my situation. But I can't give up hope. I don't think the international news elevated me to political prisoner status. That was always going to happen. Similarly, I bet the army charges were pretty well fabricated so FARC could use [them] to defend its actions. I wonder if *that* made it into the news? If so, my career as an international agriculturist is over for sure. Dinner: potato-pasta soup and two fried breads. I asked for and got second bowls of soup and *arepa*. There goes my chance to nail Mel's hide for the button incident. What will I do if she asks to share my *ají* now? A prisoner's life is degrading. I'll still refuse.

Saturday, 4 Feb., Day 135

Woke up thinking I've drifted into something heavy-duty. My situation may be, in a way, more hopeless than ever. I'm a pawn in the international game, one more item on the guerrilla table to pressure the government into what the world would consider legal heresy: give control over areas for free [illegible] and growing of opium. Not likely. Nor is my release. How long can I live like this? The humiliation of being a prisoner is as bad as the loneliness and bad food. Almost.

Breakfast: hominy. I asked for coffee. *"No hay,"* Melena said. Later Gustavo got me the last bit. I must talk with Moño regardless of the revenge Melena can inflict, especially with food. Melena has no interest in my well-being; much less comfort. No more than Daddy would have whether or not one of our cows is happy. He'd want the cow to live but nothing else matters. No, that's not right. Daddy, being a good farmer, would want the cow to be healthy. That's not a matter of high concern with me here. But you're here for a long time more, Hargrove, so accept it. You'll turn 51 in one month right here where you spent Christmas. My "taco shell" blanket arrangement worked better. By wrapping tightly and not moving, I could stay warm enough to sleep. If it weren't for the frequent urinations, one-plus liter, last night. Where does the water come from? Certainly not from the coffee that Melena brings me. Knowing that no medication is available, unless I have something obvious like a broken leg or a gunshot wound, but for nothing more sophisticated, nothing you can't see easily. The sebaceous cysts in my groin worry me the most. They're getting bigger—or seem to as I lose weight and itch and hurt more. A bad infection could be serious indeed, especially with this group. Have sore throat. Took one of the Nogripax pills [cold medicine] that I stole from Juaco's belongings after his death. Haven't had a cold yet. Am at river now, pretending to wash in this icy water. Can't refuse to bathe or they may not take me next time. Rewashed my clean, dry yellow socks—for show.

Lunch: rice and noodles; saved some noodles. Dinner: plate of rice and piece of fried bread. Brought out my mix of beans and noodles. Saved some of all for tonight. I sleep better because I think less of food if I eat before trying to sleep. Maybe I should write Miles and Tom G. instead of Susan. Will say it's not a "last letter"—but it could be.

Sunday, 5 Feb., Day 136

A long day that started with a heartbreaking analysis of my situation. Asked Moño if any news. "The government doesn't believe in peace; it only wants to fight," he said. So the Cartagena talks aren't going well. And if they were, I'm not sure they'd change my destiny. Decided I should write the boys personal letters and, yes, they may be "last letters." If I die, they should each have a personal letter from me, from my captivity. Wrote an hour or so. Then saw a machete lying around. Spent rest of A.M. and couple of P.M. hours cutting green bamboo. Hard work, good exercise.

Breakfast: *arepa*, saved one-third. Lunch: rice and peas, a lot. Saved some in a piece of plastic and in my vitamin bottle. Decided if [I was] going to save food to eat after lockup each night, must have utensils. Don't have plate, bowl, spoon, glass—almost nothing—and must return plate at night. Found half a coconut shell *manjar blanco* came in. I had hidden [it] under porch—cleaned, can be a bowl. Had Javier cut top from plastic Mylanta bottle I found. Can be storage bowl, if covered food with plastic. How long can I store cooked beans, peas here? Two days? Better be careful. Don't want food poisoning—that won't help me survive. Can't wash dishes except with bath soap and very little water. Judi asked to borrow my *equipo*. I refused. "You asked to borrow then stole the cartridge from my ballpoint pen." She got Julio Anderson to come get it. I was very upset, thought I had lost my wonderful *equipo*. That's serious because I load everything that can be stolen plus hoarded food into it and carry it when I go to river to bathe. But *equipo* was back on my bunk when I returned from cutting *chuzco*. Right now it's probably 2:30 P.M. and am lying in a pile of *chuzco* while Moño teaches a class on the porch. I don't like to be around during classes, could be interpreted as snooping, spying. I'm depressed. I can't help it. I don't think I'll leave here—or see the boys or Susan or my family again for a year or so. If I could only read books, listen to a radio, or maybe, most important, talk with a friend. Forget those things, Hargrove. Dwelling on what you don't have, on your misery, won't help you survive. Oh—I told Moño about troubles with Melena. So I'm probably up for some bad times, short food, having gone against both Melena and Judi at the same time. But the last time I told Moño, the problem seemed to get better for a while at least. Moño says next mail goes out 13 Feb.—last was 30 Jan. = 14 days.

2050h: Moño shot two *pava* this A.M. We had for dinner and—I didn't believe it—I got a leg. Tough, stringy, but meat, and delicious. It was the fourth time I've had *pava*, but my first time to taste the meat. I think Moño made sure I got the leg because he was concerned about revenge from Melena.

Monday, 6 Feb., Day 137

Noticed a plastic bottle that held foot powder in the brush but left it there and marked the spot in my mind and think could go get anytime I need it. Victor just walked past carrying it. Lesson learned: at least hide things so others won't find. Like a torn fatigue shirt I found this morning. Was it thrown away for sure or will someone come back for it? I stuck it under the porch near where it was left so it's not obvious to all, but if someone looks for it, it's not obviously hidden. If no one takes [it] in two days, I move it into my cell. I can use the cloth so many ways. A rag to move my *candela*—tear parts to make washcloths, etc. Found plastic Axion soap dish—a plate for my locked-in meal. I need a spoon but can't think of anything to use. Found a nail. I now have four. Went to bed fairly full last night and seem to have slept better for it. Breakfast was fried bread. Should have saved part but couldn't—famished. So much starch. I guess I'm so undernourished. Lunch: rice and beans. Saved 39 beans. Figured out that Colombians—or at least this FARC group—don't like the crusty part of cooked rice because I get a lot of it. My favorite part. Also saved some crusty rice for tonight. I'm getting to be a fanatic about saving stuff. Susan will be amused—or irritated—will say I'm like my grandmother who saved everything. But it pays off. I never throw away hoarded food.

Breakfast is served anytime between 6:30 and 8:20 A.M. No pattern. I guess it doesn't matter much; these guys have nothing to do but guard me. Moño has short training sessions every few days. One last week was on the space in front of my cell where I could see—and I think purposely. It was on searching for and finding people who are hiding. But *Leaving Cheyenne* just isn't very practical with only one trail out of this valley and 10 persons who know and use the trail—to chase me—and not knowing where to go if I got out of the valley. Lunch.

Writing about hoarding must have triggered luck. Soon after, I found an aluminum pan in the bushes around camp. Looks like army issue. It's about five inches in diameter, three inches deep. Bent and burned, but it has no holes. So I now have a real plate. The guerrillas are so wasteful—or maybe they just can't conceptualize, don't plan for the future. A few days after Moño gave me the food on 18 Dec., he asked if I'd eaten it all. "Eat it—that's what it's for," he said. I was hoarding, stretching it out. The attitude is most evident with fire. They all pile on as much wood as they can, build the biggest fire possible. I think of American Indians, who thought white men were foolish for building huge fires when small ones were more efficient. The [guerrillas] set fire to the forest *chuzco* groves just to watch them burn. Often they don't even do that, just set the fire and leave. I worry about the fuel for future fires. We seem to have plenty, but I'm afraid we'll be here a year, maybe longer, and use plenty of fuel, but I try to conserve fuel, feed it to the fire as the fire needs it. When I leave any log on at night, I pull out partially burned pieces. The guerrillas think that's strange. The situation looks so bleak. I wonder what Havener/CIAT would tell me if we could talk. That they're onto something that could spring me soon?

Maybe, but I suspect the situation looks about as dismal from there as from here. Poor Susan, what will she do?

2040h: Dinner: rice and beans and noodles. Five guerrillas bring around my [illegible] from five to eight. I wrote Havener re. Cuba again and why not invite FARC to send a representative to visit CIAT?

Tuesday, 7 Feb., Day 138

Awakened this A.M. thinking about my situation. The chances that FARC will release me—if that is contingent on turning the free zones over to the guerrillas—seems incredibly, dismally remote. And FARC could decide to execute me at any time. The thought of dying isn't what scares and depresses me so—but the thought of living on and on like this is pure anguish. I've lived with the thought of the real possibility of death constantly for five months. I'm prepared to face it, I think. If I learn that FARC will execute me, I'll ask to be alone for a few minutes. That'll give me time to cry—controlled crying—with no witnesses. Then I think I can face the bullets—and that is how I will do it— with dignity. I can't say I've found my peace with God or whatever force exists to counter evil and bring decency and order to the world. But I've tried. Maybe I *have* made my peace, found that solace, but just don't realize it. I seem to be strong psychologically. I cry alone sometimes, but that must be normal. Strange, I cry especially when I try to pray. (Maybe that tells me something: that I'm selfish, dwell on myself and my own family. If so . . . so be it. I can't change.) Every morning I think I can't make it through today. Not another day of nothing, of emptiness and aching loneliness. But I *do* make it. At night I try to remember how I passed all those hours. I can't—not really. But if death is to come, I'd prefer to face it now rather than continue this existence. If I knew that death in captivity will come, I could even handle suicide. I'd welcome the opportunity, but I never even think about it because there's hope that I'll be freed. What if I knew that I'll be freed—but after, say, three years of this? That's a tough one, but I'd go on living. I'd wait it out. But the pain it would cause Susan and the boys—that's hard to think about. But I know a lot about survival and I'm constantly learning more. Food at night—my special and secret meal in the cell after lockup—is awfully important. Psychologically even more than physically. Maybe my situation isn't as bad as it seems. All I really know is what Mono has told me—and that can be very selective. If my family making international news of my kidnapping is such a big deal and it began three months ago, why do I hear about it only now? And only Mono says my release is tied to government withdrawal from free zones. Problem is I suspect he's telling me the truth. I've feared that all along. Still, I hear little of what is going on. Breakfast: hominy. Leidi made a fire at seven A.M. and asked if I'd give her English lessons later. I found a plastic bag—fairly clean, no leaks. Lunch: rice and lentils. I saved some lentils in vitamin bottle and rice in Mylanta bottle with plastic sack for cover. Then bathed. It's a clear day. But discovered something at river that made me sick—my shampoo—I treasure it. Always wash hair three to four times with bar soap first to save shampoo. But like a fool I left the bottle out-side. My cell is so small and has no shelves. I could leave the bottle only on the floor. Well, someone stole most of the shampoo. I had a third of a bottle. Now only a fifth. It's my own fault, of course. And I've already written about what I think of someone who could steal from a prisoner. Oh well, I can make what's left last a couple of months, and I can live without shampoo. What if I'd lost my diary?

Washed the "new" pan that I found in the river and noticed something strange: writing scratched into the side. Hard to make out, but one line clearly says "TAPTE=TIANQU=FIANQU=DACHIN." I wrote the letters as they are. Below says, "TIP-TOP-(Yes)TUP=YAP[or QAP?]YUP and more writing I can't decipher. That doesn't seem to be Spanish. Brings to mind these stories that keep coming up about the Vietnamese who came here to train guerrillas. Strange. Dragons live on, don't they?

2025h: Moño also knew the five Vietnamese. He said they trained Colom-bians at this camp. Dinner: rice and fried beans, nothing more. I brought out and added the last of my peas. After dinner, six of the guerrillas hung around my *fogón* singing, mostly FARC songs for me. Moño said government-guerrilla fighting had broken out across Colombia. Bad. But he also said that the gov-ernment has formed a special committee in Bogotá to study demands of the guerrillas. "A cease-fire will come," he said.

"Then will FARC release all the *secuestrados*?"

"Yes."

"Including me?"

"Claro." Of course.

"When will the cease-fire come?"

Moño shrugged, *"¿Quién sabe?* A week, two months, a year . . ."

Wednesday, 8 Feb., Day 139

Awoke this A.M. thinking how ironic that to fight the alleged abuse of hu-man rights the guerrillas are using the deprivation of human rights. And worse in some ways because FARC doesn't care *who* is kidnapped and holds as long as it pressures the government. I'd like to say that to Moño and the others, but I won't. It would do no good and certainly would not help me survive. Melena found my article on kidnapping this A.M. I wrote in other notebook, camouflaged with lots of Spanish words and English—how it threw me into a near panic. But I think I did okay. It's now about eleven A.M., perfectly clear and hot. But ice formed outside in water this A.M. I've felt a strong need to write to people I love. Have written to Mrs. Sheldon, Miles Sheldon, Raford, Becky, Daddy, the CIAT Communications Unit, Bill Smith (one of the best friends a man could have), Havener, Don Fields, and now Rex and Sibyl and Dan and Joyce. They're not all "last letters," at least not in the traditional sense. But I guess they'll do if FARC and fate make them my last letters.

Breakfast: fried bread. Lunch: rice and peas. There were rat droppings in the peas, but I threw them out and ignored it. Saved some of both. My illicit prebed meal is becoming the main one of the day. That's okay. I look forward to it all day. Went to stream after lunch. Guerrillas tried to catch trout with hands in a pond. "Why not throw in a hand grenade?" I asked Moño.

"They cost Colombia $100,000 each." Wow. That's $125 each for a made-in-USA M-26 grenade.

It's now about two. I'll get through today somehow—but what will I do tomorrow?

Later. Time goes slow but I know not to slow it more by looking at my watch. I wrote about Asian vs. Western concepts of the passage of time in *A Dragon Lives Forever*. Time, here, is strange because it brings nothing: not pleasure, or utility, or knowledge. I want time to pass faster because it has no value. But the passage of time doesn't take me toward anything that I can see. I'll make it through today—but for what? Only to face a tomorrow of equal nothingness. In a way time is standing still here in the Northern Andes of Colombia. All the guerrillas have pans and cups and are headed to *la rancha* for coffee. I'm here alone and no one will give me coffee, and suddenly I'm the loneliest person in the world. Five months since I've talked to anyone—since I've had a conversation, a friend. I can't stand it. Cut it out, Hargrove. You're letting a cup of coffee that you don't get trigger all this emotion, this self-pity. Will that help you survive? Definitely not. I'll build a fire, even if it's too early. This must end someday, in some manner. I must do something to stop, counter this terrible depression. Today was bad. At 1100h Viejito came riding up on a mule from Happy Valley. As always with an unexpected visitor, I thought he might be bringing orders for my release. Why do I do it to myself? Now I'm in my cell. Javier and Melena waited till I'm locked in and are now burning my wood in my *fogón*. I would not mind so much if they weren't so wasteful like all the guerrillas. I want to be around decent people again. I want my family. Dinner was rice and lentils. I filled up—then Melena brought a piece of fried beef. Viejito had brought it. Saved most. Am about to eat. Maybe that'll cheer me up.

Later: Problem with the locked-in meal has been that I have no spoon, and it's hard to eat rice, lentils, beans with only your hands. Then I thought: We're living in a bamboo grove. I found some dry *chuzco* and made chopsticks. Work okay except the inner side is rough. Would smooth if I had a knife.

Thursday, 9 Feb., Day 140

My black pen is out of ink. The cartridge looked full but was empty. Now I have only the one "legal" blue pen. Am tempted to steal, but won't. The guerrillas are taking my wood for their own fires. I don't mind so much, for my fire, even if I'm not there, but they do it from laziness. "It's easier to take wood from the prisoner's pile than to gather it myself, and he's not likely to complain." I need a comb or a headband or both. My hair is so long. I borrowed a comb this A.M., but don't like that—fleas.

Breakfast: fried bread and a piece of beef. The meat is good but doesn't smell fresh. Am saving some. Now: if meat is spoiling, is it best to eat the meat cooked most recently or the oldest? The question is, does the meat spoil faster when raw or after cooked? Raw, I think, so best to eat the freshest-cooked first. I *must* shake this depression. I can't afford it. It's so easy to start crying and that won't help me survive. I've cried from time to time since this began and I think it's healthy. But I cry too easily now, although always in private. I can't try to pray; that brings on the crying. How do I shake it? What will I do to make today pass, go away into the past like I hope tomorrow will go? I guess I'll gather more firewood. Lunch: rice and noodles and piece of beef that was only a bite with gristle. But like before I save the gristle and tendons to use as chewing gum—a gum that eventually disintegrates. To the stream after lunch. Saved a piece of watchband as flat sharp edge last month. Used to scrape my new chopsticks smooth.

Later: Talks in Cartagena still on, Moño says, so hope there. Also he said another U.S. *secuestrado* was kidnapped in Cali. Susan still in Cali but boys are gone. Moño says other *secuestrado* worked in Jumbo [an industrial suburb of Cali]. Almost never have milk in chocolate or coffee now. Cows give little milk. They don't have enough to eat. Like me. Still coffee and chocolate are my two favorite things, the *only* sweets, sugar, I get. How long without veggies now— two months? Is it possible they may bring the *rehen* in Cali here? Then I'd have someone to talk to, but I want that only if they send extra food. We can't feed one more on what we have. Later: A terrible thought. What if the new *secuestrado* is [name of a neighbor and close friend]? How many foreigners work in Jumbo? Moño is sure he's from USA, but remember we're dealing with folks who think Japan is a commie nation. That would be awful. Especially for Susan. Pray that it's not.

Dinner: rice and lentils. Chopsticks work well.

Friday, 10 Feb., Day 141

What an anniversary: kidnapped exactly five months ago today. Breakfast: *arepa* and fried bread. Tried to save some but couldn't—starving. Didn't sleep well. 1.5 liters urine and so cold. Lunch: rice and peas. Bathed in stream. Four fires on mountain to southwest our group started. Burn many hectares but no one cares. Melena turned 17 yesterday.

Dinner: rice, spoon of pasta, piece of beef, but almost no meat. Gristle like leather—can't even bear to use as gum. Moño had first guard at eight P.M. "Would you like to sit by the fire awhile longer before [you] go to bed?"

"*Con mucho gusto*, if you don't mind." I think he suggested it so he could pass some information to me. Significant information if it's true. He first brought up that I was international news, but one month ago not two. The price of your release, he then said, is that your family agreed to pay the ransom. But the money was paid two weeks ago to a group in the Colombian army that claimed to represent or be in contact with FARC. It was a trick. This problem has delayed the negotiations, but I'm sure you'll be released soon. Wow. I didn't know what to think—I still don't. I'm sure relieved to know that something is happening—although I had prayed that my release would come without paying ransom. I feel very bad for Susan if, indeed, a group of Colombian army swindled her out of the ransom money. How terrible for her—in the midst of so many awful things. Poor Susan, I want to cry, thinking about it. If it's true—and I don't exactly have usual and reliable sources for any news—but why should Moño lie about this? Moño also said the international press was only about me not the *secuestrados* of Colombia in general. The foreigner kidnapped in Cali—the one who works in Jumbo—is definitely from the USA. The guerrillas have four foreign *secuestrados*, he says. Two are U.S. citizens, one is Belgian. Oh, thank you, God for not letting it be Ulie. That would be on my conscience—and Susan's—forever. I've tried to be careful—to protect my neighbors, will be especially careful in the future. The investigation is over and I've been cleared of the army charge. That coincides, I guess, with my being allowed outside without chains. FARC has spent 500 thousand only for food for my guards since Sept. After the charges first came up, the first orders were to assign 15—not 10—soldiers to guard me. FARC has plenty, one thousand, [one] hundred soldiers for this province alone. "So with all this you think I'll be free fairly soon—that it won't take a year like I've planned?"

"No, but your situation is *muy delicado*," Moño said as I left the fire and entered my cell for the night.

Saturday, 11 Feb., Day 142

What do I think of last night's news? I'm still overwhelmed—especially the part about paying ransom money to the Colombian group. I feel some relief, a sense that I'll survive and maybe be released in a matter of weeks with my mental and physical health still sound. Blended with that is an aching pain for what Susan must feel and a sense of guilt for having caused it all. How much money could be involved? Don't think about that now. You can do nothing about it and it won't help you survive. Now I live in the present as much as I can and want. Don't fall into that trap again, Hargrove. That of deceiving yourself into believing it's almost over, just because that's what you want so desperately.

Breakfast: rice and lentils. Washed my bowl, bean bottle with bar soap and a sock. Sunny and hot but couldn't sleep for the cold last night. River after lunch. Have learned to jump in cold water right away, make lots of noise, then sit in the sun as day goes by. What happened to Susan if indeed it did happen, but why should Moño lie about that? Seems worse and worse and so terribly unfair. How she must feel. I wish I could comfort her. Of course, I'm not with her and that's why this happened in the first place—to get me back. I've prayed for God to help Susan as much as me.

Now, how can something so cruel happen? The money part must be serious indeed; the psychological part worse. I can stay here longer, be released whenever other *secuestrados* are released. I'm neither happy nor comfortable, but I'm surviving and I know things could be a lot worse. But why, God, did you let this happen to Susan? How did you do it to her, how? I knew that many bad things would happen before this ordeal ends, but this is one of the cruelest blows yet. If it really happened, Hargrove. And you don't know that. Not for sure. But the last time—the only time—I've really felt this way before was when Bacchus [our dachshund] was killed as I was leaving for 'Nam in '69. I cursed God then. I won't do that now; but I can't understand why this cruelty to Susan.

Jhon burned a stack of my *chuzco* this P.M. Said it was a mistake, but I can't see how, and it was beside a huge pile of dry *chuzco*. Days of work! He watched and laughed as I struggled to put the fire out and keep it from spreading to the dry pile. Javier and Melena watched and laughed, too, and no one helped me, even though all use the *fogón*. Especially Javier and Melena. Cruel and senseless but not worth even thinking about compared with what they did to Susan.

Sunday, 12 Feb., Day 143

This must be the worst time since my kidnapping—even worse than the solitary confinement and the hunger. Oh, Susan. I hurt for you. I talked with Moño this A.M. "The Colombian army did it," he said. "*Nosotros no tenemos la culpa* [We're not to blame]."

"You kidnap me, yet you're not to blame?" I replied. "You can't deny responsibility for what happens as a result of your crime."

Moño shrugged. I walked away so he couldn't see my tears. I overstepped, said more than I should have. And violated my most important rule in dealing with FARC. Showing anger, contempt at Moño or FARC in general will *not* help me survive. And I want to survive, tell Susan it's okay. Nothing else.

It's sunny and most guerrillas have gone to the stream to bathe. I was not taken, probably because of what I said. Oh well. Maybe it's not so bad, maybe Moño's story is to make me hate the Colombian army. Maybe it's not so much money. Mail goes out tomorrow. Should I mention this in my letter to Susan? When I don't really know and she can't respond? I have to clear my head and think rationally, not emotionally.

Later: How stupid to have exploded at Moño—and how it hurts my pride, my manhood to admit it. If I'd gone to the stream, it would have killed this A.M.—half a day—and I'd have done the few things I did this P.M.

Also the supplies arrive tomorrow and I need so many things. How extensive will the punishment be and how long will it last? That I go to bathe had become a standard practice. It was denied this A.M. on purpose.

Monday, 13 Feb., Day 144

It's 9:30 A.M. It's cold, cloudy, windy. Winter is coming. Most guerrillas went to Happy Valley to pick up the new supply shipments. I'm by the fire, burning wood, not *chuzco*. Must shake the anger and depression that came with the news of what happened to Susan. It'll do me no good, won't help me survive. Poor Susan, and I'd have been home last week—but you're not, Hargrove, so forget it. Sent 11 letters—mostly just notes, really—with the outgoing mail. I think we have the potential for a violent showdown here in the Valley of the Shadow over women. Jhon has so little sense—and he keeps going after Melena even when Javier is nearby. *Hands* all over her. Same with Leidi, but she's sleeping with everyone, so not much potential. Jhon is so stupid—really—and I sense real violence in him. What would I do if I were alone and a rape were attempted—among two guerrillas, my captors? I'd have no love for either. And both are armed and dangerous. But the real potential for violence lies with Javier in this case. Ramiro has torn down his *caleta* and built a "tree house" in the rafters of the team hut. My fourth meal is getting to be the main event of my day—what I look forward to most. Chopsticks work fine. Somehow manage to wash "dishes" with soap each day. But must be more careful. I let rice go bad and didn't realize it at first last night. Sick this A.M.

2115h: Went to river. Moño says new talks start tomorrow between government and guerrillas in Medellín at national level. Popayán for Cauca, and *reténs* are an issue. I'll hope later. Right now, I burned out of getting my hopes up for nothing. My 11 letters will leave Happy Valley tomorrow via a mule train of two animals and in five days will reach wherever it is that the letters can be mailed. I realize that I have a rare opportunity here to express genuine thanks and love to a few people. Like the letter I wrote to John Brien today, congratulating him for receiving the ACE International Award. He'll never forget receiving a congratulatory letter from a kidnap victim, a hostage "somewhere in Colombia." Judi gave me a piece of gummy, sweet candy from the supplies that arrived today. "What is this called?"

"Gelatina."

"Made from the bones of cows?"

"Yes."

Tuesday, 14 Feb., Day 145

Happy Valentine's Day. Finally checked ink in this, my only pen. Less than half inch—not enough to last a week, and I have a list of letters to write to pass the time constructively. Plus diary notes. Pens have "appeared" as I needed in the past. Will it happen again? I have only one thing to trade—my mirror. But if I trade, how will I explain not having it when guerrillas want to borrow? Might trade my pan with Ramiro. He borrows the pan to clean his M-16. I don't know, of course, if they even have pens to trade. Next supply shipment? But how to explain using so much ink? It's always one thing or another. Out of paper or out of ink, but I must keep my record of this experience going. I often think if only I had all the *arepas* or fried bread I could eat, I'd be happy. I could not be, of course, but that's how hungry I am. Although I'd be happy, at least, tonight. Even when I eat enough, I get hungry again soon. My body, malnourished, absorbs all the food and cries for more. I don't care as much about what food I get anymore—just food. I want something to give the rice flavor, though, when possible.

Later: Ramiro [illegible] has no pen—so I keep my pen. Gustavo says he'll share a pen with me when I run out of ink. That's a relief.

Melena wouldn't look at me or say anything when she brought my lunch. "Are you mad at me?"

"No." She shook her head.

"Are you sick?" She nodded, then put her finger to her lips.

"Come to see me later if you want to talk."

She nodded. Four to five nights ago she was crying because of the fiery pain in her lower stomach. I'll bet anything she's pregnant. If so, not even those working on the O. J. Simpson case could figure out who the father is—could be anyone here or who's left except me. Poor thing. As much trouble as we've had. I feel sorry for her.

Later: Am at river, just me now and two girls, 15 and 17, in black bras and bikini panties; everyone bathes in underwear. What would Susan think? But somehow it's not very sexy. Jhon just left and I'm relieved. Judi brought me, so [she's] my guard. I almost left with Ramiro but she said I should stay. I think it's that they don't want to be alone with Jhon. But I'm a *prisoner*. Thought: In the new talks, local government can make a deal with guerrillas. Moño said maybe there's hope there because the Cauca government just might agree to "free zones." Although I'd be happy at least tonight.

Wednesday, 15 Feb., Day 146

2145h: Hot, clear day. To river in P.M. Night is hazy with smoke from fires all around, lit by the sun, they say. Must be, there's no one but us up here. The moon is full and as yellow as butter through the smoke. The bulb broke in my flashlight with no replacement available. Moño said could replace when bulbs arrive on supply train and that could be a year. Terrible. But Gustavo saw. "Wait until later," he said. After dinner he appeared and replaced the bulb. *"¡Gracias a Dios!"* Where he got the bulb, I'll never know. Not from his room, and that's where we were when he told me to wait. I owe Gustavo a lot. How could I survive without a flashlight? Hope I can send him something after I leave. If I leave. Of course, he stole my original flashlight back in the Valley of Death. Wonder if he knows I know. My lips are so chafed and cracked and my hands are like a rasp. Found a quarter sheet of absolutely clean typing paper in a grove—the largest size I use for letters—a sign? Shifting a lot of diary to Notebook 3—menu, urine at back, innocent stuff in Spanish throughout. Cow's hoof for lunch. Not bad. At first I thought some type of vegetable or maybe a root. Asked Ramiro what it was. *"Pata de vaca* [a cow's hoof]."

"¿Pero es un rais o vegetal, o qué? [But is it a root or a vegetable, or what?]"

"Pie de vaca [foot of a cow]," he said, pointing to a cow.

Thursday, 16 Feb., Day 147

Found another piece of paper—6x9 inches crumpled but totally clean. A sign to write more letters? Although there are no clouds this P.M., the sun is overcast with smoke from the brushfires. At times it gives the land an eerie strange orange glow like some of the Kodachrome photos that Tim Pages took in 'Nam.

1530h: The sun is an orange disk that you can stare at with the naked eye. The light glows softly, yellow and orange. The distant fires crackle like the crushing sheets of plastic interrupted by cracks like gunshots when bamboo explodes.

1545h: The fire in the valley sounds like a distant battle. It's hard to believe that all this fire is a natural process—or that it won't affect us—sweep through and wipe out this lonely camp.

1600h: Have made my own fire. Will I ever leave this valley? I have written Susan, full of hope. I can survive. The new talks will lead to a cease-fire and I'll be free. But how true is that? I don't even know if there are new talks. I know only what FARC tells me. But I can't give up the hope.

Later: Honestly, I feel my life—which is not a life but a joyless existence—will continue this way for a long, long time. But I don't know that, so I want to continue to live. I must shake this. Four *pava* were unfortunate enough to alight in a tree near the camp this A.M. I watched Mono shoot three of them. So dinner was rice, potatoes, and *pava*—and I got the backs. Will I ever again eat for pleasure, choose what I want to eat? Will I always be perpetually hungry? This isn't life. Stop it, Hargrove. This won't help you survive. Food fantasies for two weeks now. Malted chocolate milk mixed in a blender with fresh raspberries and strawberries. Still on a chocolate kick.

2015h: By the fire after dinner, Mono said he felt sure I'd be free by early March. He said the *comandante* wants to free me and I could be freed apart through the government-guerrilla talk. Can I trust what he says? Like when I asked Mother what she thought of things [as she was dying of cancer]. "I don't have much choice, do I?" Found still another piece of paper. But if a sign to write letters, that means I'll be here a long time yet? Maybe not. Do it, Hargrove. "It's two days by foot to the nearest populated area," Mono said, referring to my release. "Can you walk that far? It's a tough trip."

"To leave here, I'll crawl."

Friday, 17 Feb., Day 148

I certainly noted that the four-day trip is now a more reasonable two days. I wonder if Mono remembers that the official FARC line is four days? Friday Mono lent me his pen to use until Monday, when the wonderful pack train supposedly brings . . . everything, according to Mono and the others. Am reminded of the song "Mule Train." Leidi has moved in with Jhon at night, hands all over him in day. Especially when we're swimming in underwear at river. I could write a book on love and sex life of guerrillas, but I won't. Not very interested. But thought Leidi had more sense. Paper may be from Gustavo, who's moody and writes sad songs about lost love.

P.M.: Found three more pieces of paper—typewriter. Not written on, but dirty. Washed with handkerchief and drying in cell. Will write more letters. Later. Melena died this afternoon suddenly and unexpectedly of colic. It was sad, but we didn't let her body go to waste. We cut her up immediately, roasted her heart and liver, fried her loins, and gorged on the rich meat. I'm not referring to Melena the incredibly dumb guerrilla girl, but to the Hereford cow I named in honor of the human Melena. She was five years old and left behind a young heifer calf. At about four P.M. she was lying outside the team hut. Julio Anderson said it was colic and had all the guerrillas urinate in an empty brandy bottle. He then forced the urine down the cow's nose—several bottles. But Melena died anyhow. The big joke was that I was praying for Melena—to die. We skinned Melena and cut her up. I went to *la rancha* for the first time. Moño said to cut and cook whatever meat I wanted. I started with liver while Ramiro cooked heart. Later I cut away and fried a huge piece of loin. Ate until I couldn't eat anymore—the first time I've been really full since my kidnapping. Also drank all the hot chocolate I wanted. A meal I'll never forget. But *la otra de la moneda* [the other face of the coin] is Melena was the source of our only milk. So now there'll be no more milk for our coffee and chocolate. And nothing has really changed. Even though I go to bed with a full stomach tonight, I'm still a prisoner in a remote camp in the Colombian Andes with a pretty dismal future.

Saturday, 18 Feb., Day 149

Ubre, or cow udder, for breakfast. Mad. Melena couldn't find key to cell. Firetrap. Raised hell with Moño. Changed lock somewhat.

1600h: Around three P.M. was cutting *chuzco* when Julio asked if I wanted to cook meat. Went to *la rancha*, where we spent two hours cutting and cooking whatever piece of meat we wanted. We had kidney, lots of udder, tail. Reminds me of what I've heard about the American Indians. When they'd kill buffalo after lean times, would spend days gorging. Interesting afternoon. My second time to *la rancha* in two days. Will it continue? A sign of loosening up? Before my release? Don't build up hope again, Hargrove.

Sunday, 19 Feb., Day 150

Breakfast: *arepas*, piece of fried beef. After the orgies of beef, I can't help it—are they trying to fatten me up so I'll look better at release? Please, God, let me, help me quit thinking such thoughts if they're only cruel false hope. Yesterday P.M., Moño told me to take a piece of boiled beef from lunch back to my cell. I had piece of beef and of *ubre* [udder], and didn't [take another piece]. Have regretted it since. Why give up such an opportunity? Much joking about the cow. *"¡Se murió por la lucha!"* She died for the cause!

Later: Received third *arepa*, second coffee, more beef. But don't read hope into that, Hargrove. Gustavo brought the extra food. He has *la rancha*—kitchen duty—today and he's always done nice things for you. Yesterday I found a love letter Javier had written [to Melena] on typewriter paper and thrown away. Enough blank paper at the bottom to make a piece of *secuestrado* stationery. You'd think I'd say "Go to hell" at being invited to *la rancha* after 2½ months of eating 100 percent in solitude. But a person needs human companionship, no matter what the situation.

Later: The guerrillas used a piece of rope to make a swing from a large tree near the hut. (When the rope arrived, we joked about it being ordered to hang Don Tomás.) This morning I found a pair of scissors—the small folding kind, made in China—in the leaves beneath the swing. They had fallen from a pocket. What luck! I have to borrow scissors to trim my mustache and to "shave" (razor too dull). It'd be easy to find out whose scissors they are—only two or three people play on the swing. "Thou shalt not steal." But when thou art a *secuestrado*, thou can bend the 10 Commandments a bit. Are scissors a sign? But I need them for the long not the short term. In books, gorging on meat and rich food when so hungry makes one sick. Not me. I feel great. The wire I've collected could help me start a hardware store. Am using Moño's pen—hope to get a new one tomorrow. Today will write letters. One reason is to use his ink.

P.M.: What is going on? Lunch was a nice piece of beef, *arepa*, rice, and lentils. But Moño brought out a little table he had made for me to eat my meals on. Wow. In conversation he said, "You're going to be released soon. Keep your faith."

"When? In a month? A week? Two days?"

He shrugged. "I don't know, but soon." Treatment really seems to be changing. Maybe I *will* go home.

Gustavo brought coffee out after lunch. We all joked about returning to Valley of the Shadow when the war's over and opening a tourist hotel. Gustavo is in charge of the kitchen and restaurant, Caballito the headwaiter, Julio runs the disco, I run the bar, Moño in charge of the entire operation. Something is happening. Don't. Don't count on it, Hargrove. Remember what your father-in-law always said: "The show's not over till the fat lady sings." And she hasn't sung yet. Another wrenching heartache is something you don't need. "Tomás! We have another *prisionero*!" Moño said. I almost believed him. It's a mouse that Caballito caught and has on a string.

Moño keeps asking if I want a haircut. No, no one has worried about my hair until now, and I don't want it cut.

2205h: I'm scaring myself. I'm becoming convinced that release will come soon. After dinner I sat with Moño through first guard, then Julio came. It was 9:15 P.M.—1 hour 15 minutes past lockup time. I prepared my *candela* and went into cell. "Don Tomás, would you like to roast some beef?" Julio said, then went to *la rancha* and returned with three pieces. We roasted and I took a big piece back into cell, where I am now. Stranger still, they gave me a big piece of the fresh but salted smoked beef to take into cell to roast myself over my own fire when I want. Only a few days ago I thought I'd be happy if I had all the *arepas* I wanted and now have three hidden away in my cell. Am I being "fattened"— physically and psychologically—so I'll make better appearance (physically and psychologically) when released? If so, I'm falling for it, at least the physical part. I can't quit eating roasted meat and *arepas*. Tomorrow new supplies arrive. I wouldn't be surprised if *veggies* appear. But maybe this is normal treatment and it began to some degree with clearance of the army charges. Please, God, don't let this be false hope again.

Monday, 20 Feb., Day 151

Had a big piece of liver and arepa for breakfast, supplemented with fried beef and cow udder. Lit my *candela* and warmed all. Javier talked with me for a long time. When will you leave? he asked. He said all the guerrillas believe I'll be leaving right away. I told him my story of the *retén* and my kidnapping. Javier was there and said I have my facts right, as he remembers them.

Cold, cloudy. Most guerrillas to Happy Valley to get supplies. I sent 16 letters.

I try not to but can't help thinking constantly of freedom. Last night I was awake to two or three A.M., thinking not of food but how freedom will come. I think Moño—and the others—truly think I'm leaving very soon. But no orders have come. And they might not come. Lord, I hope FARC isn't waiting for another *rescate* [i.e., ransom] payment. Please not that, God, not after what has already happened to Susan. If only I could talk with Susan. But I can't influence anything, can only wait.

P.M.: Made big fire with Melena before lunch. At lunch I wanted more meat, so went to *la rancha*. Jhon will cook. One worrisome thing is: I have so much more freedom and better treatment because, I guess, all think I'll leave in days. What happens if days, weeks pass and no freedom? The honeymoon will be over. Will FARC make me resume my previous treatment? You're overdoing it, Hargrove, confusing decent treatment, what you should have had all along, with being pampered. Melena the cow's death, of course, was an unexpected windfall. But I was already getting more and better food. Had that cow died in Dec., I'd have received beef, but nothing like now. Jhon fried a huge extra piece for me—part goes into my larder, which is growing. Still have three *arepas* but not the same three as before. Melena can't stand to see me get any better treatment or freedom or independence; I could feel it strongly when I was in *la rancha* for the two orgies of beef. Not because it's her job to see that I'm fed— she hates doing that. But, I think, because it threatens her; she's the lowest person here, except for Judi. She sees anything that raises my status as lowering her own position. She's so pitiful and dumb. Later. Taught Jhon to use chopsticks. He learned immediately. Must truly be in the blood.

1605h: By fire with huge log burning. Ramiro was first back from Happy Valley. He told me to be sure to stay away from *la rancha*—*"un camarada"* [a comrade] is coming. I can't help but wonder, of course, if the visitor has anything to do with my release. Later. Roasted *sobrebarriga* [stomach meat] and drank chocolate with Gustavo and Moño from 8:45 to 10:30 P.M. Supplies didn't arrive. If Moño has such good radio contact—which I've never seen—how could he send seven people to Happy Valley to get supplies that didn't arrive? Brought me bottle of ketchup and *ají*. Wonderful! Asked Moño if this is his first command. "Yes, and I'm both first and second in command." He later [told me] Javier's his XO [executive officer], or second in command. Now I understand— Javier is obviously worthless.

Tuesday, 21 Feb., Day 152

This will be a long day. Woke up to a cold realization: I've been deceiving myself again—or letting myself be deceived. I'm not going to be released soon. No wheels are turning for my freedom. The "signs" have all been from Moño or the guerrillas. Or, are the signs real, but I'm suddenly afraid to see them because I can't bear the hurt when my delusions of freedom fall? That I lack faith? The army charges have probably been dropped; that still leaves me a kidnap victim held for ransom at least—a ransom and God only knows how much—that my family has paid, but was cheated of. I have nothing to promise, or even indicate, that I'll be released in a week or a month or a year. But what can I do? Nothing. Gather more firewood though winter rains are starting. The hurt. The pain. The cruelty. The lying to myself. I've been held 5½ months against the laws of man and God and human decency. Then I'm grateful for a fucking bottle of ketchup. Go gather wood, Hargrove, the winter rains are starting and you're going to be here through a long, cold, and wet winter. SURVIVE, Tom. [illegible] Survive. Gather wood so you can at least sit, even if always alone, by a warm fire in the winter. If you love your family, survive. That's all you can do for them. And quit crying.

Ear infection again. No medications, antibiotics, here, and none in Happy Valley. This is crazy.

Moño said he'll give me some ground coffee.

I have enough wood stockpiled to build and maintain fires every night for almost a month. I said—seriously—to Moño last night, "Considering all that's happening, do you think I should keep gathering wood?" I meant, of course, why gather more wood if I'm leaving in a day or two? Why not build a big fire with what I have and enjoy it?

"No, keep collecting wood. We really don't know how long we'll be here." I know that, of course. Well, I'm gathering wood. . . .

1830h: Today was a bad day, an awful day. I guess it had to come. I had to realize that I'd deceived myself—so cruelly—again. To make it worse the winter rain began—I think for real.

Wednesday, 22 Feb., Day 153

2015h: After writing above last night, I lost the pen I borrowed from Moño. I was terribly depressed—realizing there is no machinery for my release, then losing the ability to write. Slept well, surprisingly—depressed exhaustion often does that. Blocks the ability to think because your thoughts are all about how bleak, how hopeless is your life. Roasted a piece of the meat Moño gave me, locked in cell, over my *candela*. That helped. The A.M. was just as bad. Deep dark depression. Found the pen under porch. The sun came out and started drying wood and *chuzco*. I began to prepare for a long winter—storing dried fuel in the rafters of the hut. Spent the day at that. Had words with Moño over my jacket. "We all must sacrifice for the revolution," he said.

"It's not my revolution. You kidnapped me and I was here helping your country." I immediately regretted saying that—it won't help me survive. Later we talked for an hour about the revolution, then played "Tricky" with Ramiro and others—the whole camp is playing it. Moño told me that the *comandante* really wants to let me go, but there are others who do not. That he has been trying to get me released since the investigation, and others who helped capture me are against my release. Like I'm a big catfish and everyone who helped catch me has a say in whether or not I'm let go. I could be released any day, Moño says. Can I believe him? I must. Leidi has first guard tonight. Asked about my sons. I bragged about them, said I'd like to have her for a daughter-in-law, then asked for a piece of raw but smoked meat from *la rancha*. She brought it. I am about to roast my fourth meal. Got big shipment of maize and it's being served like rice. A welcome change.

Thursday, 23 Feb., Day 154

1100h: At the river with Ramiro and Jhon, helping build up the dam to deepen the water in the *charco*, or pond, where we bathe—although that's harder because we have more clouds and rain now and it's colder. I must be really paranoid. What Moño said makes me feel so much better, gives me hope. But the other, darker, and maybe more realistic side of my mind says, "Don't believe it. Don't torture yourself." I'm hauling rocks and logs. Better, far better, than staying at the camp thinking. Ramiro gave me a headband. A bit Rambo-ish, but practical. 2145h: Today wasn't nearly so bad as yesterday. Played Tricky with Ramiro in evening and won six of seven games. He had first guard—we went to *la rancha* and fried beef and played Tricky. I stole another piece of beef. The meat, I know, will run out someday. Meanwhile enjoy it. But it's been at least two months since I've had a vegetable.

Friday, 24 Feb., Day 155

About 1000h: Be careful, Tom. Don't let anger and a sense of justice interfere with reason and your basic rule, "Will it help me to survive?" Built a fire this A.M. Javier comes and throws my wood on, does not even stay to warm up while I'm gathering more wood and *chuzco*. I look at him then at the fresh wood piled on the fire and laugh. "*Bueno*. I'm going to collect more wood for you," I said, and went back to the *chuzco* grove. Let him take your wood in the future, Hargrove. Making enemies with anyone is dangerous when you're a prisoner held outside the laws of God, man, or decency.

Breakfast: two *arepas* and a piece of fried beef. Took one hour to eat, sitting by fire. 7:10–8:10 A.M. The beef is smoked and dried then fried. Rather tough, to say the least. But for one hour something to do. I now have a knife. Found a half of a broken machete. Stole some steel wool from where the dishes are washed and cleaned off most of the rust. Very depressed if I allow myself to think. Prayer not easy, makes me cry. Is my situation hopeless?

Later: Almost out of ink in Moño's pen. Then what will I do? My most valuable emotional resource is the ability to write, record. Borrowed *this* pen from Julio to write my wife.

P.M.: Must really be at the edge. We played *parquet*, a Monopoly-type dice-and-board game, after lunch. Unlucky roll and your piece goes to "prison." When my piece would go to prison, I would feel a strong need to *cry*. Yes, to cry because a piece of wood in a homemade dice game is imprisoned. I'm going to stay a prisoner for a long time and can do nothing to control or even influence my destiny—except survive.

Saturday, 25 Feb., Day 156

"Have you seen this?" Mono asked this morning and handed me a brochure, "*El Comite International de la Cruz Roja* [International Committee of the Red Cross]. *Lo conoce usted?*" I read *con mucho gusto*. To visit interred or detained persons is a Red Cross function. Also transmit mail when normal conditions are interrupted. I feel Moño's giving me the brochure was a cover-your-ass job of some sort. "Sure we told him what the Red Cross could offer. We even gave him a brochure." Later I asked Moño if the Red Cross is aware of me. "Yes." I show him the passages in the brochure referring to visits. "Can I ask Susan to request that a Red Cross representative visit me?" I asked. My family doesn't really know how I'm treated. They know only what I write. He said, "The Red Cross knows who has you." I'll suggest Susan formally request them to visit me, but in a second letter. I won't include it in the letter I'm writing now. That way if the FARC censor decides to kill the Red Cross request, it won't kill the rest of the letter to Susan with it. Played *parquet*, then Tricky rest of day. Javier had *la rancha* duty, so I made sure I complimented his fried bread and coffee—also suggested that he pile more of my wood onto my fire and I continued to gather wood to keep the fire burning rather than using what I've stock-piled to last through a cold, wet, dismal, winter.

Sunday, 26 Feb., Day 157

I can't help it. Despite all I've learned about ignoring or at least bypassing the wrenching heartache and throat-blocking lump that comes with it, I think I'm being released and soon. That these are the last days. The lyrics that Moño sang one lonely night around my fire keep running through my mind, returning: *"Mañana me voy de Campamento Aburrido. Adios, los recuerdos."* [Tomorrow I leave from Camp Boredom. Farewell to the memories. . . .] Late yesterday [illegible] I and five to six guerrillas sat around my fire and talked—about my freedom. There is no question but that I'll be released very soon, Moño says. "The media will ask you how you were treated. How will you answer?"

"But I'm not news."

"Yes. CNN has reported on you."

"Honestly, the good and the bad." That is about the best answer I can think of.

At eight P.M., Gustavo and I went to *la rancha* and fried some more beef and *arepa* and drank delicious hot chocolate. Eating meat often is becoming a nightly ritual. I see two reasons: to fatten me up as much as possible before my release and the fact that the unit will be dissolved with my release and all will go to other units. May as well eat that beef now. What's left may even go to waste. Suits me. I wonder how long it will be before I can leave food behind. Now I eat as much as I can hold of whatever is available, whenever I have the chance.

1735h: "Have you read that Red Cross brochure?" Moño asked. I had, but he read most of it aloud to me. Why, I don't know. Like reading me my rights? Julio's foot infected badly and no medicine here—just ampicillin. No news today, although I was hoping so. But it's Sunday. Good thing I made and can use chopsticks. Someone lost one or two spoons. Melena brought three plates for dinner. Hers, Javier's, and mine. "Sorry, Don Tomás. We have no spoon." So I have to eat rice and noodles with my hands—while they sit and eat with spoons. But I have my chopsticks, so no big deal, really. Melena and Javier are always together and are really cut off from rest of team. She really despises me—won't speak to me unless it's absolutely essential. Lord, let the word come tomorrow—and please, don't let another ransom deal be under way. Is that asking so much? Probably.

Monday, 27 Feb., Day 158

Watching my fire burn, including a hollow log. One end is burning and smoke is coming from the other end. Will orders for my release come today? If so, we march tomorrow. One long green sock fell into the fire in my cell and burned. Would have been catastrophic before, but now I don't care. Just realized

Moño said [the] radio [is] out, so orders could come and we don't get them till someone treks three hours up the mountain. Agreed to play Tricky with Melena last night. Caught her cheating blatantly and swept players off the board, ending the game. Made my point, but got only one piece of fried bread this A.M. *"No hay más, Tomás."* Did my righteous anger show her anything? Of course not. Would I rather let her cheat and have another piece of fried bread? Scruples is to show her she shouldn't cheat. Sure. Bad dreams last night about being kidnapped. Can't remember much, but was in solitary confinement and hungry. Is it that, as freedom seems nearer, mental barriers for psychological protection break down? Maybe.

1500h: Mr. Sheldon was so right—the fat lady hasn't even begun to sing although there are so many rumors that she is about to appear. Is it possible that nothing is happening, that this is just another ruse to appease me? If so, it's so nearsighted. But I never said that FARC is composed of vision and farsightedness. Meanwhile, wait and don't let yourself get depressed, Hargrove. Still gathering wood for the winter. No spoon again. Moño arranged for me to have one thermos of coffee and I'm not allowed in *la rancha*. That really improved the day. Wish I could get to *la rancha* to steal more beef—have only two pieces left. Could it be that more ransom games are being played and the worst that I fear is true? I could be in terrible debt the rest of my life to repay what others have paid in my ransom—and I have no means to pay other than a salary and maybe a book. *Something* good should come from this ordeal for which I'm paying at least half a year of my life, and this must be affecting my long-term health by now. The book had better be good; it's my only hope. Otherwise I'll leave one type of bondage—physical—only to be bound financially for the rest of my life.

1630h: Dinner: cold rice and cold *arepa*. Thank God I have the two dried beef plus some lentils I saved at lunch. When they lock me in my cell at night, I'll cook meat. But the meat will be gone soon.

2300h: Judi had first guard. Eight to nine P.M.; Leidi nine to ten. They took me to *la rancha* and cooked *cancharina*—had a *harina frita*—and hot chocolate. Had two cups [of] chocolate, three *harinas fritas*, and took four *harinas fritas* back to cell for me to eat later. Also stole another piece of dried beef, although in the darkness I think I got a piece that is all fat and gristle. What a pity to steal meat—then find I can't use it. This game of the guards sneaking me to *la rancha* to eat and drink chocolate is getting to be a regular event. Could it be on purpose to fatten me and improve my attitude? Or is it just fun, something to break the boredom? I believe Susan talked of sneaking into the kitchen to cook illicit food at midnight in boarding school. That's probably it. I certainly encourage the tradition. Leidi asked if, after I'm free, I saw her in the street, would I turn her in to the police to be killed. Strange. Moño asked the same thing—sort of. Are they really worried about it?

Depressed and losing faith that freedom will come. Started composing my own song this P.M.:

> *It's so easy, easy to cry here,*
> *Hard not to give up hope and die here.*
> *Walking the valley, the valley of the shadow,*
> *I walk the valley of the shadow of death but I won't die.*

Tuesday, 28 Feb., Day 159

1100h: Standing down, marking time, waiting for the order to release me to arrive. That's all this unit seems to be doing. There's no doubt, I believe, that everyone expects those orders to arrive at any minute. But it's been more or less like this for a while, yet the fat lady doesn't sing. Something must be wrong. All guerrillas except Melena and Javier gathered around my fire this A.M. Joking, laughing. Later, I slept in the sun for 15 to 20 minutes, then looked at my watch. It was more than 1½ or 2 hours. I'm still served with no spoon. So dumb of Melena. I could probably make trouble for her, but why bother? Meanwhile [I] can eat with my chopsticks well. I have two pens. One is Moño's—this one is almost out of ink. Julio loaned me his. It works for 20 words, then must warm it. Right now I know that someone will lend me another pen if I need it. But . . . if those orders don't arrive soon, how long will this VIP treatment continue? When will Camará Hargrove become just a dirty prisoner and a pain in the ass.

1405h: I can't believe it. I was expecting one more event, probably before release, but not this. Went to stream with Moño, Gustavo, and Caballito and en route [learned] that the guerrillas of Coordinadora Simón Bolívar* went to war with the Venezuelan army this morning. A border dispute in the *llanos.* Twenty-eight Venezuelan soldiers killed in action, fighting on 42 fronts, 5,000 guerrillas rushing to the border.

Can it really be happening? I guess so. What are the implications for me? As a prisoner of FARC? Has a guerrilla army in one country ever gone to war with the government of another country before? The guerrillas are getting ready to move out, tomorrow. All say this is good for me; they have to let me go so they can go to the fighting. I'm not so sure. Senseless things happen in war. Please, Bill Clinton, don't say a word. What scares me now is, what if the U.S.A. announces that it is backing Venezuela? And all this as I'm leaving, almost. Where will this take me? Home to Cali and Susan, I hope. Where will I sleep tomorrow? Surely not here in Campamento Aburrido? Who knows? Compará. You'll go to the *llanos* to fight with us? That's the standard joke. And we're completely isolated—no radio contact with the commander.

[Entries for March and for April 1–13 are written in broad-point soft pencil. In the months since they were written they have smudged and the paper on which they were written has darkened. Consequently many of the entries

---

*The joint force of all the Marxist guerrilla groups in Colombia (FARC, M-19, ELN, etc.). —TRH

are partially—some entirely—unreadable. For the period 1 March through 13 April, inclusive, entries written in the third person (except where the author addresses himself) are merely summaries of what could be made out of the text.]

Wednesday, 1 Mar., Day 160

Fighting ceased at three P.M. yesterday, Moño says. So it's return to normal, waiting and, maybe, fooling myself. Moño says our budget for food is Colombia $800/person per day. Rate was Colombia $830=USA $1 when I was captured. To *la rancha* with Moño and [?] last night [illegible] I secretly returned the last piece of meat I stole. We're now virtually out of meat. [illegible] Virtually out of ink in both pens. No one has—or will lend me—another. What will I do if I can't write? Our meat supply is gone but out of ink is worse.

Thursday, 2 Mar., Day 161

Yesterday was a dark day of loneliness, depressions, with forebodings of worse days to come. Gustavo had *la rancha* and that made it a little better because he brought me extra fried bread for breakfast then more coffee through the day than I could drink. But maybe that made the day worse because orders came in the evening by radio—it's working again—for Gustavo to leave today, probably to Mellanos. That little Indian has made my life so much better. He's the closest, by far, to a friend I have here. We went to *la rancha* and he fried *arepas* again last night. I did something stupid, if I stuck to my guiding principle (which has worked okay so far) of: "Will it help me survive?" Gustavo borrows my pocket mirror two or three times a day. In the darkness, I pressed it into his hand. When Gustavo's gone, having given him the mirror won't help my life—in fact, it deprives me of the option to lend it to others, and I need a way to give favors to others. But what involves survival maybe I need to give to others. I have so little to give. But giving almost my only possession—maybe that's what I need to do. I should care for the health of my spirit as well as that of my body. After all, survival is more a mental than a physical ordeal. That's also why I need the mirror—to make others at least partly indebted to me for something other than my time. Later Moño had other bad news—the *"comisión especial"* guarding me will [remainder completely unintelligible]. They will probably move out as a unit to *llanos* in a couple of days. A completely new group will come in to replace [Moño's group] as [Hargrove's] guards.

Friday, 3 Mar., Day 162

"Happy Birthday to Me!" It's Hargrove's birthday. Builds La Rancha Tomás with Ramiro's help. Has mixed feelings because it is as if he's settling in for the long term.

Saturday, 4 Mar., Day 163

Moño told me that Javier leaves Monday and he [illegible]. His replacement is Martín, an Indian, so I'll be left alone but Moño insists I may leave with them. I asked if it's *really* true that my release is imminent. Yes, he assured me. I do appreciate what he did to get La Rancha Tomás built—it will make my life more livable. But what an empty, lonely feeling. [illegible] back in cell. An interesting talk but ended in terribly depressing way—when he assured me again that I'll be free soon, he mentioned that the talks were at the national level. "About me?"

"No, about all the *secuestrados.*"

Then it hit me: "You mean—when I'm freed it will be along with all the others?"

"Yes."

"Ese día no viene," I said.

"Why not," he said. "One [illegible] has already been released. *¿Es posible que el gobierno de Colombia puede cambiar un prisionero que ha capturado de la FARC por mí?"*

He anticipado esta reunión con un mezcla de agradecimiento [illegible] *miedo y* [illegible]. Aeogo=David Marcus, *Dallas Morning News*? [illegible] *oportunidad a acelarar los* [*puntos en dísputa*] *asustados de confusión* [illegible] *lo que podría pasar. Si no me crea* [illegible] *Uds. pueden* [illegible] . . . *en avance.*

"Who?"

"The one from Sumas."

"But he was captured only a short while ago. Why was he released instead of me?"

"I don't know the reason."

The reason seems perfectly obvious to me. Ransom money. And to me, it seems obvious that FARC isn't going to release all its *secuestrados* because we're being used, one by one, as collateral. So, from being up, I fall down again—way down and hard. I guess my disgust showed. Moño left, and I went to bed a few minutes later without even saying good night. Is Moño deceiving me or am I only deceiving myself? Am I still able to look at things objectively, analyze my situation? Maybe not. When Moño assured me earlier that, yes, people are really coming to get me free, right away, I assumed he meant me, Tom Hargrove. I've gone up so high then fallen down so hard, so many times recently. How many times can I soar so high then crash so hard before I have the ability to go with [Moño?] again? Have I lost my rationality? Am I going crazy, and everyone but me sees it? Am I unfair to Moño? Or only to myself? Is there really hope that my release may come in a few days? That I'll leave with [illegible]? Or does being realistic mean planning on at least six more months here? When I discover sign-writing . . .

Sunday, 5 Mar., Day 164

Tom reflects on his earlier bitter thoughts about a recently released *secuestrado* who was freed after only two months of captivity.

Monday, 6 Mar., Day 165

Guerrillas return from Happy Valley with supplies. Moño cuts Hargrove's hair.

Tuesday, 7 Mar., Day 166

Because he fears they have gone bad, Tom throws out bottle of lentils he has been hoarding.

Wednesday, 8 Mar., Day 167

Moño tells Hargrove that the Colombian army is only a three-hour march away.

Hargrove's infections seem to be clearing up, but he is out of toothpaste. He has been out of toilet paper since January. There are few matches and almost no chocolate left in the camp.

Thursday, 9 Mar., Day 168

[Unreadable]

Friday, 10 Mar., Day 169

Hargrove's six-month anniversary: 24 weeks of captivity. He borrows a knife to sharpen his pencils. He is down to a total of three inches of pencil.

Saturday, 11 Mar., Day 170

Cold, raining. Everything has been wet for days and I think will be for months. Winter has come to these desolate mountains. I use my stock to [illegible] dry *chuzco* stored in the rafters only for starting fires, and move pieces into cell at night to dry more. Moño and five guerrillas went into Happy Valley to try to get more supplies. Gustavo is [illegible] and brought me a full cup of coffee and an extra can [illegible].

0920h: Brushed my teeth for the first time in four or five days, and the last time unless my toothpaste arrives with the supplies today. Lord, I live filthy, but no choice. Other than vitamins or mail, which I won't get, I hope for 1. oil for my skin, 2. toothpaste, 3. chocolate (for the camp), 4. a pen. Not in that order. The pen comes first. I'm going to get caught with this stolen pencil—it's too obvious. Fat with "Made in China" across the top, and running out fast. Again the guerrillas obviously think I'm on my way out of here. They sat in La Rancha Tomás around the fire last night and talked about sentimental times. What have I liked most here? That's a tough one. What did I like least? Being honest wouldn't help me survive here another six months, so I said, "Jhon's singing," nothing about solitary confinement, the chains, being starved. "It was M-19, not [illegible] decision, made by the *jefe* of *Simón Bolívar*—like your release will be," Moño said. That makes me feel better. Manuel Marulanda, Secretary of FARC, is also secretary of C[illegible]. But the show's not over until the fat lady sings. I translated the phrase, explained how [illegible]. I don't think the battle will come. At least not here to camp.

Sunday, 12 Mar., Day 171

0735h: Was awakened early this morning by lots of noise, activity. Then Melena brought coffee, unlocked my cell at six A.M. [illegible] 6:45–7:15 A.M. Something's going on, I thought. Then became more realistic; it's to impress the visitor. Still, I don't [illegible] and saw [illegible] were building a fire in La Rancha Tomás. I dressed—but then—*undressed* is a better term because I stripped down from wearing [illegible] trousers and three shirts to only one of each. The visitor brought [illegible]. "[illegible]," Moño said. "And a new jacket and one that will fit." [illegible] but it's just as warm as a new one. My jacket fit perfect [illegible] holding out [illegible] arm. The torn sleeve halfway between my elbow [illegible]. I changed the subject [illegible] camp is up earlier than normal. Do you think [illegible] is the reason? To wake me early? I can't sleep. [illegible] The fire didn't burn well. What the hell [illegible]. I brought out extra [illegible] my arrest and [illegible] wood. Because Julio brought an extra [illegible] brought a [illegible] Then, later, other types of [illegible] and [illegible]. "Where's Papá Noel?" Gustavo came to La Rancha Tomás, wore a new ski mask. Last night Jhon was wearing a [illegible] guerrilla high-fashion dress for a special occasion? The sun came out at 7:45 A.M.—the softest [illegible] I've seen. [illegible] the clearest day I've seen in the mountains for weeks [illegible]. 8:15 A.M. What is going on? I know what to surmise but I tell myself that *muy engarda* hasn't [illegible]. The fall down from what already has been this A.M. will be bad enough. God, not again . . .

Viejito is getting in the sun with [illegible] hut. I borrowed his Brazilian hunting knife and take it to the cell to sharpen this pencil and cut candles for tonight. "How's life in the Valley of Happiness?" I ask. *"Bien,"* Viejito replies.

"I hear it's like heaven, that they have strawberries and cream for breakfast and beefsteak for dinner and whiskey and beer in between."

"That's right, Don Tomás."

"And *mujeres*?"

"Oh, lots of women."

"But I think the women are nicer here," I say nodding at Leidi. "It's the pure mountain girl."

Ramiro borrowed my scissors which makes me uneasy. I've been feeling like a real thief, hiding both the, get this, pencils from their true owners. "Did you lose a pair of scissors two or three weeks ago?" I ask when Ramiro returns them. "Here on *la rancha*?" He nods.

"Here, these must be yours."

"Keep them. Give them to me when you leave."

"What a wonderful idea. It may bring me luck!" I think. Okay, Hargrove. I put the scissors in my pocket. Now I have only one stolen item to hide. Why didn't the visitor bring ballpoint pens?

1015h: Tomás [illegible section]

"*Sí.*" I ask if she'll wash some clothes. And especially plain dry socks. If I may be marching for two days. I give her two pair from my cell, then remove my boots and strip away my third pair. One sock is green, the survivor of a fall into a fire. The other is blue. I found it months ago by the stream. "Blue and green, it's the latest style." She grins and takes the socks. Caballito wanders by. "Did you bring me luck with the other presents?" I ask.

"*Veremos.*"

If this is not it, I'm in for the cruelest, hardest fall yet. I've tried not to let it happen.

A.M. Lunch. This is a strange day. The sun is so warm and bright, it brings out all of the deep colors of the mountains. You can count the ridges on Mt. Perran, capped and shining in the distance!

[illegible] My freedom finally arrived, sort of. Moño told me at [illegible] orders to release the [illegible] from Marulanda himself, I guess. But I'm not going home, not yet. Fighting and [illegible] soldiers surround us, and FARC can't escort me through the net, so we're trapped in Valley of the Shadow until [illegible] army pulls out. So . . . am I free? Or still a prisoner? Will they lock my cell tonight? Pretty anticlimactic after all that I've been through. "You may stay here another [illegible]," Moño said. "Your wife is still waiting in [illegible]," Moño said. "Our visitors talked to her only four days ago."

"Does he speak English?"

"No, through your son."

So Tom G. probably is in Cali with Susan. I'm glad, but I'm sorry to have disrupted his university program. Now, is it possible that this is all a trick for some reason? Of course, but I really don't think so. This changes some things. Suddenly, instead of wanting the Colombian army to attack, I hope they can't find us. What will I do if the army attacks? Before, it was perfectly clear. Escape if possible. Now my objective is what? To survive [illegible]. Try to escape if that seems safer than staying as the [illegible]. Don't risk your life if you can avoid it.

My new jacket and *ruana* are somewhere en route and should arrive in a few days. It seems a shame to waste the [illegible] guess [illegible].

[The very bottom of the page is illegible.]

Monday, 13 Mar., Day 172

Today is hot and clear—unusual weather for winter in the northeastern Andes. We've actually been trapped here, without the option of moving, for a week, but it seems different now that I have orders for release. If the army weren't below us, somewhere, I should be arriving back home in Cali sometime tonight. Instead, I'm sitting in the sun in a bamboo grove. I've wired together five pieces of dried beef that I snitched from *la rancha*—the kitchen—a couple of weeks ago. I have it in the sun. I figure the sunshine will make it last longer.

The detachment of 10 guerrillas who are guarding me have dug trenches all around the camp for defense—I helped. Is that like digging my own grave? I don't think so. Those trenches might save my life, too. Until yesterday I was hoping desperately that the army would find and overrun this camp—there's no way that 10 guerrillas could defend it even if figures for [the size of the] army are exaggerated vastly. I was figuring I might escape and get to the army in the confusion. The guerrillas told me, of course, that they're defending me. The army will kill me, they say, if I wind up [illegible].

Tuesday, 14 Mar., Day 173

Hargrove notes that the camp is visible from high ground on three sides and that a sniper or heavy machine gun could cause a lot of damage. He then details how a blocking force could be placed and how an assault would be handled. He wonders if the guerrillas would surrender. He feels the camp cannot be defended.

Wednesday, 15 Mar., Day 174

Hargrove has bad infections in both ears. Again no antibiotics are available.

Thursday, 16 Mar., Day 175

Hargrove's ears are a little better. Moño tells him that new fighting has broken out across Colombia, including nearby—which means Hargrove's release will be delayed yet again.

Friday, 17 Mar., Day 176

[illegible]

Saturday, 18 Mar., Day 177

Hargrove mentions that El Valle de la Muerte—the Valley of Death—is a cold, steep, wet swamp—the high mountain ridges trap the clouds and the sun almost never shines there.

Sunday, 19 Mar., Day 178

Melena steals Hargrove's coffee cup and openly uses it to serve Javier while bringing Hargrove his coffee in a plastic cup. Hargrove speculates that she's probably been kicked around most of her life. He's read everything in the camp there is to read. Gustavo returns from a fishing trip for which he had borrowed Hargrove's pack with a 30-page computer catalog (from a Bogotá computer outlet) for Hargrove to read. Then Gustavo gives Hargrove a Mongol #2 pencil, which means Hargrove can now admit to owning a pencil and write with it in the open.

Monday, 20 Mar., Day 179

[illegible]

Tuesday, 21 Mar., Day 180

Cold, raining. Using my new pencil to make personal [illegible]. The "team hut" is 20 steps long and 9 wide. The guerrillas were blackening weapons with a tube of printer's ink. Gustavo had the idea of filling empty ballpoint pen cartridges. This is test. Pen #1 doesn't work well. This one seems to—but it's the one I borrowed from Moño—and Moño was there when Gustavo filled the cartridge. So I guess this goes back to Moño. Alternating all day between bright sunshine and cold rain. I've never seen weather that changes so much, so fast. Doesn't look like refills will work. Moño says the *chulo* operation is still under way. "How long can an operation last?"

"Maybe two or three months."

"If so, you'll keep me here two or three more months?"

"Yes."

How depressing. I'm torn. If I knew they were telling the truth . . . it would be so much easier to buckle down to last it out. But if the *chulos* [work over] this area for several months, they'll surely find this camp. Something has to happen.

Wednesday, 22 Mar., Day 181

Javier and Melena spent the morning in La Rancha Tomás burning my fuel and feeling each other up. I don't know why they piss me off so much. That sick feeling. I know, I keep writing it but that empty hopeless feeling won't go away. Turning me loose would cause news, so I'm being put on ice indefinitely until FARC can release me with minimum publicity. Lunch was rice and lentils. A true luxury will be to someday be able to eat whatever I want. But I don't spend [illegible] fantasizing about food. [illegible] painful. I keep enough leftovers hidden and always eat something after lockup. I can't prevent the food fantasies. I try not to think of Susan and my family.

Friday, 24 Mar., Day 183

Hargrove is very disappointed. Javier starts a fire to burn a big pile of *chuzco* but doesn't even stay to watch it. Melena asks Hargrove the time, so he shows her his watch; she can't tell time.

Saturday, 25 Mar., Day 184

Hives break out on both Hargrove's wrists. Javier spent four hours talking with Hargrove the night before. Javier says he was at the roadblock when Hargrove was captured. He confirms that the guerrillas at the roadblock concluded Hargrove was a CIA officer when they saw his CIAT identification card. Leidi comes to say good-bye.

Sunday, 26 Mar., Day 185

Mail goes out. Hargrove sent 21 letters. The night before, Moño tells Hargrove again that the *chulos* are the reason he is still being held. On Sunday, Moño and Gustavo go to Happy Valley and don't return that day. Hargrove ran out of candles two days earlier and got two more from Gustavo. Melena came for Hargrove's plate to get him dinner but never returned.

Monday, 27 Mar., Day 186

The infection in Hargrove's nose gets much worse. Moño and Gustavo return from Happy Valley. Moño tells Hargrove that they are going to move to a camp even more remote than the one they are in.

Tuesday, 28 Mar., Day 187

Tom learns scuttlebutt at his fire—that there are only two other camps in the area. Speculation is that the most likely move will be to Happy Valley.

Wednesday, 29 Mar., Day 188

Hargrove sits too close to the fire and burns a hole in his right boot, which he attempts to patch using strips of rubber from a castoff boot. Hargrove tells Judi that there's no communism anymore even in Russia, but she doesn't believe him. Hargrove recalls that Moño thought it possible that the USSR would give the guerrillas planes if they fought with Venezuela.

Thursday, 30 Mar., Day 189

Julio and Caballito are going to Happy Valley to prepare for switching the camps.

Friday, 31 Mar., Day 190

Hargrove is anxious to get to Happy Valley because, he speculates, the large numbers of guerrillas who were stationed there probably left behind a goodly amount of usable trash. Perhaps even some reading material. Hargrove rages at Melena in English, calling her a slut. He talks with Julio about Happy Valley. Julio makes it sound like the Garden of Eden.

Saturday, 1 Apr., Day 191

Happy Valley is supposed to get supplies every week to 10 days. But apparently the Colombian army has put a force of 2,500 troops in the area, which are blocking the guerrillas' lines of communications, so not enough supplies are getting through.

Hargrove is chagrined that he saved a piece of meat so long it spoiled. He reflects that a guerrilla would never do something so stupid.

Sunday, 2 Apr., Day 192

Hargrove writes to the Director General of the International Red Cross in Geneva, requesting that a representative be sent to visit him, and asking for mail, vitamins, medicines, a shortwave radio, and books. He wrote the letter less with the idea that it would actually be mailed than with the hope of impressing FARC, which he thought showed a modicum of admiration for the Red Cross. So he went to the top. . . . He also hoped to impress FARC with CIAT's international status.

Monday, 3 Apr., Day 193

Moño confirms that Hargrove and Moño's people are trapped in the Valley of the Shadow. He says that the nearest town in the opposite direction is eight days' march. He also says FARC won't turn Hargrove over to the army.

The infections in both of Hargrove's ears are better.

Hargrove writes: "A few days ago I thought I'd be perfectly happy if the pain in my ears and nose—and the fear that comes with it—would go away. The pain's almost gone now, but I'm not a happy camper in the Valley of the Shadow."

Tuesday, 4 Apr., Day 194

More talk of moving to a new camp.

Wednesday, 5 Apr., Day 195

Hargrove and "his" guerrillas do move to a new site, but the "camp" is just a grove of *chuzco* bamboo deep in the forest, near a river. The guerrillas are hiding from the army, but the new spot is damp, cold, and dark. Hargrove's tent is very small, just big enough to cover his bed, and is less than one meter high. "The most miserable camp yet," he concludes.

Thursday, 6 Apr., Day 196

Moño tells Hargrove that the only reason for the move was to hide him. Hargrove makes a cross from two pieces of bamboo tied together with twine and strips of cloth from a camouflage uniform. He is very cold at night, even after he receives the two blankets left behind earlier in the Valley of the Shadow.

Friday, 7 Apr., Day 197

Hargrove is told by Rambo that he is confined to his tiny tent.

Hargrove ruminates on his dealings with Judi, who treats him with cruelty and contempt when he is confined; when he is not, she is driven by loneliness to confide in him and he must take part in the conversation or she will take it out on him at the first opportunity.

Hargrove feels it is clear that the guerrillas feed him only what is necessary to sustain his life, while eating better—if not well—themselves.

Weather cold and rainy.

Saturday, 8 Apr., Day 198

The weather is sunny, but at the new camp the sun can reach the ground in only a few places. Hargrove writes letters to Susan, his father, Havener, Cam Lan Lock.

Judi came to Hargrove's fire that night and said she was very homesick. When Hargrove asks if she writes letters home, she says that FARC doesn't deliver them. Hargrove is outraged by the implications of this statement for his own letter writing.

Hargrove falls into the icy river. Even with ". . . covers, four trousers, four shirts, four socks, and a ski mask and wool cap, I'm very cold at night."

Sunday, 9 Apr., Day 199

Cold weather continues. Some of the guerrillas go somewhere to play *fútbol*. Hargrove surmises they've gone to La Playa.

Monday, 10 Apr., Day 200

Hargrove sees Erika, the beautiful guerrilla he'd originally been introduced to as La Italiana. She arrived with Rambo.

Tom's bamboo cross draws the guerrillas' attention. He hopes it reminds them of the inhumanity of kidnapping and regards the cross as a kind of psychological warfare.

Tuesday, 11 Apr., Day 201

Guerrillas come to visit the camp, but not the VIPs Moño says he was expecting. Erika is there but she has not brought the magazines she promised earlier.

Wednesday, 12 Apr., Day 202

Hargrove is depressed because he clearly won't be freed by Easter. He can't get anyone to bring him a knife to sharpen his pencil, which sorely needs it. Moño and Ramiro bring Tom new boots, but the left boot is too tight a fit to march in and it won't stretch. Hargrove recalls with fondness the Easter egg hunts that Susan arranged every year even after the boys were grown.

"We may be leaving soon," Moño said by the fire in La Rancha Tomás #2 last night.

"To go where?" I asked cautiously.

"To an area where we can free you. The *comandante* is studying how we can leave!"

"No!"

Moño looked surprised and puzzled. "You mean—you don't want to leave?"

"No . . . Yes . . . I want to leave more than anything in the world!" How does one explain in Spanish that in English you sometimes say no to mean something is too wonderful to be true. I also meant, Please don't lie to me, Moño. If it's not true, don't say it. I don't know how many more of these trips—up so high, then falling so hard—I can take.

"You'll like the new camp," Jhon said. "There's lots of *chusque* to burn." That pisses me off. About all I do—all they let me do—all day, every day, is gather fuel for my fire, or sit and burn it—so he thinks that's what turns me on.

"Would we cross to the other side with the permission of the Colombian army? Or go around them?"

"Around them."

"That may be more than two days' march."

"Yes. Now we must wait and see."

How many times does this make, Tom? Can you risk it—the fall? Once more? Yes, I have no choice. *I have no choice.*

But even if Moño is telling the truth, Tom, the fat lady hasn't sung yet; you're still a hell of a long way from freedom. To march around the Colombian army in a cease-fire could be . . . interesting. And dangerous, of course, but that doesn't worry me. I'm truly afraid not to believe this. . . . How many times, now? FARC has told me I'll soon be free four times, and I've convinced myself on my own at least another dozen times. But a couple of other hints: the guerrillas are so transparent. This A.M., around my fire, Gustavo joked about Don Tomás killing him.

Ramiro then asked, "Would you have us killed, Don Tomás?"

"Who killed?"

"The guerrillas."

"Why?"

"Because of anger."

I assured them I would not. What else could I say?

Thursday, 13 Apr., Day 203

[illegible]

Friday, 14 Apr., Day 204

Hargrove gets wet in the night's downpour because his tent isn't staked properly.

Jhon suddenly gets orders and leaves, the way Leidi did earlier.

1315h: It's Black Friday, and it's dark, wet, raining. There has been sun to-day. We have a cease-fire and a truce between the government and guerrillas, Moño said last night, "If it lasts, then I could be escorted back and be released?" "Maybe." I'm trying not to think about it too much, but, please, God, let the cease-fire continue successfully. Guerrillas around my new fire all last night. Used all my *chusque*, used my bed as a bench. I could run them off—but I'd better be careful about that—would I rather be alone with no one around the fire, or have too many people taking advantage of me? The latter, I think. Gustavo brought me an extra *cancharina* this A.M., which I'm saving for tonight. Moño brought a copy of *Semana* [*"Week"*] for 28 Feb., so only five weeks old. Wow! Real news; where did he get it? How kind. Maybe they're getting ready—yet again—to let me go. Don't even think about that, Hargrove. *No more hurt*—not unless it's absolutely necessary.

Later: The Marlboro Man is featured in an advertisement at the front of *Semana*. And by him is written *"Cuando tu eres triste, recuerdes que Erika existe."* [When you are sad, remember that Erika exists.] So she didn't forget— Erika sent the magazine. How nice. Why didn't Moño tell me? What could that have hurt?

1505h: Am by fire trying to dry the trousers I'll wear to bed tonight. But everything gets wet faster than I can dry it. Lots of [illegible]. Saw Leidi.

1715h: It's so wet I can hardly keep my fire going. Even the flames seem damp and won't dry my wet socks. Am eating cold rice—[finished] a cup of hot chocolate—love it. I wish I could do something for Easter, wish I could watch *Jesus Christ, Superstar* or read the Easter part of the Bible. I wish so much I had Susan, could talk with her. Will it happen? Will I finally walk through, and out of, the Valley of the Shadow of Death?

Two men about 30 [years old] appeared at my tent, first to see who I was. Apparently, [they] are very familiar with much of the team. They were headed to Corintho to spend Easter. [Both are] farmers, who live six hours away. "What do you grow," [I asked].

"Potato, marijuana, and opium poppies."

Saturday, 15 Apr., Day 205

Sábado Santo Supplies must have arrived. Got this pen last nite. It's been at least six weeks since I have a pen. *"¿Cómo amáneció?"* [How did you sleep?] Moño asked. Not worth a damn. I'm cold. The others have tents. I'm sleeping here in the open. I can stand anything for a little while. But I must prepare for the long term because it is obvious that they have no plans to free me! *"No sabemos, Tomás."* Moño agreed to bring me another blanket and the *plástico* to keep part of my area partly dry.

"Why can't we take advantage of the cease-fire to move me out of here?"

"We don't have orders for that. And the cease-fire hasn't changed things. The army has moved closer."

What can I do? Nothing but survive. Should I write to Susan to go back to Texas? I don't know. Tomorrow is Easter Sunday. That symbolizes hope, new life. I'll think about it tomorrow.

0830h: Am by river. Wonderful sun this A.M. Hard to even let my fire die. After days of fighting, coaxing to keep it going. How ironic that fires start easily and burn hot when the sun shines brightly and it's warm. Lesson in life.

Jhon left his knife. Judi, with Melena, gave [it] to me to keep. This A.M. Judi borrows [the knife]. Not normal. I'll bet Jhon left the knife for me. Julio Anderson asked to borrow my *equipo* this A.M. I refused. No dry place except the *equipo* to store my things. I shouldn't have. But when I called him back, he was gone. Strange that Thursday and Friday were so dark and cold and today is warm and clear. Can it be Easter? Christ rises tomorrow. He lives and so will I. That all changes tomorrow? That God, or his equivalent, has planned Easter as the vehicle for the change, that I'll rise and march out of these mountains? Careful, Tom, you can't give up faith, but you don't need the hurt either. Three P.M.: This afternoon was so beautiful. I bathed and washed all over, in the river. First time in two months, I guess. Washed clothes. Then weather turned cold. Raining again. Moño brought *plástico* and we covered the front of my tent. Will make big difference.

Maybe when I'm free I can quit lying, stealing, and hiding, especially of food.

Had soup of potato and beef for lunch. Ate two-thirds, poured one-third in pan, for tonight. Hid [it] under bunk, covered with dirty rag [made] from fatigue uniform someone had thrown away. Then asked for more. But no more potatoes, so I mixed the broth with rice I had saved from last night.

Easter Sunday, 16 Apr., Day 206

I had planned to have my own private service for Easter Sunday by my rugged cross of bamboo. I even remember the words to "He Lives," but hadn't sung them. I'd save that for this morning. Maybe it'll be clear like 15 Apr. and I can have a sunrise service as the sun appears over the mountains. But it wasn't like that. I'm disappointed, but can't complain. It was raining, and Moño appeared by my fire with a big piece of black plastic. He called Julio and Judi. We all sat by my fire 45 minutes waiting for breakfast. While I was trying to think about New Life, Moño was feeling up Judi, being an obnoxious ass. Poor little Judi, no one has ever paid any attention to her, I'm sure.

Julio had caught 64 trout yesterday with the *chilo* [throw net] and breakfast was two big trout and 1½ *arepas*. Judi gave me one, then we put up the plastic. What I now have is not a tent like the others, but it's far superior to what I had before. Closed, more or less, three sides. I can sit up under the roof. I also managed to cover, with brush, a piece of rubberized canvas and later put it on the mattress as a base for my bed. Cut my hand with the machete, not deep but wide. If I were in Cali, I'd probably go get a tetanus shot. Forced more blood, washed well in the cold stream water. Don't need infection here.

1200h: Was it—or is it the start of a new life for me? If I live, I'll have to start a new life. I can't resume life where I left off on 23 Sept. '94. But no, Tom, you can't let yourself hope, expect anything more hurt, more pain if you're foolish enough to hope for something special to happen to you. You spent the A.M. working without thinking too much. That's all the blessing you can hope for right now. That plus the extra cover Moño promised. "The Colombian army isn't going to pull out, because the cease-fire is successful," I told Moño yesterday. Even before a cease-fire, armies grab all the terrain they can. They don't abandon ground in a cease-fire.

"*Veremos,*" Moño said. We'll see.

1415h: I think I saw the Phantom of Shadow Valley two days ago, then again today up on the hill where I'm not allowed.

A lot of my friends must have attended church services this A.M. I wonder if any prayed for me. God knows I need it. Do people think about me, wonder where I am? What would they think if they could see me, dirty and bearded, sitting on the edge of a bamboo cot set among the trees in the forest, warming myself over a fire with the rain falling all around.

1600h: Tried to have my Easter service today, but it is hard. When I sing "He Lives," I start crying. I sing "The Old Rugged Cross" to my cross of bamboo sometimes. But the fact is, I feel abandoned. The despair is deep and as cold as the rain that's fallen on and around me for days.

1755h: What an Easter. Nothing like I'd fantasized. The coldest, wettest, most miserable day yet. But the spirit of Easter, and what happens, is what counts—not the weather.

Monday, 17 Apr., Day 207

Woke up warm and snug this A.M. Couldn't believe it. Was almost toasty. It's because of the plastic cover over my tent. This is the first time I've slept under dry tent with dry covers since moving to the forest. Also the canvas on top of the foam rubber mattress seems to help a lot.

Breakfast was okay—two *arepas* and one small fried trout. Then came a surprise: a third *arepa* and a piece of fried intestine and [a piece] of beef. The difference is that Gustavo is *ranchero* today and he brought the other [i.e., additional food]. I've always known I don't get the same food as the others, of course.

The river is high. Washed away the latrine we built, plus the bridge I built to cross to other side. Still cold, dark, rainy.

Judi is sick. Fever. Two nights ago she had guard, came to La Rancha Tomás and asked the time. [It was] nine, time to change guards. Ten minutes later a single shot rang out from the direction of her tent. Oh God, another suicide, I thought. Then Julio appeared. "I tripped in the dark and my rifle went off," he explained. Lord, walking in the dark with his AK-47 not even *on safety*. What a sin, to my way of thinking.

Mail went out today. Four letters including one to Miles Sheldon, one to Russell Galen [literary agent in New York] care of Lee Lanning [one of Galen's clients, and an old friend]. Told Moño that Russell Galen is an old friend. I'm sure he'll read between the lines—that I want to talk about a book when I'm free. If I'm free. Ironic, but I may be worse off with a cease-fire than a war: if neither side moves, FARC can't move me out of here. If FARC plans to free me. Hell, I don't even know for sure if there is a cease-fire, although I don't know why Moño would lie about that.

In the dark last night I felt a strange cloth. Put it away. This A.M., sure enough, it's an olive hand towel, 2x1 feet. I need that towel badly, have only one towel and I use it as a pillow. At river this A.M. I found a sock. Not bad, just the toe end missing. Will dry and wear at night so can't be seen and recognized. Stealing? I hope not. I'd rather see these things as gifts—or reallocations—from God, or fate.

Tuesday, 18 Apr., Day 208

1010h: Sitting by my spot by the river. The sky was navy blue, clear, this A.M. Now clouds are coming, but maybe winter is nearing its end.

Crawled and cut my way through brush toward the bigger river this A.M. Hit a trail and heard voices. Didn't try to hide; that could cause even more problems. Up rode Erika on horseback. Then I saw, following on foot, Ramiro and

Joanna. "What are you doing here?" Ramiro demanded. The illiterate twerp bristled; he was partly showing off for the girls, too.

"Walking."

"You're not allowed here," Ramiro said.

"I could walk this way along the river."

"You're too far—go back to the camp." He added something about *regaño*, which means to "reprove" or "scold." Erika looked at me and smiled. Wish I could have thanked her for the magazine. Joanna smiled at me, too. Like they were saying, We understand. We see what's happening to you and it's too damned bad.

I was reading a magazine article to Ramiro last night. He's really illiterate. How sad.

I must quit hoping or thinking about freedom. I don't think I can try prayer any longer. When I try to open that dialogue—which never becomes a dialogue that I can recognize—I start crying. My situation seems so hopeless and I'm so helpless, so unable to change it. But crying won't help. I've still never cried in front of the guerrillas, although I get so choked up I can't talk when I must read my letters to Susan to Moño. How humiliating.

1200h: Back at tent, built fire, drying clothes from crossing river. Found a space to lie down on the rocks at "The Beach," and dozed off for an hour. The sun came out of clouds in bits—but those snatches of sunlight were as warm and delicious and sweet as a cup of the best very hot chocolate. And I felt that my body needed—and absorbed—the sun's nutrition like that chocolate.

A lot of my prayers are to help Susan, to give her strength, judgment, faith. And to give me strength. I don't know if I should pray for faith or not. I don't want to go on if there's no hope. If it's not written that I'll survive, I'd rather die now. I pray for Daddy, to make this easier on him, but I fear it already is, because I'm afraid he's dead. I pray for my boys, too, but more for Susan than anything else. I try to pray sometimes for the guerrillas, but maybe only because I think I'm supposed to. I really don't hate them; my feelings lie somewhere between pity and contempt. A far cry from the Old Testament words of hate and revenge I think I wrote six months ago. An improvement? I'm not sure as far as survival is concerned. The 28 Feb. '95 *Semana* has an article about human rights violations of the Colombian guerrillas and guerrilla failure to comply with Protocol 2 of Geneva [Conventions]. The author estimated that in the past five years, more than 7,500 persons have been kidnapped, of which 4,000 kidnappings were commanded by different guerrilla groups. Of those, 430 victims were murdered.

Wednesday, 19 Apr., Day 209

Both ears infected again and hurt terribly last night. We still don't have antibiotics, eardrops, etc. Both ears opened in the night and may be getting well again.

Javier left yesterday, Moño says. Back to his unit. I'll bet he was glad to get out of the Melena situation. Replaced by Natalia. The *"comisión especial"* is now eight: five males—Moño, Gustavo, Ramiro, Julio, Caballito—and three females, Melena, Judi, Natalia.

Moño saw a piece of blue rubberized wire I tied my packet of cotton with this morning. Insisted on taking it, giving me a piece of twine as trade. "Do you know what we use this wire for?" he asked.*

Was last night the sign I prayed for yesterday?

Later. I hate taking orders from 16-year-olds. Worse, I hate taking orders from 16-year-old illiterates. I mean Ramiro, of course, who first told me I can't cross the river—which means I can't go sit, read, write sleep at The Beach. But Moño said I could. We'll see . . . I may lose. Moño hates conflict.

Thursday, 20 Apr., Day 210

I probably lost. Ramiro saw Moño first. Moño came to my tent last night raising hell about my going far from the camp. "We don't shut you in a cell and we don't tie you up," he said. Thanks a lot, I thought. I'm not a criminal. Besides, you did lock me up and chain me for a long time. [Moño] says he's afraid the *comandante* will come and see me away from camp. He doesn't know where The Beach is and I want to show him today. That I don't want to lose. There's no place where sun can even reach around my tent except the rocky place where everyone does laundry.

1120h: Saw the Phantom yesterday and again today. Gray jacket and blue woolen cap, jeans, boots. P.M.: I wrote that I might lose. Boy, did I! The Beach, my spot in the sun, is off-limits. My new world is restricted to 20 feet from my tent to the river, then 30 feet to the right. How depressing. That'll also cut back on my exercise. But what can I do now? Sit by my tent, feed *chusque* to my fire all day. Moño seems paranoid that the *comandante* will come and either see me out of camp, or want to see but can't find me. "But there's no dry place to sit in the sun."

"I'll give you another piece of *plástico*," Moño said. "You can put it there," [he said,] pointing to a clear spot that is perpetually wet. No matter how p.o.'d I am, I can't be fool enough to turn down anything that can improve my life or slow its deterioration. "Okay, give me the plastic."

And *that* caused the next problem. Within 30 minutes, Gustavo appeared, asking if *I'd* give *him* the plastic so he can enlarge his tent. What could I do? I said no and pissed Gustavo off. Careful, Hargrove, I thought. As a friend, Gustavo makes your life a lot easier. You can't afford to have him as an enemy. It's not fair, I said. Moño just gave me the plastic and now you want it. You can have anything I have, almost, Gustavo, but if I'm to remain a prisoner in this little spot, I must make my life as comfortable as possible. Finally appeased Gustavo, I guess, and we're still friends.

Anything that dulls the pain of all this, makes it a little easier to take, is

---

*"To make bombs with," Moño then said, but I didn't want to write that in the diary.—TRH

still more sign that I'll be freed soon. What a fucking fool you are, Hargrove. You are falling for it again. What else can I do? Julio had [the] 9-to-10 P.M. guard last night and came to sit by the fire at La Rancha Tomás #2. "Do you want to eat meat, Don Tomás?"

"Of course."

He went to *la rancha* and returned with a huge piece of fresh beef. We cooked [it] on the coals, but he wouldn't eat any. "It's for you, Don Tomás. I know that you love meat. Do you want more to eat tomorrow and the next night?"

"Of course." He brought three more pieces. Beautiful meat. So much I'm afraid part will be spoiled before I can eat. Julio told me several interesting things, including that the guards have orders to leave La Rancha Tomás and not talk with me, after 10 P.M. That's good. Now I know I can cook illicitly at 10 P.M. "You're to be freed very soon. Don Tomás, we're only waiting for the order. You're to be taken to a town, and FARC will hire you a car to take you home. But that's a secret. Don't tell anyone I told you."

"Moño already told me the same thing."

He [Julio] also told me stories of fighting for five months with the Sixth Front [of FARC], and that was extremely interesting and encouraging.

"When you need more meat, tell me and I'll get it," Julio said.

All in all, very encouraging. I can take what[ever] comes if it's almost over. And I've already selected and washed the beef I'll grill at 10 P.M.

1600h: The afternoon passed somehow. Partly my talk with Julio. No one is doing much, and Julio tells me all are waiting for orders re. what to do with me. Standing down. But still digging trenches around the perimeter of Camp Loneliness. Something has to give. They have to get rid of me and move on. This is [now] a group with no mission.

Friday, 21 Apr., Day 211

0740h: Rained all night and is still raining. Miserable, cold weather. Right ear clearing up, but left is still infected and hurts terribly.

Natalia, the new girl who replaced Javier, wants to study English all the time. Good. But when will orders come? We must get out of here soon to re-lease this group to fight. That's what Julio told me. FARC will either release me or kill me or continue to hold me. The last option is least attractive. Later: Natalia gave me an apple. The first fruit I've had since the kidnapping. Today is the official day for the Texas Aggie Muster. I wonder if there'll be one in Cali? Well, I won't be there. This also marks 7½ months since I was kidnapped. And it was 40 days ago that Moño told me I'd be free. Lies. Then I think, God, don't give me that information if it's not true; it's too terribly cruel. I'm afraid, I guess, that I can't foresee the future. It would be awful to look far ahead in a crystal ball and see myself still here. And three, four months, a year. I wonder what Susan has thought when I've written letters with hope? What does she know? Do I look naive, ridiculous in Cali? Have I ever had a choice? But this time, both Gustavo and Julio have told me—but what do they know? And Moño—but is he lying? Oh God, let it end. Let it end.

1625h: This has been an awful, terrible, agonizing day, sitting here mostly and doing nothing but think. And thinking exactly what I've thought about for so long. When will it end? If only I knew. If I just knew that they're not lying, and my freedom *will* come. If freedom isn't coming, let me die, God, let me die. Quit it, Tom. You have a piece of beef under your bunk to cook at 10 P.M. tonight. You can look forward to that. Your ear infection is much better and it was so bad last night, you could hardly chew your illicit beef. This day is almost over—only another five hours or so. Maybe the order to march will come tomorrow. *NO!* Don't think that, you fool. Tomorrow will come but not the order. Then what will you do? Cry, be more depressed. If only I could do something to influence my destiny. If I knew. If I knew I won't be freed, I—well, I wouldn't kill myself. I'm not ready for that. At least most of the time I'm not. But I'd start making plans for how to do it. Ending this life wouldn't be suicide.

1645h: Pull yourself together, Tom. Rage, anger won't help. Neither will anguish, if you can avoid it. Tomorrow will be better. You'll still be here, but it will be better. Better days always follow the truly bad ones. Things would be so much better if I had some form of communication with Susan. My God, I haven't heard from my wife or, for that matter, from anyone I know, for 7½ months. If only I could talk to Susan, know that she's all right, exchange assurances that this horrible period, this interminable nightmare will end someday. The cease-fire broke several days ago. I hope that I may be better off. Worse, I want whatever will free me to happen, be it stop the war or intensify it. I'll deal with my conscience about the issue later.

Saturday, 22 Apr., Day 212

0715h: Waiting for breakfast on this our 17th day in Campamento Soledad [Camp Loneliness]. This time I had the guerrillas name the camp. Campamento Soledad was the suggestion of Julio and Melena. I face a real challenge: to make the day pass and go away as quickly and painlessly as possible. Not to do anything constructive. That's too much to ask, but not to fall into that terrible, deep, dark pit of anguish and despair. I spent yesterday in that pit, that's enough. Does it help to write these things or does that trigger the despair, catalyze and make it worse? I don't know. I asked Moño last night if there's any news about the plan to free me. His answer was awful: "We're analyzing the situation, Tomás. Studying it. The problem is the army won't leave; they're on all the routes." What a nothing answer. Gustavo told me, again, that he was sure they'd leave to fight soon, and must free me first. I see signs that it's true—but I'm looking for those signs. If anyone does anything nice or throws me an extra *arepa*, I think they're getting me ready for freedom. They're preparing to set me free. I've thought that a thousand—no, thousands—of times in the 211 days they've held me. But that day never comes.

Later: The day is miserable, one of slow, cold rain that soaks and chills, a day so damp it's a challenge to keep my fire going without using an entire forest. Maybe it's better this way. If the day were warm with sunshine, I'd want to go sit and absorb the sun in my spot—my special spot, now forbidden—by the river, instead of spending it in my wet world of 20x30 feet. I started to pray this A.M., but I can't afford to start off such a dismal day with still more depression. How can prayer give strength and comfort to so many yet it tears me down, breaks my spirit. Or so it seems. It makes me cry, and I can't avoid that. I haven't been forgotten. CIAT must be trying somehow to free me. And I know that Susan is doing whatever she can even if that's nothing but waiting. What a miserable day. I tried to sing, but I break down. I don't cry much—just a few seconds. Is that bad or good? I don't know.

Lord, what a difference a radio would make in my life. Especially a shortwave radio. But even with a regular radio, I could listen to news in Spanish. There's been a bomb in Oklahoma—I heard snatches on a guerrilla radio. Apparently a big one. The guerrillas shot down two choppers in a battle near Tolima, someone told me, and a defoliation plane somewhere else. . . . Should I hate, like I did before, I wonder. To go back to hatred would be easy; it's only a step from the contempt I now feel for these vermin who hold me. The question is, Would hatred help me survive? I don't think so. Just like I never argue with the guerrillas, almost never criticize or tell them what they're doing is wrong. They may be holding me partly because they're afraid of what I may say to the media when I return. Why add fuel to the fire? I'd use the media as a threat, I guess, to demand better treatment. But that could easily backfire—I don't like to think about the consequences.

1325h: Got through the A.M., now only the afternoon to survive, then I have something to look forward to . . . a clandestine steak dinner after the guards leave my fire at 10 P.M. tonight. Like I had last night. Have worked some teaching Natalia more English—she seems bright, eager to learn. Hope so; it would be nice to do something of value to someone for a change. Natalia has a [high school] degree from Bogotá, 10 years of school—that makes her seem like an Einstein in this group.* She seems to have come from a good family. Maybe that's why she seems kind. Life hasn't kicked her around like it has Melena and Judi, so she understands basic rules of kindness, courtesy. At noon I asked Judi a question. She wouldn't speak to me, or even acknowledge that I had spoken. For no reason. Maybe someone has been especially mean to her today. So she passes it on down. And I'm the only person "on down" for her. 2:55 P.M. I'm [lucky] that I still don't have bad dreams. Maybe that's why I consider the nights so much easier than the days. Drifted off to sleep for 10 minutes and woke up laughing. Dreamed I was shooting the bell with a 30-30, ringing it with bullets in the bell tower of the church at Hermleigh, Texas. Why? I don't know but it was a fun dream. How I wish I could master "lucid dreaming." . . . Today between 2 and 2:30 I thought deeply about Susan. I tried to contact her mind-to-

*I later learned that she hadn't actually graduated from high school.—TRH

mind through mental telepathy. Thought hard then tried to squeeze the message from my mind into the air to her. I've tried to pray that way, too.

Julio told me about guarding prisoners from the Colombian army, *chulos*, the other night. "We became good friends, like you and I are, Don Tomás," he said. "We never killed them. We always let them go after three months."

Then why have you held me for seven months? I thought. Julio also assured me that I won't be killed. I still didn't think they'll kill me either. But I'm not sure. FARC is composed of some very cold and ruthless bastards that aren't very smart. If they're afraid to release me, don't want to continue committing the human and financial resources to hold me . . . and we're so remote here in Camp Loneliness [that] killing me is possible . . . and they can always blame it on the *chulos*. 1620h: I just tried mental telepathy to Susan again. Wish I had a specific message to send. All I could send was, "Susan, can you hear me? Please listen. I don't know if I'll return or not, but I'll try. I love you and I'm trying to make sure I return in good health—sane and in good mental and emotional health as well as physical health. Please hear me. I can't advise you what to do, whether to stay in Cali, return to Texas. I don't even know where you are. But do what you think is right and know that I love you and I'll try my best to survive and return. Someday." What else can I say? To say that I'm coming home soon would be as cruel as Moño's lies. I start the messages with singing, like the opening of the song "Cindy": Susan . . . Oh Susan. Hear me, Susan . . . am I crazy right now? I don't know. Maybe.

Later: The sun came out, but you could catch its rays within my 20x30 world only at one spot along the river. I stood on the rocks and also my bed [to get] as much sun as possible.

Also tried to reach my mother via mental telepathy. "Mother, you were such a good mother, and you loved me so. If you can hear me, and you are able, please send me any help you can. I don't know what kind of help, just whatever you can offer. I may see you soon." I thought about praying, then thought: No, that doesn't help—and maybe you've been praying through two intermediaries with better communication channels, who can reach God better than you can.

Is my diary changing to a chronicle of [my] going crazy? Has it always been a log of insanity? It's hard for me to know. I feel something is near, it's heavy and all around me, and it may be death.

Later: Last night, Judi had guard duty 9 to 10. I certainly couldn't risk cooking my steak while she was on duty; the bitch would love to bust me for stolen meat. She sat here till ten. Then she told me she had duty again ten to 11 P.M. Traded, I guess. I was so pissed. Blew out candle, which I rarely use anyway (and I use the fire for light), and did not add fuel to the fire. She sat in darkness for a while, then went away. I sprang from my bunk and cooked and ate my fourth meal—my steak dinner—in darkness, except for the glow of coals. Just saw the Phantom. He walked off the hill (strickly forbidden to me, of course), to *la rancha*.

Sunday, 23 Apr., Day 213

Today started off bad. Beautiful, warm sunshine, the first sun we've had in eight days. But it's not for me. I can't enjoy it because there's nowhere in my 20x30 feet where [I can] catch rays as they filter through the trees. That's it.

Now it's 9:35 A.M. and [it] looks like clouds will block away the sun and the rest of today will be typically cold and dismal. Good. If I can't enjoy the sun, I don't want them to either. A positive thought came to me last night. If this unit is dissolved and guerrillas sent back to their units, or if it goes to fight as a unit, its last act would be to free me. They'll be concerned that I could tell where this camp is, so they must disappear as soon as I'm freed. That could help explain delays. Maybe. If the unit is to fight. FARC/Cauca has 1,500 soldiers, Mono said, and it's hard to find work for all of them. So these nine could sit out the fighting as my guards. There's nothing new about the idea that my freedom will be the last act of the unit. I've known it all along. Mono has even told me that. It's just that the idea seemed to explain so much, to give me new reason for hope last night in the dark. Grasping for straws, I guess.

1530h: Well, I've gotten through the worst of the day pretty well and I haven't even lit my fire yet. (Have to wait till someone brings me coals; I ran out of matches ages ago.) I cut away the brush around the nearest grove of *chusque* to my tent and made a place where the sun can reach. No one was around, so I cut some tall *chusque* that threw shade where I want sun. Mono said not to cut tall plants because they're camouflage against aerial reconnaissance. But I want the Colombian army to know where we are. An air strike might change my mind, of course. I also cut a little cave out of the brush behind my tent. Thank God I have the machete.

None of what I did today is of real value. It's "make-work," to make the time pass instead of sitting and thinking like I did yesterday. And it's to exhaust me so I'll go to sleep without thinking. Tried mental telepathy again to Susan at 12:20 P.M.

Monday, 24 Apr., Day 214

Was helping Natalia to study English when Mono called a meeting. She left her pen and notebook for me to write words and tenses. Mail goes out tomorrow, so used her pen to address and write the opening sentence of six letters and now this. In other words, to use her pen and her ink, because there is no way to know how long I'll be a prisoner, so must make my own ink last as long as possible. Similarly, I still have some pieces of typing paper that I found in the Valley of the Shadow that I tear to pieces for stationery. It's dirty, but I can't use any of the notebook while I have another option. I may still be in this cold forest "waiting till they can free me" a year from now. I'm damned serious about that.

1355h: Spent the A.M. with Natalia's English lesson, interrupted now and then by guerrillas coming to warm by my fire. The A.M. went pretty fast. No one in this camp is working. I hope they're standing down, killing time while waiting for orders—meaning, orders for what to do with me. But keep in mind, Hargrove, that this unit has seldom done much.

P.M.: Mail leaves tomorrow. Read my letters to Moño, then asked if he had any news. "No, they're still fighting."

You lying son of a bitch. I almost said, You have no plans to free me; why don't you kill me now and get it over with? It's raining and so cold. It was better yesterday, but today I want to die. No, Hargrove, you're not ready to die. Not yet. But when does hope run out? They can keep me for years—or until time to kill me—always making me think I'm about to be freed. Moño probably tells Gustavo and Julio to tell me those things, that plans are being made to free me. I'd love to talk to these bastards honestly one day—but that must be the day I truly give up hope and accept that I'll never see Susan and my family again. Because what I'd say would not help me survive. I must be awfully careful not to say those words now. I come awfully close sometimes.

Later: Stole four pages from Natalia's notebook. I feel bad about it, but that's 16 letters or more I can write without using potential diary pages.

1635h: Spent entire day sitting on the edge of my bunk by a fire. No choice. Raining straight down, so cold. Am depressed but I've survived. The guerrillas haven't sent me any coffee, chocolate, or anything. Which further convinces me there are no plans under way to free me. Oh God, what have I done to deserve this punishment? What will Susan do when I'm gone? Hell, I've been gone 7½ months. She'd be better off once it's final. But when they kill me, will she know? Or will I just quit writing? But they may not kill me for a year. And how do I know that she's received any of my letters? Or that anyone else has? I don't. I have only the word of my FARC kidnappers.

1730h: Something horrible just happened. I can't bear to think of it, but must write it now. I lost my bowl, the one I found in the Valley of the Shadow, with what I think is Vietnamese writing scratched into it. How could I? I used to keep rice [in it] for my locked-in meal. I went to the river after dinner to dump some old rice and replace it with fresh. I went to throw the old rice way into the river so no one would [see it and] know. It's so cold and I was in a hurry. I threw—flung, and the bowl slipped, went flying into the river, which is up, swollen. It floated 10 meters or so and sank. I saw where, but the river is high, fast, and will surely carry the bowl downstream. How could I be so stupid, so thoughtless, so clumsy, Hargrove, after so long. My evidence of Vietnamese training [of FARC]. I must think this out. What does it mean? If there's a God, why did he let this happen? Could there be a purpose? This is awful. It would also be awful even if it weren't for that Vietnamese text. I need that bowl. I regret, terribly, not somehow bringing the other one to Camp Loneliness. I'm numb. This can't have happened. No, let it sink in, Tom. No, what can I do? I can't scream, but why, God? Is that a sign that it's time to die? I'm so shocked, I can't even cry: WHY? WHY? God, God.

Later: I'm numb; this hasn't sunk in yet. Let me eat, let me survive.

Tuesday, 25 Apr., Day 215

"*¡Puta!*" I heard, and rolled over to look through one of the dangling tent flaps. Gustavo was standing by my tent bunk in the forest. "*Un día puta.*" It's raining and the sky is dark gray.

"Yes, a whore of a day," I agree. "Like yesterday."

"*¿Quiere tinto extra, Don Tomás?*"

I find my battered cup under my bunk, hold it out, and Gustavo fills it from the battered tin pot of coffee he's brought. "But we have a good *ranchero*, we'll eat well today. . . . *Puta*," Gustavo mutters, and turns back toward *la rancha*, where he pulls today's kitchen duty. Thank God for Gustavo and Julio and sometimes Caballito. They do a lot to make my life better. And today can't be as bad as yesterday. It may be as cold and miserable, and it may look like an-other day of only sitting here watching the rain fall, but it'll be better than yes-terday. It has to be. A few more yesterdays and I'll be over the wall, flipped out. I can't let yesterday happen again. But what will I do today? Brush my teeth, for one thing. It's been three days. I still have Natalia's pen, so I better write while I can use her ink. Start letters to Susan and Daddy, and address letters to everyone I might write. And update that backup key-word diary that I keep on blank checks in the——belt [i.e., the money belt, which TRH avoided mention-ing in his diary to prevent it—and its contents—from being confiscated—ed.]. And I could write some in the diary, which is what I'm doing now.

Losing that pan yesterday was such a shock—such a *tragedy*, and that's an appropriate word—that I've shut it from the thinking, contemplative section of my mind, and haven't dwelt on its significance. The pan was my second most valued possession—after my diary. But maybe that explains it. Maybe I had to lose something—and loss of the diary would be the most devastating, anguishing blow of all. Maybe I lost the pan so I'll leave here with the diary, complete. Well, the pan is gone. It's like a friend died. I'm sad and I'll miss him every day. But I can do nothing to change the situation, and life must go on. And maybe something good came of it. The loss shocked me so, it wrenched me out of the deep depression I was in. Maybe. Today my attitude is more positive. That's partly because of a conversation with Moño last night. Again, he assured me that [they] were just waiting for the order to get rid of me and return the troops to their units. "This is a *campamento movimiento*," he said. "There's no work to be done here."

Yeah. That makes sense. Moño expects orders any day. . . . But what if FARC decides to keep me and turns me over to another unit?

"Why would FARC do that? We don't like to keep *rehenes* long."

So . . . I believe again—sort of. Again, what are my options? Only anguish and despair.

Had a big problem with Judi on her 9-to-10 guard last night. She said that I had to lie down and go to sleep at 10 P.M. I refused. Of course, I wanted to cook a piece of beef and had to keep that secret. I won in the end. Or did I? Why must she be so stupid? Why can't the pitiful thing have me as a friend?

P.M. I'd try to contact Susan by mental telepathy again, but I don't want to put myself in that mental state. When I tried 22 and 23 Apr. it was a call from the deepest depression and despair. Somehow I think such a call has a better chance of getting through than one from a "normal" state of mind. Right now I'm lonely, bored, and uneasy, but my mental condition is far better than before. Must keep it that way.

1730h: Got through today okay. I feel a great nothingness and try not to think of the future or home. That helps. It numbs.

Either Rambo or the Tall Stranger visited Camp Solitude this P.M. (couldn't tell from the distance). Made me hope, of course, to arrange my freedom.

2005h: *"Mañana nos vamos, Tomás,"* Moño said 15 minutes ago. "Tomorrow we leave."

"What?" My God. Finally I'm going home. I can't believe, can't fathom it.

"Arriba." We're going back up, returning to the Valley of the Shadow. That stunned me.

"To *live?*"

"Yes. The Colombian army is nearby." Oh God, I can't believe this. How much more delay does that mean? I have to let this sink in. I can't bear the thought right now.

Wednesday, 26 Apr., Day 216

A.M. Am sitting on the skeleton of my bunk ready to march. Every thing I have is in my backpack or roll of covers. It's pitiful. I've thrown away parts of old magazines that I probably won't read for the 15th time no matter how bored I get. Like the 1988 *USSR* magazine. Have saved all wire and string I can. I took off the cloth strips that hold the arm of my rugged cross of bamboo. It still stands, held by vines, but not for long. A pity—I wanted to leave that cross behind, as sturdy as possible. Maybe if the army hits this camp, they'll find this cross and figure out I was here. I'm wearing all four shirts and jacket, using *ruana* as padding for the backpack. My *candela* and other pan and cup are wired to the pack. The tent I lived in and the rubber canvas cover were packed in my backpack. I put [in both canvas] bases for my bed.

I wrote earlier that one more thing would happen before my release. Is this it?

I've dreamed, fantasized of leaving each camp. This is my fourth time [to] leave camp and, as before, it's only to more imprisonment, Why? I wish we'd start the march so I can quit thinking.

1115h: This is hard to believe, but I'm locked—with a padlock, from outside—in my dark cell in Camp Aburrido again. Locked in darkness, where there's barely enough light coming through the cracks to write. Why? I don't know, but I can't let it get me down and I must push the claustrophobia from my mind. My God, I spent weeks locked in this cell. How did I keep from going crazy? Or did I? Did a little bit of my mind twist here in the cell? Is that how I've survived so long?

Before leaving I built a fire, from last night's embers, at Camp Loneliness, and threw on armfuls of *chuzco*. My last sight of Campamento Soledad was [of] my blazing fire with my Rugged Cross of bamboo standing behind it in the forest. Made first part of trip on horseback, then climbed the mountain's 60 percent slope, wet, slippery, carrying pack of at least 50 pounds, with Caballito and Natalia. They say soldiers have been living near Camp Aburrido, but I saw no evidence. The little aluminum bowl that I regretted so much not bringing was sitting by La Rancha Tomás, where I left it. Also a *costal* [bag] and a plastic sack. My cell looks just like I left it.

1630h: *Grief.* That's the only word I know to describe how I feel. No, there are others. *Despair, heartbreak.* Those words are generally used to describe human relations. Well, I guess that's what this is. I miss Susan terribly, and I'm not sure—at all—that I'll ever see her again. Things keep getting worse and worse. Every time I think I'm finally to be freed—something else is thrown at me and my life becomes worse, not better. Guerrillas *were* here and they cut almost all the *chusque* and wood. It's going to be hard to stay warm. And I'm further than ever from release. It's raining and cold.

1810h: Still waiting for dinner. So cold. This P.M. I was released after 30 to 40 minutes. Then was left alone by my room. The others hadn't arrived yet. Went into Jhon's room. His bunk had lots of straw. Lots. I moved two armsful to my own bunk. Then went to Melena's room. There was a sheet of typing paper, which I took. Also four packs of Kotex and a roll of bandage. I took one Kotex and cut two feet of bandage. What will I use it for? I don't know, but one always needs clean cotton.

Lunch was cold rice with a teaspoon of sardine. I will write future letters in pencil, save this ink for diary and backup.

Thursday, 27 Apr., Day 217

Awoke this A.M. thinking I don't know what's going on, but things are getting worse. I have a feeling that life in Camp Aburrido will be worse than before—and life [then] was no *retozo* [frolic] before. It must be true that the Colombian army was getting closer to Happy Valley—otherwise two moves would make no sense. Also the pressure on the guerrillas may make me more valuable as a prisoner. Thus, plans to disband the unit and release me have been dropped. I have no idea, of course, what's going on back in Cali. Are there still ransom negotiations that have gone bad? Is FARC using me (and maybe my life) as collateral insurance—against army operations? P.M.: It's obvious that the unit is doing its other mission. Is that why we returned?

After the others left this morning, Ramiro came and started locking my cell from outside with a padlock. "What's this? Why?"

"Orders."

I said I had to go to [the] latrine.

When I returned, I talked Ramiro into letting me stay on the porch to La Rancha Tomás—20 feet away. He's told me I must be back in the cell when

Moño returns. Did Moño really order me in solitary confinement all day? If so, he hasn't told me and that's strange. Of course, Ramiro also left me in the tent till one P.M. before—and Moño said he didn't order it. Ramiro said that Rambo gave Moño a bad time because I went so far from camp at Camp Soledad. But that was a week ago. I'm in La Rancha Tomás right now trying to keep a fire going. Will I be locked in the cell all day tomorrow? This is bad and getting worse. I haven't let myself think much about my situation today and somehow have stayed busy keeping the fire going, making repairs on La Rancha Tomás, etc.

1400h: Don't want to work more because Ramiro says he has to lock me up again so I'll be caged when Moño returns. So I'll need something to do. Now I can sit here by the fire in La Rancha Tomás while it rains outside. My God, what levels I sink to.

1600h: I guess the solitary confinement is Moño's orders after all. Ramiro locked me back up at three so I'll be under lock when Moño returns. My mattress was dirty yesterday and wet so I left it out to dry. Still was pretty warm last night with the tent and canvas base plus the extra straw. Ramiro brought me plastic today and we nailed it over two walls to stop the wind and the third piece went on my bed under the mattress. I should at least be warmer than before. It's funny that his nine-person team has three women and one homosexual—and two of the women and the homosexual are the ones I have the most trouble with. The women are pitiful. Judi is a psycho; she'll do what she can to be cruel.

Both ears are infected again. They've been infected for two to three months now and get better and worse. The sores inside the ears swell and fill with pus and it's extremely painful. Then the *granos* [sores] burst, and it doesn't hurt so much. I've done okay today. I've managed generally not to think beyond here and now. Width of cell: arms extended, palms up. Length: arms extended, fingers and six inches arms and palms and fingers of other hand. Height = me plus two inches. I'm afraid to think, afraid to pray, and afraid to sing, at least until I get out of this cell. The black plastic on the walls makes it warmer, but also darker, more claustrophobic, and scarier.

1715h: Was released after two hours of solitary confinement. But Moño thinks it was 21 hours. Wow. Dinner last night included green beans—also tonight—the first vegetable, or anything green, since early Dec.; delicious, although only a couple of bites.

2015h: Locked in at seven P.M. Asked Moño if there is a problem. Yes, an operation *muy serio*—nearby. All these precautions, I guess, are to make sure I don't try to escape.

Stuck a big piece [splinter] of *chusque* in my right wrist—deep. Hurts. I'm afraid, of course, of another infection here, with no antibiotics.

Is FARC holding me to trade for some sort of army—or government—concessions? Proposed or potential?

Friday, 28 Apr., Day 218

This is my third day back at Camp Aburrido in the Valley of the Shadow. Am sitting in La Rancha Tomás. It's cold and cloudy, but not raining. Not yet. What will I do today, to keep sane? It's time to count my blessings. 1) My wrist, where the thick sliver of *chusque* stuck deep yesterday—doesn't seem to be infecting. Thank God! 2) My bunk with the new straw and tent and plastic as a base is warm, almost cozy. It seems almost sinful to wake in the night and not be cold. 3) I'm not locked in solitary confinement today. 4) I have my broken machete, and can cut some *chusque* later. 5) I have a pen with ink. 6) I've never had a cold since being kidnapped. I have a few complaints, of course, but counting my blessings is better. I'll add as more come to me. 7) The nights aren't so bad, partly because I generally have nice dreams. But last night [I dreamed I] was kidnapped [and] trying to escape. Oh well . . .

Later: I paced off the areas to which I can go. They form a teardrop pattern of 105 steps, door to door, from my cell and returning. One step = 1½ feet; this includes up- and downhill, backtrack, etc.

Something else will happen: I have one more test before this ends. I wrote that weeks ago. Is this, my return to the Valley of the Shadow and whatever hardships it brings, the last test? Will they free me when this ends? The bigger and more impossible question is, I guess, is there a plan to all this, a reason? And that question means, is there a God? Men and women have sought the answer to that question for ages. The answer would come, clearly and strongly, in a time of extreme test and need, I thought. But it hasn't. If there is a God, then prayer should give me strength. But maybe that doesn't follow. I'm alive and, I think, sane after seven months, three weeks of pretty awful conditions, and trials of the spirit and soul. Is there a book in all of this? Is it wrong to hope for one? Could I pray for one? How else could all this torture make sense? As I wrote the previous, the embers of my fire started smoking. Is that a sign, or do I read too much into coincidence? Like finding the pencil while crying on my birthday.

Ten minutes ago Ramiro walked by. "Let's start a fire," I said, meaning would he bring some coals. My matches ran out weeks ago. *"No, Tomás, me enfermo."*

"I'm sorry, but if you're sick, a fire would be good."

"No, Tomás," he said, and walked away. In other words, he wouldn't bring me coals. It's only 60–70 feet to the permanent fire at *la rancha* and he could do it easily. Why are they so damned cruel? I thought, and cried a little. Wow, the fire is really smoking now. I must close this and help it.

1140h: Spent the morning keeping the fire going and gathering cold, wet, slimy *chusque*, and trying to figure out where I am in life. The guerrillas have never been terribly nice, but they're getting worse—cruel and insulting. I guess it's because no one wanted to come back here, all wanted this to end. But here we are, and I guess Don Tomás is to blame. The novelty of the *gringo* wore off long ago. No one stops to talk to me anymore, and it's not because of something

I've done. The war seems to be going bad for the guerrillas and that's not going to help me. I should write something positive or funny, but there's nothing funny or amusing about this life. I haven't laughed sincerely since 23 Sept. Yesterday, I started to laugh out loud, but alone and to myself about something; I don't remember what it was, and it doesn't matter. My laughter turned to crying in the same breath, the same exhalation triggered by the irony of the same thought. That scared me, and I went back to cutting *chusque* like hell. Another funny thing: yesterday I searched—but didn't find—my chain, the one the guerrillas used to chain me [with] for so long. Found the leather dog collar that went around my wrists, but not the chain. I was going to propose to Moño, if he planned another two hours of solitary confinement, that he chain me again instead. Fortunately, it wasn't necessary because I think he's here in the camp all day. Wow, is that funny? Searching for my own chain to give to my kidnappers? Yeah, it is in a way, here in el Valle de la Sombra [Valley of the Shadow]. What, oh what, is going on? For dinner, I got a spoonful of green beans and a dish of rice. Finished it and asked if I could have more. No. Not "We don't *have* more," just no. Are we out of food? I don't know. It seems that I'm being deliberately punished. And I honestly don't know why. To make it worse—a cup of chocolate came with dinner. Delicious. But I spilled it all after only one sip. I'll bet Judi and Melena lock me up at six P.M. tonight. Thank God I have this machete, even if the blade is broken. It lets me cut wood and *chusque*, gives me exercise, and numbs the mind. Well, what would I do without the machete? God, what is happening?

Saturday, 29 Apr., Day 219

Start: I feel a great deal better than earlier this A.M., but I feel I should write my situation. I'll try, as objectively as possible.

My situation is probably worse than at any time since the kidnapping with the possible exception of the days of solitary confinement and chain, but I am only a hair away from that, too. I don't know what's happened, but three days ago I was in a transit camp with all the signs that freedom was almost here again. Suddenly I'm stuck back in the Valley of the Shadow and freedom doesn't seem even a remote possibility. We've reestablished a permanent camp and the guerrillas are working. Things are tough for the guerrillas; the army must be pushing hard. We've scarcely any supplies. Everyone is p.o.'d about being back here—and I'm the only one to blame it on. Judi lit a fire in La Rancha Tomás—used three full, new candles. I almost cried, watching. Three candles would last me 10 days to two weeks. Typical of guerrilla wastefulness, inability to look ahead: we have candles—use 'em. Monitoring of my daily life has been turned over to Judi and Melena—pitiful sick women who are taking vengeance on me for the cruelties life has dealt them. Moño doesn't want the problem of dealing with me. Not only has he turned the responsibility over, he's also now screwing Melena and, I think, Judi—always has his hands on her. So I can't complain to Moño. My ear infection is serious. The pain last night was excru-

ciating, yet I have no medicines, nor any access to medical attention. It's cold
and we live in mud. I can move about 30 feet. I slept last night some, but with
dreams of pain. Felt better at 6:40 A.M. when Judi brought breakfast. Wanted to
stay in bed, it was so warm and comfortable, and escape from it all. But if I'm
inside the cell, Judi can easily slip the padlock over the latch and lock me in
solitary confinement all day. Especially if Moño leaves. That's not idle
speculation—she'd do it. So I got up so I'd at least be out of the cell if she decided to try it. Am drinking from the plastic thermos lid. Melena has obviously
seen this as the opportunity to get even regarding the cup incidents. This time
I can't fight it. I belong to her and Judi. I'm not going to die, not immediately.
At least I don't think so. But death hovers over this valley, circling and always
on call. The ear infection may be my most serious problem. But a *chulo* [i.e.,
Colombian army] attack is not out of the question. And—oh no—I've used 60
to 70 percent of the ink in my new pen. Maybe only make backup notes in
future?

P.M.: Problem with eltbe [i.e., the money belt in which the author hid the
backup notes to his notebook diaries]. What to do? Terrible . . .

Sunday, 30 Apr., Day 220

The pain in my left ear was excruciating last night. Finally took my
Ponstan 500, although I don't know when I can get another. Had a long, happy
dream that I'd moved to India for some reason. It was so warm and the food
was so good. The sores in my ear burst in the night, and when I woke, my ear
was encrusted with dried pus. Maybe that ends the ear problem for a while. A
lot of the new measures I've figured out are to isolate me. Judi sends me to bed
early so I won't talk to the first guard. None of them come by La Rancha Tomás
anymore. I'm more alone than I've ever been; it's really scary to think why. But
if they were to kill me, I guess they would probably already have done so. But
I see no end. Saw Moño this morning. The army *el gobierno* has broken, etc.,
"all has broken down," he says, and they're protecting me from the army and
still plan to free me. I thought, If Moño tells the truth, I've had one hell of a
lot of bad luck—like it was programmed to lift me up, then crash me down. But
he is lying. I have to quit thinking about home and Susan or I'll go crazy.
Maybe I'm already crazy.

A nice thing. Gustavo went to Happy Valley [La Playa] yesterday. He
brought and gave to me in ultimate secret a bottle of ketchup, hot sauce, and
mayonnaise. Wow, I'm living almost entirely on rice and fried bread. This is
Day 3, so I brushed my teeth Saturday night, and ate more beef—but it smelled
a lot. It had been 17 days since we killed that calf. Mice in my room; I find
droppings in bowls where I keep food. Never mind. I wash the bowls and heat
food. Some sun. Dozed, trying to think of things that I haven't thought about,
new and positive things instead of thinking only of freedom, my family, my
luck. No luck. Remembered two songs I haven't sung in weeks: "Fraulein" and
"Geisha Girl." I'll save them for tonight.

Monday, 1 May, Day 221

Today will be long and hard. It appears that the cold, drizzly rain will never stop. Breakfast was one *arepa*. *"No más,"* Judi said. Most guerrillas have left, and Julio is my guard. He got me another *arepa*. Delicious and I'm hungry, but I saved half for tonight. Must maintain that last meal, especially now that I'm locked in by seven P.M. Judi took most of my dry *chusque*. Asked permission as she was taking it; what choice do I have? She controls my food, my schedule, and the medicines, including those pain pills I've taken to sleep with. My ears fill with pus during the day; [the cysts] burst sometime during the night, but after terrible pain.

"My wife is very cynical," I told Moño. "She's not going to believe that you really plan to free me."

"But we have another delay!" [he responds].

"But she won't believe it after so much false hope. I have trouble believing it, too."

"The *ejército* [army] has—"

"I know, I know. Anyway, I want to write her a very honest letter and tell her exactly the situation as you tell me. Do you agree?" Moño agreed. So that's my project for today. But I can't set out to convince Susan because I don't know what to believe myself. But it's going to be a long sad time before I see her or my family again. I still have hope, so I'll live, but I'm not sure that living is the best thing anymore.

Later: I worry so much about Susan, the boys, too, but especially about Susan. Whenever I pray, I always pray to give her strength and guidance. If only I knew that she's okay, where she is. But it's like worrying about my father. I can do nothing to help them except survive, and write when I can. Why so cruel, God? Or is it hope? I know better, but it takes nothing. I said something meaningless to Moño: "Is there hope?"

"Maybe we'll receive news tomorrow," he replied. Now all I can think is the work of the guerrillas is done. Now maybe they'll release me. Tomorrow the orders will come.

Tuesday, 2 May, Day 222

My ear is better and didn't hurt much last night, but still I didn't sleep. I couldn't help it. I thought about my "monel" all night. Tried to pray this morning, but can't. Unless I'm in a state of total anguish, it's like talking to myself. And I can't afford to start a day in total anguish. But getting to that state is easy; all I have to do is stay still. I've prayed this morning, but not deeply. For two things other than for Susan and Daddy, and my captors and strength and judgment for me: to protect my diaries and to not let me fly so high and crash so hard again. But I'm going to, I can't help it. The news that comes today, will it bring freedom? "We receive news today?" I asked Moño.

"No, tomorrow."

"Why the change?" [Yesterday Moño said news would come] today. "Do you think orders will come soon to free me?"

"I don't know, Tomás. I didn't want to build up your hopes," he said, "but it's best to hope for freedom. Another summer comes, the roads and trails will be clear, and it will be easier to move you." My heart dropped. Late May should bring summer, they say. My letters to Havener and Susan were full of "they say." I hope they catch that. In other words, I'm not saying it's true I've been moved because the Colombian army was approaching, but that's what FARC told me. We grew short-staple cotton on the Hargrove family farm in West Texas. I've discovered where the shortest staple cotton of all is used. Kotex. Wonder how many of my cotton-industry friends know that? I put cotton from the stolen Kotex in my ears. Had a hell of a time removing it later because the lint was too short to pull so I wrapped it on a stick. Guess I'll find another use for the Kotex. Gustavo brought me from Happy Valley a third cartridge of ink yesterday. How nice. But it's red ink, so will use sparingly. Too conspicuous, easy to see.

Later: What a bumbling fool I am. Judi saw my bottle of ketchup in my pocket at noon and insisted that I give her some. No choice. "But you have to do nice things for me." Sure. My cell is full of rats. One ran across my face last night for the second time. With [my] ski mask on, they can't tell it's a human.

1650h: Oh, ye of little faith! Is that me? For the past two days, Lord protect my diaries has been a fervent prayer. Only Ramiro knew, although I've literally been sick at heart since the compromise [since Ramiro may have seen the money belt]. Removed [my diary pages] and have been carrying them in a coat pocket. Only a few hours ago I was thinking as [I had] over [the] past few days maybe Ramiro will be transferred out before I've—no, that won't happen. He's been part of unit since the day I was kidnapped. Well, at about three P.M. today Ramiro walked up wearing his pack and held his hand out. "*Me voy* [I'm leaving], *Tomás*."

"What, permanently?"

"Maybe. I'm sick." He's being sent to a clinic somewhere—is that an answer to a prayer? I'll transfer all [of the pages] back—the most secure [place] of all [the money belt]. Later Gustavo told me [Ramiro] has an infection of the groin. Could be AIDS, of course. Well, if he has it, who else on this team has it?

Wednesday, 3 May, Day 223

Transferred all backup back to eltbe [money belt] last night. But in cell, after lockup, [I] feel such relief. Thank God.

Red pen for backup. Most guerrillas gone to work or to Happy Valley. Okay, I can't help it. Thought all night. Maybe job [the guerrillas] came for is finished. Best get rid of prisoner. Only two ways, and I'm banking on the more humane. You must be strong, Hargrove. Prepare yourself for the news—the no news. Eventually I'll have to ask, and that'll be the answer. Be strong, have faith, don't let the crash hurt you so, this time.

Later: The last sliver of beef last night—amazingly it was still good 20 days after butchering the cow. I kept pieces in a plastic bottle buried in wet leaves. I buried my two pads of Kotex. With such short-staple cotton it was of little value, and the flesh-colored packages and outer part made it too dangerous to keep. That color could be spotted anywhere. Last night cold and clear—like summer coming. Ramiro threw away piece of plastic. I stuck it under the porch and this morning [used it] as more base for [my] bunk.

P.M.: Emptied half inch of hot sauce into empty bottle so supply won't be obvious if someone sees it. Oh God, don't let me crash so hard this time.

El Templo [a "power spot where I went to pray"] looks so bare, but it's my power. . . . I haven't put up a cross because at the U front there's a thick broken stake of bamboo standing straight. It looks a lot like the base of a . . . cross on which the arms on top have been broken. At least it looks that way to me, and it stands in exactly the right place where the altar should be. It's a war-torn and shattered cross that still stands. It's my Broken Cross of Bamboo.

1425h: Why, God, why? Why? I had only two pairs of trousers I can wear. Both denim. Drying the wine-colored trousers and wearing the blue ones 15 minutes ago; the wine trousers caught fire. In an instant they were virtually burned away beyond salvage or repair. I can't wear them. What will I do now? This also affects my nights. I wear all four trousers to bed. These have been drying the last two nights and I've been so cold. God, why? Is this a test? I wasn't careless—not really. There's no chance of replacement. Is this punishment? For what? I need only one pair of trousers. I'll live and I won't go crazy.

1515h: I've been cutting bamboo—and thinking I'll laugh about this. I'll not let it get me down. I'm too close to the edge. I'll survive. It could be worse. Far worse. What if I'd broken my glasses? That would be a real catastrophe. What if I'd lost—or burned, somehow—my diary. Maybe this is partial payment for giving back my diary backup. This I should consider funny and a nuisance but nothing to break or even crack my spirit.

1530h: Of ultimate importance. I must put out of my head all thoughts of orders for my freedom arriving tonight. They won't [come] and I can't push my spirit further. New goal: I'll leave at the end of one year [of] kidnapping. Until then, Hargrove, survive.

1700h: The no news arrived. No news. But I should be thankful I have the security of my backup again. I couldn't expect that and freedom to arrive at once. I must find a better way to use, or shut off, my mind. How much solitude and loneliness can a person take? Tomorrow is Day 3! I brush my teeth. I'm getting too careless. Two days ago [I] dropped watch in the fire. Ten minutes. I worry that the longer they keep me, the harder it is to release me. Maybe it's partly like they say. FARC thought it had a real prize when they captured me and took me deep, deep within its territory. Too deep to get me out easily.

Thursday, 4 May, Day 224

A rat drowned in my piss bucket last night. Hope it's the rat that keeps running across my face at night. Seems that with the ski mask, they can't tell I'm human. Some sun yesterday afternoon. This morning it's cloudy, with no sun, but not raining. Signs that summer is coming. Hope for release when summer comes, Moño said, because it will dry the trails and make them easier to travel, and open other trails. Summer should be here by the end of May. Escorting me out of here on these trails might, of course, be the most dangerous time of all. An army ambush is possible. But what I fear even more is that it will be a time to kill me and blame it on the army. I've composed a final letter, or at least a letter telling what I fear will happen. If that's written, God, please have them kill me now. In my mind I'm nowhere near ready to send the letter, but it goes like this:

Dear Becky and Raford (or Susan, depending on whether I should tell her):
It looks like the guerrillas are finally getting ready to set me free [forever], so I expect to be coming home within a few weeks. Would you tell our cousin Darrell that I really look forward to visiting with him again. I also want to spend time with Marlin, and Willene Field and Buddy Day and Ed Tout and some of my old Texas Aggie buddies like Joe Bush and Gene Oates. Coming home will be a relief.

All those mentioned are dead, of course. I can't include Mother because I mentioned her death in conversation with Moño.

Later: Having written that makes me feel better, like I'm not really going to die. That makes me want to pray or to sing, but I don't dare because that would throw me back into hopeless despair and depression. Why? It's not supposed to be this way. Maybe I'm truly crazy.

P.M.: Judi brought lunch. The procedure was typical. It was gruel of corn and potato and my shallow bowl was filled, thank God, to the brim. *"Tengo,"* take it, she says. She's standing on the porch looking down at me. I try to take the shallow bowl gingerly, so as not to spill a drop, but thrusting it at me and sloshing a precious spoonful on the ground, she then turns and walks away, laughing. Why? She's truly cruel, but I doubt the others ever see it because they don't receive her cruelty. Well, another cross to bear. I can't let her get me down. I pity her. Her life must have been so cruel. I'll try to help her. I'll try more. I must beat back despair or it will kill me. I've been thinking I'm going to try hard to be more positive. "Joy" is the word that keeps coming into my mind. There hasn't been much joy around here, but I'll search for it. I'll find it. Maybe finding that rat this morning was a fortunate sign: I can't be like the rat that drowned in my piss. What do I have to be thankful for, joyous for? Last night I had a good locked-in dinner. I heated rice until it was hard—crisp and oily—then added beans. Later ate [with] ketchup and *ají*—there's something to be thankful for. And heated half an *arepa*. It was delicious. And then I slept like a rock. Maybe it was emotional exhaustion, but I didn't lie awake thinking. This morning wasn't so bad. It's raining now, but the day's been drier than usual. I think I can still wear my red jeans to bed. Only the front and seat of the right side [are] missing. I can still use them as extra pajamas, take advantage of the warmth. I'll try joy.

"I need to work," I told Moño, instead of sitting here hour after hour, day after day with nothing to do but think. Can I help with the kitchen? Peel potatoes? Anything? Cut firewood? The answer: "*No. Punto* [Period]."

1725h: Got through another day. Rained all P.M., dammit, so I had to sit by the fire, go out and cut wood when the rain stopped. But thought nothing but positive. Joy was the theme. Although not really on purpose. Sang every song I knew about joy. "Jeremiah the Bullfrog," even the Christmas song "Joy to the World." It worked. But really, Hargrove, it's [as] if you'd taken a pill, you can't keep it up. Never mind. I got through today; one day at a time, remember?

Friday, 5 May, Day 225

Today is 32 weeks, 8 months a *secuestrado*, two-thirds of a year except [that] calendar year is 12 months, 26 days. Windy and with intermittent sun today—also note that the ground is crawling with flies—both signs that summer's coming?

My cell crawls with rats and mice. I listen to them all around me in the straw in the bunk at night. Lay in my bunk and dozed until 9:30 A.M. with nice dreams. What a wonderful way to kill two hours. Now let's see if I can sleep tonight. They have been washing clothes. Melena tries to make me feel bad for asking them to wash some socks and a shirt—I have no choice. I can't go to the river, or even to the spring. Joy, Tom, remember? How will I squeeze some joy out of today? I must believe FARC believes that no more games are being played, and I'll be taken to freedom in the next few weeks. God, it hurts; I miss my boys and Susan so. But I can't think about them; I can't afford the grief. How can these people be so cruel? There's trouble between the USA and Colombia, Moño said. President Clinton says Colombia is not doing enough in the drug war and [Moño] claims he "has threatened to *invade Colombia*?" Surely not. Nothing could be so naive. But what if the U.S. pulled something like that while I'm still held? That might even give FARC some degree of legitimacy, and increase my value as a prisoner.

1620h: Turned cold and rained all afternoon. Haven't sung my three songs [that I wrote about life as a prisoner] yesterday or today because I'm afraid they're too depressing. I'd like to write a song about joy, and have been trying. Something to pick me up. But nothing comes, I guess because there is no joy, no laughter, no love here. Mail leaves on Sunday. Awfully hard to write. What do I tell Susan? That I'm coming home soon? I can't do that to her. I can't really write about the misery and anguish here. If only I could believe. But I have a deep fear. So bad I can hardly bear to think of it; that I'm part of FARC's package for peace. That freedom comes when the Colombian government pulls out and recognizes the guerrillas' "free zones," for example. If that's what's happening, there's almost no hope. If I knew that was happening, I'd be getting ready for suicide and writing that letter to Raford and Becky.

Saturday, 6 May, Day 226

[Continuing the above thought]: On the other hand, if this were a trick all along, we wouldn't have moved to Happy Valley, then to Campamento Soledad for three weeks, then back up here. That would make no sense. That's not to say, of course, that my status didn't change while at Camp Soledad. When we moved back up here, Lord, I don't know.

1130h: I'm not even going to try to fight it this time; I've learned that it's useless and I can't fool myself. I know I'm going to crash again, and it'll hurt like hell, but . . . About 20 minutes ago Viejito and two other guerrillas arrived by surprise—at least a surprise to me. One guerrilla is, I'm almost certain, the VIP who came on 11 March in civilian clothes and brought the news which I was told on 12 March, that I was to be freed. They all disappeared, then Moño came and brought me a new purple *ruana*—remember the civilian was the one who promised the *ruana*? He's a VIP and represents the *comandante*, I know. Oh God, please, please, please, God. No, it won't happen. I won't hurt myself like so many times before. But what can I do? I'll survive, no matter what; it won't destroy me or my mind; I'll live.

1220h: Señor VIP brought other goodies; Gustavo just brought my share: six pieces of chocolate candy, a pack of four chocolate cookies, two suckers, two cans of sweet condensed milk. Couldn't help it—ate one candy. So absolutely, divinely delicious—and two of the cookies. I'll now be able to use my old *ruana* as a pillow—a big improvement over my bath towel . . . hey . . . that means I have a towel that I can use—*as a towel*!

1230h: Julio confirms that Señor VIP is the same who brought the news 11 March. Went to El Templo. Oh God, if this is not it, stand by me, stand by me, stand by me, because I'll need more strength than ever. But nothing is going to happen, except that I have some candy and a new *ruana*, and I'll be okay. I won't go crazy, grief and anguish won't get me; I'll survive; I'll live through this new trial. But God, isn't it stupid to hope so much? No, I can't help it. I'll be okay.

1255h: Moño just brought me a new pair of socks, which, God knows, I need.

1505h: Well, it's over, I guess, and for a while, and I know what it's about, *más o menos*. Moño brought me a legal-sized sheet of clean paper and said I must write a letter to Susan in Spanish, but with a last paragraph in English. Said that Susan does not believe I'm still alive, and I need to add that to convince her. I must write about how bad my life is, Moño said, and that I'm sick. I argued a little, but there was really not much I could do. I wrote with big letters, and wide margins, to fill the page with as few words as possible. I wrote only the truth about the miserable life; I only repeated things I'd already written without being forced: the boredom, the loneliness, how I'm alone almost all the time; the worry for my family; the cold and rain. The only *new* thing in the entire letter was the part about being sick. I had not told Susan this before, but wrote simply can she send medicines because both my ears are infected; I can't cure them because I lack both eardrops and antibiotics. The ears are painful and sometimes it's hard to sleep at night. It's entirely true and I might have written it earlier had I thought it would do any good. For example, if Susan *could* send the medicines. I read the letter to Moño and he seemed satisfied. Said the letter could go immediately to Susan, not via the mail, like other letters.

I feel sick, but I had no more choice than the day I had to make the video. Are they trying to squeeze ransom? I don't know; can do nothing about it. I only hope CIAT is behind us on this.

1605h: Now it's truly over for a while. Señor VIP has left. But I talked with him twice. "Yes, *rescate* [ransom] will be paid," he said, "but I don't know how much. All arrangements have been made, and your family and FARC are in agreement. All that is lacking is this letter—it's proof that you're still alive."

But if the letter was only for proof, why did they make me write that I was sick? I'm glad I had the ear problem to describe, so I didn't have to lie. "Then I can expect to leave soon?"

"Yes." I believe him. I should be ecstatic, but I'm not. The ransom issue leaves an especially sour note to a bitter experience. But I don't know why I say that. I've always known that I'd never leave alive unless ransom was paid. I even wrote that ransom must be why they won't simply turn me over to the army. The Colombian army cut off escape from here once. I believe there was at least some truth to the story. It could happen again. Wouldn't that be a bitch? To be stuck here another month, with the guerrillas telling me again that it's the army's fault and me not knowing what to believe. I feel depressed, in a way, but not really; more than anything, I feel numb. Numb and exhausted; maybe I'll be home in a week. I'm not counting days. I know better. But I've taken some of the dry wood I had saved in the rafters, and put it on the fire. Maybe I don't need to hoard firewood anymore. Caballito brought three more candles.

Sunday, 7 May, Day 227

I'm still stunned by the news. Rather than joy that this horrible time will end soon, I feel a sadness that it all had to happen. Why? How will I feel when I'm finally home with Susan again? But the fat lady hasn't sung yet. I'm not counting on anything; even if everyone is honest and there are no lies, we're still in the mountains and in purgatory. The trip out of here is a long one: two days by horse, four by foot, they say. And dangerous. The Colombian army will still be hunting guerrilla. And I can't trust FARC. It won't end until I'm out of FARC's hands, beyond their control. In a taxi to CIAT that I hire in Palmira, maybe. My biggest concern, now, is getting my diary out. How awful, how devastating it would be if, after all this, they took my diary. It's the only thing that gives a little meaning somehow to this awful experience.

Judi brought me an extra *arepa* this morning. Wow, when things are going well, when you're treated well, people give you better treatment. But not when you're down and need help. When I was at my lowest, the same Judi would deliberately spill my food, to watch my face, the pain it caused. And she'd laugh. Moño gave me a new throwaway razor this morning. I'm going to be extravagant and brush my teeth, even though it's only the second day.

Around 10 A.M. Melena brought me the thermos of coffee—with milk, sweet and warm and rich and so delicious—and two more *arepas*. That makes three extra *arepas*, for a total of five, this morning. Three are stored for lock-in meals. The fat lady has been announced, but she hasn't set foot on the stage yet.

P.M.: Is raining but the morning was sunny. Cut wood and *chusque*. Need for fire and still need to exhaust me. Now raining a lot and cold. Got a new roll of toilet paper.

Monday, 8 May, Day 228

How to make time pass is still the major problem. May be worse than before. What if this drags on weeks and I don't hear anything? I lost six tablets of Ponstan 500. Looked everywhere. Scares me. With it, I can tolerate the ear infection. Will have a hell of a time getting more. Must take better care than ever of ears. I did nothing today except gather and cut some firewood, and sit by the fire. Nothing to do, less than before.

Tuesday, 9 May, Day 229

0800h: Cold, rainy, nothing to do except think. Maybe plan, for the 100th time, a trip to visit friends. Ears okay, itchy and wet with pus, but no pain. If only I can make it until it's time to leave without that awful pain. Thinking about the trips I'll make in the USA to kill time. [To visit] Rex and Sibyl, Dan and Joyce, Lee and Linda, Larry and Debbie, Don and Ginger is a good one. Also about to start cutting up this diary to smuggle part in plastic bag, part in my underwear, plan to leave backup in eltbe. Don't think Ramiro told Moño— anyway am using better places for parts of the real diary. Please, Tom, do this right. And please, God, protect my diaries. Am in El Templo, Moño giving training on *la rancha*; don't want to stay around. My broken machete is dull. I could find a file and sharpen it, but having a dull machete gives me more exercise.

Later: Cut diaries, washed shorts, especially larger ones with bar soap and a little water. All is part of preparing for departure.

1705h: Another day of doing absolutely nothing but wait.

Wednesday, 10 May, Day 230

Such a cold miserable day. Thank God I have hope and anticipation or it would be so much more depressing. Two fears permeate everything, my life, my existence. One is that nothing will happen. It'll be like before. I'll wait and wait and nothing will change, and I'll finally realize that it's another trick, another crash. I can't bear to think of that. The other fear, of course, is that they will search me and take my diaries at the very end; I can't bear that thought either. How will they release me? I also think a lot about that. By taking me to a town and hiring a car to take me to Cali? I don't think so. By taking [illegible] ransom to be paid. There'll have to be a meeting of the two sides, an exchange of a satchel of money for me. And that could be dangerous. I wonder who'd carry the money for me? Hugo Melo?

P.M.: This is the coldest day ever. An icy wind with rain. About all I can do is sit by the fire, try to keep it going. Judi has learned a new trick. She now whistles for me to come when she brings meal, etc. Cute. [In] *Semana* 28 Feb. '95: "The guerrillas have reached the extreme of charging for the return of the lifeless corpses of kidnap victims."

I count, oh God, how I count. Señor VIP left Saturday P.M. Two days to Cali by horse, four by foot. Sun. Mon. Tues. Could be making arrangements on Tuesday; today is Wednesday. But maybe by foot. Arrive tonight. Don't expect anything before weekend, Tom.

FARC released two Swedish *secuestrados* in Medellín two days ago, Moño said.

1750h: Another day is ending, another day of nothing. What these bastards have stolen from me, I'm thinking, is my time. Almost a year of my life. And as the autumn of life commences. That to me cannot be brought back or replaced. Time to work, to laugh, to love; in its place they gave me anxiety, not only for me but for those I love. And immense boredom and what a waste, waste of time, like today. The son of a bitches. The vermin. The slime. They also took, in a way, my book away from me—the chance to enjoy being an author. They took away the last remnants of my sons' youth from me. A year makes a big difference. I've lost that time with my young sons—the bastards took a lot, and have no regrets.

Thursday, 11 May, Day 231

0900h: Breakfast came late. There was a single *arepa* and a cup of chocolate. The chocolate was full of dregs, which means it was from the bottom of the pan. That's okay—more nutrition. But one *arepa* isn't much, and I'm hungry. I asked for more. Judi's answer was, *"No más."* Got the same answer when I asked for more dinner last night. Is it true or has Judi just decided not to give me any more? Are we really short of food? I'm thinking. For the third time FARC has told me I'll soon be released, it looks like for real. But the other two times my treatment improved vastly—to *la rancha* at night to cook extra *arepas*, singing, etc. "We want you to be happy," Moño said. This time it's not that way—why? Is it because they're burned out of preparing to release me, then it doesn't happen?

I could interpret this more ominously, of course—that FARC plans to kill me before releasing me—I prefer not to. But I sure hope—and assume—that "my side" has some assurances built into the deal to make sure I'm delivered alive. The "exchange scenario," trading a black bag of money for me somewhere in the night—is looking [illegible] all the time. Demands for the letter to prove I'm alive is an indication that my side is being cautious, of course. My response to Judi is often in English: fuck you. She doesn't know what it means, of course—probably thinks it means thanks! I heard her repeating it the other day: "Fuck you. Fuck you."

P.M.: Asked Moño if I could go to spring to wash my hair. "No, Judi will bring water to wash your hair." It's so obvious that I'll never see *la rancha* again. My last bath was on a Saturday, either 26 or 33 days ago, in Camp Soledad. My arms, elbows, and wrists are breaking out in a rash from being dirty, I think. 1725h: Judi brought hot water, and I washed my hair and upper body. I hate it, having her bring me things.

Well, orders to leave to start the march to freedom didn't come today. Saturday is when I'll really start watching. Don't be ridiculous, Hargrove. You've watched, waited all day today and yesterday, counted the hours and remembered what was said again and again. This hurts a lot. But waiting like this is better than no hope. Dinner was rice and lentils. I got seconds and refilled my plastic water bottle. That means I have a food reserve beyond what I'll eat tonight. Food security, prisoner style. It means a lot.

Friday, 12 May, Day 232

Today is eight months, one week. Summer looks further off than ever. So cold, so wet. I try not to watch, try not to hope, but it's hopeless. My worsened personal treatment is actually only a reflection of being left alone and entirely in Judi's care. I keep telling myself that again and again. It's not because they plan a double-cross that will mean my death in the end. No, but I can't help but think that. The problem is also partly worsened because I'm hungry all the time, and that's bad for morale. But why haven't orders to leave come? It's probably 10 A.M., but I haven't lit a fire. I'm saving my fuel, especially scarce dry wood. The guerrillas are tearing down Ramiro's house in the rafters plank by plank. Have managed to steal three planks from the rafters for firewood. [I] cut and hide them for my own *fogón*. Even dead *chusque* is almost impossible to find. I no longer wish for something different to do; I wish for something even to think about. I've been through every [Pen starts to run dry—TRH switches to faint pencil]. Oh no. Out of ink! Only have part of a red pen. No more backups. [To repeat: I've been through every] song quote, thought about every book, movie, every friend, enemy I ever knew. I've been stealing wood from the team hut. Took two pieces this morning, also two pieces from Ramiro's house.

P.M.: Found broken piece of mirror, about one inch by one inch. Haven't seen myself for some time. There are yellowish-red—almost red—streaks through my hair [normally gray white] and beard. Why? Surely it's not malnutrition? What will I think when I read these diaries and letters later? To say I was half-crazy when I wrote some of this may be only half-right.

Saturday, 13 May, Day 233

[TRH switches to his red ink cartridge] A.M.: What, oh, what is going on? I'm sitting in the darkness of my cell in solitary confinement, writing by candlelight. Today is the day. Orders for my freedom will surely come today. That's what I thought when I woke this morning. Judi brought coffee at seven A.M. "I'm locking you in," she said. "You can't leave here."

"What? All day?"

"Yes."

"Why?"

"Orders."

"But why?"

"We'll have visitors."

Anguish—worse—sheer panic gripped me, and tore at my chest and throat. No. Anything but to be locked in darkness in the cold damp cell. I once spent 48 hours in solitary confinement, 36 hours another time, 23 and 21 hours lots of times. But that was five or six months ago, and I can't stand to think about those endless terrible hours of grief and anxiety, listening to every footstep outside, hoping, praying, that someone is coming to let you out. I got permission to go to the latrine and stopped at El Templo, on the way and coming back, but I didn't pray that God give Susan and Daddy strength this time, nor for forgiveness for these pitifully cruel, ignorant bastards that hold me. There was no time. I prayed only for strength, for myself, if possible, the ability to sleep through some of the dark hours that were coming. Two *arepas* and coffee were waiting when I returned. I emptied my piss bucket and my *candela* of ashes, and grabbed some *chusque* from my stack outside. Judi ordered me inside and shut the padlock. That cold sound of metal grating against metal—I've heard it every day for eight months; it will lurk in the darkest recesses of my mind as long as I live. I poured the coffee through a crack in the floor. Sleep is the greatest blessing I can hope for today, so I don't need stimulants. I wrapped back up in my blankets, cried a little, and tried to push it all from my mind so maybe sleep could come. Then metal scraped metal again outside my cell door. Judi had returned with a bucket of water and a mop made of rags. "Throw all your *chusque*, and everything [else] on the floor, outside. I'm going to wash the floor." I did so, but in the process hid as many sticks of bamboo as possible under my blankets and inside my jacket. A fire later will not only be warm, lighting and feeding it will be something to do, to make time pass. The visitors, I know, don't concern me. If they had something to do with my freedom, I'd be outside looking well treated. "Move up."

"Will the visitors see me?" I asked as Judi splashed water on my floor.

"*Sí.*"

"Will they meet with me?"

"*Sí.*" Then I was locked back inside. But really, that means nothing. What does Judi know? Besides, she only answered yes to my question; she volunteered no information. I'll wait, and I won't let this drive me crazy. I'll survive, I'll be out of here someday. But it's been so long.

1020h: I'm sitting on my bunk with the door open. Moño came by to play feelie for a while with Judi. I asked if we could talk. The visitor is a FARC commander. Does the visit concern me, my future, my freedom? The visit might concern that. *También.* Also. Actually, Moño doesn't know the reason for the visit. He said he agreed that I could sit in my cell with the door open and stay on the porch—2x2½ steps. So here I am. It's cute. The way FARC worsens your conditions. First by making things far worse, then by loosening up. The result, you're far worse off than before, but grateful because FARC could have kept up the even worse treatment. This move is a good example of the process.

Judi took all the dry wood I had cut and stored so carefully. Thief. Bitch. Try not to hate her, Tom. Hatred does you no good. Okay, I'll try. [TRH switches back to faint pencil.]

1030h: Gustavo took my *equipo* at 7:30 A.M. to go to Happy Valley for supplies. Just now returned. Also Julio and Melena later made a fire. Waiting but not hoping. Bullshit, Hargrove; you're hoping like hell for something, but don't expect much. You'll still be here a month from now.

P.M.: Melena is at La Rancha Tomás, burning all the dry *chusque* I collected, all the wood I dried. I can watch her. She asked Moño if I could come sit in La Rancha Tomás with her. No. Why? Don't let them get to you, Tom. The bastards.

2200h: Waited all afternoon. *Comandante* never showed up! What a terrible letdown. I'm sure the visit concerns me. Moño didn't deny that when I mentioned it.

Sunday, 14 May, Day 234

A.M.: What an emotional and disappointing day yesterday was. The weather must have caused the delay—it rained almost continuously all day. Now waiting again. It rained all night, but now it's cloudy, cold, windy, but not raining. Can this all be about to end? Do I have the courage to hope? Hardly slept all last night, and when I did, I dreamed of life as a prisoner. I know better, but . . . The trip is four days by foot, two days by *bestia* [animal]. Will I be with Susan by this weekend? Stop it, Tom. That's only hurt, it brings nothing but pain. How many times have you already been this close. Or so you thought.

1025h: Still waiting. Do you expect the visitors today? "I hope so," Moño said. No radio communications again. Moño said I could sit in La Rancha Tomás, 16 or 17 feet on the porch until the visitors appear, then return to my cell.

1240h: The commander still hasn't shown up. The entire camp is just waiting for him and trying to stay warm in the cold drizzle. Lunch was rice and a couple of spoons of noodles. I asked for more. *"No más,"* Judi said. Maybe she's telling the truth. No one's gone "downstairs" for supplies lately. Maybe because Moño expects to break up this camp after the visit—meaning that I'll be gone. I only hope the commander hasn't been ambushed or that the delay has in no way been caused by an action of the Colombian army. That might put me back on ice again. My God, this is the fourth time to be right at the wire, waiting to be freed. If it doesn't come, can I take it again? Of course you can, Hargrove. You have no choice. I'll survive. For my family, I'll survive.

Later: We're burning anything that's wood. The *chusque* is so waterlogged it's almost impossible to burn it without wood. Melena throws wood on like there's no tomorrow. No, Tom, at least in the Valley of the Shadow. It drives me crazy. I'm way too afraid there will be a tomorrow in this miserable camp, and it will be as cold and wet and dreary as today and we won't even be able to build a fire.

1400h: Javier arrived an hour ago from Happy Valley. Came around not by La Rancha Tomás. I'm sure he's escorting the commander, who must be at *la rancha* with Moño, but I don't know that. "Has the visitor arrived?" I asked Judi. She walked away without answering, but that's not unusual. Oh please, God, please. No more tricks. One hundred and fifty million pesos is the price paid FARC for each [Colombian government antidrug] spray plane or [army] chopper, according to *Semana*.

Later: Oh no. Moño walked by alone. The *comandante* hasn't arrived, and he doesn't know why. When will this all end?

1645h: I'm hungry, and I'm worried. Can't get any seconds, not even plain rice. P.o.'d the guerrillas by walking to end of hut to ask if the commander still hasn't arrived. Two days overdue. Something's wrong. And remember, he's bringing my future, my destiny. Is it just that there's a delay, and no commander? I don't think so; Moño seems worried, too. I don't like any of this, not one bit. I may be more scared than I've ever been since all this began.

2045h: In cell. I'm worried about tomorrow. Ironically, solitary confinement worries me more than being shot. Well, there's little I can do to prevent either one. Whatever comes, I must have strength and I'll try not to worry because it can do no good. This is a very sad life. If it's destined to end here in the Valley of the Shadow, well, so be it. I'll try to live as long as I have strength to face whatever is coming.

Monday, 15 May, Day 235

0900h: I'm not locked in solitary confinement, I'm sitting in La Rancha Tomás vastly relieved. The way of these bastards—if they're not being cruel, you interpret that as being nice. But I'll be extremely careful from now on; I'm truly in that lonely and deadly valley. Talked to Moño. He's still waiting—the whole camp is waiting—with no idea what's wrong. He said it's likely this is it, that I'll leave after the commander's visit. Moño is worried. Fresh fighting across Colombia, he says. Six government soldiers killed last night. Later: Julio returned my two pencil stubs. Thank God. I gave them to him yesterday to sharpen. Was afraid Moño confiscated them, maybe because he's seen me writing too much, is suspicious.

1045h: After eight months seven days, the man is to come with my freedom. For the fourth time. Now he's three days overdue and probably won't arrive today. Why? It's like a great and cruel trick is being played on me. Freedom is dangled before me again and again. As I reach for it—it's snatched away. *Why?* I won't go crazy, I won't. But when will this end? My new concerns make it even worse.

1420h: Judi borrowed my backpack. My stomach has knots thinking about getting it back. She'll probably try to switch an old one on me. I pity Judi; life and people have obviously been cruel to her to make her so sadistic and cruel to me. I'm a man who represents all that was denied her, I guess. A good life, intelligence, enough money, respect, education.

1610h: What could have gone wrong with the visit? I'm so scared there's trouble with the negotiations and I'll be here months more. And I'm afraid I might not survive months more here—not because of me and my weaknesses, but because of circumstances beyond my control. Poor Susan. What does she know, think, expect right now?

1710h: Judi tried to force me to trade packs. Hers is crude; she made it herself. I refused and very nicely said I couldn't trade because my *equipo* is a personal gift of friendship from Julio. She got mad, left in a huff. Did I win? No, I still don't have my *equipo* back, although I guess I'll get it. I'll probably be sent to bed at seven tonight. And get one *cancharina* instead of two for breakfast. A prisoner doesn't win against his guard and master.

2030h: In cell. Judi wouldn't give me my *equipo.* Finally opened door and pushed in—her *equipo*—and locked the padlock again. What can I do? Nothing tonight. See Moño tomorrow? He'll do nothing, and even if he did—this is the person who brings my food. Maybe I'll do nothing. Survive, Hargrove. When will this end? I feel so helpless. An illiterate 16-year-old girl, who I've tried to help, can just take my things. What humiliation. What should I do? I may be here a long time yet, and this will continue. But if I'm here a lot longer, I'll need to eat.

Found a radio speaker and a belt buckle, somehow in my bunk. How? Could someone have planned to set me up for stealing? Don't think so. Only Judi would do that, and she's not that sick. I carefully threw both in the brush around the hut.

Tuesday, 16 May, Day 236

Breakfast was one—not two or three—*cancharina*, and Melena—not Judi—brought it. I talked with Julio, [the one] who gave me the *equipo.* "Take the other *equipo* and forget it," he advised.—Judi didn't steal from me. He also said [illegible] she left the *equipo* [here].

Later: Waiting. If another problem and have to start over, I'm not sure I'll survive. I had no idea when I named this valley, how much truth the name would carry. Would things be better if I had named it the Valley of Hope? No, I'd still be in the Shadow of Death; maybe I had some guidance when the name came to me. Remembered two new songs that I've never sung, last night: "Your Cheatin' Heart," and "Jambalaya." I know most of the words. I'll save them for tonight. I'm writing a new song, a prayer for strength and wisdom to survive. But death hovers; it's close. If this fourth time fails, they may not even try to keep me alive much longer. I don't want to die, but I guess I'm ready if it's destined.

1045h: Oh God, oh God. The *comandante* arrived at about 10. I didn't see him; they must have gone around. Oh God, let it be, let it happen. I haven't met the *comandante* yet; he's with Moño at *la rancha.*

But something frightening also came. He's escorted by Ramiro—the only person w.k.a.m. eltbe [i.e., who knows about (the diary in) my money belt]. I haven't decided what to do about that yet. I'm sitting on my bunk hoping and praying.

Later: Still waiting. This is it. If it doesn't happen, I'm dead.

1100h: There was shooting of AK-47s this morning, but that doesn't mean much. Moño says he hasn't even discussed me, which I find hard to believe. Please, God. Please.

1505h: This is too horrible to think about—no, it could be worse, but . . . The guerrilla with Ramiro was *not* the expected *comandante*, or his representative. He was just a friend of Ramiro's. Ramiro is cured and has been reassigned and has come to tell us of it. So I'm back where I was this morning before the visitor arrived. Except another day—the fourth—has passed, and that's [bad.] So cruel. Did I jump the gun? Am I flipping out? I don't know. Think of things, Hargrove. At least Ramiro is not back here [permanently]. So I don't worry about the eltbe.

Later: How many more times can I go up and down like that? Well, the *bad* news hasn't come yet. If it does, I will not think about suicide. I'm going to live. Later: Maybe it all wasn't so bad. I was almost happy for five hours, sure that today would be my last in the Valley of the Shadow, and tomorrow I'd start my journey home. It didn't happen, and now [that] the shock's over, I don't feel so bad. I feel numb all over, but at least the worst news didn't come. I'll live. How could I make such a screwup? I don't know. I'm hungry and worried most of the time, and lonely all of the time. So lonely, it often makes my throat and chest ache.

Wednesday, 17 May, Day 237

A.M.: Two distant shots echoed through the valley about 10 minutes ago. Caballito and Gustavo took rifles and have gone down the trail to Happy Valley. Maybe it's the overdue *comandante* on the fifth day of waiting. My two pencils are down to 1½ inches each, and the pen with red ink will dry up anytime. Julio said he has another pencil that he'll give me. I asked this morning. Once again the [illegible] of having no way to write, record. Gustavo got a new jacket and gave me his old one. Cotton, pockets mostly torn away, but larger and fits better. I'm grateful.

Moño and crew cut wood this morning—including the branches on the log that was the only dry place that I can sit outside. I asked him not to but he laughed. Cruel; it wasn't necessary.

1100h: It is, it is! Señor VIP in civilian clothes. Hold it, Tom. Don't hurt yourself again.

1120h: Am shut back in cell but happy about it. The visitors are arriving, Julio explained: "I'll let you out when I can." Ramiro and Viejito are with Señor VIP. Have fire in candela. Waiting: Please let it happen. Let it.

1330h: Still in cell. This is it. I'll know something soon. Will I leave the Valley of the Shadow alive? I assume so. Will I walk back to Cali or ride a horse or a mule? Will I be with my family again in three days? Five days? What changes will I find in Susan, the boys, myself? CIAT? Is my father still alive? That one could be tough.

But like almost everything in my life in the past eight months 12 days, I can do nothing to influence any of it. I'll take what comes.

1420h: Moño and others play *fútbol*. Where are the VIPs?

1500h: Still waiting. Why can't they tell me?

1510h: Oh no. Señor VIP, if that was him, and three guerrillas just left back down the trail to Happy Valley. Was it all another false hope? Why hasn't Moño said anything? Please, God, please, please.

1515h: Julio brought me some hard candies the stranger brought. And yes, that was the expected visitor, he said.

1544h: It won't happen. I know, I feel it. Otherwise Moño would tell me and the guerrillas aren't getting ready; they would if we march tomorrow. God, God.

1625h: This is the worst it's ever been. I'm scared, for me, for my sanity. For my life? Not really. If I'm not going home, not to be freed, death will be another liberation, another way to escape this terrible camp. But I won't even think about suicide. The bastards will have to kill me.

1736h: Moño, why don't you come? I know what's coming, but we have to get it over with. I've been to El Templo five or six times. I pray for strength, wisdom, guidance, courage, to get through this. I've cried deeply; I'm ready. Getting it over. The [illegible] hard truth. The reality will be a relief. I can't stand the waiting. This is too cruel. They'll kill me if I stay too much longer; I'm ready for that, too. I wonder what that'll be like. Waiting for it? Maybe, like this.

2005h: It's happened again. What I thought could not happen again has. Moño didn't see me until 7:30. I'd convinced myself I'd been mistaken again. That today's visitor was not the one with my destiny. But he was.

I won't be released, Moño said. It's just a delay because the trails aren't se-cure. This was the fourth time that I was ready for release then everything crashes. Why? Why? Moño says no trouble in Cali, with CIAT, or my family. Just a short delay. I don't believe him, of course. I'll live. I'll be very, very care-ful and won't give the bastards a reason to kill me. Will that matter? I don't know. My position is awfully dangerous. How do I feel? Numb like last night.

But this is worse because I did get the news and it was the worst news. I'm sick to the soul. But I'll start all over again tomorrow. Can I protect myself from the hurt? No, probably not. Only if I give up hope—and that means suicide. But it's like God is torturing me on purpose. Why?

2035h: I'm okay now, and warming beans and rice. I'll make it through tonight, but tomorrow it'll be tough. Starting over for the fifth time. If only I could hear from Susan—a letter, anything. Later: Judi doesn't have my *equipo*; said they gave it to someone. I don't understand. But my beautiful pack is gone. I have to accept that.

Thursday, 18 May, Day 238

A.M.: Have spent most of the morning playing with my *candela*, trying to make a fire burn in the rain and cold. Thinking constantly but not feeling much. Now I'm in La Rancha Tomás and I feel, Oh God, how it hurts. Never been religious, but I've tried to learn to pray, to believe in God here, to believe in Divine Justice. It's never worked well, but now I feel totally alone, abandoned by CIAT, by God, by Susan—no, not by Susan, Miles, Tom G., and my family. If I felt that, I could end it now. I could do it; I could grab an AK—the guerrillas are pretty careless. Would I try to take some of them with me? That would be a delay and might blow my chances. I'll think about it. I have wire and . . . But no, suicide is not for me, not until I'm sure there's no hope.

"This isn't another delay, Tomás," Moño said to me this morning. "But the visitor told me—12 days ago—that everything was arranged, that only the letter"—proof that I'm still alive—"was lacking. But we're still waiting for a response to the letter."

That has to be a lie because last night I asked if there was a problem in Cali with Susan or CIAT. Moño assured me there was none, that we must wait until the trails are open. I think I'm being held for bigger stakes. Maybe political. And they keep telling me I'll be freed to keep me happy.

But one consideration: they can't hold me in the Valley of the Shadow forever. If they want to hold me and keep me alive, they need to move me from here. A new shipment arrived yesterday. I got a new pair of trousers, a shirt, and shorts. No, this can't happen, but I dropped my pencil stub straight into the fire. Was frantic. Got it out, but . . . Am I losing my mind?

Later: Yesterday, I prepared my "new" *equipo* for the march, fixed my diaries, sorted what I could take, etc. Went to El Templo in the rain. Jesus of the Broken Bamboo Cross, guide me in the Valley of the Shadow of Death, grant me strength, faith, judgment. Help Susan; guide her. Help my father, if he's still alive. Forgive these ignorant, contemptible bastards, they don't even realize what they're doing. Bring peace to this tragic country so permeated with evil. And Lord protect my diaries. And thanks, God.

Later: I can't give up faith, prayer just because it doesn't feel like I'd expected, because I don't feel prayer or just God like I'm supposed to. Maybe that's like saying I don't believe in love because she doesn't make me feel like they describe in songs and books. Faith in God, in some sort of supreme power—I have nothing.

Later: Did I overdo it? My belief that the visitor would bring orders for my freedom? No, Moño said everything was arranged and agreed a letter was the last step.

Did FARC raise the price? Was [Moño] lying all along? I must bounce back, or I'll die somehow. I can't die—I have Susan and Tom G. and Miles. I have love and responsibility. I have years of enjoyment, satisfaction ahead. I have another book to write. Yes, if there is a God, and He has a plan for this, it must be a book. Faith, Tom. Survive. The rain will stop someday. I stole and cut another board from Ramiro's rafter house.

P.M.: I got through the morning doing nothing but sitting feeding the fire, walking through the mud around La Rancha Tomás, thinking and writing the above. How will I make it through the afternoon? But I will. Happiness is a thing of the past. It Mrs. Heathington, the teacher at Rotan High School who said that. I believe that her fiancé was killed in World War II.

1645h: Moño came and sat by the fire for an hour and a half. We talked and he admitted he doesn't know why the delay on my release. Señor VIP didn't say. I wish I could believe him. Moño stressed that he said I'd be released pronto. Time for dinner. Gosh, time passes so much faster when you're with, and talking to, someone, even if it's your kidnapper.

Friday, 19 May, Day 239

P.M.: Rained through the night but woke up thinking, You must think positive. But the morning was a long one. I awake in the night with my hand around my genitals, I notice. I've read, but not seen, soldiers in great danger who sleep with their helmets over their crotches. Part of the survival instinct? That why I started doing something similar?

Later: Judi amazingly asked to borrow my pen, after having borrowed, stolen, my earlier pen, then my *equipo*. "I don't have a pen." *Nada más.*

Have been thinking about an incident I witnessed by ICESI last year. I bet it was a kidnapping, and I didn't even think about the police.

Later: "Are you going to say bad things about the guerrillas after you're free?" Gustavo just asked me. Now, what kind of answer could he expect? I assured him, of course, that I have no such intentions. But the question worries me. Is that why I haven't been freed?

Saturday, 20 May, Day 240

P.M.: No rain today, and sun in P.M. Cold last night. Signs that summer's coming. Wrote Susan and told her exactly the situation of the 6 May letter, and my freedom that didn't come. Decided it's best. Have thought a lot. The situation looks hopeless, except for that 6 May letter and my freedom that didn't come. Something must be going on (or have been going on).

Melena took over my care and feeding again from Judi. Have had no problems and want to keep it that way.

Sunday, 21 May, Day 241

Verano, adiós [Summer, good-bye]. Rained steadily all night. Cold and drizzling now. Am faced with the terrible morning thought: What will I do today? Damn! Gustavo borrowed my comb. He has lice or fleas. I've seen other guerrillas picking them from his hair. They can spread via leaving their eggs on the comb. What to do? Can I boil a plastic comb? I live in filth, but thank God I've avoided lice and fleas. Am I being paranoid? My left ear is infected and swollen outside. I have four antibiotic capsules, but I'm not going to use them yet, because there's little pain. Maybe it will go away. I want to save the antibiotics in case I have a really bad infection. I've thought about death in a practical way as I lay in the bunk dreaming this morning. My death, if it comes here, will solve a lot of problems. It would resolve for Susan, CIAT, or both the matter of ransom. It would make Susan a widow and that has to be better than what's happening now. It would save pain and anguish with me. My death might even cause problems for her. Bad *panela* at least. There, I've written the unthinkable: the practicality of suicide, despair, and hopelessness. Maybe writing it down will exorcise that evil and frightening thought.

P.M.: I boiled water over my fire at La Rancha Tomás and boiled the comb. No damage.

Monday, 22 May, Day 242

A.M.: Cold, steady rain. No hope for summer, ever. Sitting by the fire. Nothing else to do. How to keep faith and hope like this? Gustavo borrowed *equipo* to go to Happy Valley. Maybe, oh God, maybe, I thought in fear, how could Moño *not* have talked with the VIP about my situation? He *must* have, which means he's lying. And that means something I don't know about is happening about my destiny. And it must be bad.

P.M.: Lunch was beef intestines (must I say tripe?) and rice. Part tied in my two plastic bags to keep it away from the rats and save it for tonight. I also have two *arepas* saved.

Tuesday, 23 May, Day 243

Javier brought me this red pen from Happy Valley—used, no cap. Stole it, I guess. Gustavo returned from Happy Valley. Used pencil. Grateful for both. But he didn't bring what I want desperately. Last night after dinner was terrible—those thoughts, my deepest fears—if they are true, that I'm being held indefinitely. If only I could read a paper, hear the news, I'd have something new to think about.

1005h: "Inside quickly, Tomás, visitors." I was cutting wood when Melena and Gustavo shoved me into my cell. I saw the visitors arrive through cracks in my wall. A man and a woman. Guerrillas. Both strangers. Moño, in his greeting, didn't act like he knew the visitors. They could be bringing—but I won't pray for that. If there's a God—there must be—He knows what I want so desperately. Maybe praying for it is selfish. And I dare not lose hope. Especially locked up in my dark cell. Thank God I have candles. Am writing by candlelight.

Later: I cut the two separate legs from my burned jeans. Wear them as leggings at night. Ear infection stable, maybe going away. Melena has a magazine, *Chrono*, December '94. Moño showed me this morning. Showing an ad for transparent panties, but she won't lend it to me, not even while I'm locked up in my cell. Cruel bitch. Later Melena sent me the magazine, held door open at lunch so I can have light. Javier spent day sitting in my bunk, in cell the door is cracked to let in some light most of the time. Just found out some visitors will spend the night here. I need to move, stretch, get at least some exercise. How long can I stand this? As long as I must I guess.

1900h: Was let out at 5:30, but Judi sent me in again at 6:45. Why does she hate me so?

Wednesday, 24 May, Day 244

Last night Moño said that I could have antibiotics and a pain pill for my ear. Judi could bring them. But she refused, and there was not much I could do about it. She's a sick cruel person. They came to tell me I'm being freed. That's what I thought when Moño and the visitor, wearing a brown ski mask over all but his eyes, appeared at 10:15 A.M. But no! Moño handed me a notebook and said I must write another letter to Susan, about like the last letter, including that I'm sick. I did and wrote about my ears once more. I pretty much wrote what they wanted, but included "*me dicen* [they tell me]," so that maybe Susan will know that the letter was forced. Also that they'd deliver the letter to her soon. Will it never end? The visitor used the *tu* form when talking with me and said that CIAT has no interest in my case, doesn't respond to FARC's communications. That doesn't surprise me. It would make sense to have all messages via Susan. Also phoned to her—via CIAT, I'd assume. Interestingly, he said, when all is arranged I'd be given a ticket to Bogotá, then later that I might be sent to Brazil because we're close. Said my family was in contact with [FARC], and had me add a sentence that the army could not find and rescue me. My letter would reach CIAT in four days, the visitor said. Start again, wait again. Guards all around. Don't want to borrow Melena's magazine because I have something to do, to think about what just happened. That should keep me busy all day. Oh Lord, I'm getting weird. But the magazine has an article about O. J. Simpson published in December. I must read that. Maybe tomorrow. I'm glad that Susan is no longer in Cali. Made no sense for her to stay there. I'd have written advising her to return to Texas, but I knew it wouldn't be delivered. I assume that Susan and CIAT are working together.

1600h: Now that the letter's written and on its way, I'm having doubts if

I did the right thing in downplaying it all. The fact is I don't fear that I'll die of disease, as they implied. I should write—but I do fear they'll kill me. Should I have stressed that the letter may be my last? Was I too brave? Was I foolish? What is different in this letter [compared with] the last one? Should I have begged, have conveyed fear for my life? If ransom isn't paid, I'm not leaving here, that's obvious. Well, I can do nothing but wait and pray [the] Lord [will] help Susan do the right thing. And if that means I die, let it be soon. Don't let me stay here for years.

1615h: Oh God, I'm getting scared and feeling sick. Why didn't I write that I think I'll die?

Thursday, 25 May, Day 245

I'm starting the agonizing process again—of waiting, hoping, praying for my release. This is, I guess, the sixth time, and the previous five times have ended with hard crashes and vows to not be so foolish in the future. But I have no choice. In addition to my letter of yesterday, they made me prepare three other items this morning. All are proof that I'm still alive. Susan doesn't believe that I'm still living, Moño told me yesterday afternoon. First we made a Polaroid photo; for that I had to remove my boots and pose barefoot, to hide the fact that we're in the cold mountains, I guess. Next, a cassette recording in Spanish that Susan is not to trust the army, and a repeat about my ear infections. Third, I had to copy a passage from the 23 May 1995 edition of *El País*. I can't believe the paper can reach here so rapidly—and someone had to have brought it last night. Civilization must be closer than I thought. In the photo I tried to hold my right hand so that I'm giving the "finger." But I had to be subtle, too. Javier snapped the photo as I was moving my finger, so it doesn't show—damn! But maybe it's for the best. Am using Moño's pen and ink that he left with me to write the *El País* summaries. "These are the last days, Tomás," he said. Maybe. All of this goes to the Red Cross, which will deliver it to Susan, Moño says. Also that Susan has left Cali, but is still in Colombia. Where? At a friend's *finca*? In an apartment at CIAT? The *comandante* said my letter will reach Susan in four days if all goes well. FARC will release me in Bogotá or in Brazil, Moño says. We can reach either in two or three days by foot. Says we're near the border of Brazil and can enter the country by the mountains. I can't believe that. Even if we went east after my kidnapping, we traveled no more than 3 to 3½ hours by truck and van, then two days by horse, and Moño says we're 14 days from Cali by foot and 12 by horse. Makes no sense.

Funny thought. My photo [of me] sitting in my *ruana* reminds me of a portrait of Susan's great-grandfather sitting in his *ruana* in Bogotá in the mid-1800s. Except he wore boots and a hat.

Maybe I'm wrong. Maybe we are in the Bogotá part of the Cordillera Central and can go down across the valley and climb into the third mountain range and from there cross into Brazil. Hardly slept last night thinking about walking to Brazil and my release there. How? Money? I don't think there are any major cities in that part of Brazil, but I don't really remember. I'm glad of one thing: I haven't lied in my letters. My ears are infected and that situation may be worse than described—I have never thought the army might rescue me—that possibility seems so remote it hasn't even been a fantasy. I've never seen any evidence of a military presence since arriving in this area. And though I don't say it clearly, I think I'll die here; they'll kill me if I don't leave here soon. Too many complicating factors.

Later: Julio gave me six pieces of dried beef this morning—that's better treatment, more food. Another sign that freedom is coming? Am I being naive, foolish? I wonder if one of the boys is still with Susan? I've thought a lot about my conversations with them in the future, especially Tom G., if he still doesn't know what to major in. I plan to use verbal probing as we learned at Heemskirk.

P.M.: The letter, photo left three hours ago. Like yesterday I'm suddenly terrified I didn't say enough, sincerely enough. I stressed twice to Susan that I hope to see her again (not "again soon"). But I don't know that I was sincere enough in conveying the true message that I will return only if she plays ball with the guerrillas. I'm paranoid, I guess, but I feel sick that I didn't add a P.S. stating that more [forcefully] in my words. But I'm afraid my letter and tape will sound like I repeated what they told me to say—which is true. Take it easy, Hargrove. You said clearly that relying on the army wouldn't work. That the only way to arrange my return was through *ell que metienen* [those who have me]. I said, they might hold me four to five years, but including *"me dicen"*? Tom, it's okay, your tape to Susan was an absolutely honest tape saying that the army couldn't rescue me and without cooperation from FARC I may never return. I think it was the right thing; I don't feel uneasy or guilty. Moño sending someone to Happy Valley to include in packet for Red Cross tomorrow. . . . Washed hair. Now reading the 23 May *El País*.

2005h: Has been raining more than one hour in cell. I think a lot, of course, about the letter. I feel sad that I had to write it but feel that I had no choice. And it was only honest. I feel that something will happen this time. But if nothing happens, I feel that I'm in for a very rough time, maybe death, but certainly incarceration for an awfully long time. In other words, I think this is pretty much the last chance.

I've never talked with anyone wearing a ski mask except at ski resorts—and I've never been to a ski resort.

Friday, 26 May, Day 246

1100h: Interesting to watch steam rise from the roof of the hut when the sun finally comes out. I'm emotionally exhausted, but still feel I did the right thing. If I could talk to Susan, I'd have to tell her the situation as I understand it, and would never think it was wrong. Judi gave me three Ambramycina for the boil on my ear yesterday afternoon—take one each four hours. I opened it myself and took only one—so now I have five antibiotics and one pain pill. I don't want to be caught again with a serious infection and no antibiotics. Having antibiotics could mean I live instead of die. I never intended it, but a song from the late fifties runs through my mind again and again for weeks: "The Man Who Never Returned," by the Kingston Trio. Especially the part "Will he ever return? No!" etc. Depressed by the rain and cold, went to El Templo and cried. Imagined Jesus was there—unplanned. But in a different way—jeans, red plaid flannel shirt, high leather boots, the lace-up kind. Looked like Sunday-school paintings, with a Kris Kringle beard. Laughed, told me to sit on a log. Said I could cry there if I wanted. Opened a bottle of Gallo Hearty Burgundy, had a few drinks. Said I could visit again, but I might include Him more when I'm having fun after I leave here. Felt better.

1700h: I worry too much—now it's that my letter to Susan wasn't included in the package. Mono assured me this morning it was, but I never saw anyone going down to Happy Valley. I still feel this is a turning point; if I don't get out this time, it's going to be bad. But I can't hope for freedom in a week. This is tough waiting. We're eating a lot of plantain and cassava lately.

2000h: Locked up. Asked Judi for water. She filled the bottle, shoved it into the cell, locked the door, and left. I took a drink. It's soapy water; full of soap. Mistake or on purpose? The latter, I think. Why?

[*A Proof of Life Polaroid of Tom in a hammock, and a letter in his handwriting quoting a 23 May newspaper, was retrieved from behind a toilet in a fast food restaurant.—SSH*]

Saturday, 27 May, Day 247

I lay awake thinking before dawn this morning, thinking. In the next two weeks my destiny, or at least the foreseeable future, will be set. I see only three distinct possibilities. The new initiative is a major FARC effort; things can't just continue afterward. First, freedom. That seems the least likely, given the history of the partisans' efforts, especially the last one. I worry also about Susan's move. I hope it's not to a "safe house" provided by the army or police, where her mail and movements will be monitored. The second option seems the most likely and the least disagreeable in many ways: continuation of this nonlife as FARC's prisoner. If that happens, the way will be long, hard, and have little hope. FARC seems to have a way of punishing me for whatever happens in Cali. The third option—death—doesn't scare me so much. I'm as ready as I'll ever be to face death. I agonize over things I wish I'd done before I was kidnapped, but can do nothing about that. I'm not really afraid of death itself. I don't lie awake and think about and dread it like I fear an indefinite life as FARC's prisoner. I'm rather curious about death, in fact; if it comes, I hope it's quickly—like a bullet in the back of the head, with little delay and agonizing. I'll stay alive as long as I can, but I can do nothing if they decide to kill me. And it's a strong possibility, given what I can't write about plus the fact that kidnapping is selling of life with death as the alternative. I don't feel the comfort and closeness to God that is supposed to come when facing death, but maybe it's like love; it doesn't necessarily feel like it does in books and the movies, but that doesn't mean one should reject it. If FARC kills me, will I see Mother and Ed Tout and Darrell and other friends who went before me? I hope so. I don't want to die, but an indefinite continuation of this life seems worse. My death would also be easier for those who love me. A double cross: that's what I fear most about death; that FARC takes the ransom money, then kills me. I hope Susan takes the right precautions. If the ransom is paid, and the money doesn't change hands without my delivery alive. If I'm destined to continue this nonexistence, then it's time to seriously plan *Leaving Cheyenne*. But my chances of success, I fear, would be less than 10 percent. I would consider *Leaving Cheyenne* a desperate gamble with suicide—meaning to be killed in the process—the most likely outcome. And suicide would be far preferable to capture. Nor would I rule out actual cold suicide as an alternative to life without hope. I'm writing this while sitting in a natural cathedral—El Templo—and maybe some divine company and guidance. What I dread most about dying is the things I'll miss in life—like seeing Susan and the boys again, and the pain that my death would cause for those who love me. The pain and uncertainty and fear of facing the unknown and whatever comes afterward—those things worry me less than the joys I'll miss here on earth. If I'm freed, I want to see Jim Lanning and Earl Martin again. Those two men may represent two extremes of what I hope to find in life. Sort of Jesus to Jack Daniel's but leaning toward the former. These thoughts are not off the top of my head; I've thought them for a long time. And I am not writing in a state of despair—I'm writing calmly and trying to be as detached as if I were writing about the possible death of a friend who has been dangerously ill and threatened by death for almost a year. My story since 23 Sept. 1994 is sort of a modern-day South American *Heart of Darkness*: a journey far further upriver, deeper into the wilderness, physical and mental. Especially further into the evil and darkness of the soul.

Sunday, 28 May, Day 248

1205h: Something is happening. Moño has called a formation and has lectured for one hour. I try to stay away, of course. But it's something about new dialogues between FARC and the government.

Hints this morning: Melena and Caballito's letter—just heard Moño refer to "revolutionary communist countries" such as Cuba, China, and Japan. I've told him several times that Japan is hardly a revolutionary communist country, but it doesn't sink in. Later: We could be in Tolima, to the north. If so, Bogotá and Brazil don't seem so out of the question.

The weather has been like summer's trying to come, but the winter won't give up. The sun fights and forces its way through the dark, heavy lining of clouds and shines light from all sides. Then the clouds smother the sun and it's cold and wet for hours.

[*After retrieving a map from behind a toilet of a bakery, ransom was delivered for Tom's freedom. He was not released.—SSH*]

Monday, 29 May, Day 249

Today is Day 4 since packet left. It's going to be tough from now until I hear—waiting for the response. Always with that hollow fear that pushes its way as a lump into your throat and chest—what if no answer comes? If only I had something to do besides sit or walk in tiny little circles and think. The extreme limit of my domain—El Templo—is 50 muddy, roundabout steps from my cell. "Do you think you'll fight again soon?" I asked Gustavo as he sat on his bunk. "*Sí*. That's why I'm preparing." He pointed to a stack of cartridges. He was cleaning ammo.

"That means I'll be freed soon?"

"*Sí*."

But that means nothing. Down to the last candle, but Gustavo gave me two more.

Can't sing. I save that for the late afternoons or night by the fire. I'm in El Templo. Why do I let it bother me that Melena and Judi yell at me and treat me like a dog? I should have some compassion. Their words can't hurt me and my life has been so much more fortunate than theirs. But they will not respond to courtesy, even kindness. They take what they can from me. But Gustavo and I made a new flashlight for me on Saturday from three broken ones. What a luxury after two to three months without light other than candles. I found that the plastic bag I use to store food for the night to keep rats away had been clawed through and the food was littered with rat droppings. I brushed the droppings away and ate the beans, rice, and *arepa* anyway. What diseases can you get from rats here in the mountains? Anyway, I at least wash all before eating. Then I changed all to another bag I'd saved; the rats ate through that and I had food wrapped in both bags, but it's hopeless.

P.M.: Sun came out. Took off shirt and lay absorbing that wonderful, beautiful warmth for 15 minutes. Then the clouds took over and another cold rain fell. If only I knew these were the last days. If I could only lose and chase away that terrible fear that they're not coming. Keeping my spirits and my hopes high is even harder in the cold rain.

1715h: At the slowest pace, the packet should have reached Cali today. Unless the army intercepted it. Freedom must come this time. If not? Well, I find myself praying, unplanned and without thinking—Oh God, if it doesn't come, kill me. Kill me, God, kill me.

2025h: I can neither believe nor understand this. I'm locked in and both Judi and Melena refuse to give me water. Why? What can I do? Does FARC plan to kill me and they know it, so they treat me as they please? What is going on? I can't let them get to me. Not while locked in this coffin of a cell. I'll go crazy.

Tuesday, 30 May, Day 250

0845h: Julio came on guard duty and gave me water. I'm okay. "What are you going to do with me?" I asked Melena. "Why do you always yell at me and treat me this way? I'm a prisoner, but not a criminal."

"I'm bored, Tomás," she said.

"I'm sorry, but that's not my fault."

She said, "*Sí.* It is, Tomás—because of *you*, we're here." Is she really that simple? I'm afraid so.

P.M.: The morning went fast, maybe because I had things to do. It doesn't take much. I think a lot before, during, and after doing anything. Rinse and dry clothes was my main activity. Wrote above in diary and backup. The guerrillas and being kidnapped are in my dreams now, not necessarily good or bad—I can seldom remember. But if I'd been in, say, Disney World for nine months, Disney World would also be in my dreams. I taught Natalia English.

Something hilarious. Or is it even funny? She's the only guerrilla who's been halfway serious about learning English. Moño says government and Simón Bolívar [Front] are in talks in Urubá. Natalia explained Melena to me. "You must understand that she's been here in the mountains for almost a year and it's affected her mind." Funny? What about Judi?

"She's just *mal* [evil or sick]." [Side passage in Spanish:] *¡El termia a la inverte nos aleja de la vida y no de la muerte!* Natalia, 30 May. Nice, but not describing my problem. I fear continuing life here not death.

Wednesday, 31 May, Day 251

Day 6, so news could arrive. What will I do today? I'm almost crazy with worry. I can't help that deep sick feeling: Nothing will happen. I'm here for months more or until I die? Spent the first hour this morning trying to think of things to do or even to think about. No luck, but that killed an hour. Lists to make. Moño came by to talk. It's obvious the camp is on hold. Waiting for an order. I'm so afraid to hope too much. There's that sickening terror of despair another crash would bring. But I can't help it. I've already cried. So afraid, so helplessly, terribly afraid. [?Gustavo?] is cleaning a saddle. For a trip? Where? I ask Moño. He grinned. Just found another red pen on porch with full cartridge. Don't hurt me again. God, not again.

1220h: Oh no. Yes. No. I'll cry, laugh, scream. I've already cried. I'm so afraid, so helplessly, terribly afraid—three guerrillas just arrived from Happy Valley, below. Two women who I don't know, and Leidi. Can they be bringing [illegible]. The news? The orders? Don't hurt me again, God, not again.

1230h: Just found another red pen on the porch, with full cartridge. Oh God, that scares me. Have always found [?wire?], pencils when out of ink or to prepare for a long time. With the blue pen Moño left (accidentally?), I have three. God, does this mean I won't leave here? [illegible] God left the pen for me. I'm scared.

1240h: They brought hard candy like all VIP representatives. My stomach hurts. It's in knots.

An absurd primitive thought. I'd like to sacrifice a pig or a goat or a sheep while waiting. A totally spontaneous thought. I never thought it before. Back to basics of life . . . "Gustavo, I've noticed representatives of the *comandante* bring *dulces*." Maybe it makes sense. That's what I'd do if I were in the Old Testament and had a fat sheep. And my life is as primitive and basic as life in the OT. Is my attempt at religion completing a circle? Remember, seven to eight months ago my thoughts, instincts of Old Testament vengeance.

1300h: Well, Moño just told me the visit has *nothing* to do with me. No news regarding orders. I stay here. Meanwhile I'd been to El Templo and prayed. Oh, how I prayed, but at least I know without waiting 4½ hours like the last time. What do I think? I can't think. I'll think later. Thank you, God, for not letting me think. It suddenly turned cold and is raining hard.

1405h: Why do you do this to me, God? Or do I do it to myself? What's the difference. The pain is the same. But I know deep inside that this wasn't my freedom. But I'll always know that. The truth is, I don't believe my freedom will come. I can't go back to El Templo and pray. Not now. Later, but not now. Found half of a Ponstan pain pill on porch. Laying in provisions. Also an army belt buckle that I'm using on the canvas strap that I wear under my belt to hold up my trousers. Have been tying knots in strap.

1420h: Am in El Templo. The only praying I could do was scream, "Why, God, why?" silently in my mind again and again. The rain has stopped and there's a little sun. I realize that is not yet a failure; it's just that those [illegible] didn't come for me. My situation is no different than if they hadn't come at all. But what happened—when and how—was so cruel. No one just drops by without a purpose. One of the guerrillas was the farmer who visited me at Camp Loneliness [*Soledad*].

1544h: Have lit my fire. I don't know what I can do, but I must divert myself from doing that again. I can't keep going so high, then crashing so hard. [Several largely illegible sentences discussing lines written by Natalia, in Spanish.]

Later: Regarding today's crash: had forgot, I did same two weeks ago, and with Señor VIP.

Thursday, 1 Jun., Day 252

0800h: A long day ahead. Melena locked me up, she started screaming about the *chusque* I had stacked on the floor. Said [she] would clean out all today. I can't keep the *chusque* anymore. Got up this morning to move all I want hidden, like the precious firewood I keep under the bed. Coffee. I think Melena is on drugs. Maybe *basuco* [cocaine by-product in common use by the guerrillas] and that's why she gets so high and hysterical.

0830h: Have lit a fire and waiting for two things—whatever will happen with Melena—but maybe nothing, because she's not stoned now. And, of course, news of my freedom. No, Tom, not again. How do I handle hope, faith? It's like they're enemies, not allies.

P.M.: Sometimes when I have hard times, especially when Melena and Judi treat me so, someone does something nice. Gustavo brought me two cans of sweet condensed milk after lunch (plus two candles three or four days ago). Now I'll have dessert tonight. This morning was long. Can't stand the wait. Everything the *comandante* said goes through my mind again and again. They need only the last proof that I'm alive, he said. That proof left 16 days ago (today is Day 7). Why doesn't word come? Of course, I have only the *comandante*'s word that's true. I really know nothing of my situation. My kidnappers are my only information source.

A year ago I was in Uganda, waiting to get into Rwanda.

Later: Moño said the package left on Saturday, not Friday, so today is Day 6. Told me he is only waiting, like me. Cold rain.

1602h: Melena and Judi sat by fire and [the] afternoon went faster than I feared. Strange, just to be around people, even those I despise and have no choice but to fear, makes the time go faster. I've been almost ready to give up faith, were it not for Susan. I know that Susan won't rest until somehow I'm out of here.

Friday, 2 Jun., Day 253

I was kidnapped nine months ago today. Dark, wet cloud cover. Waiting, waiting, we're waiting for something. Find it difficult to believe in my freedom or heaven. It won't happen. Maybe it's because I've been hurt so many times. To be with Susan and the boys and the dogs and go to bed when I wish, to the supermarket, sit in the sun. Cook, laugh, see friends, buy a magazine, rent a video, drive a car—it all seems unreal, sometimes, from a dream of the past. That will never happen again. I did those things once. But I have hope that they'll return even if I don't believe it, yes, but I didn't appreciate them before. Without hope for that, I'd have no problem ending it all now. I could pull that trigger easily. It'd be far easier than going off the high-diving board or plunging into the cold river water, back when I could bathe.

And I'd have to do it quickly because I'd have to grab a guerrilla weapon. I have another infection in my nose. Have been in a quandary. Should I take two of my five antibiotics? No, not yet. I don't want to use something that could save my life just to end some discomfort.

P.M.: Made it through morning, now to make it through 4:30 and dinner, then lockup. Will brush my teeth later when the taste of the sugar cookie has gone away. (After lunch had one of the sugar cookies that the last visitor brought.)

Later: That deep despair. To the depth of the soul, it's coming again. Hope, faith, Tom. But I've had that for a month. Lies. Lies. Why, God? Why? If I'm not going to be free again, God, let them kill me.

Later: Raining, cold yesterday, and Melena asked me to pull some threads from my *ruana* for her weaving. I wasn't happy, but let her. I just saw that she cut—yes, *cut*—a square foot from the *ruana*. And she will not bring me water. Maybe if I beg enough. But maybe someone else will fill my bottles. Why must I take such humiliation from a half-wit? What have I done to deserve this?

1700h: I always consider the day over after dinner, which was rice and macaroni.

Today was terrible—one of the worst in a few weeks. The depression. I talked with Moño regarding Melena. What will he do? Who knows?

2015h: Should I believe any of [?Moño's?] . . . I must believe some. Moño says that FARC or Simón Bolívar launched a new offensive four days ago. Almost in control of Bogotá: 64 fronts, 2,000 soldiers each. And that is good for me, Moño said. "Colombia will soon be a revolutionary communist country like Cuba." Moño said total guerrilla [forces] are 180,000. Gustavo brought me water, says he has replaced Melena. "What will happen to *secuestrados* like me if FARC wins?" I asked Moño.

"You'll all be free. We'll have no more use for kidnapping."

Saturday, 3 Jun., Day 254

Gustavo brought hot coffee at 6:45 then breakfast. Later: He brought *colada* and took me to the spring up the trail to Happy Valley. I washed [my] hair. So he really must have replaced Melena. He must have volunteered. Won't bring freedom but, still, should make my daily life more bearable.

Julio came to tell me not to walk far on trail—in sight of *la rancha*. Reminded me how dangerous my situation is. Haven't written, and tried not to think much of what Moño said last night because I wanted to save it to think about later. Can guerrillas really be close to taking Bogotá? To winning the war? I can't believe [this], but have no other news. The offensive must have been the topic of Moño's talk last Sunday.

P.M.: Terrible thought. What if the USA gets involved in the renewed fighting? Maybe not directly, but supporting the government against the guerrillas. My position might suddenly become much worse.

Sunday, 4 Jun., Day 255

Don't think the guerrilla offensive is as extensive as Moño described it. Moño was less jubilant when I asked about it last night. Remembered a new song last night with a tune that's easy to carry: "Misery Loves Company." But I sing it cautiously. I don't want to use it up like I used up "Long Black Veil" and "Streets of Laredo." Two other songs came to me this morning! "He'll Have to Go" and "Peace in the Valley."

Later: The order won't come today; nor do I expect, deep down, orders to come at all. Not on this round. Trial 6. And that means I'll be here at least a year. Right now I sort of accept that. It makes me sad, deeply sad. The kind of sadness that, if I turn loose, will evolve into tears; then, if I'm not careful, deep

284 Thomas R. Hargrove

aching, despair. But it's not that bad right now and I can't let it take that kind of control. Having Gustavo in charge of my personal life makes things so much better [than with Melena]. Thinking I'd like to work with someone like Tom Clancy [the writer] to write a novel when this ends. I'll write an autobiographical book myself, too, of course.

Later: The main mechanism I've used for survival is to make time my main enemy. But I always have to block off the progression of my thoughts, prevent them from entering that dark realm of despair. It's a terrible race and it never works, not really, because whatever I think of is no longer, no longer exists, and maybe—probably—will never exist again for me. How I wish I could take an opposite route—and block off thought altogether. I've tried to enter self-hypnosis, but with no luck. Like this morning. Thinking about the 1995 ACE meeting has given me so much pleasure and escape in the past. Washington, D.C., old friends, CG HQ, maybe go to New York City and see Owen Lock [my editor] and Lee Lanning and Russ Galen [Lee Lanning's literary agent], Boston to see Khang, Weiner. But this morning I realized: the ACE meeting is around July 4, and today's June 3. My chances are *slim* of making it. Hoping will only bring pain. Now, what do I do about that? Every pleasant, even whimsical line of thought merges into the hard path to reality. The past haunted, tried to drive me crazy, once before. Only then it was terrible, tragic memories and the past forcing the realities of Vietnam on the present. Now the past tortures me again, won't leave me in peace. "We two kept house, the past and I . . ."

P.M.: Despair is closing in, tightening, choking, and I'm so alone. I went to El Templo and prayed to God, to Mother, to Susan. Help me. I don't know what you can do, but if you hear me, try to help me. Thank you, God, for letting me use your phone.

Later: Another day is almost over, but does it bring me closer to anything? Yeah. There are only two alternatives: release, eventually, or death as a prisoner. If I'm to be released, this [day] took me one day closer; if I die, the same. Whichever is destined, I want it to come as soon as possible. So getting today out of the way was good. Natalia helped.

Monday, 5 Jun., Day 256

Still no summer. Cold and wet. What to do, how to keep from going insane today?

Gustavo is wonderful and Natalia helps. Maybe it's just the contrast with Melena's constant harassment. I'd grown used to it as normal. Gustavo calls me Dragon and I call him Dragon or D2. He loves military things; I showed him the German salute and we use it all the time. Also the single rifle-drill trick I remember from years ago. I refused to demonstrate with a shovel; he finally removed the clip and I taught him with his AK-47.

Later: Took an imaginary Susan on a real tour of my little *secuestrado* world—the 50 feet of camp I can visit. She considered the latrine—a hole in the ground—disgusting. I was embarrassed because I started crying when I showed her El Templo. Have been having imaginary conversations with others. It doesn't work very well. Last night Moño told me again that my freedom is imminent. The delay may be because of weather or soldiers or the new offensive. "Then I have no reason to worry?"

"No. Just have patience."

I always believe him at the time.

1645h: If I stay here five years, I'll never learn. Gustavo and Caballito went to where the radio is this morning. So I waited, hoping they'd return with orders for my freedom. The anguish, when they returned with nothing. But Natalia and Melena were at my fire and asked about the dangers of scuba diving. I shut out the anguish.

My ear is infected again. "Why is your hair turning blond?" they asked. So it's true; they see it, too. Actually, I think it's reddish-blond streaks, and it must be a vitamin deficiency.

Later: I went to El Templo. When I returned, Melena had left my fire. But first she threw all my dry *chuzco*—that I'd worked all afternoon to cut and dry—into the fire. I save some, but most burned. I'd dried the bamboos to use in my *candela* at night and to start a fire tomorrow. Melena did that for only one reason: to destroy what I'd done. Why? The drugs.

Tuesday, 6 Jun., Day 257

Both ears are infected. Bad pain last night. Left ear opened. Got six anti-biotics this morning. Took one. One year ago went to Rwanda. What a disappointment, but had I only known what lay waiting a few months ahead. My memories—they're like a bank account of joys and grief, achievements and failures. Memories, I draw on the interest, memories are all I have to keep me going, but I'm also eating away at the capital. No new memories are going into that account, except those of grief and anguish. How long can I keep reusing them? If I could only hear a new song, for instance, to add to that account, then sing it later. If I could see Tom G. or Susan again, new memories for the bank.

When I'm free, I hope people won't say, like they do of Michael Benge,* "He's crazy because he spent nine months without a friend, etc." Only Susan saw the truth about Michael Benge. "He survived seven years as a prisoner—four in a cage without seeing another American—because he *was* crazy before he was taken prisoner."

Wednesday, 7 Jun., Day 258

So cold and wet today. Where is summer and the sun? Ears opened in the night, infection clearing, and I used only three of six antibiotic pills. So now have three. Am trying to quit watching, hoping for the guerrilla coming up the mountain from Happy Valley with orders for my freedom. It's not going to hap-

---

*A personal friend who was a prisoner-of-war in Vietnam for seven years.—TRH

pen. I live one day at a time with hope but not much faith. What else can I do? I brush my teeth every day since I got a tube of toothpaste two weeks ago. We're all out of candles and I really can't warm a fourth meal up without a light, but fortunately have had enough *cancharina* and *arepas* to warm on the coals.

This morning passed okay—spent almost all of it teaching Natalia English.

Seems I eat nothing but rice and bread now. At night I sleep in four leggings made from remnants of my burned jeans.

P.M.: I call Gustavo *"Cumpa"* [Compadre] or *"Cumpa* Dragon." Pleases him. We don't have supplies because the *arrieros*, or mule trains, haven't come for weeks. Moño says because of rain and mud. If true, maybe it's true that's why I'm not released? No, I don't believe him. Gustavo gave me a whole candle. I had seven stubs, a total of 1½ inches, and one 2-inch candle.

Thursday, 8 Jun., Day 259

Rained hard all night. Still raining. So cold. Out of coffee, candles, don't know what else. Moño sent Julio and Caballito to Happy Valley to see if any supplies are available. Mule trains have not been able to get through the mud for three weeks. I slept better last night than in months. Maybe it's because I realize that I won't be released soon. The winter isn't going away and we're more isolated than ever. I can't hope, until the trails dry somewhat. Can I learn to accept and survive? When Julio and Caballito return with no news, I'll be disappointed, but maybe I can skip the deep depression. If only I had something to read for a few hours, some new stimulation that would give me something new to think about. We get *colada* twice a day usually. A drink of, I guess, flour, sugar, powdered milk. It's like a liquid bread. They say that about beer, too, of course. Beer: I've always loved it so much, but here I hardly miss it. Maybe because it's so cold. I need meat and vegetables, steak and eggs and tomatoes and lettuce. I wish I were like the guerrillas. They've never read so they don't miss reading. They never thought much either.

1605h: Julio and Caballito returned and, as expected, no news. But it didn't hurt so much. Bullshit. It hurts like hell and I could cry for an hour. But that would do no good. I can't give up hope. All communication with the outside world seems to have been cut off. Moño says no idea when the next mail leaves. But how do I know what to believe?

I want to walk, but not through mud. I can take nine normal steps on the porch. Rocks are still wedged between the wooden boards—rocks that I placed there to prevent my chain from hanging up—six months ago when I walked the same route but dragging my chain but the porch route gets boring after a few months. Lord, I'm lonely.

The only supplies were candles and toilet paper. I got two candles and two rolls of toilet paper. That does give me confidence of plans to free me soon. The song "I'm So Lonesome I Could Cry" keeps going through my head, but

I can't sing it because of the part about the mourning dove.* Susan is all I have faith in.

Friday, 9 Jun., Day 260

Moño, Gustavo, and Julio went down to Happy Valley for supplies this morning. I wish they hadn't; hurt's coming and I don't know how to prevent it. Went to El Templo but dreaded it. Said, "Hi, God. Stand by me. I'll need strength today. Help Susan. Have to go now. I don't want to cry, to bring on the despair. Bye. Amen." It bothers me that my diary is so bleak—few good things, nothing funny. Only despair, fear, depression. But that's life here in the Valley of the Shadow. *"Aquí no hay mucha risa."* [Here, there is not much laughter].

P.M.: Spent the morning thinking about where we might go live after my release. Best = Granbury, Australia one year; Washington, D.C.; Mexico? Later. They returned. No news, no freedom. This is Day 13. I don't expect to be free for a long time. How long, Lord? Does it hurt a little less each time?

Saturday, 10 Jun., Day 261

Dreamed—clearly—that Daddy was dying and I was back in Rotan, taking him around to say good-bye to old friends. Julio stopped by my cell to tell me he was going down to Happy Valley—and that he might return with a mule. A mule! That could mean only one thing. When we leave to free me, I'll ride a horse, or a mule, Moño said. "The others will walk—*puro infanteria* [pure infantry]"—Julio was joking, Natalia said later. Funny joke.

Later: Moño got batteries for a radio and was talking last night and this morning. *"Bueno, bueno,"* he said, and acted pleased. Later he, Judi, and Natalia left and went down toward Happy Valley. To meet Julio? No, probably to other site. Here I go again. I can't help it, and God, help me. Gustavo took me up to the spring and I bathed with a rag for the first time since Camp Soledad, and washed socks, etc. Filth encrusted on legs felt like yellow stain that won't wash off.

1300h: No rain for 43 hours. "Summer has come," I told Gustavo. "Will freedom follow?"

"No sé," he replied.

1540h: Damn Julio, damn him. I said I wouldn't, I knew better—but I spent all afternoon watching the trail, waiting, hoping yet not daring to hope, thinking of the trip out of here, of freedom, of Susan. Moño has returned; so have Judi and Natalia. No news. Nothing has changed. Except I've done it to myself yet again. I can't help it. This is worse than yesterday.

Later: Tom, you can't let this continue. You're going to lose—or destroy—your sanity. Tomorrow I cannot hope or build myself up again. I must accept that I'm not leaving here. But . . . if I do that . . . why live? I'm not afraid to

*". . . a mourning dove who's lost its mate in flight? . . . I'm so lonesome I could cry."—TRH

die. Last night Melena left her M-1 carbine, loaded, on a bench. I could have grabbed it. No, Tom, you can't think about suicide either. But how will I survive?

Sunday, 11 Jun., Day 262

Clear and beautiful this morning. Makes 2½ days without rain. If it were true that FARC is waiting for the trails to dry, freedom should come soon. But it's a lie, of course. I can't allow what happened yesterday to happen again. It will kill me or drive me insane or, maybe, to suicide. But how can I keep hope and faith yet not watch for signs and hope—desperately—that they mean freedom?

P.M.: Found a drowned rat in the jug of drinking water I keep in the cell. The last rat drowned in my urine bucket.

1706h: Got through another day. Didn't let myself think much.

Monday, 12 Jun., Day 263

Rained last night. Day has started badly. "Let's kick the *fútbol*," Judi said. Okay, it's exercise, then I realiz[ed] it's [also] something to do. We started. The only flat place to play is *la cancha* and all but a couple of meters is strictly off-limits for me, so we quit. I swore no more depression, but I was suddenly so depressed that I went to El Templo. I was so despondent that prayer didn't hurt me more.

Breakfast was one little *arepa*. Few supplies getting in, Moño says, and they are only via the civilian *arrieros*. The FARC *arrieros* have stopped. That's why no outgoing mail. The FARC *arrieras* carry mail. I could—and will—interpret that as encouraging. Many things have been put aside, including my destiny—in a time of semicrisis for FARC. Later: The police have arrested Miguel Rodríguez-Orejuela, one of two capos of the Cali Cartel [illegible]. The Cali Cartel planted a bomb in Medellín yesterday that killed 29, wounded 200. "How will this affect my destiny?"

"It won't. There's no interest in this."

"What is FARC's policy toward the Cali Cartel?"

"We have no policy. That's not our concern." Interesting. FARC's policy toward the government police, army . . . is all all-out war, yet no policy for the Cali Cartel?

None of the guerrillas are doing anything. "We're all waiting for orders," Moño says.

"Orders for what to do with me?"

"*Claro.*"

The moon was full last night, but tonight there'll be no moon. That's why the weather has changed, Moño said.

1610h: It's been a long day. A bad one, even though I managed to avoid deep thought. Thoughts on hymns. I remember only a few, but I don't find them relevant. They're all about salvation, being saved, everlasting life. Those values don't concern me much. If I die, I accept what lies next and I'm ready for that right now. Again, dying doesn't scare me so much, but I can think of nothing more frightening and depressing than the thought of living like this indefinitely. *Strength* is what I need. Strength and the will to continue. But I know no hymns that help much. I sing "Stand by Me," but is that the chorus of a hymn? Or is it from "Let It Be" by the Beatles—which is the tune I use.

Tuesday, 13 Jun., Day 264

Rained last night and is cold, cloudy. Maybe summer is not here. What will I do today? I made a list of favorite jokes. That was fun. I laughed a little. Thought of making a list of foods I'll eat when free, but that might be demoralizing. Moño sent two guerrillas to Happy Valley this morning. I will not let it happen again. Orders for my freedom may or may not come someday, but they won't bring them. No more, Tom. I'm the only friend I have. I can't continue to hurt myself so cruelly. There are enough other people who will do that. Today is Day 17 since package left. Scary thought. Susan may not believe photo because hair has changed from white to reddish. Should write, tell her it's probably malnutrition. I don't want to write that; she could do nothing to help me. It might upset Susan.

1516h: Damn Moño. "What are you doing?" I asked two hours ago.

"Waiting for Gustavo and Judi to return. Maybe they'll bring the orders." So what did I do? That set me off again. Watching the trail, hoping to see them return with a mule. It won't happen, and maybe thinking and writing it destroys it. God help me stand the hurt that's coming. Help me. The wait. It's terrible.

1536h: They returned. No mule, no news, no freedom. I'll survive. I'll survive. Oh God, help me. I'll survive.

1655h: Was terribly depressed but feel a little better now. Gustavo brought a surprise in my dinner plate. A little jar of mayonnaise and a bottle of ketchup he smuggled up from Happy Valley. I was surprised—happy—I hugged it and almost cried in front of the little bastard. Mayonnaise goes as well with boiled cow's hoof and rice. That's what we had for dinner.

Later: Got a box of matches, also welcome. Have 1½ candles. "New" flashlight quit working after one night.

Later: I don't feel anything except numb. That happens sometimes after these crashes. How long can I continue this?

Wednesday, 14 Jun., Day 265

A sunny clear day, but still it seems a day without hope. Night is my favorite time of day. That's so strange, but being locked in my cell in darkness is better than [being locked in the cell] in midmorning or early afternoon, the worst times. My happiest time is in the twilight hours when I'm dreaming. Especially if I'm also warm. Dreams are the only escape and they're seldom bad. If I could only learn to control my dreams.

P.M. I'm terribly afraid Round 6 [of the ransom negotiations] will result in nothing, like before. What's happened, in my mind, is: FARC's seen the CIAT budget, maybe in the Annual Report, and is asking a ransom impossible to pay. Especially if it's only to be paid by my family. So I'm going on ice again. Maybe they'll try again in three to four months. Maybe FARC will release me in two to three years without ransom if I'm still alive. I think of suicide, but not as something I'm ready for now. But in the future? Maybe, if I see no hope. With a rifle, definitely. I could grab one easily while the guerrillas are playing *fútbol*—as they are right now. I'd only use an M-16, because I know that weapon and don't want any chance of failure. Grab rifle, chamber a round, turn it to fully automatic (last setting). Muzzle under chin, push firmly on trigger with thumb. That assures a burst of at least three rounds through the head and a fast, painless passage on to . . . whatever follows.

Raining now, and cold. A bad day. I think about suicide too much. Later: I wish prayer would help, give me strength. But it doesn't. Or maybe it does and I just don't recognize it. I'm very afraid that there is no God. I'm not afraid because of heaven, hell [illegible]. If there is Divine Justice then Divine Power must exist to guide it. That's God. But with no Divine Justice, my fate is in the random numbers. And I'm afraid the cards may be stacked against me. Here, I've written what I've thought all this miserable, cold, rain-soaked afternoon. Selfish and shallow? Probably, and maybe that's why I'm not free. Actually, I hope that's right—because it would prove that Divine Justice exists. But I've certainly prayed and will continue to pray.

4:20 P.M. I must shake this horrible depression. I've lit a fire. I saved beans from lunch and Gustavo has *la rancha* today. He gave me two extra *cancharinas*. I'd forgotten about the ketchup. I'm going to have a real feast after I'm locked in my cell tonight.

Thursday, 15 Jun., Day 266

Scary. I awoke in the predawn this morning, crying. Why? In that state of half dreaming, I thought of what Moño told me last night: "Don't worry, Tomás, FARC will never kill you, no matter how long you're held prisoner." That kind of good news I don't want.

P.M.: Maybe "I will survive" seems contradictory, with thoughts of how to commit suicide, but not in my mind. I'll survive while there's hope, but I want the option of ending it if I see nothing in the future but the nonlife I'm now living.

1505h: Still raining.

1530h: Have been reading Melena's *Chrono* again. It has an ad for Hush Puppies shoes. No matter what my mood, I can't look at that without breaking into tears. Then I turn the page quickly. You see, the ad has a basset hound that looks exactly like Cuchara. Nothing is so painful as a dog because nothing says *home* like a dog. Especially home with Susan. I'm glad Orejas and Ranger and Oso are no longer around. I can hardly bear to even write this, but I must record certain things because I'm afraid I'll forget them—erase them from my mind—when I'm free. If I'm ever free again.

1700h: Tried to contact Susan via mental telepathy. Simple message: "Susan, I'm alive and I love you," several times. Hurts so much—mental pain—to do that. Usually sent from El Templo.

Later: A *secuestrado* was released in Cali yesterday, Moño said. For a ransom of Colombian $600 million. That didn't make me feel any better (800 Colombian pesos = 1 U.S. dollar).

Friday, 16 Jun., Day 267

Today is 9½ months and another day of clouds and cold rain. Haven't written much in my diary about the problem of CIAT [i.e., its troublesome acronym] and CIA because [I] have explained [it] in letters. The guerrillas would never have arrested me were it not for the CIAT acronym, Moño says. Today, I'm going to write Havener [CIAT's chief] again asking that the CIAT board review the matter. But no mail has left in three weeks and [I have] no idea when next will be. The problem, Moño says, is that the FARC *arrieros* [mule trains] come here no longer because the other guerrillas have left the area.

P.M.: Gustavo gave me a bottle of *ají* hot sauce. All night I heard rats trying to chew into the double plastic bags where I store food. Now I see that actually a plastic candy bag with my last *cancharina* was partly outside the bags. The rats ate it completely, right beside me. That was my last reserve of *cancharina*. How I wished I'd eaten it last night. Oh well, I still have rice.

Rice and bamboo. Food and fire. Strange how my life revolves around two very Asian plants, as a *secuestrado* here in the Andes Mountains of Colombia. Mental telepathy to Susan at 8:15 A.M. Left ear infected again; right ear will follow, I'm sure. No more medicines. Moño gave me Visine—yes, Visine for the eyes—to use as eardrops. Well, *algo es algo* ["something is better than nothing"]. Gustavo jokes [?] that he wants to be my *guardiaespalda* [bodyguard?] someday. Does he mean it? Maybe.

1700h: Got through today better than most, maybe, but I must push heavy thoughts of freedom and family from my mind. Mostly, and accept that I'll be here a long, long time. Moño still tells me freedom is coming at any moment, but I don't believe him. Diet is back. Breakfast: one *arepa*. Lunch: rice and pasta. Dinner: rice and lentils.

Saturday, 17 Jun., Day 268

This is the worst kind of day. Rained all night, raining now. Gustavo brought *brasas* [coals] and made a fire, but to sit by fire all day thinking is bad. No alternatives. Twenty-one days since packet left. Should CIAT start publicity again? I wouldn't, but I don't know what's right. Will not think freedom is com-

ing, will fight the depression and despair. That means: Don't go to El Templo
to pray. How will I get through the evening? I don't know, but I will. Left ear
opened last night, but was very painful. Didn't use antibiotic: I have eight and
there are no more medicines in the camp. I hope I never use those because I'm
saving them for a real emergency—life or death, maybe. All activity, except
waiting, seems to have ceased (or slowed down). . . . Group of 15 FARC kidnapped a congressman yesterday in Caquetá. I always knew there was a lot of
kidnapping here, but not like now—every time I see news, it includes another
kidnapping.

Sunday, 18 Jun., Day 269

Ate little dinner last night, saved my rice and beans to eat in cell after
lock-in. As I was getting ready, I heard a rustle in the plastic bags where I keep
food. Opened the bag and a rat jumped out onto my stomach and bounced away.
He'd chewed through the plastic and was inside with the food. I warmed and ate
the rice and beans anyway—didn't have much choice. Wrapped what food was
left, including two *cancharinas* that Gustavo gave me, in the plastic and put
under the foam pad under my head like a pillow. Worried that rats would swarm
around my face in the night, but they didn't. Mental telepathy to Susan several
times yesterday and 9:30 A.M. today. The food and discomfort are not the worst
things here, although I wonder when my teeth will start falling out. It's the
worry about Susan and family, the excruciating loneliness, the boredom. The despair's so *heavy* that you could cut it with a knife.

Monday, 19 Jun., Day 270

Today is a special date. I'll always remember 19 June like, I guess, I'll always remember 23 Sept. in the years to come. Twenty-six years ago today I left
Susan at Carswell Air Force Base and the army flew me to Vietnam in a char-
tered baby-blue Braniff DC-8. Well, I survived the year that followed and I'll
survive this (if only I knew it would be a year). Rained all last night, and this
cold gray morning seems like the sun never existed. Summer was to begin on
7 June, but except for three glorious sun-filled days, the weather has been as
cold and wet as the worst of winter. Winter is still here.

Moño sent guerrillas to Happy Valley today for news. If only I could hope
without the hurt and despair that inevitably follow like the three were one giant
powerful emotion. Moño said this morning that FARC took me to a camp so remote because I was considered a very special prisoner (CIA). Also, that there are
no more horses, so we'll walk to Bogotá. If orders come. That helps confirm,
I guess, that the main units have left Happy Valley. Had a bag of *yupis* (corn
chips) that I have saved since the *comandante*'s visit. Rats chewed through them.
Why didn't I eat them myself? A rat crawled across my face last night. May be
trying to get to the food I was using as a pillow. Mental telepathy to Susan, only
the two messages: alive and love. Nothing else seems very important. So cold

[illegible] deep, wet cold with wind to push it through your clothes to the bone. Have thought a lot lately about a Fields family [my mother's side of the family] reunion. I'll do my share to help, if such a blessing is possible. When this terrible time is over I want to maintain better contact with families.

1600h: Gustavo came back.

1610h: Julio returned with supplies and waving a checkerboard. This camp needs a game, but that means we aren't leaving. I said it couldn't happen—I controlled it all day, but I can't help it. I can't stand it, but I have to.

1655h: Gustavo told me Moño's orders. I read articles and ads from the *Crono* magazine to Gustavo. We looked at ads together, especially for refrigerators, and divided shelves of food between us. I get the top shelf with the turkey and ham. You get the next one with the desserts, etc. It's rained cold rain for eight days. I'm wearing socks three days at a time without washing them. I'm abandoned, left to die here. No, worse, to not die. No, Susan can't have abandoned me. If I thought that, I'd truly end it. Right now I must block out my thoughts: they'll drive me crazy. . . . What did I do, God, to deserve this? Right ear infected.

Tuesday, 20 Jun., Day 271

If waiting for good weather to dry the trails and for the march out of here is a factor in my supposed release, then even God seems to have lined up against me. (Seems that way a lot, lately.) This is the ninth straight day of dark gray clouds and cold rain and drizzle. Last night around my fire, Moño gave some new information. 1) I am the only foreign *secuestrado* in FARC custody in Colombia since two Swedes were released two to three months ago. 2) Marulanda, the FARC commander in chief himself, ordered for my release, so there should be no problem with new negotiations. 3) Susan knows I'm to be released soon and is waiting. 4) He has no idea why the delay, but [it] should not be a matter of ransom negotiations. 5) "They" have told me that we will not be in this camp in August (but a few weeks ago Moño said that "they" planned to wrap up my case by the end of June). 6) Still no idea when the next mail will leave. (The last mail out was 27 May.)

Later: Learned that I can sing "I'd Rather Be a Texas Aggie." I've tried but can't sing "Spirit of Aggieland" or the "Texas Aggie War Hymn." Too many memories, mostly very happy memories, but also some incredibly sad ones. Too much emotion, either way. I can't handle that. I don't need to torture myself mentally on top of all the rest.

1310h: Two guerrillas—total strangers—just arrived—climbed up from Happy Valley. No . . . no. I don't want this, God. I don't need this. I was surviving today. Okay, please don't do that to me again. Oh, please, God, please stop the hurt.

1335h: The two guerrillas walked by, so I asked. No, they brought no messages. So that's that, I guess. I cried, first alone [?] Couldn't help [it], and I knew what the answer would be. The rain has started again. Must think of wonderful things, the family reunion I hope to help organize. I was down to three inches of candle, but Gustavo gave me two new candles. Found red pen visitor threw [away]. Not working but has ink. Saved.

More cloud, sun chased it away. Mental telepathy [to Susan]: alive and love and I'll return to you if I can.

Wednesday, 21 Jun., Day 272

Day 10 of cold rain. Natalia talked to me for the first time in days. (I think she's scared to be friends with me [because of] Melena and Judi.) "Something is happening. You're to be released very soon." I wish she wouldn't say that. Especially since Gustavo and others have gone to Happy Valley again. If I could hope without the hurt that follows.

Do I think they're going to release me soon? Sometimes, especially after talking with Moño. He seems so sincere about it. But when I look at the situation coldly, as an outsider, well, it doesn't seem likely. Saturday will make one month since the last "final" step was taken—the package to Susan. They're holding me to exchange for something that's not coming. Why wasn't I freed by May, like you said? I asked Julio last week. "It's not our fault, Tomás. The government won't cooperate with FARC." That answer scares me. Not because Julio is smart and astute but for the opposite reason. He's not, so was probably repeating what he heard. And maybe from someone who knows. Left ear opened Monday night, but right ear now infected again. The weather seems colder than ever. *Hope without hurt*, if only that were possible, but I'm afraid it isn't. I could spend the day *hoping* that Gustavo will return from Happy Valley with the order, and be fairly happy. I've done it so many times. Hours thinking about how they'd tell me ... about how and where I'd meet Susan, seeing my staff and friends at CIAT, returning to Texas, etc. But it's not worth the crash when Gustavo actually returns with no orders and nothing has changed except I've been high for hours. I prayed at El Templo this morning for hope without hurt—this ability to hope without that awful hurt. Now look, Tom, you're working yourself up again. You'll never learn—*I will survive*, that's the only philosophy to help you now. And false hopes of release won't help you survive.

1250h: Oh no, oh no. I'll die. I'll die. Gustavo and Caballito just returned from Happy Valley with a horse and a mule packed with supplies. What a shock. Oh God, you can't be—you can't let it happen again. Not with a horse and a mule. I'm sitting in La Rancha Tomás—what will happen next? The worst crash ever? I can see the animals. I'm crying. I can't help it. God, please, God.

1425h: What do I write? I don't know. I've been up and down. I've soared and crashed and been battered. ... Well, the scene was exactly as I'd imagined it. Gustavo and Caballito led the two mules—both are mules—to *la rancha* and unpacked them. Moño appeared. "How do you like the mules?"

"They're for the trip? The orders have arrived?"

"No—they're to work for the group, to carry supplies. The orders haven't arrived, but they will."

What happened next? I don't remember. I didn't cry. I think I went to El

Templo. Later I saw Moño again. "I just learned that your family has paid half the *rescate* [ransom], Tomás," he said. "The orders should arrive anytime."

"Then . . . the mules are also to ride out of here?"

"*Sí.*"

So, here I am. But I'm high again. The end must be in sight. But the fat lady hasn't sung yet, Tom, as Buck Sheldon would say. I'm still far from free. The two mules are grazing on *la cancha*—they're the most beautiful animals I've ever seen. Which would I ride to freedom? The white mule is named Paloma. Both are females.

Later: I'm letting myself think. How dangerous.

1540h: I could be home in a few days. No, Tom. Think in terms of a few weeks—but you'll return alive! But what happens if a few days, then weeks, pass and . . . nothing? I'm still here. No, I can't think of that—but I *must* stay out of the euphoria trap.

1900h: No rain today, only drizzle. Got crackers and seven new candles.

Thursday, 22 Jun., Day 273

Last night was bad. At 4:30 A.M. I still had not slept. First was the excitement, thought of freedom, seeing Susan and the boys—what it will be like. The exchange of other half of the [ransom] money? (Alex?)*[1] But both cars are now infected and the pain grew worse and worse. But I *will not* take my eight antibiotic pills unless the car infections grow life-threateningly serious. They are to save my life, my last reserve. If I leave here having never used the antibiotics, I won't regret it. I'll be grateful. They're insurance to sustain my philosophy, my belief, my strength. *I will survive.* Gustavo took both mules back to Happy Valley. "But they'll be there when we start the trip out," Moño assured me. This camp once again has no medicines. Not even alcohol, not any type of disinfectant, or cotton. That disgusts me, the [lack of] intelligence of FARC to kidnap and bring a 50-year-old man—now well into 51—to a place like this with no medicines. What if I had a bad heart condition or diabetes. I'd die, I guess. FARC wouldn't be sophisticated enough to recognize it and take the right actions. Idiots. Haven't seen the Phantom for weeks or months, and [illegible] seems not so important now. [illegible] irresponsible.

1630h: The day is so cold and gray, raining slowly, I wonder how FARC will decide it's time to release me, assuming the story regarding [payment of] half ransom is true. I don't know when it's [illegible]. I guess.

Later: Melena said I'll be free within 15 days, that Moño told her that. Also, this is 19th not 6th Front of FARC, and that she and Judi will stay here to work.*[2] I don't believe [her].

*[1] A reference to Alexandra Walter, a personal friend and CIAT employee. I was speculating that Alex might be the person to deliver the ransom money.—TRH

*[2] During this time the guerrillas repeatedly told me that they would remain in the Valley of the Shadow after my release. I think they assumed that I would reveal the location of the camp to the Colombian army, and were planning to ambush whoever followed up my lead.—TRH

Friday, 23 Jun., Day 274

Sun early this morning, but gray clouds chased it away. Julio took me to wash hair, socks. "When will we leave?" I asked.

"In 15 days."

"In or *within* 15 days?"

"*In* 15 days." So the magic number, 15 days, which is 7 July, arises again from a different source. Moño must have told the guerrillas that, as Melena said. Do I dare set 7 July as a target date, a goal? I can't have hope without hurt. Thought, if we were not in Cauca [valley], then why is "6 frente" [Sixth front] painted in big green letters on the large rock en route to *la rancha*? It was there when we arrived.

P.M.: Raining steadily, cold, dreary. "When does the next mail leave?"

"There'll be no more mail out," Moño said.

"What if I'm here six more months? I can't write my family?"

"*Veremos.* Now we're waiting." I guess that's good. Means something must happen.

1440h: "Let's light a fire. Can you bring coals from *la rancha*," I said to Gustavo.

"We have candles now," Gustavo said. "Don't. You can use a candle."

"But we should save the candles, only use them for light."

Gustavo looked disgusted, went to [illegible], handed me a three-inch candle stub, which I'm using to light the fire. (Actually I'm not. I have another stub, only half inch, which I was saving. I'll use it and save the three-inch one, which is probably good for 40 minutes of light.) Typical of guerrilla wastefulness. Disregard for tomorrow. "We have candles, use 'em." The boil or sore in left ear just opened. Lots of pus and blood; it's draining. Gustavo asked again what I'll say about guerrillas when free. What a question.

Saturday, 24 Jun., Day 275

Day 13 of the resumption of winter after a false three-day start on summer. Cold, raining. Both ears so infected. Terrible pain, last night. This morning, Moño brought booklet, *"Normas Fundamentales del Convenio del Ginebra y Sus Protocoles Adicionales Conscimiento del Derecho Humanitario."* He read to me from a page, then had me read to him. It's obvious he doesn't understand it, but why bring the booklet if it will show FARC in total violation of *my* rights? A prerelease requirement? Remember, I had some questions earlier when [illegible] brought and read to me the other Red Cross literature.

Later: As I thought: kidnapping is specifically prohibited, without exception, in at least four places. It also specifies that a prisoner of war has the right to receive mail.

1700h: Ears better. Natalia spent most of the afternoon with me. Drew me and La Rancha Tomás. Asked if I wanted sketch of the hut. No. I'm afraid if it was found, I'd get her in trouble, "intelligence value" [I feared], although it has none. The day was awfully cold: so cold and raining all day. Heard that the two visitors of last night would escort me from here. Everyone expects the orders at any time. I can't; I've been through this too many times before. Five times to be exact. Awful pain in my ears last night.

[*A letter instructing the family to start new negotiations via radio was received by courier mail.—SSH*]

Sunday, 25 Jun., Day 276

Sun early in morning, but fat, wet clouds covered it by 8:30 A.M. I can't help but think they—FARC—may be waiting for dry weather to take me out of here. This is the dry season. Two weeks of sun. Rain isn't normal. It's like something is working against me. This is Sunday morning. I sent mental telepathy to [Susan]. Alive, well, will return if I can. She may sleep late, without distractions. Twelve days until the magic date of 7 July.

Later: 15 to 20 more days, Moño says. Thought: True despair is when the thought of continuing to live, as you are, causes more anguish than the thought of death. I've walked through that part of the valley and hope that I never return there.

1310h: Damn. Just as I'm philosophically accepting [the news of the delay], Gustavo tells me we're expecting a visitor. I won't let myself fall into that trap, walk that dead-end road to despair again.

1600h: Damn it. The visitor has been here all afternoon, but I know nothing. I don't see the arrival, but Melena and Natalia also confirm [that he's] here. I need to know something. I don't want to be hurt, but I can't ignore that he's here. Of course, Moño probably doesn't now that I'm well aware of a visitor.

1630h: Now shut in cell as the visitor leaves. Later, saw visitor through crack in wall. Wore guerrilla uniform with white straw cowboy hat. Pretty sure was Señor VIP. No news, Moño says, but freedom coming soon. No choice but to believe.

Monday, 26 Jun., Day 277

"When you're free and they interview you on the radio, will you say '*Hola, Julio*' for me? We'll all be listening for what you say," Julio said by my fire last night.

Then Moño appeared. "We won't take you out. We'll turn you over to a group of guerrillas who will take you to another part of Colombia and free you."

This was after he said there was no news. He was, as usual, playing tickle-and-feelie with Judi. "What will you tell people about us?"

"It depends on the question."

"If they ask which front had you?"

"The Sixth."

"No—FARC only. FARC. You don't know about fronts."

"Okay."

"What if they ask you the name of the *comandante* of the group that guarded you?"

"I'll say that her name was Judi." That got some laughs. "In any case, you're not using your real names, you all have *noms de guerre!*"

"How do you know that?" Moño snapped.

"It's obvious. It only makes sense." Moño was touchy and I didn't like it. Careful, Hargrove, I finally feel it's coming. Too many things. I'll be out of here in a few days.

But to be turned over to another group of guerrillas—that's scary. It's the scenario I've always had in my mind for my execution. Another group, not those who've had me for 10 months, would do it and these guerrillas would probably never even know. But I don't think that will happen. If it does, there's nothing I can do to change it. I'm as ready for death as I'll be. *Qué será, será* [What will be, will be]. This morning I change to black shorts because they are larger, easier to stuff part of my diary in. Tore pages from this notebook to include. Found the letter with the army charges to hide separately. I want to be ready to march. By that I mean to have my diaries as ready as possible. I have nothing else of value to worry about. I'll be free, or dead—another form of freedom—in no more than two weeks. I feel it. Whichever, I hope it's soon—today, or tomorrow. And yes, I am concerned that I'll be killed, but I'll try not to let it worry me. Sent mental telepathy to Susan.

Gustavo has *la rancha* [duty] today. Gave me six *cancharinas*, "To make you fat and strong."

"For a long hard trip?"

"*Sí.*"

"By foot or by horse?"

"*No sé* [I don't know]."

It's cloudy, and very cold, but not raining. Not yet.

Later: Cutting *chuzco*, trying to keep my mind from whatever's coming. I'm ready, whatever it is. P.M.: Lots of activity. Julio and Caballito went to Happy Valley this morning, returned with Viejito and Leidi. "I still have the four-leaf clover you gave me," I told Leidi. "But it doesn't work." "Keep it. It will work—soon," she said. Later: The visiting guerrilla brought a black dog named Rambo, but I can't pet him. I'm not home yet and I'm not ready to handle a dog. Nothing says home, family, like a dog. Carlos Upequi Zapata was kidnapped 22 Aug. '93. What happened to him?

1546h: Should I believe them? How terribly depressing. I'm to be released between 4 and 11 July—8 to 15 days from now. "I don't know," Moño says. "That's the *plazo* (deadline term)," set for the final payment of the ransom. Says Susan is aware—and set the date, to raise the money. If that's so, then CIAT has abandoned us. Can it be? How *much is* the ransom? I feel awful. Maybe my earlier idea—that it would be better if I die here—isn't so bad. Murder, not suicide. Later: I don't really know what's true. I asked, sort of, if Susan set the deadline, to raise the money. There may be other reasons. But I won't know until I'm free and see Susan again. What hell, what a terrible thing. I must have strength. I mustn't feel that all have abandoned us. What poison for the mind. Later: I said Susan must have set the *plazo* and Moño agreed. I went to El Templo and prayed—God, help Susan, stand by her, help her. And protect me from myself. It's raining and so cold.

1730h: I asked Moño. He does not know why the *plazo* was set, or how. Very specifically said that. Also that the *plazo* was set three to four days ago, after payment of 50 percent of the ransom. That makes me feel a little better. Moño says he has no idea if it has anything to do with raising money. Now I can only wait, hope, pray. Sent mental telepathy to Susan.

Later: I'm exactly where I was before I hit the panic button. Actually, better off—I know the *plazo* begins in eight days. But I'm scared of myself.

Tuesday, 27 Jun., Day 278

What happened yesterday scares and worries me. I expressed my very deepest fears—put or imagined the words in Moño's mouth, then just about flipped out over it. Thank God it scared me so. I grabbed hold of myself. If I hadn't, I'd be terrified and in a state of near-suicidal depression. What I feared so could be absolutely true, of course. But I don't know that and torturing myself with the worst of my imagination is awful, sadistic, suicidal. FARC almost definitely set the *plazo*, to arrange logistics, etc. This is Day 16 of cold dark clouds with rain. Why? It's not like I'm asking for sunshine in midwinter; we're 27 days into summer.

P.M.: Through all of this I've never given up faith, never even faltered really, in Susan or my family. If I had, I'd have gone mad. I've never prayed without praying for Susan, mainly asking God to give her strength, courage, judgment. I have never cried in front of guerrillas. Natalia drew a sketch of me in La Rancha Tomás, and it's essentially correct except for the proportions of La Rancha Tomás. She made it too big. It's really 6x8 feet. Clouds, sun all day. Cold but no rain. Maybe summer's coming.

Wednesday, 28 Jun., Day 279

P.M.: Rained all day till 3:30 then some sun. At five took two machetes, rope, shovel to trail. Hurry. Moño said I may leave—by foot—in five days. Natalia and I named seven wonders of ancient modern world. Studied Spanish a lot.

1740h: I don't like this. Something has happened and it probably involves Gustavo, who, I guess, went to Happy Valley. This morning, Moño, Melena, Judi all went down the trail. Anything out of the ordinary can only be bad for me.

1820h: Scared, so scared, that whatever it is will mean I don't leave. Please, God. Please, please.

Thursday, 29 Jun., Day 280

I'll probably never know what happened last night, but it wasn't what I feared most. I pictured Gustavo dead and a grave being dug along the trail in the forest. And I was desperately hoping the *chulos* [soldiers of the Colombian army] hadn't ambushed him. Soldiers around here could put us into deeper hiding and stop all plans for my release. All guerrillas returned around 7:30 P.M., but most left again early this morning. It's some kind of problem at the other site. The weather is terrible, the camp is a mire of mud. Our summer dry season began with rain, then three days of no rain and some sun. Then 15 days straight rain, one day without rain (27 June), then solid rain since evening of 27 June.

Our diet terrible. My consumption of solid food is rice 60 percent; bread 20 percent; lentils, beans, peas 20 percent. Plus three cups coffee or chocolate with sugar, and usually 1 cup *colada* from oatmeal, daily. Along with the cold rain, life is as miserable as it's been since my kidnapping 10 months ago with the exception of the days of being chained in solitary confinement. But it's almost over so I can take it. No, that's not right. I can take it whether the trial is really over or not. I have no choice because I will survive to return to Susan and the boys and my family and friends, and to resume life again. I have no choice; I've thought several times: Thank God the end is here, because I couldn't take any more. But the rug was always pulled from under me. The end never came. Yet I survived. If Round 6 fails, I'll survive somehow.

Later: I broke three planks for firewood from the floor and wall of the team hut when no one's around to see. The place is so dilapidated, I don't think anyone will notice. Need the wood to keep the bamboo burning in this weather. I have enough wood saved away to do okay if I were sure to leave by 2 July. But I know better than to count on leaving. I've learned the hard way to table all my fear, concentrate on my release, not my death. At 12:45 clouds parted, for a couple of brief minutes the sun shone on this valley. Spontaneously I remembered and started singing a song I hadn't thought about in years—"Let the Sun Shine In," etc.

P.M.: Sitting by fire as it rains. Nothing else to do. Do I dare think? I could be home in six to seven days. It's best not to. In a way, this is the furthest I've ever been from home. Even if I were in Xian, China, I'd get home in two days. But not from here. This is bad. If I'm still here July 4 without a date, I'll be half-crazy.

1735h: I thought as freedom came nearer it would all get easier. But today was awful. Never talked—not one word—to anyone, and I'm so lonely. Moño came by, said two North Americans—professors—were killed in Medellín, and also a *rehen* [i.e., a hostage] was killed. Why tell me that? Seemed less positive about my release than before. A month ago there was mostly no hope, but now there's much hope. Now what does that mean?

I'll almost definitely miss the ACE meeting. What a shame. It would have been a good way to reenter society and reestablish contacts that I may need. See old friends. I'm scared. So terribly scared that I won't go free. A deep sick fear in my throat, my chest. Kill me. That thought doesn't scare me. Holding me here longer does. God help me. Have sent many mental telepathy messages to Susan. Mainly that I'm alive and the last mail left a month ago, so she has no evidence and may think I'm dead. Especially if FARC is behind all the delay.

Friday, 30 Jun., Day 281

Today marks 10 months—40 weeks—of captivity. I remember when I hit 40 days and thought of considering the sign. If [a person suffered for] 40 days in the Bible, that would be the end of my test. Rained all last night and all day today. Of 30 days in June—summer, the dry season—26 have been cold, cloud-covered, and rain-soaked. July 2 is two days away. That's when Moño said we might start the trip out of here. I can't bear to think about that because I know it won't happen. Whenever the rain ceases, I rush out and cut more wet bamboo. Anything to push aside the thoughts, fears, hopes which go hand in hand. The anguish, the pain. I sent mental telepathy message to Susan: it's okay because the pain is already here. I'm alive, I'm alive, and I love you and I'll return if I can. How terrible Susan's life must be. If I were dead, she'd be a widow and that's that. Maybe I will be soon.

But why am I thinking that way? The *plazo* is 4–11 July, if I can believe FARC. And half of the ransom, they claim, has been paid. And the two guys came from below to set arrangements. The problem is, I can't really believe any of these things. I have hope, but little faith almost gone. Both have caused only hurt in the past. And the cold cruel rain keeps falling.

"Do you want to go for a walk?" Moño asked at eight A.M. Of course. I haven't left my 50-60-foot confinement area except to go to the spring up the trail twice since we came back here 26 April. And thus, I learned what happened two nights ago. A cow had slipped off the trail to Happy Valley, into a deep gully. She couldn't get out. Nor could the guerrillas get her out. We went to kill the cow to bring meat back. But my luck! When we arrived, the cow had somehow gotten out. [We] built a fire, then returned. The trip killed 2½ hours. For that I'm grateful. A good break, good exercise and preparation for the long march out of here. All the walking was in mud, ankle-deep or deeper, in drizzling rain. But I did okay. Never stopped to rest. Now I'm trying to dry my jacket and *ruana*. Haven't taken it off for a week. The last time I took off my clothes was when I bathed in the river by camp. Fifth weekend after Easter.

Saturday, 1 Jul., Day 282

The day is cloud-covered with a sharp cold wind. But there was no rain last night and no rain by midmorning. Today Gustavo washed my clothes. They were just too dirty to go on. I'd hesitated because if I march tomorrow, I want my clothes dry. But if that will happen, I can dry clothes with all the dry firewood that I've been hoarding. I'm sick with fear and anxiety as the morning passes and no one arrives with orders to march tomorrow, 2 July. That would probably get me near Cali or Bogotá in time for a 4 July release. I have so many fears. They're all deep hurting fears, and they all concern my release. What if 11 July passes and I'm still here? Can I continue to fight the despair? Hope without hurt. If only that were possible.

Later: Melena came and lit a fire. Used a full candle. "Should I leave my clothes outside to dry in that cold wind, or bring them into La Rancha Tomás, where there is a fire?" I asked Melena.

"Outside, Tomás; if you bring the clothes inside, they get smoky."

"I don't care. I want my clothes to be dry when I start the march out of here."

"But you won't wear those clothes, Tomás."

"What? Why not?"

"They're bringing you all new clothes for when you're released."

Now that's something new and encouraging. No one had mentioned new clothes, not to me. That means they're talking about my release, and I guess new information is coming in. Positive signs. Or am I groping at every straw? But with enough straws you can make a raft. Profound philosophy, Hargrove.

Later: Rice and peas for lunch. Will I ever again eat for pleasure? Here it's to push hunger away. To keep strength up. But very little is good. The *arepas* and *cancharinas* are still my favorites. I think of the funniest things. This morning it's been the watchbird from *Ladies' Home Journal* or one of the magazines from the fifties. And how Mother read it to me each month. There is a watchbird watching you. Guess I've run out of relevant themes to think about.

Showers late afternoon but no real hard rain. Now sun. It's [absurd] to believe I'm kidnapped by Colombian guerrillas in South America. But it's harder to believe I'll ever be free. The idea seems unreal. Something too wonderful, of too much happiness to be possible.

[*The Colombian military started an offensive against the Sixth Front of FARC. The kidnappers stopped scheduled radio communications with the family. The U.S. Embassy repeatedly requested to the Colombian government that they cease operations in the area where Tom was being held. Although the Embassy was assured that they had, the media continued to report activity.—SSH*]

Sunday, 2 Jul., Day 283

This is Day 2 of what I fear will be the Long Wait. If [it] really [takes] two days to get to Cali or Bogotá, then I must leave in the next seven days to be released by 11 July. If they're not lying. Cold, cloudy, still no sun. Rain last night. If I think about what they've done to me—to us, Susan, and my family, and me—hatred and anger swell inside me. But I can't do that because the anger turns to frustration and frustration to despair.

I can't afford the emotion. I must keep pulling myself from despair. I can't think of what I'll do if I'm not released in this, Round 6. I could kill myself easily—the thought doesn't even scare me. But I won't. Not unless I'm sure I won't be released. But in what time period? Six months, one year, three years?

At what point would I kill myself? I'm not sure. I'd prefer that the bastards kill me so I don't have to make that decision. It's time to study Spanish. To think of something else. Mental messages to Susan, this morning: alive. The simpler the message the more likely it is to go through. At least it seems that way to me. And the most important message for Susan now is: I'm still alive.

P.M.: "You'll be home next Sunday," Moño said, without my asking or coaxing. That makes me feel wonderful, it lifts my spirits immensely. But how cruel if it doesn't happen. I'm afraid to hope. Too much hurt always follows. Showers then sun, late afternoon, then rain.

Later: "*Regáleme su ruana azul*, [Give me your blue *ruana*]," Judi said, like we're the best of friends. She won't remember when she was guard and I needed water. She brought water all right, but put soap in it, then laughed.

Monday, 3 Jul., Day 284

Day 3 of the Long Wait is cloud-covered and very cold but not raining. Not yet. The eight-day period to my release starts tomorrow. I should have been traveling yesterday, but I'm still here. I feel, I really feel—deep inside—that I won't be released. I don't understand why, but this is all a cruel test. I can't let myself feel that way, but I do. Oh God, why? Will any of it make sense someday?

1030h: Moño just told me and I'm sick. I'm deep sick. Can I pull myself out again? New fighting yesterday; three brigades of Colombian army and of FARC Sixth Front (Cauca). Four soldiers and two guerrillas KIA [killed in action]. "Between here and freedom?" I asked. "Sí." Claims to have heard on the radio news. True? Probably. But doesn't matter. Maybe FARC raised my price. Means doubtful release and my freedom is off, and this is what they tell me. Either way, he was telling me freedom is not coming. Not now. Not likely at least. *Why?* I know it'll be a year. I've always known. It's so cold, but I can't use my firewood, except to keep wet wood burning. Not now. Mental message to Susan: Still alive. What does she know? Think? How can she believe I'm alive? I scream the message mentally into the atmosphere. Let it swell from my mind, clench and tighten my body, my jaws, then concentrate my energy on that. Force it from my head. Whatever medium may carry the message. When I got/found four pens—three red—I knew that meant I would be here much longer. All pens were found or stolen. Not one had a cap. Have used 1⅔. No thoughts of suicide, Hargrove. No. Too dangerous. Oh God, give me strength. Susan, hear me and keep faith. Word of honor.

Rain began again. Cold rain seems to go with hurt and anguish.

1120h: Went to El Templo. Cried and prayed, both deeply. Is this the end of Round 6, I prayed and asked, or just a delay?

"Delay," something seemed to say. And it seemed calming. I must cling to that. Fight despair and the deadliest of emotions.

1500h: Rained all afternoon, so cold. Natalia came to La Rancha Tomás and we studied Spanish and English. Melena joined. Thank God. I guess there really is a battle going on between the guerrillas and the Colombian army. Natalia gave the same story.

Later: Battle is still going on with helicopters and gunships, Moño says. One brigade = 2,000 soldiers, so [with three brigades] 6,000 soldiers. Casualties now 15 soldiers killed, 2 guerrillas. What will I do now? The only thing I can do—survive. Survive. I'll survive, and maybe I'll be free someday.

1655h: Dinner like almost every night for a week or two was a plate of rice with a couple spoonfuls of *carve* sprinkled over it. Supplies ceased coming a couple of weeks ago because of my pending freedom, Moño said. None will come soon, that's for sure. What will tomorrow—the day I expected to return to Susan—be like? Well, I won't be watching the trail. Is that better? I must think positively, somehow. I'll survive. But why does God—if He exists—wave freedom in my face then yank it away? So cruel. More mental messages. Must calm myself; I'm on the verge of doing something stupid or self-destructive. I could attack someone or say something that will cause me trouble. Stand by me, God. And Susan.

Tuesday, 4 Jul., Day 285

Happy Birthday, Raford! Cold steady rain fell all night and this morning; freezing even wrapped in blankets like a cocoon. This is only a delay. I can't let myself think anything else. Maybe there's some guidance and some sense to it all. If I'd left 2 July, we might have been ambushed or caught in the battle. Still, I'd take my chances. Gladly.

The Fourth of July. Not a big holiday for me, but it was—Stamford Rodeo and Cowboy Reunion, Ft. Benning, and Krebs picnic at IRRI [in the Philippines], the parade then fireworks on lake at Granbury [Texas]. Hamburgers cooked outdoors. Susan always made holidays special. Did I appreciate that? Not enough but I never appreciated anything in life like I will if I'm ever free again.

Later: The battle continues into Day 4. Moño says FARC made a commitment to free me between 4 and 11 July. Will FARC honor that commitment? I asked. "We'll see. All of the areas are militarized." You lying son of a bitch, I thought, although a battle probably is going on. I can't think of a word to express my contempt for the guerrillas. Careful, Tom. That won't help you survive. The guerrillas are loyal to FARC because they aren't too bright and know nothing else. Most joined at age 15 or [younger], probably from homes that aren't really homes. All they know is FARC and they believe what FARC tells them. They won't change. They can't.

1115h: Broke down and built a fire. It's so cold and wet. *I think the unthinkable.* I can't help it. What if there is no battle, if it's another lie? Then Round 6 is over and I start again? They'll kill me eventually. I can't think that. The battle is a fabrication. Natalia told the same story about the battle. If so, I lose all hope and go crazy.

P.M.: It's rained almost steadily [illegible]. I guess there really is a battle.

Julio just told me about it. Six soldiers, six guerrillas, six *policia* KIA in Cauca. Julio said we were to have official visitors on Saturday, but they canceled because of the fighting. I guess they were to have sent me off on Sunday, 2 July. . . . Also today—Gustavo still calls me Viejo [Old Man]. That's okay, I guess. He's only 15—no, probably 16 by now . . . hint that [we're in Tolima] again.

Later: Moved my reserve bowl of rice to tin bowl for tonight. Afraid we may get real hungry soon. Lunch was rice and two to three spoons of peas. Dinner was rice and some pasta. I should be home by now. That thought makes me sick.

Wednesday, 5 Jul., Day 286

Rain all last night and this morning. I don't even hope for sunshine because it's not coming. Gustavo went down to Happy Valley, but I'm hoping for food, not good news. The battle continues, Moño says. I haven't heard, even in the distance, a radio for several days. It's probably because news of the battle will include its location, and that would help tell me where I am. Moño said that FARC will inform Susan of the delay. But if they say it's because of fighting, that tells more about where I am. Of course, there is also the unthinkable—that radios are kept away because there is no battle, and it's another trick. But I can't think that way. I send lots of mental messages to Susan with the alive message. Only when I'm depressed, but that's often enough. I feel sure that Daddy has died. I wonder what he was thinking about me? I'll never forgive these bastards for that. Well, that did it. I'll go to El Templo and send a mental message now. Pray some, too, maybe.

I have a terrible sick feeling, a deep fear the battle is a fabrication invented because there's another problem, another delay. Was freedom ever coming or was it always a trick to keep me calm a few days at a time? Oh God, please, no, no. Went to El Templo. Prayed for mental messages. Oh God, how I long for someone to talk with, someone to calm such fears. It's been so long. Dear God.

Thursday, 6 Jul., Day 287

And the rainy, gray, leaden skies continue into Day 6 of the Long Wait and the battle and Day 5 of the *plazo*. Lay awake an hour before dawn—thinking hatred for the vermin who have me, and fighting those thoughts because they lead to despair, my worst enemy. If I'm to survive, and I will survive. "We may move in a few days," Moño said last night, "because the fighting may reach here. Also, the Colombian air force may reach this camp," he claims, because a spotter plane flew over a few days ago. What if the camp is bombed and strafed while I'm in my cell? Think of something else, Hargrove. My overwhelming thought is: Is the battle and resulting delay a lie? Yes or no, I can no longer hope to leave here soon. I must prepare myself to move. Hope I can bring my *coacho*. At least I'm fairly warm at night and that means a lot. Started wrapping my foot in my handkerchief and two socks, because the socks are 50 percent holes. Will cut more rags to substitute for socks. My God, I read about Confederate soldiers wearing rags for socks, and now I'm doing the same thing. *"¡Venga, Tomás! ¡Pronto!"* Gustavo called at 12. Moño had called a formation and I had disappeared—was by El Templo. "Pack your things—clothes only. The *chulos* are coming. We're leaving."

Melena had taken my *equipo* to Happy Valley to get supplies. I threw things in the rucksack and was marching down the trail to Happy Valley in 5 to 10 minutes. I'm sitting in an abandoned shack at the edge of Camp Alegría. At the foot of the trail, a saddled horse named Paloma was waiting and I rode two to three kilometers, then walked the rest of the way. It's now 2:45 P.M. Apparently, we left just ahead of the soldiers, but I don't know. What awaits next? I have a real sick feeling that the future's not going to be much fun. I'm shut in this bamboo hut, sitting on a little bunk of bamboo and straw. The "door" is open, so I can see out, but can't go out. My hut is 4 feet wide (length of bunk) and 6 feet deep and 4½ feet high, so I can't stand up. Lined with black plastic and some comic pages and a leaflet titled, ironically, *"Actividades del CIGR (Red Cross) en Colombia!"* I keep darting to the adjacent hut to grab a handful of straw from the bunk. I stripped a cardboard box away, too, to line the bunk. Tonight will be cold. I brought my *candela* pot and have four candles and matches, most of my clothes, one thin blanket. Caballito came by—said 4,000 soldiers were at the other camp. I don't believe, especially not the number, but the situation looks serious, especially for me. We march again tomorrow, Moño said. Gustavo made me remove and throw away my cotton jacket—the one he gave me—before arriving at Camp Alegría, because one side is olive? Because he's not allowed to give it to me? I don't know; I argued, but it was no use.

Later: Juaco came to see me. One of the original group who left before the *other* Juaco killed himself.

1730h: Despite all, I am so grateful that Gustavo replaced Melena. He has brought me three blankets and even a mattress of sorts—the cushion from a sofa. But I don't even like to think about my situation—the guerrillas running from the government troops, [like] the VC running from U.S. [troops] 25 years ago.

Friday, 7 Jul., Day 288

Had to wake to rain in Happy Valley. Hardly slept—bed so short that I had to stay doubled up all night. But I have three huts to choose from tonight. We stay here today. I'm restricted to a small area but still could do some scrounging. Got lots of cord by tearing up the other hut. Found an old T-shirt with long sleeves, and Gustavo brought a spoon with a serrated handle—someone cut notches in it. It cuts things like cord fine. The T-shirt is too small, but I can cut out the arms with the spoon, and they will make fine socks, far better than what I'm wearing now. Found a Pepsi bottle, plastic, and scrounged a second bowl. Leidi is here. She and Viejito visited me last night and we made a big fire. She gave me a comb. I can't believe it. If I can keep my hair fairly straight and cut a bandanna from the T-shirt, maybe I can put off having my hair cut. Found three candles.

Later: Any change is great—have spent about eight months in the Valley of the Shadow. But make no mistake. My situation is awfully dangerous—more dangerous than before. It's obvious that I won't be with Susan by 11 July. But I plan to survive till that day arrives. Tore magazine article off walls to read. One haunting question answered. Yes, there is fighting, it's not a lie. Makes me feel relieved, free of a terrible fear. That relief even makes up for the new fears that replace my fear that the battle was a fabrication. Ironic, the danger makes me feel good—because it's real. (*Semana* 20 Dec. '94. Protect fields = Col. $10,000/mo/hr; run a lab = 10,000,000/mo; *gramaje* in lab = 5,000/kg processed; shipment = 20,000/kg; *peajer fluviales para insumos* 1,000/gal; use of airstrip = 13,000,000/flight.)

P.M.: It's really cold and wet and no, you can't sit by the fire in La Rancha Tomás. The guerrillas here have been very friendly. Paola told me that she was told I was to be released this week, but the fighting stopped it. So I guess I just wait and freedom will come. Statistics above from magazine page pasted to wall to block wind leaks. Cows, horses, fat black hogs, and chickens wander through.

1730h: An awful day of sitting in the cold and rain, confined to 20 feet of cold mud. But better than most because I'm out of the Valley of the Shadow. To-morrow we march to some high, mystical site by a lake. The guerrillas here killed a calf. Had beef, three or four meals. Delicious. Found a machete, rusty but intact.

Saturday, 8 Jul., Day 289

Three-hour march, mostly uphill, to El Valle Escondido. [Hidden Valley].

Sunday, 9 Jul., Day 290

My campsite is terrible. El Campamento de Viento [the Camp of Wind] in a ravine on a side of the mountain. Isolated, no friends. But I'll survive. Every change I make seems to be for the worse. Rain, no dry places—alone.

Rained last night and raining all day. Gathered wood and sticks for a fire. I miss the bamboo. Sent lots of mental messages to Susan. She won't believe I'm still alive.

Monday, 10 Jul., Day 291

Viejito gave me a piece of plastic to make a cover over my fire. It's now 5:30 P.M. I haven't talked with anyone all day. Terribly lonely. God, stand by me and stand by Susan. Let Susan get my mental messages. The last she could have heard from me was my letter of 27 May—44 days ago. Rain all day. So cold, so lonely.

Tuesday, 11 Jul., Day 292

Last day of *plazo*. Poor Susan, what she must think. Am drying blankets and towels now. Rain last night and this morning; now it's noon and high wind. I'm filthy. What Susan must think. Sent mental messages, to hell with anguish and despair it causes. Susan, I'm alone and I love you.

Wednesday, 12 Jul., Day 293

Rain last night. Tent leaks and so cold. I'm glad Susan can't see me. I wonder if Mother can. Eighty percent of diet now just rice. Still fighting.

Thursday, 13 Jul., Day 294

Last night guerrillas killed pigs. Rain all night, but not so much this morning. We had pork. Viejito and Caballito took me to stream, and I washed my hair and head. Both ears are infected. Mental messages to Susan. She must think I'm dead.

Friday, 14 Jul., Day 295

Terrible night last night. Diarrhea—had to crawl from my tent through mud to a latrine. Sent Susan mental messages in predawn—maybe get through to her dreams.

Saturday, 15 Jul., Day 296

Moved to other site, maybe 200 meters at two P.M. yesterday. Lucero arranged and she and Jonathan prepared. Side of mountain behind a knoll. High bed but can't shut the plastic [front of the tent] so awfully cold. Still raining.

Don't see my three guerrilla angels—Leidi, Lucero, Paola—so much. Maybe that's because I don't need them so much now.

Sunday, 16 Jul., Day 297

I'm truly afraid of going crazy. I went 20 yards uphill to gather *chuzco pequeña*, the only thing that will keep a fire going. I was yelled at from below, then a guard was sent to tell me to stay right by the tent. "How can I even keep a fire going? There's no more *chusque pequeña* here." Moño has already warned me that he'll have me tied if I don't follow the rules.

If I flip, I'll do something stupid and if I'm chained or tied again, I may go insane. I fear I'm close to dying, in some manner. Or close to that downhill slide that leads to death. But I'll survive. I have Susan and my family to return to. I've been crying. Must stop that. I pray, but it increases the anguish. Lucero came to my camp. Cut *chimesas* in front of the tent, where I can't go. More important, she said I could gather *chusque* at the front of the tent. She intervened on my behalf, and I think she intervened to change my tent and campsite. Thank God for a few guerrillas like her, with feelings. I feel better a little, and I'm not going to lose control of my mind. I will survive. Oh, Susan, I love you so.

1615h: Something has changed, I think. Jonathan, commander of the Campamento Alegría *comisión*, appeared with Lucero. He inspected my campsite and dug a trench to drain the water standing in front of the tent and a well one by one meter to collect clear water. He gave me the heavy wool *ruana* he was wearing and one-third roll of toilet paper. He set boundaries for an area where I can gather wood and reasonable boundaries, or, at least, compared with the previous lines. He dug a latrine up the hill. "Has the responsibility for me changed?" I asked. "Are you now in charge of me?"

"*También* [also]," he said.

"How much longer do you think we'll stay here?" I also asked. Maybe I shouldn't have. One month, maybe two; the army has us surrounded.

Monday, 17 Jul., Day 298

Eyes burned last night. Very painful. Lucero, then Levaron, then Viejito brought Visine. Helped a lot. This morning I can tell I did some damage to the left eye—all is blurry, even with glasses, but the damage probably isn't permanent. Leidi and Viejito were kind—helped me prepare my bed and tent. I brought another piece of plastic from [Happy Valley]. Moño brought a piece of foam rubber for my mattress. Herman brought a quilt. Lucero said she told him he must. As nurse, she must have authority over matters of health. Rained all last night. Wasn't cold but kept having to go out because I was sick. From the pork? Lord, I hope not. I need the meat for psychological as well as physical reasons.

P.M.: Trimmed away all fat from the pork I'll cook tonight, with my dull machete. All the pork that the guerrillas have served me with meals has been 100 percent fat. Gustavo said, "That's what we're all eating—the pigs were fat." But the stolen meat I've received has lots of lean [meat]. Lucero gave me a clean handkerchief. "But I can't keep it clean," I said. "Give it to me when it's dirty. I'll wash it for you." She also offered to patch the big hole in my boot that lets water in. It's just now sinking in; I've lost a lot of vision in my left eye— and very suddenly. What if it's not temporary damage from the smoke, but caused by, say, malnutrition? Will I regain the vision? Worse, what if my right eye goes next? Oh God—2:50 P.M., Just learned from a guerrilla that Colombian army has set a base at Santo Domingo, which is the entrance to get to this area. "Then we're trapped?" I asked.

"*Sí, sin salida* [Yes, without an exit]."

"Then we'll be here a long time more?"

"*Sí.*" Yes. I asked Jon if there's a way I could send a note to Susan, in my handwriting, telling her that I'm still alive. "It's doubtful," he said.

Tuesday, 18 Jul., Day 299

Awoke trapped in the valley I call Hidden. Other guerrillas confirm we're trapped and all say there'll be a battle here—and I'll be caught in the middle. It only makes sense that if the army has us bottled in here, it mounts operations to find and clean out pockets of guerrillas like this one. I hope for a battle. I think it might give me a chance to escape—although the chances of dying seem more likely than those of escape. But I can influence nothing, so I have no choice but to wait and try to survive whatever comes. Ten more guerrillas joined this group last night. Julio brought a shortwave radio he borrowed from [some-]one. Spent morning listening to some preacher. No news.

The pork gives me diarrhea, but I have no choice. Must keep eating it. I'm served nothing but pork plus some potatoes, pasta, *cancharinas*, peas. Beans only once. Plus pork fat, which is worse, of course. Right ear infected. Lucero gave me four Ponstans—I take only half a pill. Does only half the job, but that lets me sleep when ear's infected. What a pity it [illegible] so much. But if I die, I die.

P.M. Paola sat with me by the fire last night. We talked about what we would do if we were in Cali and a little about the situation. "I don't want to die," she said, half crying. Later, asked Jon if I could send a radio message to FARC in Cali to deliver to Susan—with a message [bearing information] that only I could know, as proof that it's from me. He agreed. "I still live," it began, and ended with her grandmother's maiden name and father's nickname. Lord, let her recognize and believe the message. Jonathan and Lucero repaired and patched three holes in my boots. Also learned of new fighting with Venezuela at the border. I project that'll keep the army away from here. Both ears now infected.

Wednesday, 19 Jul., Day 300

P.M.: Cold rain all last night and all day. Natalia spent two hours in my tent. "You'd better leave. Won't you get in trouble?"

"Probably."

She doesn't care. All think a battle is coming, and it makes sense. We're surrounded and trapped, no question. But I don't know how big an area we're in. Still, army's search-and-destroy operations [are] the only option that makes sense. I'm staying ready to march.

Should I hope for sun and clear weather? That might help my infected ears but would also enable the army to use observation planes and choppers and find and hit this camp. Do I want that? I think so. A battle here could be my chance for freedom—or death. They'd probably tie me, of course. If I must move quickly, the diaries go in my boots, where I can't lose them unless I'm hurt really badly. Matches, candles in coat pockets. Try to wear both jeans; I always wear all four shirts. And two *ruanas*. Backpack always ready. I'm ready to die, I guess, if that's what comes. I just hope I don't do anything stupid, and please,

God, don't let them chain me again. Rain has stopped twice—for five minutes—all day. Each time I dash out to gather more wet *chusque pequeña*. Otherwise, just sit here. Rice and dried peas for breakfast, lunch.

Thursday, 20 Jul., Day 301

Yesterday was terrible. Never quit raining, so could only sit in tent by fire. Smoke burned eyes, ears so infected, painful.

"Could I stay with you and visit, hide in Cali?" [a guerrilla asked last night after telling me he wanted to defect.]

"Where should I go?"

"The plains [Llanos] the Amazon," I said.

Cold, true, but no rain yet. I have some bad dreams, but not about here. About being free, then kidnapped again, occasionally. I look forward only to sleep—my only escape. God, I hope Susan got my message. Ears so bad I took five antibiotic pills yesterday, but didn't help, so stopped. Will I die here? I just don't know. Often, I don't care. But I know I must survive, survive. How could all of this have happened and at the time of—and instead of—my being freed? Can't pray. Must stop the depression. It's too early in the day, and I face an entire day of nothing. I think, I've seen the Phantom seven times, including several bathing. Another reason for my seclusion—how long would it take to die if I really give up? Die, not suicide. Not long.

1705h: Another day almost over without the battle that could bring freedom, but death would probably be more likely. The fighting is six hours away—not far in the mountains. Rained from midmorning all day. Breakfast: rice and potato chunks. Lunch: rice and two small boiled potatoes. Dinner: rice and potato slices.

Friday, 21 Jul., Day 302

Rain. New tents going up. Must be other guerrillas who've escaped the fighting. Two white geese on lake. [INS change name to el Valle del Cráter] There are two dogs here, but I won't let them near my tent for two reasons. First, I can't stand the emotion and pain a dog brings. Second, I still have a couple of pieces of pork hidden in my bunk. Can't take a chance on the dogs' smelling and stealing it.

Later: Paola gave me a bottle of Visine, how kind. I want to keep a fire going for warmth, and I like for the guards to stop, warm, talk. But sitting in my tent with rain pouring outside like now, the smoke accumulates and is terribly painful. Jon said the fighting seems to have decreased.

P.M.: Lucero brought me two trout, one hand length, the other smaller. Wonderful. Will roast it before I go to bed tonight.

Later: I play a game, every day, with both Lucero and Paola. We go to a restaurant in Cali and order exquisite meals.

Saturday, 22 Jul., Day 303

Calendar full but can't quit writing, even though I'll probably lose all this.

Sunday, 23 Jul., Day 304

New boots. Fit well, but both right feet. Wife says I have two left feet. [Given a jacket to wear to] confuse *chulos.*

Monday, 24 Jul., Day 305

[?About?] to leave. Breakfast: meat. [I hope the guerillas will] butcher [another] hog. Hear explosions in far distance? Seven P.M. We fried, roasted beef. Felt better.

Tuesday, 25 Jul., Day 306

Late breakfast. Good news. Also [illegible]. Later. Paola, Lucero agree to help me survive. Marta appears. Wrote two letters to Susan and Carlos Lascano—final proof [of life]. [Guerrillas] say all think I'm dead.

Moño and a dark-haired female guerrilla—a stranger—appeared at my tent in the Valley of the Volcano late in the afternoon of 25 July.

"This is Marta, and she's come to take some letters from you to your family," Moño said.

"Proof that I'm still alive?"

"Yes, for the last time." Moño and Marta sat on my bunk.

I sighed. "Okay." I knew better than to build up hopes again.

"You're to write two letters. One is to your wife. Tell her you're still alive, but nothing that hints at where this camp is. Don't mention the cold or the mountains."

"I know that."

"Write the second letter to a Colombian friend—someone whom both you and your wife know and trust."

"But I don't know my friends' mail addresses," I replied. "I've visited their homes—but I don't write them letters."

"Just give the name and neighborhood," Moño said. "We'll find the address and deliver the letter."

No way, I thought. I can't direct FARC to the home of a Colombian friend. That letter must go to a Colombian friend at the CIAT research center.

"Here, use clean paper." Moño stood and tore two sheets from his notebook. "Tell the guard when you finish, and Marta will return to get the letters."

I stared at the mountain, then began to write:

25 July 1995

Dear Susan,

I'm sorry that so much time has passed since the last letter, but I never had the opportunity to write to you. I worry much that you will think I am dead, especially since the deadline for my delivery passed two weeks ago. I hope that this letter of proof will assure you that I am still alive.

We're still hidden, and waiting for the day that the guerrillas can escort me safely from here with security. They tell me that this trial will not last much longer.

I miss not only you and our family, but even our dogs, especially our basset hound Gabriela del Carmen. After my freedom is given, I hope that we can return to the United States soon. I worry so much about my father and your mother, and I want to see Tom G. and Miles so much. I love you all.

I love you more than ever.

Tom Hargrove

P.S. As proof that this letter is from me, the name of your mother before her marriage was Marjorie Nell Day. Your uncle in Texas is Bill Day. His wife is Elaine, and their children are Debbie and Hank.

I gave my letter to Marta. The next day, I saw Moño, then others from the group that was to leave to fight the Colombian Army. They couldn't escape the Valley of the Volcano. That meant that my letter hadn't gone out.

I'll write another letter, I thought. On 26 July, I wrote:

Dear Susan,

I'm sitting beside my fire, thinking of you and the day when we will re-unite once again. Sometimes, it is difficult to believe that is possible. They kidnapped me 10 months and 26 days ago today. [NOTE: the author was counting in terms of four-week months.]

Sometimes I try to send you mental messages, mind-to-mind. Do you receive them? The messages are very simple, mainly: "I'm still alive." "I love you." "I'm going to survive and return to you—if it's possible."

... Give my love to my father, your mother, Miles, and Tom G., and the rest of the family.

I love you, I love you.

Tom Hargrove

P.S. I wonder what has happened worldwide in the past year. I have received almost no news.

Proof: Our friend in England is called David Canfil.

Wednesday, 26 Jul., Day 307

Marta, who came just to get letters, didn't leave—too much rain. Wrote two more letters, to Susan and W. Correa. Marta spent four years in prison cell, four paces, no windows. [Marta] has clippings referring to me. [Said she] would check if can show me. But didn't.

Thursday, 27 Jul., Day 308

Gustavo told me last night [that he and the other guerrilla] will leave to go fight today. Stood formation at nine, then Moño, Gustavo, Julio came and said good-bye. *"Tengo cuidado* [Be careful],"* I said to each, *"Vaya con Dios."* But with Moño I thought: I hope they take you prisoner.

Friday, 28 Jul., Day 309

Saw Javier. He's with a new group of FARC which arrived this morning. Came back alone tonight. We'll roast some beef and [illegible] but keep it a secret. I think [illegible] this morning. All seemed to pose [illegible] I should feel something with Moño and the others going after 10 to 11 months together. But I don't and don't think I'd grieve any if learned all were killed. I'm so much better off with the new team. The difference is leadership. Moño never gave a damn about me so long as I stayed alive. P.M.: Must be 30 soldiers here now. Food not so abundant. The females here—they've been the cruelest (Judi, Melena). And the kindest (Lucero, Leidi, Paola) of all the guerrillas. Little or no in-between.

Saturday, 29 Jul., Day 310

Rain all night, this morning. Ice on peaks around us this morning—just a little higher than us. Ramiro showed up last night with new group—also Roberto (new name)—the guerrillas who brought my chain and gave me a mirror, in the Valley of Death. Last night Jonathan mentioned CIAT again—he understands that I work for the Centro Internacional de Agricultura Tropical—but thought that is a part of CIAT, which means CIA. The guerrillas are semiliterate, don't understand acronyms. The Phantom is alone most times. Looks as lonely as me. Wish I could talk with him.

1700h: Oh no. A military plane flew over—low to our camp. Someone fired three shots at it. Does that mean we abandon this camp? Bombing, strafing could follow? Another delay in my release. I played dominoes with Herman all afternoon. [Weather] was terrible this morning but sunny in the afternoon. My punishment for wanting a sunny day?

Sunday, 30 Jul., Day 311

Cold, clear morning—just what I dreaded. But no strafing. All say ground-attack aircraft can't work here because of air currents. Still, I can't see where a little high-altitude bombing wouldn't be in order. Maybe plane didn't see us and so here is [a] Gato Negro from [illegible] My well: 1x1x2-foot bed of mud, and pigs drink from it. P.M.: Moño and group returned. Why? More trapped than before? No freedom? Oh God, please, please.

Later: Herman said release was planned. Please, God.

Later: Guerrillas passed with plants for treatment of diarrhea. "What is that plant?" [Apo.] Leaves looks like celery, tastes like it, too! I wonder if celery is native to South America.

Monday, 31 Jul., Day 312

My worst fear. The group returned yesterday because it couldn't move out, including Marta, who was sent here only to get letters that prove I'm alive. The letters were to reach Susan and CIAT no later than today. Now we're really trapped. Lucero borrowed my watch and Julio my [illegible]. And neither returned. A sign they now really plan to kill me? They can't sell me, I'm a burden. Not afraid to die, but thought of not seeing Susan and the boys again is terrible. Gustavo woke me at five A.M. New [illegible] all ready for attack. I hope *chulos* hit, but with soldiers, not an air strike. Seems about only hope.

Later: A squad left with full packs. Another attempt to break out?

Later: Lucero returned watch, asked if I'd be *padrino* at baptism of her 1½-year-old daughter if we get out of here alive. Katarina Magdalena. Yesterday Lucero said that the plane two days ago was around Mariano—observation/photo.

Later: Grief is what I feel again. I want to cry and I do. How can I start again, there's no hope. But I must. Not ready to give up and die . . . I can hear planes passing but can't see because of clouds.

Tuesday, 1 Aug., Day 313

Rained all day. Deep despair. Hurts so to be alone. Mental messages. Fried *baje* [cow's lung].

Wednesday, 2 Aug., Day 314

Marta visited, and thank God! She gave the letter to another guerrilla, who was to take them into Cali. So there's hope after all. If that guerrilla got past the army, through the lines. Oh God, please, please. Can I believe her? I must. My despair has been too deep. If attacked, I'll carry the diaries out of here as priority.

P.M.: Viejito, Leidi came, and we roasted meat and ate . . . Viejito brought an egg from the hen I killed last week. The first egg since 20 Oct., the night Juaco killed himself. I've dreamed of eggs so many times. Must be getting ready once again to free me. Marta was 16 when [in] prison. Drugs?

Thursday, 3 Aug., Day 315

Treatment improving a lot. Jonathan and Lucero brought meat. (Killed third calf.) Fried liver, intestines, lungs, heart, kidneys at my fire. Left pan with oil. Also gave me coffee, *panela*, soap, plus permission to go to lake afterward to wash hair in muddy water. Marta is kind. Helped clean my well. Jon and I played dominoes.

Later this morning: What a difference it makes to not be alone.

Later: Am definitely being fattened. "Would you like some potatoes, Don Tomás?"

"No, I get enough with meals."

Later: "No, to fry at night [with] your meat." My beef supply is two weeks old but still good. I could throw it away and they'd give me a new stock of fresh beef, but I couldn't bear that, not after being so hungry so long. Received two more blankets. Dreamed again—kidnapped. Free . . . but return to kidnapped at night. Second dream.

Friday, 4 Aug., Day 316

How much longer to wait? The letters, one proof, left eight days ago. I try not to think, but I'm scared. God, I'm scared—that something's wrong. Nothing will happen. I'll go on as I am, but treatment will revert to the former. That FARC's raised the ransom [amount] . . . that plus I don't know and I can't let myself think about it. Please, God. Made coffee for myself, for the first time, at my fire.

P.M.: Sent four *arepas* and breakfast three *cancharinas*, one *arepa*. Lunch, then enormous supply fresh beef—three to four kg and chocolate, *panela*. Rain all day, sit by fire, do nothing. Alone! Alone! Cry a few seconds, but that does no good.

Saturday, 5 Aug., Day 317

Letters not yet reached Cali, Jonathan says. May take one month . . . I don't know. Jonathan and [illegible] came this morning and dug well 60 to 70 meters above tent, hose to my well to bring water. Improves well. Am glad but worries me. How long will I be here? Don't worry, Jonathan says. Means nothing. Could all leave immediately but can't count on anything. I'm weak after one month here with little exercise. Radio messages went by foot. No radio communication. One month, 15 days to Cali, and 15 days return. If Susan gets messages, answer must be delivered by hand. Feel awful to learn that. Grief.

Sunday, 6 Aug., Day 318

[I think there'll be] no release until [the guerrillas] move camp.

Monday, 7 Aug., Day 319

High cold wind. Last night: Made chocolate *panela* candy. Hard words with Moño this morning. I see no end to this.

1730h: Marta came, said Susan received messages. She sends me *"muchos saludos"* and is waiting for me—the first message since I was kidnapped. She sent a question as proof: Who is my favorite writer? I thought of saying Thomas R. Hargrove or Michael Lee Lanning [a good friend and another author published by Ballantine Books], but decided now is no time for jokes. Moño and Gustavo came, fried beef, ate candy. My candy is a big hit.

Tuesday, 8 Aug., Day 320

Cold, rain. Do not think message will free me unless FARC [illegible] abandoned their campaign. But the question itself convinces me it's really from Susan. No one in FARC would think of asking me for my favorite writer's name. Would never occur to them.

[*Four Proof of Life letters, written by Tom on 25–26 July, were retrieved from behind the toilet of a fast food restaurant.—SSH*]

Wednesday, 9 Aug., Day 321

[The guerrillas] building new *rancha* 100 meters from tent. Gather all *chusque* and wood I can because all will soon disappear.

Later: Jonathan says can't visit *la rancha* without permission. That triggered crying alone in tent for an hour, first time in a long time. I've been so brave, but how much more can I take, why is this happening to me? Will it end? Why? What did I do? Will I see Susan and family again? Why, God? Why? No, Tom, you must drive on, you must survive. Survive.

Thursday, 10 Aug., Day 322

Terrible despair, but must fight it somehow. Can't allow deep despair like yesterday. It's deadly for the spirit and soul. Cry too much. Must stop. Can't hope for all. The pain is too great. Wish prayer would bring comfort. Trouble with Gustavo yesterday. And crying too much. [illegible] stop.

Friday, 11 Aug., Day 323

Rain, awful depression. I can't stop it. Feel FARC is holding me to trade—someday. Cry suddenly. Can't think about freedom [illegible] Maybe worst ever.

P.M.: played four dominoes, thank God. Depression is terrible. Dom = lost G1, win G2, lost G3. Always keep score within 20 points, if possible.

Saturday, 12 Aug., Day 324

I will not go crazy. I'll get through today, then tomorrow may be better. Cold rain. Can't think about freedom, family. My strength, my courage, I seem to be losing them. I must take hold of myself. I must fight grief and despair.

Sunday, 13 Aug., Day 325

Kidnapping. The deliberate creation and marketing of human grief, anguish, and despair. Last night dreamed I killed with hands a female VC prisoner. Broke neck. Woke up exhausted. 5–26 Apr. = Camp Loneliness. No leave soon. Army near, looking for me, Julio says.

[*After picking up a map from behind the toilet of a fast food restaurant, a second ransom was delivered to FARC with the agreement that Tom would be released to a mutually acceptable intermediary.—SSH*]

Monday, 14 Aug., Day 326

Live today, only today. Maybe be here capt. me more [illegible] fight despair. Letters to Susan, Dad, Lascano, etc. Explain [illegible] Jonathan [illegible] relieve [illegible] Depression, worry. Cut dominoes. 27. Again, 27-27. Then 28-28-28. Good. It felt better. Is talking to myself like praying? Jonathan gave me *Verdades* magazine, Jan. 95 [illegible] A pencil, two candles.

Tuesday, 15 Aug., Day 327

0745h: Twin-engine observation plane circled, then a single-engine. One hundred shots [fired at it by guerrillas]. Silver chopper flew over. Hundreds more shots. (UH-1)? Planes circled until 8:20 then stayed in distance till almost nine. Photo, I guess. [A]pproaches to Volcano Valley Jonathan appeared. "Abandon camp?" I asked.

"Looks that way."

"I'll only be trouble; wouldn't it be better to get rid of me—one way or the other?" I pointed finger at head, like a pistol.

"If you want, we can arrange that," Jonathan said, drawing finger across his throat. Careful, Hargrove, this may not be time for jokes. But seriously, it would be same risk to assign two guerrillas to escort me to Cali. I stood outside tent and watched [as the planes and helicopter circled the camp], the only one with a beard and without a weapon. I held my almost white dirty handkerchief in my left hand in case we're photographed.

0915h: Backpack ready, can march in minutes. Bombing, strafing may follow. Clear day for a change. No gather wood, exercise. Save energy for march. Diaries stuffed in boots.

1200h: No abandon camp, Jonathan says. Has faith in the wind [illegible]. Says all my *rescate* paid, absolutely no problem. Only waiting for army to leave. FARC opened new fronts in *Tolima* and Quetaua to draw army away.

P.M.: Feel much [illegible]. Yesterday count of dominoes was turning point? I'll make it.

Wednesday, 16 Aug., Day 328

The air strike didn't come at dawn, but a lone chopper appeared on the horizon at seven A.M. If yesterday's planes took photos, I wonder if [illegible] will analyze and recognize me. Tried to [illegible] with this tent. Cat—Niño—loves meat. Slept with one last night. Maybe I can make into a pet—Niño isn't a dog.

0930h: Hear [illegible] plane in [illegible] range [illegible]. Why don't they bomb by map coordinates? But . . . is fogged in. Killed calf.

[*The intermediary went to pick up Tom at the agreed location in a nearby town. Tom was not there.—SSH*]

Thursday, 17 Aug., Day 329

Country in "*conmoción, bien caliente* [confusion, good and hot]," from Cordillera Central to Botero, Manuel says. Rain. No idea when [I'll be] free, Jonathan says. Spirits up, Tom, don't let yourself get depressed. Rain, sit in tent. Second greatest pleasure is playing dominoes, although must work hard to lose two of three games, but that's most of the time, so my greatest pleasure is to dream at night. Last night I dreamed P. Roger and I [were] on a cattle ranch in Texas; second time only Herman do I play for real. None of guerrillas know their basic 1–5 addition scales. For example, we all know $2 + 3 = 5$, but they must count each number. Rain. I read only when it's raining and then only when I can stand the nothingness no longer. Can't use up what little reading material I have. Five hundred shots were fired at chopper on 15 Aug., Moño says.

Friday, 18 Aug., Day 330

So cold. Marta returned.

Saturday, 19 Aug., Day 331

Rain. I've felt and I feel grief for Susan and the boys, especially Susan. Not loneliness and missing them, but grief like Susan has died. But it won't . . . continue [illegible] Think of [illegible] about loss of a spouse being like drug withdrawal. Noted that most guerrillas—even old group—call me Don Tomás. Jonathan's [?influence?]. I may die, but that doesn't bother me—not like the grief I feel for Susan. Time doesn't lessen the pain—it sharpens it.

SCRAPS

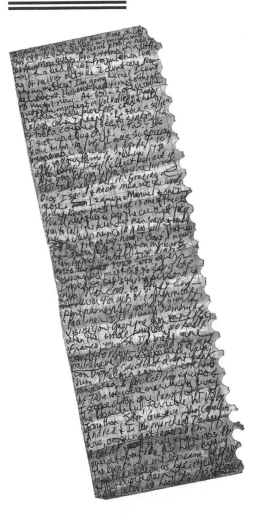

Sunday, 20 Aug., Day 43 in Volcano Valley

Rain. Alone. Oh God, help me or kill me. Or take my mind and memory . . .

Afterword

"Le toca de salir," I heard, and glanced at my watch. It was 6:30 A.M. on 21 August. Then the significance of those words hit me, and I sat up in my bunk. Two *guerrilleros* stood in the mist outside my tent.

"What did you say?" I asked, in Spanish. The answer was the same: "It's your time to leave."

"Leave . . . to where?" I remembered, too vividly, my joy the evening that Moño said I'd leave Camp Loneliness, then the pain when I learned that I'd go back to the Valley of the Shadow.

"To your family, in Cali."

"When?" I was suspicious, afraid to believe it.

"This morning, after breakfast."

"Is this a joke?"

"No. In two days, you'll reach an area where you can hire a car to take you home. This is to cover expenses." The *guerrillero* handed me a bank note for 10,000 Colombian pesos—about 12 US dollars.

I barely had time to gulp a tin bowl of coffee and a *cancharina* as *guerrilleros* appeared at my tent to say good-bye. "Here are my dominoes," I said, hoping to leave the precious game with Herman, who'd appreciate it.

"I'll take them," Moño said. What could I do? I handed the dominoes to a man who couldn't count.

By 7:20 A.M. I was marching down from the Valley of the Volcano with five *guerrilleros*: Jonathan, Gustavo, Caballito, and two others from Jonathan's unit whose names I've already forgotten. At the river below, we walked through the now-deserted camp, La Playa. Che Guevara's portrait, spray-painted across its single wooden building, was fading fast.

An hour farther south, we began to climb steep mountains, leaving the Valley I had named Happiness. We reached a high mountain plateau, and I realized that we were opposite the Valley of Death. I could barely see the distant hut where we lived those first two months.

"Is Juaco still buried there?"

"Of course. Now move fast!" Jonathan said. "Only guerrilla come here, so army helicopters will gun down any human on the ground."

We reached a fast-flowing river, and the *guerrilleros* cut poles from a thicket of brush. "We'll catch trout for lunch," Jonathan said, tying a line and hook to his pole, then selecting a worm from a pouch in his pocket. He dropped the line into the river and, within seconds, landed a hand-length trout. Caballito caught another trout as Jonathan and I slogged a hundred meters forward.

The distant roar of an airplane interrupted the fishing.

"Hide! It's the military!" Jonathan shouted as the roar grew louder, more menacing. Herman and Caballito crouched in bushes as Jonathan and I tried to blend into the riverbank.

A single-engine Cessna passed overhead, circled, passed again, then flew away. "He spotted us!" Jonathan shouted. "Move! Helicopters may be on the way!"

Surely I won't be gunned down by friendly choppers, I thought. Not after I've survived so much, and freedom seems so near.

We slogged through the mud for 20 minutes. Then a single helicopter gunship appeared and circled the area where we had been. We were safe.

A high mountain range loomed ahead. "Do you want to stop and cook lunch, or wait until we cross the mountain?" Jonathan asked.

"Let's keep marching." I can't make it across that ridge, I thought. But I knew I could.

At the ridge's crest, I could easily see 50 or 60 kilometers from horizon to horizon. In the treeless savanna below lay a shallow lake, about three kilometers long and one kilometer wide.

We passed the lake, then pitched tents and made camp by a stream at 3 P.M. Jonathan and Caballito cut new poles and set out fishing. Gustavo cut *frialejong*, started a fire, and fried trout and *arepas*—our first food since breakfast nine hours earlier.

Hard rain soon began to fall, and we couldn't keep the fire going. By 6 P.M. we were all in pup tents. There'd be no dinner that night. That's when I wrote, by candlelight:

Monday, 21 Aug.

1643h: Am sitting in a little tent on a bed of wet leaves as it rains outside. I don't care. Nothing matters: I'm going home! I can't believe it. Haven't had time to think until now. At 6:30 A.M. guerrillas were outside my tent in Volcano Valley. I was hidden under blankets, cold and half-asleep, when I heard: *"Le toca de salir."*

It took a couple of seconds to sink in, then I sat up. *"¿Qué dijo?"*
"Le toca de salir." It's your time to leave!
I was suspicious; remember Camp Soledad. *"¿Adónde?"*
"To Cali, to your family."
"When?"
"Today, after breakfast."
I still couldn't believe it. "Are you joking?"
"No. You're leaving today."
I finally believed it. *"Gracias a Dios,"* I said, and never meant the words
more. Two guerrillas, Manuel and one I didn't know but I think is one of the
leaders. "You'll need this to pay the car that takes you to Cali," the bearded man
said, and handed me a crisp new cold Colombian 10,000 bill. That was US $12
a year ago, but now I don't know. The two guerrillas left and I put on my boots,
then immediately stuffed my diaries into the boot tops. Soon guerrillas surrounded my tent to say good-bye. I tried to say something personal to each.
"Natalia, continue to study. And I'll never forget the afternoon we spent naming
the seven wonders of the world. Paola—I'll always remember the Visine you
gave me for my eyes when the smoke burned them so badly. Franco—I wish I
would have made more candy for you—you loved it so much." Moño appeared.
"Vaya con Dios," I said, but didn't thank him. Melena came, shook hands, ran
away. I packed my equipment and by 7:20 A.M. we were marching away. I
stopped for one last look at the beautiful, terrible Volcano Valley. Jonathan,
Javier, Gustavo, Caballito, Andrea, and I. We marched 7½ hard hours, covering
at least 20 kilometers. Today, a Colombian Air Force single-engine observation
plane flew over at about 10 A.M. We hid, hugging the banks of a mountain
stream. The plane must have seen us because it circled and flew over again.
Then disappeared. Thirty minutes later, we heard a chopper, but I never saw it.
And I'm awfully glad. This area is a free-fire zone, Jonathan says. Only guerrillas roam here, so the choppers shoot at any human on the ground. We finally
crossed an incredibly steep mountain range, then passed a mountain lake and
pitched camp here on [illegible] at 3 P.M.

1930h: Back in tent for the night, warming my feet by two candles—no
need to conserve them now. Lunch was rice and a finger-size trout and *panela*.
Dinner was only a few bites of *panela* because I couldn't keep a fire going. Awfully cold and only two blankets, but I'm happy. I don't think [illegible] soaked
in [illegible]. Can this really be my last night in these miserable mountains? And
tomorrow I'll be with Susan? Take a hot bath—my first bath of any kind since
17 Apr.—and sleep on a bed. Am I terribly lucky to be alive? Or terribly unlucky to have been kidnapped and held 11 months? I should probably consider
myself lucky. Somehow I'd always had a feeling that 11 months would be a
magic number—maybe because that's how long I was held. I wonder if I'll ever
return to these mountains. I returned twice to Vi Thanh, the village in Vietnam
where I spent a dangerous and sad year so long ago. It was an incredibly re-
warding and fascinating experience. But I doubt that I'll ever want to visit the
Valley of Death, Valley of the Shadow, Camp Loneliness, or Volcano Valley

again. Almost all memories [of them are] bad. What will I think about all this
a week, a month, a year, five years from now? I don't know. I don't think I remember much now. And I still have one more tricky, maybe risky challenge: to
get my diaries out. Well, I'll do the best I can. What will Susan think of all this?
What will she be like? Has the trial changed her? Of course, as surely as it's
changed me. But how?

I folded my last diary entry, stuffed it into the packed money belt, and tried
to sleep. I had only two blankets, and was cold. But I didn't care. I felt sure that
I was finally going home.

Our tents were coated with ice when we rose at daybreak on 22 August.
We were marching through the free-fire zone again by 6 A.M.

A clump of trees and boulders on a mountain slope offered cover. We
stopped there and cooked *arepas* at 9 A.M. A spotter plane flew by, but didn't
see us.

An hour later, we approached another lake. Gustavo and I stayed on the
slope above while the other *guerrilleros* went below to check at an Indian's hut.
They'd signal if no army units were in the area.

"Unpack your *equipo*," Gustavo said. Nervously, I opened the rubberized
canvas backpack.

"You can't take any clothes, except what you're wearing," Gustavo said.
"You can wear your light *ruana*, but leave the heavy *ruana* here. Also, your
other clothes and blankets."

The denim jeans I wore were filthy. My other jeans, in the *equipo*, were
clean, but had holes in the knees.

"Put on the clean trousers," Gustavo said.

"No, see the holes? That would look terrible, when I get home." I talked
as calmly as possible. Anything to avoid changing jeans in front of Gustavo—
and giving him a chance to notice my greatest secret, my money belt stuffed
with the precious diary. A notebook was stuffed in my underwear, and another
in my high rubber boots.

That's when Jonathan signaled, from far below, to move forward. Gustavo
forgot about my dirty jeans and we left my worn jeans, backpack, extra clothes,
and blankets lying on a rock. Gustavo allowed me to keep a yellow notebook
whose pages were blank except for the English and Spanish words and phrases
I was studying, some domino scores, and draft radio messages to Susan that
were never sent.

"Cover your face!" Jonathan ordered as an Indian woman with a baby appeared on the trail ahead 30 minutes later. I put on my ski mask.

We met an Indian man a few minutes later. I waited at the crest of a hill
while Jonathan talked with him. Then the five *guerrilleros* approached.

"We leave you here, Don Tomás," Jonathan said.

"What?" Could this really be true?

"We go no further. The risk of running into an army patrol is too great. Follow the trail, and you'll reach a *carretera*, a road. Turn right. You'll find houses

of Indian *campesinos* along the road. Maybe one will lend you a mule or a horse to ride to Tacueyo, the nearest town. There, you can hire a car to Cali."

Each guerrilla shook my hand. *"Tenga cuidado. Vaya con Dios,"* I told each. Be careful. Go with God.

I started up the trail again, then stopped, pulled my broken wristwatch from my pocket, and scribbled in the notebook:

1047h, 22 Aug. 1995
I'm free at last!

I walked on. At 11:20 A.M. I met three more Indians. Yes, continue on this trail, they said, and you'll hit a road.

"Then maybe I can catch a ride in a passing car?"

"Maybe . . . I saw a truck pass yesterday afternoon."

I continued marching. I was tired, but never stopped to rest. If I got lost, I might have to spend the night in these mountains with no blankets. It would be easy to freeze to death. I developed a marching cadence in my mind:

> *Each step takes me closer to Susan*
> *Each step takes me closer to home*

I repeated the cadence again and again. I hoped desperately that I'd find Susan at our home in Cali, even though the *comandante* of the Sixth FARC had told me that she'd moved. I repeated the cadence for Miles, Tom G. and my father, even though I knew they were all in Texas.

My next notebook entry was:

1155h. Reach road. Sign. Parque Nacional de Nevado del Huila.

So I had reached the road, my first sign of civilization, via a national park.

Turning right on the gravel road, I soon reached a hut. There, I explained my plight to an Indian couple and their friend. The Indians had no transport, not even a mule, but the woman served me a bowl of delicious potato soup.

"The road will lead you to Tacueyo—but it's eight hours by foot," the man explained.

"Then I'd better start. I won't stop until I reach home."

The friend introduced himself as Regulo Paya Corpus, a guide in the national park.

"I can guide you over the mountains for a couple of hours," Paya volunteered. "That will shorten your trip, because I know all the trails, the shortcuts."

The Indian guide and I climbed over two more mountains, then reached the road again. I was amazed by how easy it is to walk over a hard gravel road. As we walked, I told him of my life over the past year. This was the first person I'd talked with in almost a year who had no reason to hurt me. Maybe I'm talking too much, I thought.

At last, Paya had to turn back. "Stay on the road," he said, "and you'll finally reach other houses."

"Did my story bore you?"

"No, but it makes me sad to know that these things happened to you when you were here to help our country."

We shook hands, and I marched on.

My next notebook entry was:

450p. Reached house. Motorbike, Honda

I explained my situation to an Indian potato farmer in the house. He showed me his identification card—it said his name was Yovany Alvarez and he was 20 years old. Yovany gave me a plate of rice and pasta, then offered to take me to Tacueyo on his motorbike. We coasted down the mountainside, never even starting the motorbike, for 30 minutes.

Tacueyo, a poor Indian village with a Catholic church on the square, looked vaguely familiar. Was this the same village that FARC took me to the day I was kidnapped? Maybe; I couldn't tell.

"Where can I hire a car?" I asked a group of men loitering in front of a cantina. They beckoned me to a Jeep parked by a store. How do I explain this?

"I want to hire transport to Cali," I explained to a man who was loading the Jeep with sacks of coffee. "I don't have much money, but my family or my neighbors will pay you. I'm a North American who's been living in the mountains for a year and . . . you see, I was kidnapped by the guerrilla, by FARC, and—"

"Are you from CIAT?" the man asked. I was amazed.

"Yes . . . but how did you know?"

"I've read about you in the papers, seen your family on television—" An Indian woman interrupted him.

"Dr. Tomás Argro!" she said. That was close enough. Few Colombians can pronounce my family name.

A crowd soon gathered. Lord, and I thought the entire world, except for Susan and my family, had forgotten me. If I could only have known, during those achingly lonely days in the Valley of the Shadow, Camp Loneliness . . .

"Get in! I'm going to Santander and once there, I'll arrange a car to take you to Cali!"

I climbed into the Jeep with two other passengers and two bags of coffee. A curious passerby climbed in beside me, for the ride. As we left I noticed that Yovany and a friend were following on the motorbike.

The trip to Santander took an hour and a half. There the driver, José Elder Canaral, took me to his home. His family, curious and kind, surrounded me.

"What can I offer you to drink?" José said. "¿Aguardiente? Beer?"

"How about a Coke?" My first carbonated drink was delicious.

"Would you like to wash?" José opened a bathroom door, and switched on an electric light. A strange sight startled me. I stared—at myself—in a mirror.

I was filthy and thin—very thin. My hair, silvery white when I was kidnapped, was shaggy and had turned a garish orange. My beard was also orange and scraggly.

A friend of José's soon arrived in a sedan, and we loaded in for the drive home.

Forty-five minutes later, we approached Cali. I knew that I wouldn't find Susan—she'd moved, the *comandante* had told me, months before. But the Greiners, our neighbors, would know where to find her. I directed the driver to Pance, our neighborhood in southern Cali.

Enrique, the security guard, stood at the gate to the four-home compound where we had once lived. He didn't recognize me at first, then grabbed me in a bear hug.

"Where is the *señora*?" I asked.

"In your home."

"What? Why?"

"Because she lives there."

Susan is still here? Thank God . . . but can I believe it?

The garage door was open, so I entered that way, into the kitchen. I saw no one.

"Is anybody home?" No one answered. I shouted again.

"Oh my God! Dad!" Miles stood, stunned, then crushed against me. "Mom! Geddie! He's here, Dad's home!"

"Dad!" Another pair of arms—Tom G.'s this time—wrapped around me.

"But . . . why are you here? I thought you were at Texas A&M, TCU—"

"We dropped out of school when you were kidnapped," Tom G. said. "We came back to Cali to be with Mom."

"Where *is* your mom?"

"Talking with Raford." I rushed into our bedroom, where Susan and my brother in Texas were talking on an encrypted phone, to scramble messages.

"He's here!" Susan screamed, and dropped the phone on our marble floor. "He's here!"

Raford and his son Mark were listening on a conference phone on Raford's farm. It was 15 miles west of Rotan, Texas, but about 3,000 miles north of Cali, Colombia.

To: FRIENDS-OF-TOM@cgnet.com

SUBJECT: LETTER FROM TOM AND SUSAN HARGROVE

Dear Friends,   23 August 95

Did you hear Gabriela del Carmen [Tom's basset hound] barking? Yes, we got him out. Will get back to you later. Thanks for everything.

Susan

Just got back after two days hard march through the Central Cordillera, Colombia's most rugged mountains. Also walked alone, physically at least,
through that proverbial Valley of the Shadow of Death—but I'm alive. Thanks
to all for the support you gave Susan and the family. Will send more news
later.

Tom Hargrove

SUBJECT: LETTER FROM RAFORD HARGROVE

*Dear Friends of Tom, 22 August 95 (transmitted 23 August 95)

Thank you all for all your support over the last 11 months. Your support has
made a terrible time more bearable. In regard to Bill's account of tonight's
(Tuesday, 22 Aug. 95) events, it is accurate in all respects except Tom walked
in the house at 8:15 CDT, not EDT. He had been released Monday morning,
at which time the guerrillas said they had gone as far as they safely could, and
he was on his own.

They left him directions to the nearest village. He arrived there on foot in
midafternoon, and was greeted by people who recognized him from news reports. They insisted on taking him to his home in Cali. It was another three-
hour ride. My son and I were on speakerphone in my home with Susan when
Tom simply walked in their house.

We had just finished an hour or so of making more plans. Never during this
ordeal was Susan without another plan, and we were constantly discussing
them. We were in the middle of summing up the current next plan, followed
by three more plans, in order, when the dogs started barking up a storm. Susan started screaming, "What is the matter?" then went wild. I thought Tom's
body had been thrown out onto the sidewalk. My son thought Susan had been

---

*The Friends of Tom (FOT) e-mail list was started within a week of Tom Hargrove's abduc-
tion when Susan Hargrove asked Bill Smith to send a message to about 40 friends. That message became the basis for a series of status reports that Susan sent periodically throughout
Tom's captivity. From that start, FOT grew to a list of about 175 names, and with the help of
CGNET it was finally put on a listserver. Included in the FOT list is the professional organization Agricultural Communicators in Education (ACE). ACE in turn sends the messages to the
400 of its 600+ members who have e-mail. So, the FOT list effectively amounts to about 575
persons worldwide. Those people then share information with their own circle of friends or
post the messages on bulletin boards where they work.

The FOT list for the most part is composed of friends Tom Hargrove has made through his
nearly 25 years of professional work (nearly all of it in international agriculture), former classmates and professors at Texas A&M and Iowa State University, former military personnel
Tom served with, and even children of friends (mostly children of associates at IRRI who
grew up there during the 18 years Tom worked in the Philippines). Their time of association
with Tom ranges from 30+ years (college classmates) to associations of 5 years or less.

kidnapped herself. Then we heard Susan yell, "It's Tom," and in a minute Tom picked up the phone off the floor where Susan had left it, and said hello. It was an incredible moment, made more so by the fact that my son and I shared it on the speakerphone.

Tom says that the last 11 months compared to what it might have been like living with the Viet Cong and running from the South Vietnamese Army. He said it was worse than anything he had been through in Vietnam. They had very little to eat until the last month, when they started killing cattle to eat.

He said he felt very lucky to be alive.

He was elated to learn our 84-year-old father was still alive and well. He had had absolutely no news in 11 months. He had written letters to us in Spanish every two weeks, none of which were delivered until we got two of them two weeks ago. According to both him and the boys, Tom is thinner and looks awful. But it is apparent to me and them that he is normal in all other ways, and will fully recover from the weight loss.

This is about all I know about the situation for the moment. I will share more news of this later, as I get it. Thanks again for all of your support.

Raford

Saturday, 26 Aug.

0848h: Take off—

El Dorado, Bogotá—Continental 714 nonstop to Houston—fogged in—left Cali at five A.M.

I realize I am very tired. Really tired. [thinking of] Kashmir kidnap victims

New in-flight games, video programming

Those son of a bitches—did I do wrong? Those SOBs—how long will I have that fear?

What does future hold? I have no idea what the future holds

Worst part is leaving Robert and [Greiners] and all those people who did so much for us. I didn't want it to end this way either. But when you think— you're damn lucky—loved it so much that [illegible] in Colombia. Thought would always come back.

0936h: It's all over and I feel a terrible guilt—will it ever go away? A terrible need to cry. To cry—alone—was okay a few days ago.

flight 710

1 P.M. Houston

Letters Unsent

In addition to this list I also wrote to my wife Susan, my father Tom, the CIAT Communication Unit, and Robert Havener, Director General of CIAT, whenever the mule trains left the guerrilla camps.

This list is compiled from notes and from memory; thus it is incomplete. I apologize for names I omitted and I'm sorry that the guerrillas destroyed all my letters, so none of these good friends received them.

Al App, David Arnovitz, Steve and Cheli Bonta, Randy Barker, Hank Beachell, Steve and Nancy Breth, Tony Bellotti, Tim and Mai Bertotti, Norman Borlaug, Bob and Rae Bourquein, Allycen Brady, Nyle Brady, John Brien, Mike and Lucy Bonman, Rob Briggs, Vicky Cabanilla, David Canfil, Bob Chandler, CIAT Administration, Robert Clerx, Jerry Cooper, Jesus Cuellar, Ronnie and Charlotte Coffman, Walter Correa, Richard Critchfield, Santy Culala, Bill and Elaine Day, S.K. and Vijji DeDatta, Dick and Jean Disney, Bart and Baby Duff, Jill deVille, Deding Dimatelis, Dan and Joyce Fields, Debbie Fields, Don and Ginger Fields, Rex and Sybil Fields, Alice Flinn, Myles and Pam Fisher, Dennis and Faridah Friesen, Pauline Fleming, Porter Garner III, Jack Gaden, Russell Galen, Frank Gillespie, Uli and Claudia Greiner, Henry Green, G. Habich, Bill Hardy, Miles Hargrove, Geddie Hargrove, Raford and Lana Hargrove, Tiff Harris, Gene Harter, Bob and Lorna Herdt, Guy Henry, Derk and Kathy HilleRisLambers, Bob Huggan, IRRI Communication and Publication Department, Keith Ingram, International Red Cross, Lynn Johnson, Mike Jackson, Julia Kornegay, Mike Kelly, Bob Kern, Nguyen An Khang, Vrinda Kumble, Harold and Jean Kauffman, Ranjiv Khush, Larry Klaas, George Krajcsik, Klaas and AnneMarie Lampe, Doug Laing, Carlos Lascano, Jim and Marge Litsinger, Lee and Linda Lanning, Jim and Judy Lanning, Mila Lapitan, Owen Lock, Earl and Judy Martin, Art and Ellen Maurer, Bruce McAllister, Eric McGaw, Ian Montagnes, Kinney and Becky McKinney, Hugh and Joanne Murphy, Gustavo Nores, Uli and Uschi Neue, John and Sharon O'Toole, David Patton, Ricks Pluenneke, LaRue Pollard, Ed and Allethaire Price, Manuel Pina, Pierre and Chantel Roger, Ruth Raymond, Walt Rockwood, Shirley Roman, Barbara Rose, Naomi Rock,

Nathan Russell, Marjorie Sheldon, Miles and Hilda Sheldon, Merle Shepard, Bill and Marlene Smith, Ed and Linda Sulzberger, M. S. Swaminathan, Lee Sanders, Hal Taylor, Harvey Weiner, Elizabeth Wilson, Ashley Wood, and Vo Tong Xuan.

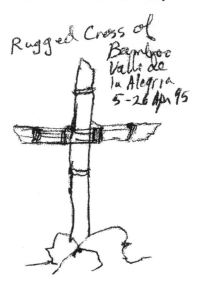

Rugged Cross of
Bamboo
Valli de
la Alegria
5-26 Apr 95